MW00329653

Directory of
SCOTTISH SETTLERS
IN NORTH AMERICA

1625-1825

Newfoundland ca. 1620

Directory of
SCOTTISH SETTLERS
IN NORTH AMERICA

1625-1825

By
David Dobson

VOLUME V

Baltimore
GENEALOGICAL PUBLISHING CO., INC.

Copyright © 1985 by
Genealogical Publishing Co., Inc.
Baltimore, Maryland
All Rights Reserved
Library of Congress Catalogue Card Number 83-82470
International Standard Book Number 0-8063-1124-X
Made in the United States of America

*Abstracts from documents in Crown copyright
are published by permission of Her Britannic
Majesty's Stationery Office.*

Introduction

Although this volume identifies Scottish settlers throughout North America from the seventeenth to the nineteenth century, the emphasis is on Scottish emigrants to Canada, and to a lesser extent East New Jersey and Virginia.

In the aftermath of the Napoleonic Wars the British government actively encouraged emigration to Canada. This was done partly for strategic reasons and partly for economic reasons. The War of 1812 clearly indicated the vulnerability of the frontier between Canada and the United States, and it was partly for defensive reasons that the British government settled former soldiers, including many Scots, in Upper Canada. At the same time the post-war depression coupled with rapid industrial change led to poverty and unemployment in Britain, affecting such groups as the hand loom weavers of central Scotland, for example. These weavers established emigration societies with the object of organized large-scale settlement in Canada. In the spring of 1821 four ships sailed from Greenock to Quebec with 1,883 passengers for settlement in Upper Canada. Among other matters, this volume identifies many of these emigrants and their places of settlement in Canada.

I should like to express my appreciation to the following whose help has made this volume possible: Dr. Bruce H. French, Princeton, N.J.; Richard Dell, Strathclyde Regional Archivist; Scottish Record Office; National Library of Scotland; St. Andrews University Library; Public Record Office, London; New Jersey State Archives; Public Archives of Nova Scotia; and Public Archives of Ontario.

David Dobson

References

ACA   Ayrshire Collections. Ayr, 1961.

AEG   Harvard Encyclopedia of American Ethnic Groups. Cambridge, Mass., 1980.

AG   Annals of Guelph. Guelph, 1877.

AP   American Presbyterianism. Edinburgh, 1885.

APB   Aberdeen Propinquity Books (MS)

ASA   A. S. Alexander Library, Rutgers University, N.J.

AUR   *Aberdeen University Review*

BAF   Burke's American Families with British Ancestry. London, 1939.

BCB   Biographies of Celebrated Canadians. Quebec, 1862.

BES   The Story of the Beveridge Families of England and Scotland. Melbourne, 1923.

BGC   Biographical Sketches of Soldiers and Patriots in the Battle of Guilford Courthouse. Greensboro, N.C., 1958.

BM   *Blair Magazine*

C   The Cherokees. Oklahoma, 1967.

CC   Clan Campbell. Edinburgh, 1912.

CCAI   Clan Cameron Ancestral Index. Raleigh, N.C.

CD   Clan Donald. Inverness, 1904.

CFG   Chronicle of the Family of Gairdner. Taunton, 1947.

CFR   Cockburn Family Records. Edinburgh, 1913.

CG   Clan Gillean. Charlottetown, 1899.

CK   Chronicles of Keith. Glasgow, 1880.

CMF   History of Clan MacFarlane. Tottenville, N.Y.

CMM   *Clan MacMillan Magazine*

CMN   Clan MacNair. New York, 1923.

CMR   Clan MacRae. Dingwall, 1899.

CO   Colonial Office (PRO ref.)

CP   Canada and Its Provinces. Toronto, 1914.

CPD   Consistorial Processes and Decreets, 1658-1800. Edinburgh.

CR	Clan Ranald of Knoydart and Glengarry. Edinburgh, 1979.
DCB	Dictionary of Canadian Biography. Toronto, 1966.
DD	Dunlops of Dunlop. London, 1939.
DF	Family Record of the Name of Dingwall and Fordyce. Toronto, 1885.
DNY	Documents Illustrative of the Colonial History of New York. Albany, 1856.
DP	Darien Papers. Edinburgh, 1849.
DRF	Domestic Papers of the Rose Family. Aberdeen, 1926.
DSP	Darien Shipping Papers. Edinburgh, 1924.
DU	Duke University, N.C.
EHG	Erskine Halcro Genealogy. Edinburgh, 1899.
EFD/EJD	East Jersey Deeds
EMR	Edinburgh Marriage Register. Edinburgh, 1908.
FC	Family of Cassels. Edinburgh, 1870.
FF	Forbes of Forbesfield. Aberdeen, 1905.
FKC	From Kintail to Carolina. Glasgow, 1976.
FKK	Families of Kerr of Kerrsland and Montfode of That Ilk. Edinburgh, 1881.
GC	Grants of Corrimony. Lerwick, 1895.
GD	General Deposit (SRO ref.)
GFH	Glasgow and West of Scotland Family History Society Newsletter
GG	A Roll of Graduates of the University of Glasgow, 1727-1897. Glasgow, 1898.
GOT	Genealogy of the Orkney Traills. Kirkwall, 1883.
GR	Glasgow Records. Glasgow, 1881.
H	*The Highlander*
HAR	History of the Ancient Ryedales. New Hampshire, 1884.
HB	Haigs of Bemersyde. Edinburgh, 1881.
HBRS	Hudson Bay Record Society
HBV	History of Bristol County, Virginia. Richmond, 1879.
HCA	History of County of Ayr. Edinburgh, 1852.
HCS	History of Clan Shaw. Oxford, 1951.
HD	History of Dumfries. Edinburgh, 1867.

HF	House of Forbes. Aberdeen, 1937.
HFH	*Highland Family History Society Journal*. Inverness.
HG	House of Gordon. Aberdeen, 1912.
HGM	Historic Graves of Maryland and the District of Columbia. New York, 1908.
HGMI	History and Genealogy of the MacKenzies. Inverness, 1894.
HGP	Hayden Guest Papers (MS)
HHG	History of Hutcheson's Hospital. Glasgow, 1881.
HKK	History of Kemp and Kempe Families. London, 1802.
HOM	History of the Mathesons. Stirling, 1900.
HOT	History of Old Tennent [New Jersey].
HPC	History of the Presbyterian Church. Toronto, 1885.
HSNC	The Highland Scots of North Carolina, 1732-1776. Chapel Hill, 1961.
IG	Index to Genealogies, Birthbriefs and Funereal Escutcheons Recorded in the Lyon Office. Edinburgh, 1908.
JAB	Jacobites of Aberdeen and Banff. Aberdeen, 1934.
JRC	Pedigree of J. R. Campbell and Sir G. D. Gibb. London, 1872.
KCA	King's College, Aberdeen
LC	Lamont Clan. Edinburgh, 1938.
LGR	London and Guildhall Record Office
LM	The Lyon in Mourning. Edinburgh, 1895.
LOC	Livingstones of Callendar. Edinburgh, 1920.
LP	List of Persons Engaged in the Rebellion. Edinburgh, 1890.
MB	MacKenzies of Ballone. Inverness, 1941.
MCA	Records of Marischal College and the University of Aberdeen, 1593-1860. Aberdeen, 1898.
MCC	McClung Clan. Knoxville, Tenn.
MCF	The McCaskill Family, 1770-1984. Irmo, S.C., 1984.
MCFI	Memoirs of Clan Fingan. London, 1899.
MGL	Memorials of Gordon of Lesmoir. Inverness, 1893.
MHR	Maryland Hall of Records (All Hallows Parish Register)
MIBWI	Monumental Inscriptions in the British West Indies. London, 1875.

MMT	Memoir of Families of McCombie and Thoms. Edinburgh, 1890.
MNJ	History of Monmouth, New Jersey.
MR	The Muster Roll of Prince Charles Edward Stuart's Army, 1745-46. Aberdeen, 1984.
NER	*New England Historical and Genealogical Register*
NHP	Nisbet's Heraldic Plates. Edinburgh, 1892.
NJA	New Jersey Archives
NLS	National Library of Scotland (MS-RyIIb8(19))
NRAS	National Register of Archives of Scotland
NRP	Narrative of the Rise and Progress of Emigration from Lanarkshire and Renfrew to Upper Canada. Glasgow, 1821.
NYGBR	*New York Genealogical and Biographical Record*
NYHS	New York Historical Society
OD	Scots in the Old Dominion. Edinburgh, 1980.
ORIII	Official Roster of Soldiers of the American Revolution
OS	Oliver Surname on the Scottish Borders. Galashiels, 1982.
OSC	History of Old Scots Church, Freehold, N.J. Freehold, 1895.
PANS	Public Archives of Nova Scotia
PAO	Public Archives of Ontario (MS-154)
PC	Register of the Privy Council of Scotland
PNS	History of Pictou, Nova Scotia. Montreal, 1877.
PRO	Public Record Office, London
PRSC	*Proceedings of the Royal Society of Canada*
PWD	Life, Letters and Papers of William Dunbar. [Mississippi.]
RAF	Robertson's Ayrshire Families. Irvine, 1825.
RCF	Records of Clan Ferguson. Edinburgh, 1899.
RH	Register House (SRO ref.)
RRW	*Raleigh Register Weekly.* Raleigh, N.C.
RT	Roster of Texas Daughters of Revolutionary Ancestors. Texas, 1976.
S	The Simsons. Glasgow, 1867.
SA	Scotus Americanus. Edinburgh, 1982.

SAE	Stewarts of Appin. Edinburgh, 1880.
SC	Stirlings of Cadder. St. Andrews, 1933.
SF	Scotland Farewell. Edinburgh, 1980.
SFG	Stewarts of Forthergill. Edinburgh, 1879.
SG	*Scottish Genealogist*
SHC	Scottish Highlander Carmichaels of the Carolinas. Washington, 1935.
SHR	*Scottish Historical Review*
SNF	The Scot in New France. Montreal, 1881.
SO	The Scots Overseas. London, 1966.
SOF	Some Old Families. Birmingham, 1890.
SOP	Seton of Parbroath. New York, 1890.
SP	The Scots Peerage. Edinburgh, 1904.
SRA	Strathclyde Regional Archives, Glasgow
SRO	Scottish Record Office, Edinburgh
TC	The Covenanters. Glasgow, 1908.
TDD	The Darien Disaster. London, 1968.
TML	The MacLeods—Genealogy of a Clan. Edinburgh, 1969.
TO	Toronto of Old. Toronto, 1966.
TPC	The People's Clearance. Edinburgh, 1982.
TRA	Tayside Regional Archives, Dundee
TSA	The Scots in America. New York, 1896.
TV	*Tay Valley Family History Society Journal.* Dundee
TWS	The Wardlaws in Scotland. Edinburgh, 1912.
U	History of the Usher Family in Scotland. Edinburgh, 1956.
UKA	List of Persons Admitted to the Degree of Master of Arts in the University and King's College, Aberdeen from 1800. Aberdeen, 1856.
UNC	University of North Carolina
VI	Viri Illustres Universitatum Abredonensium. Aberdeen, 1923.
VMHB	*Virginia Magazine of History and Biography*
VT	Valley of the Trent. Toronto, 1957.
WM	Unrecorded Wills and Inventories of Monmouth County, New Jersey
WS	The History of the Society of Writers to H.M. Signet. Edinburgh, 1890.

To

Robert Barclay of Urie, 1648-1690

Co-Founder of East New Jersey

Directory of
SCOTTISH SETTLERS
IN NORTH AMERICA

1625-1825

ABERCROMBIE ALEXANDER
Son of Robert Abercrombie,
minister of Leslie, Fife.
Alumnus of University of
Aberdeen 1745. Graduated
M.D. in Aberdeen 30 July
1753. Surgeon of a
military hospital in Nova
Scotia.
(MCA)

ABERCROMBY GEORGE
Surgeon and later a
merchant in Jamaica and
Mexico c1729-1744.
(SRO/GD345)

ABERNETHIE JOHN
Skinner. Strathbogie,
Aberdeenshire. Jacobite in
Lord Lewis Gordon's
Regiment 1745-1746.
Transported to Plantations.
(MR)

ADAM ALEXANDER
Born in Scotland c1655.
Indentured servant imported
into New Jersey by James
Johnston, merchant, on the
Henry and Francis during 1685.
Settled in Pitcataway in 1685.
Resettled in Freehold in 1694.
Quaker. Married Margaret Eube.
Father of Thomas, Alexander,
Cornelius, Mary, Margaret,
James, Ann, William and David.
(MNJ)(EJD/A226)

ADAM DAVID
Emigrated from Scotland to
Canada on the Earl of
Buckingham during June 1821.
Received a land grant in
Ramsay, Upper Canada on
26 July 1821.
(PAO)

ADAM ROBERT
Scottish servant of
Lord Neil Campbell in
New Jersey. Settled
in Perth Amboy and at
Raritan River, Somerset
County, New Jersey c1690.
(ASA)

ADAM ROBERT
With his wife, emigrated
from Scotland to Canada
on the Earl of Buckingham
during June 1821. Received
a land grant in Ramsay,
Upper Canada on 25 July
1821.
(PAO)

ADAMSON JOHN
Born in Scotland. Former
Sergeant in the Glengarry
Fencibles. Wife, son and
two daughters. Military
settler. Received a land
grant in Kitley, Upper
Canada on 21 July 1817.
(PAO)

AFFLECK PETER
Born in Scotland during
1733. Shoemaker. Settled
in Isle of Wight County,
Virginia, during 1753.
(OD)

AFFLECK ROBERT
Wife, five sons and two
daughters. Emigrated from
Scotland to Canada on the
Prompt. Received a land
grant in Lanark, Upper
Canada on 21 December 1821.
(PAO)

1

AIRD JAMES
Born in Ayrshire. Fur
trader in Canada. Died
on 27 February 1819 at
Prairie du Chien,
Wisconsin.
(DCB)

AIRD JOHN
Planter. Died 'of
decay' on the voyage from
Scotland to Darien on 28
October 1698.
(NLS)

AITKEN ROBERT
Born in Perthshire during
1724. Emigrated from
Scotland to America.
Printer and publisher in
Philadelphia, Pennsylvania,
from 1769. Died during 1802
in Philadelphia.
(TSA)

AITKEN ROBERT
Born in Scotland. Emigrated
from Scotland to Canada.
Received a land grant in
Beckwith, Upper Canada, on
30 October 1822.
(PAO)

AITKEN ROGER
Episcopalian minister in
Aberdeen. Received an
honorary M.A. from the
University of Aberdeen on
14 February 1809. Later
settled in Canada.
(MCA)

AITKEN Rev THOMAS
Emigrated from Scotland to
Nova Scotia during 1828.
Minister in Halifax, Nova
Scotia.
(HPC)

AITKENHEAD JAMES
Wife, three sons and three
daughters. Emigrated from
Greenock to Canada on the
George Canning during May
1821. Received a land
grant in Ramsay, Upper
Canada, on 16 July 1821.
(PAO)

AITON WILLIAM
Strathaven. Applied to
settle in Canada on
27 February 1815.
(SRO/RH9)

ALEXANDER Dr ADAM
Born in Inverness during
1758. Studied medicine
in Edinburgh. Emigrated
to America. Surgeon in
the Continental Army.
Married Louisa Frederika
Schmidt during 1802.
Father of Adam Leopold
Alexander 1803-1883.
(DU/Cab81/1940)

ALEXANDER ANDREW
Emigrated from Scotland to
New Jersey with three
indentured servants during
November 1684. Married
Jean Campbell. Father
of Jean Campbell Alexander.
Schoolmaster in Elizabeth-
town, New Jersey. Settled
in Middlesex County on
1 May 1690.
(ASA)(EJD/D325)

ALEXANDER DAVID
Indentured servant who was
imported from Scotland to
New Jersey by Lord Neil
Campbell during December
1685.
(EJD/A225)

ALEXANDER GEORGE
Emigrated from Scotland to
America. Settled in Blew
Hills, Essex County, New
Jersey. Land grant dated
22 February 1688.
(EJD/B426)

ALEXANDER JAMES
Born in Scotland during 1733.
Married (2) Margaret Clarke
Ross. Revolutionary
soldier. Died 9 May 1817.
Buried at Flushing, Ohio.
(OR)

ALEXANDER JAMES
Inverkeithing, Fife.
Applied to settle in
Canada on 2 March 1815.
(SRO/RH9)

ALEXANDER JOHN
Emigrated from Scotland
to Virginia in 1659.
(OD)

ALEXANDER JOHN
Emigrated from Scotland to
America. Settled in Blew
Hills, Essex County, New
Jersey. Land grant dated
22 February 1688.
(EJD/B426)

ALEXANDER JOHN
Emigrated from Greenock to
Montreal during 1825 on the
brig Niagara, Hamilton.
Settled in MacNab, Bathurst,
Ontario, during 1825.
(SG)

ALEXANDER PATRICK
Four year indentured
servant imported from
Scotland to New Jersey
by the Scotch Proprietors
before 1 December 1684.
(EFD/A)(NJA21/61)

ALEXANDER PETER
Emigrated from Greenock to
Montreal during 1825 on the
brig Niagara, Hamilton.
Settled in MacNab, Bathurst,
Ontario, during 1825.
(SG)

ALEXANDER THOMAS
Son of James Alexander,
tailor in Aberdeen.
Educated at Aberdeen
University 1820-1824.
Graduated M.A.
Presbyterian minister
in Cobourg, Canada.
(MCA)

ALISON JAMES
Leith. Applied to
settle in Canada on
1 March 1815.
(SRO/RH9)

ALISON WILLIAM
Leith. Applied to
settle in Canada on
1 March 1815.
(SRO/RH9)

ALLASON DAVID
Son of Zachariah Allason
and Isabel Hall, Gorbals.
Emigrated from Scotland
to America during 1757.
Indentured servant to
Archibald Ritchie at
Rappahannock, Virginia.
In Falmouth, Virginia
1760-1762. Storekeeper in
Winchester, Virginia, 1763.
Died after 1815.
(SRA)(VMHB,1931)

ALLASON ROBERT
Son of Zachariah Allason
and Isabel Hall, Gorbals.
Emigrated from Scotland
to America during 1761.
Merchant in Virginia.
(SRA)

ALLASON WILLIAM
Son of Zachariah Allason
and Isabel Hall, Gorbals.
Emigrated from Scotland
to America during 1737.
In Britain from 1752 to
1757. Factor for Alex
Walker and Company in
Virginia. Merchant in
Falmouth, Virginia.
Married Anne Hume, daughter
of Captain John Hume, in
Virginia. Naturalised
American.
(SRA)

ALLASON WILLIAM
Son of John Allason,
tanner in Glasgow.
Surgeon in Port Royal,
Virginia. Died during
1768.
(SRA/B10/15/7345)

ALLAN HUGH
Born in Ayrshire on
29 September 1810, the
son of Captain Alexander
Allan. Emigrated from
Greenock to Canada on
the Favourite on 12 April
1826. Merchant.
(BCB)

ALLAN JAMES
Emigrated from Scotland
to Canada on the
Garland during October
1819. Received a land
grant in Bathurst, Upper
Canada, on 22 July 1820.
(PAO)

ALLAN JOHN
Born on 3 January 1747
in Edinburgh Castle, the
eldest son of William
Allan and Isabel Maxwell.
Emigrated, with parents,
from Scotland to Nova
Scotia c1750. Married
Mary Patton on 10 October
1767. Politician and
public official. Died on
7 February 1805 at
Lubeck, Maine.
(DCB)

ALLAN JOHN
Born during 1777 in
Kilbirnie, Ayrshire.
Emigrated from Scotland
to New York in 1794.
Settled at 17 Vandewater
Street, New York.
(TSA)

4

ALLAN WILLIAM
Emigrated from Scotland
to Canada with his wife,
two sons and a daughter,
on the Commerce during
June 1821. Received a
land grant in Dalhousie,
Upper Canada, on
27 July 1821.
(PAO)

ALLIE JOHN
Shetland Islands.
Surgeon in the Royal
Navy from 1798 -
Later a farmer.
Applied to settle in
Canada during 1818.
(CO384/3)

ALSTON JOHN
Emigrated from Scotland
to Canada on the Peace of
Hull on 16 July 1817.
Received a land grant in
Burgess, Upper Canada, on
7 April 1818.
(PAO)

ALSTON JOHN
Born in Scotland. Formerly
a Lieutenant in the 70th
Regiment. Military
settler. Land grant in
Elmsley, Upper Canada, on
7 October 1818, and in
Larder, Upper Canada, on
26 September 1819.
(PAO)

ANDERSON ALEXANDER
Emigrated from Scotland to
Canada. Received a land
grant in Beckwith, Upper
Canada, on 29 September 1821.
(PAO)

ANDERSON ALEXANDER
Son of Alexander Anderson
in Drumblade. Educated at
Aberdeen University c1825.
Surgeon in America.
(MCA)

ANDERSON ANN
Born c1792, daughter of
Laurence Anderson, 1761-1813,
shoemaker in St Andrews, Fife.
Died in New York on
24 November 1825.
(St Andrews GS)

ANDERSON DONALD
Emigrated from Scotland to
Canada. Received a land grant
in Goulburn, Upper Canada, on
30 November 1820.
(PAO)

ANDERSON GEORGE
Indentured servant imported
from Scotland to New Jersey
during 1684.
(EJD/A)

ANDERSON GEORGE
Born 1798 son of George
Anderson, Ironshill, 1767-1841,
and Agnes Kerr, 1770-1843. Died
in New Orleans 7 October 1827.
(Inverkeiller GS)

5

ANDERSON HARRY
Natural son of Harry
Anderson, merchant in
Glasgow. Emigrated from
Scotland to Barbados c1665.
(GR)

ANDERSON HUGH
Emigrated from Scotland
to Canada on the George
Canning during June 1821.
Received a land grant in
Ramsay, Upper Canada, on
16 July 1821.
(PAO)

ANDERSON JAMES
Kilmarnock, Ayrshire.
Covenanter captured at
the Battle of Bothwell
Bridge on 22 June 1679.
Banished to the
Plantations in America.
Drowned off Orkney.
(HCA)

ANDERSON JAMES
Carpenter. Inverness.
Settled in Georgia c1737.
(HGP)

ANDERSON JAMES
Born c1785 in Falkirk,
Stirlingshire. Applied
to emigrate to Canada
in 1817.
(CO384/3)

ANDERSON JAMES
Born c1797, son of
Lawrence Anderson, 1761-
1813, shoemaker in
St Andrews, Fife. Died
in Newark, U.S.A. on
12 April 1830.
(St Andrews GS)

ANDERSON JAMES
Emigrated from Scotland
to Canada on the
Commerce during June
1820. Received a land
grant in Dalhousie, Upper
Canada, on 3 September
1820.
(PAO)

ANDERSON JOHN
Born in 1665, son of
John Anderson. Captain
of the Unicorn. Settled
in East New Jersey.
Married Anna Reid, born
in Scotland during 1680,
daughter of John Reid.
Father of John, James,
Kenneth, Jonathan, Margaret,
Helen, Anna, Elizabeth and
Isabella. Judge and
Governor of New Jersey.
Died on 28 March 1736.
Buried Manalapan, Monmouth
County, New Jersey.
(MNJ)

ANDERSON JOHN
Planter. Emigrated from
Scotland to America.
Settled in Fredericksburg,
Virginia, pre 1755.
(OD)

ANDERSON JOHN
Born in Scotland. Military
settler. Former Corporal
in the Royal Artillery.
Wife, son and daughter.
Received a land grant in
Drummond, Upper Canada,
on 29 May 1817.
(PAO)

ANDERSON JOHN
Emigrated from Scotland,
with his wife, son and
three daughters, to
Canada on the Earl of
Buckingham during June
1821. Received a land
grant in Dalhousie,
Upper Canada, on 20 July
1821.
(PAO)

ANDERSON JOHN
Yeoman. Emigrated from
Scotland to Canada.
Received a land grant in
Eldon, Newcastle, Upper
Canada, on 8 March 1826.
(PAO)

ANDERSON ROBERT
Indentured servant
imported from Scotland to
East New Jersey during
October 1684 by John
Forbes. Land grant 1 May
1690. Servant of Colin
Campbell.
(EJD/A266,D325)

ANDERSON ROBERT
Kilmarnock, Ayrshire.
Covenanter captured at
the Battle of Bothwell
Bridge on 22 June 1679.
Banished to the Plantations.
Drowned off Orkney.
(HCA)

ANDERSON ROBERT
Indentured servant
imported from Scotland
to East New Jersey in
1683 by Gavin Lawrie,
Governor of East New
Jersey.
(EJD/A,E330)

ANDERSON ROBERT
Emigrated from Scotland
to Canada on the
Commerce during June 1820.
Received a land grant in
Dalhousie, Upper Canada,
on 3 September 1820.
(PAO)

ANDERSON THOMAS
Born c1795 son of George
Anderson, 1767-1841, and
Agnes Kerr, 1770-1843,
Ironshill, Inverkeilor,
Angus. Died in New
Orleans on 1 August 1835.
(Inverkeilor GS)

ANDERSON WILLIAM
Gardener in Edinburgh.
Applied to settle in
Canada on 8 March 1815.
(SRO/RH9)

ANDERSON WILLIAM
Emigrated from Scotland
to Canada on the Commerce
during June 1820.
Received a land grant in
Dalhousie, Upper Canada,
on 3 September 1820.
(PAO)

ANDERSON WILLIAM
Emigrated from Scotland,
with his wife, three sons,
and three daughters, to
Canada on the Commerce
during June 1820.
Received a land grant in
Ramsay, Upper Canada, on
9 September 1821.
(PAO)

ANGUS ANDREW
Emigrated from Scotland
to Canada in the
Commerce. Received a
land grant in Lanark,
Upper Canada, on
4 September 1821.
(PAO)

ANGUS JAMES
Emigrated from Scotland,
with his wife and four
daughters, to Canada.
Received a land grant in
Dalhousie, Upper Canada,
on 2 April 1821.
(PAO)

ANGUS JOHN
Emigrated from Scotland,
with his wife, son and
two daughters, to
Canada on the Commerce
during June 1821.
Received a land grant in
Lanark, Upper Canada, on
6 August 1821.
(PAO)

ANGUS JOSEPH
Glasgow. Merchant in
St Kitts c1763.
(SRA/B10/12/2)

ANGUS WILLIAM
Son of William Angus,
Aberdeen. Educated at
Aberdeen University
1784-1788 - graduated
M.A. Surgeon in Jamaica.
(MCA)

ARBUTHNOTT ALEXANDER
Brother of Rev. James
Arbuthnott, minister in
Inverbervie, Kincardine-
shire. Merchant in
Philadelphia, Pennsylvania,
c1720.
(SRO/B51/12/1)

ARMOUR JAMES
Merchant in Glasgow.
Emigrated from Scotland
to East New Jersey on the
Henry and Francis during
1685. Merchant in Perth
Amboy, New Jersey, 1687,
in New York city 1690,
in Westminster, London 1724.
(EJD/B472/E89)

ARMOUR JOHN
Emigrated from Scotland,
with his wife, son and
daughter, to Canada on the
Earl of Buckingham during
June 1821. Received a
land grant in Dalhousie,
Upper Canada, on
19 August 1821.

ARMSTRONG WALTER
Emigrated from Scotland
to Canada on the Lord
Middleton 20 July 1817.
Received a land grant in
Elmsley, Upper Canada,on
4 December 1817.
(PAO)

ATKINSON GEORGE
Emigrated from Scotland,
with his wife, two sons
and three daughters, to
Canada on the Earl of
Buckingham during June
1821. Received a land grant
in Lanark, Upper Canada, on
20 July 1821.
(PAO)

AUCHMUTY ROBERT
Emigrated from Scotland
to America. Member of
the Court of Admiralty.
Agent of the Colony of
Massachusetts in
England. Father of
Sarah, born in Boston
16 January 1722. Died
in Boston during April
1750.
(NYGB.XXVI.186)

AVERY BENOIT
Born in Scotland.
Former Sergeant in the
104th Regiment.
Military settler.
Received a land grant
in Young, Upper Canada,
on 31 July 1817.
(PAO)

BAILLIE ALEXANDER
Born in Scotland.
Formerly in the 10th
Dragoons. Military
settler. Received a
land grant in Drummond,
Upper Canada, on
16 September 1817.
(PAO)

BAILLIE CHARLES
Emigrated from Scotland,
with wife, five sons and
a daughter, to Canada on
the Prompt. Received a
land grant in Dalhousie,
Upper Canada, on
21 November 1821.
(PAO)

BAILLIE HUGH
Former Customs Collector
in Orkney. Emigrated
from Scotland to America.
Settled in Josephtown,
Georgia, in 1735. Trader.
(HGP)

BAILLIE KENNETH
Son of John Baillie of
Balbrobert. Emigrated
from Scotland to America.
Signed treaty with the
Creek Indians in Georgia
on 11 August 1739.
(HGP)

BAILLIE ROBERT
Planter. Died on voyage
from Scotland to Darien,
of fever, 21 September
1698.
(NLS)

BAILLIE ROBERT
Yeoman. Emigrated from
Scotland to Canada.
Received a land grant
in Thorak, Home, Upper
Canada, on 8 March 1826.
(PAO)

BAILLIE THOMAS
Scottish trader.
Settled in Josephstown,
Georgia, in 1735.
(HGP)

BAIN ALEXANDER
Emigrated from Scotland,
with wife, seven sons
and three daughters, to
Canada on the Earl of
Buckingham during June
1821. Received a land
grant in Dalhousie,
Upper Canada, on
20 July 1821.
(PAO)

BAIN DUNCAN
Emigrated from Scotland,
with his wife and two
daughters, to Canada on
the George Canning during
June 1821. Received a
land grant in Ramsay,
Upper Canada, on
16 July 1821.
(PAO)

BAINE HELEN
Indentured servant
imported from Scotland
to East New Jersey by
Charles Gordon during
October 1684.
(EJD/A255)

BAIN JOHN
Educated at Aberdeen
University c1823. Author
and minister in Galt,
Ontario.
(MCA)

BAINE ROBERT
Indentured servant of
James Millar, merchant in
Greenock, Renfrewshire.
Emigrated from Scotland
to Williamsburg, Virginia,
in February 1759 on the
Peggy of Glasgow. Factor
in Williamsburg, Virginia.
(Robert Baine's Book 1758-
1759 in Library of
Congress)

BAIN WALTER
Emigrated from Scotland,
with his wife, son and
daughter, to Canada on the
George Canning during June
1821. Received a land
grant in Ramsay, Upper
Canada, on 20 July 1821.
(PAO)

BAIRD ALEXANDER
Son of Robert Baird, merchant
in Edinburgh, and Elizabeth
Fleming. Emigrated from
Scotland to America. Settled
in New York. Married
Magdalena Van Vleck, a
widow, in New York in 1700.
Father of Wilhelmus and
Robberd.
(NYGBR)

BAIRD ANDREW
Sailor. Died of flux on
voyage from Scotland to
Darien 29 September 1698.
(NLS)

BAIRD ARCHIBALD
Rutherglen, Lanarkshire.
Applied to settle in
Canada on 3 March 1815.
(SRO/RH9)

BAIRD JAMES
Emigrated from Scotland,
with three sons and four
daughters, to Canada on
the Brock during 1820.
Settled in Lanark, Upper
Canada, on 23 October 1821.
(PAO)

BAIRD JOHN
Born in Aberdeen c1665.
Four year indentured
servant imported from
Scotland to East New
Jersey during 1683 -
landed on Staten Island.
Married Mary Hall during
1684. Settled in
Monmouth County, New
Jersey. Father of John,
David, Andrew and
Zebulon. Died during
April 1755. Buried at
Topenemus, Marlboro
County, New Jersey.
(HOT)(MNJ)(EJD/A)

BAIRD JOHN
Son of John Baird of
Easter Muchrofts,
Glasgow. Merchant.
Settled in Greencroft,
Prince George County,
Virginia. Father of
John. Died before
15 September 1738.
(Petersburg Deeds,
DB2.387)

BAIRD ROBERT
Emigrated from Scotland,
with his wife, four sons
and two daughters, to
Canada on the George
Canning during June 1821.
Received a land grant in
Ramsay, Upper Canada, on
16 July 1821.
(PAO)

BAIRD WILLIAM
Sailor. Died at Darien
on 24 November 1698.
(NLS)

BAIRD WILLIAM
Emigrated from Scotland
to Canada on the George
Canning during June 1821.
Received a land grant in
Ramsay, Upper Canada, on
16 July 1821.
(PAO)

BALFOUR WALTER
Born in St Ninian's,
Stirlingshire, in 1776.
Emigrated from Scotland
to America during 1806.
Minister. Died in
Charlestown, Massachusetts,
during 1852.
(TSA)

BALLANTYNE DAVID
Emigrated from Scotland,
with wife, son and daughter,
to Canada on the Commerce
during June 1820. Received
a land grant in Lanark,
Upper Canada, on
8 September 1820.
(PAO)

11

BALLANTYNE PATRICK
Ayr. Tobacco merchant.
Died in Virginia c1770.
(ACA)

BALLENDEN JOHN
Born in Orkney Islands
during 1810. Hudson
Bay Company employee
from 1829 to 1856.
Chief Factor 1848.
Died 7 December 1856.
(HBRS)

BALLOCH JAMES
Born in St Ninian's,
Stirlingshire, during
1764. Emigrated from
Scotland to America in
1790. Married Sarah
Chase during 1796.
Father of James, George
W., Francis H., Charles,
William, Margaret, Mary,
Sarah and Janet. Died
on 27 February 1831.
(CFG)

BANKHEAD JAMES
Scottish doctor.
Educated in Edinburgh
c1733. Settled in
Virginia.
(OD)

BANKHEAD JAMES
Emigrated from Scotland,
with wife and four sons,
to Canada on the Earl of
Buckingham during June
1821. Received a land
grant in Lanark, Upper
Canada, on 26 July 1821.
(PAO)

BARCLAY HUGH
Sailor. Died at Darien
on 5 November 1698.
(NLS)

BARCLAY ROBERT
Emigrated from Scotland
to Canada on the David.
Received a land grant
in Lanark, Upper Canada,
on 24 September 1821.
(PAO)

BARCLAY Rev THOMAS
Born at Collairnie Castle,
Fife, c1663. Educated at
University of St Andrews,
Fife, - graduated M.A. in
1688. Ordained during 1707.
Emigrated to America in
1708. Married Anne
Dorothea Deauyer during
1709. Rector of St Peter,
Albany. Father of Henry.
Died during 1734.
(BAF)

BARR JAMES
Emigrated from Scotland,
with a son and daughter,
to Canada on the Commerce
during June 1821.
Received a land grant in
Lanark, Upper Canada, on
8 August 1821.
(PAO)

BARR NEIL
Emigrated from Scotland,
with wife and two daughters,
to Canada on the Commerce.
Received a land grant in
Lanark, Upper Canada, on
10 September 1821.
(PAO)

BARR PETER
Emigrated from Scotland,
with wife and a son, to
Canada on the Commerce
during June 1820.
Received a land grant in
Lanark, Upper Canada, on
1 October 1820.
(PAO)

BARRETT NATHANIEL
Emigrated from Scotland
to America before 1754.
Settled in
Northumberland County,
Virginia. Planter.
(OD)

BARRETT WILLIAM
Emigrated from Scotland,
with wife, son and two
daughters, to Canada on
the Prompt. Received a
land grant in Dalhousie,
Upper Canada, on
21 November 1821.
(PAO)

BARRIE JAMES sr.
Emigrated from Scotland,
with wife, son and
daughter, to Canada on
the Prompt. Received a
land grant in Dalhousie,
Upper Canada, on
21 November 1821.
(PAO)

BARRIE JAMES jr.
Emigrated from Scotland,
with wife, two sons and a
daughter, to Canada on the
Prompt. Received a land
grant in Dalhousie, Upper
Canada, on 21 November 1821.
(PAO)

BARRON WILLIAM
Planter. Died at Darien
on 17 December 1698.
(NLS)

BARROWMAN JAMES
Emigrated from Greenock,
Renfrewshire, with wife,
two sons and five
daughters, to Canada on the
George Canning during May
1821. Received a land
grant in Lanark, Upper
Canada, on 26 July 1821.
(PAO)

BARROWMAN WILLIAM
Emigrated from Scotland,
with wife, three sons and
a daughter, to Canada on
the Commerce during August
1820. Received a land
grant in Lanark, Upper
Canada, on 5 September 1820.
(PAO)

BASSET JOHN
Emigrated from Scotland to
Virginia pre 8 January 1754.
(OD)

BAXTER Rev JOHN
Emigrated from Scotland
to Nova Scotia. Minister
in Onslow, Nova Scotia, 1832.
(HPC)

13

BAXTER KENNEDY
Emigrated from Scotland
to Canada on the
Commerce during June
1820. Settled in
Ontario.
(PAO)

BAXTER PETER
Emigrated from Scotland
to Canada on the
Commerce. Received a
land grant in Lanark,
Upper Canada, on
7 August 1821.
(PAO)

BEATTIE FRANCIS
Born in Dumfries(?)
during 1796. Died at
Port Hope, Upper
Canada, on
29 September 1828.
(Dumfries GS)

BEATTY JOHN
Emigrated from Ayrshire
via Ireland and Holland
to America. Settled in
Marbletown, Ulster County,
New York c1691. Married
Susannah Asfordby.
Father of John.
(BAF)

BEATTY (?) JOHN
Born c1785. Shoemaker.
Emigrated from Scotland,
with wife, to Canada.
Settled Pictou Town,
Nova Scotia, c1815.
(PANS/RG1)

BEATTIE WILLIAM
Emigrated from Greenock,
Renfrewshire, with wife,
two sons and a daughter,
to Canada on the David of
London during May 1821.
Received a land grant in
Ramsay, Upper Canda, on
17 August 1821. (PAO)

BEDDIE BENJAMIN
Son of David Beddie,
smith in Wigtown,
Wigtownshire. Manager
of Clare Valley Estate,
St Vincent. Died there
28 September 1810.
(Wigtown GS)

BEGG ARCHIBALD
Born c1777, son of Hugh
Begg and Margaret Taylor.
Died in America during
April 1816.
(Lesmahowhow GS)

BEGG HUGH
Born c1776, son of Hugh
Begg and Margaret Taylor.
Died in America during
November 1806.
(Lesmahowgow GS)

BELL DAVID
Glasgow. Merchant and
planter in Virginia c1745.
(SRA/B10/15/5959-60)

BELL Mrs DAVID
Sister of Alexander Spiers.
Manageress of her brother's
plantation in Virginia c1754.
(SRA/B10/15/6653)

BELL JOHN
Emigrated from Scotland to
Canada c1830. Settled in
Quebec.
(NLS/MS7198.7)

BELL ROBERT
New Abbey, Kirkcudbright-
shire. Applied to
settle in Canada on 2 March
1815.

14

BELL WILLIAM
Glasgow. Applied to
settle in Canada on
27 February 1815.
(SRO/RH9)

BELL Rev WILLIAM
Emigrated from Scotland
to Canada on the
Rothiemurcus during June
1817. Received land grants
in Elmsley, Upper Canada,on
31 October 1817, and in
Drummond, Upper Canada, on
18 September 1820.
(PAO)

BELL WILLIAM
50. Farmer in the parish
of Balmaghie, Stewartry
of Kirkcudbright.
Emigrated from Scotland,
with his wife Janet 40
and five children, to
Canada during 1818.
(CO384/2)

BENE JOHN
Royalist soldier captured
after the Battle of
Worcester. Transported
from Gravesend, Kent, to
Boston, Massachusetts on
the John and Sarah, master
John Greene, 13 May 1652.
(NER)

BENNET ADAM
Midshipman. Died of fever
on voyage from Scotland to
Darien 22 October 1698.
(NLS)

BENNETT WILLIAM
Emigrated from Scotland
to Canada on the
Commerce during June
1820.
(PAO)

BENNIE JAMES
Emigrated from Scotland
to Canada on the
Commerce. Received a
land grant in Ramsay,
Upper Canada, on
9 September 1821.
(PAO)

BERRIE JAMES
Emigrated from Scotland,
with wife, son and two
daughters, to Canada on
the George Canning during
June 1821. Received a
land grant in Lanark,
Upper Canada, on 15 July
1821.
(PAO)

BETHUNE JOHN
Born during 1751 at Brebost,
son of Angus Bethune and
Christian Campbell. Educated
at King's College, Aberdeen
c1770. Loyalist chaplain.
Settled in North Carolina
during 1773. Married
Veronique Waddens in
Montreal on 30 September
1782. Minister in Glengarry,
Upper Canada. Father of
nine children. Died on
23 September 1815 at
Williamstown, Upper
Canada.
(DCB)

BETHUNE Rev JOSEPH
Former minister of the
Church of Scotland at
Renton. Died on 5 June
1800. Buried in
Kingston Cathedral,
Jamaica.
(MIBWI)

BEVERIDGE JOHN
Born in Scotland.
Schoolmaster in
Edinburgh. Emigrated
from Scotland to New
England during 1752.
Professor of Languages
at the College of
Philadelphia,
Pennsylvania in 1755.
Died in 1769.
(BES)(TSA)

BEVERIDGE JAMES
Emigrated from Scotland,
with wife and son, to
Canada on the George
Canning during June 1821.
Received a land grant in
Dalhousie, Upper Canada,
on 15 July 1821.
(PAO)

BEVERIDGE THOMAS
Born at Eastside,
Fossaway, Fife, during
1748. Ordained in
Edinburgh on
23 September 1783.
Emigrated from Scotland
to America in 1784.
Minister in Cambridge,
Washington, New York.
(BES)

BIGGAR JAMES
Born c1789 in Dumfries.
Merchant in Kingston,
Jamaica. Died on
25 June 1814. Buried
at Kingston, Jamaica.
(MIBWI)

BIGGAR JOHN
Dumfries(?) Died on
13 July 1829. Buried
in Kingston Cathedral,
Jamaica.
(MIBWI)

BINNIE AGNES
Indentured servant
imported from Scotland
to East New Jersey by
Thomas Yallerton
during 1684.
(EJD/A)

BINNIE JOHN
Born in Edinburgh during
1793. Died on
6 December 1830. Buried
in Kingston Cathedral,
Jamaica.
(MIBWI)

BIRNIE JAMES
Born in Scotland c1799.
Emigrated from Scotland
to Canada. North West
Company employee from
1818 to 1821. Hudson Bay
Company employee from
1821 to 1846. Died in
1864.
(HBRS)

16

BIRRELL GEORGE
Born during 1800 son of
George Birrell of the
Honourable East India
Company Service.
Apprenticed to (1)
Henry Moncrieff, (2)
James Stuart. Admitted
to the Society of
Writers to the Signet
on 1 July 1824. Married
29 December 1832 to Lucy,
daughter of Hon. Charles
Chipchase, Controller of
the Customs in St Lucia.
Barrister of the Inner
Temple and Senior Member
of the Legislative Council
of St Lucia. Attorney
General of the Bahamas.
Died on 9 March 1837.
(WS)

BISHOP ROBERT
Surgeon's mate. Died at
Darien on 8 December 1698.
(NLS)

BISHOP W.
Falkirk, Stirlingshire.
Applied to settle in
Canada on 27 February
1815.
(SRO/RH9)

BISSETT ANDREW
Mariner in New York.
Father of John, Eleanor,
Jane, Margaret, Elizabeth,
and Andrew in Queensferry,
Scotland. Will 1728.
Probate 1 June 1734.
(NYHS)

BISSETT ROBERT
Leith, Midlothian.
Applied to settle in
Canada on 1 March 1815.
(SRO/RH9)

BISSETT THOMAS
Emigrated from Scotland,
with wife, son and three
daughters, to Canada on
the Earl of Buckingham
during June 1821. Received
a land grant in Ramsay,
Upper Canada, on 20 July
1821.
(PAO)

BLACK ...
Born in Scotland. Formerly
a soldier in the Glengarry
Fencibles. Military
settler. Received a land
grant in Drummond, Upper
Canada, on 29 December 1818.
(PAO)

BLACK DAVID C.
Cousin of Janet Soutar,
Arbroath, Angus. A sea-
captain based at
Alexandria, Virginia,
during the 1820s.
(UNC/Black PP 2530)

BLACK GEORGE WATSON
Son of Thomas Black,
pharmacist in Aberdeen.
Educated at Marischal
College, Aberdeen, from
1809 to 1813. Graduated
M.A. Settled in America.
(MCA)

BLACK JAMES
Parkhead. Applied to
settle in Canada on
4 March 1815.
(SRO/RH9)

BLACK PATRICK
Emigrated from Scotland
to Canada. Received a
land grant in Cavan,
Newcastle, Upper
Canada, on
10 October 1818.
(PAO)

BLACK THOMAS
Educated at Marischal
College, Aberdeen, from
1815 to 1819. Merchant
in Canada.
(MCA)

BLACK WALTER
Emigrated from Greenock,
Renfrewshire, with his
wife, four sons and a
daughter, to Canada on
the George Canning
during May 1821.
Received a land grant in
Ramsay, Upper Canada, on
16 July 1821.
(PAO)

BLACKBURN JOHN
Glasgow(?) Merchant and
shipowner - latterly in
Norfolk, Virginia. Died
c1750.
(SRA)

BLACKWOOD JAMES
Emigrated from Scotland,
with his wife, to
Canada on the Commerce
during June 1820.
Received a land grant
in Lanark, Upper Canada,
on 3 September 1820.
(PAO)

BLACKWOOD JOHN
Son of John Blackwood of
Airdsgreen, Lanarkshire.
Emigrated from Scotland
to Canada during 1780.
(NRAS0097/1)

BLAIR DAVID
Giffordland, Ayrshire.
Settled in Georgia in
1736.
(HGP)

BLAIR DAVID
Born in Angus during 1740.
Emigrated from Scotland
to Virginia. Settled in
Spottsylvania County,
Virginia. Merchant.
Died in Fredericksburg,
Virginia during 1801.
Buried in the Masonic
Cemetery.
(BM)

BLAIR HENRY
Emigrated from Scotland,
with wife and three
daughters, to Canada on
the Alfred in September
1820. Received a land
grant in Bathurst, Upper
Canada, on 25 February 1821.
(PAO)

BLAIR JAMES
Born in Crombie, son of
Robert Blair, minister of
Alvah. Educated at
Marischal College in
Aberdeen from 1667 to
1669. Commissary of
Virginia.
(MCA)

BLAIR JAMES
Son of James Blair,
merchant in Ayr and in
Glasgow, and Mary
Davidson. Died at
Hopeton Estate,
St Elizabeth, Jamaica,
in early 1800s.
(RAF)

BLAIR JAMES
Emigrated from Scotland,
with wife and son, to
Canada on the Alfred
during September 1820.
Received a land grant
in Bathurst, Upper
Canada, on
25 February 1821.
(PAO)

BLAIR JAMES
Emigrated from Scotland,
with wife, two sons and
two daughters, to
Canada on the Brock
during 1820. Received
a land grant in
Dalhousie, Upper
Canada, on 25 October
1821.
(PAO)

BLAIR JEAN
Daughter of Archibald
Blair, writer, married
John Blair jr., son of
John Blair, councillor
in Virginia, in
Edinburgh on
26 December 1756.
(EMR)

BLAIR Dr JOHN
Brother of 'Inchiron'
in Angus. Resident in
Port Royal, Jamaica,
c1700.
(DP)

BLAIR JOHN
Born 1718. Emigrated
from Perthshire to
America c1735. Settled
in northern New Jersey.
Married Mary Hazlett.
Father of James born in
1769. Died on 20 May
1798.
(BAF)

BLAIR JOHN jr
Son of John Blair,
councillor in Virginia,
married Jean, daughter of
Archibald Blair, writer,
both in New North parish,
in Edinburgh 26 December
1756.
(EMR)

19

BLAIR JOHN
Emigrated from Greenock,
Renfrewshire, with wife,
two sons and four
daughters, to Canada on
the David of London in
May 1821. Received a
land grant in Lanark,
Upper Canada, on
3 September 1821.
(PAO)

BLAIR JOHN
Emigrated from Scotland,
with wife, son and three
daughters, to Canada on
the Prompt. Received a
land grant in Dalhousie,
Upper Canada, on
21 November 1821.
(PAO)

BLAIR SARAH
Daughter of David Blair
of Adamton, married ....
Watkinson. Settled in
America during eighteenth
century. Mother of David
Watkinson, merchant in
Hertford, Connecticut.
(RAF)

BLAIR WILLIAM
Born in Scotland.
Former army lieutenant.
Military settler.
Received a land grant
in Bathurst, Upper
Canada, on 23 July
1816.
(PAO)

BLAIR WILLIAM
Born in Scotland. Former
lieutenant in the Glen-
garry Fencibles. Military
settler. Wife, son and
two daughters. Received
land grant in Upper Canada
on 23 July 1816, and at
Oxford, Upper Canada, on
31 July 1817.
(PAO)

BLAIR WILLIAM
Emigrated from Scotland,
with wife and two sons, to
Canada on the Alfred in
September 1820. Received
a land grant in Sherbrook,
Upper Canada, on
25 February 1821.
(PAO)

BLAKE WILLIAM
Edinburgh. Applied to
settle in Canada on
28 February 1815.
(SRO/RH9)

BLOUNT ROBERT
Son of James Blount, 1756-
1816, farmer in Rosehall,
and Minnie Kissock.
Surgeon. Died in Jamaica
on 23 July 1833(?)
(Dumfries GS)

BLOUNT SAMUEL
Born during 1794 son of
Lieutenant David Blount.
Died in Jamaica during
September 1828.
(Dumfries GS)

BODY WILLIAM
Born c1726. Farmer.
Emigrated from Scotland
to Virginia pre 1756.
(OD)

BOG DAVID
Born in Scotland. Former
Clerk of the Field Train.
Military settler.
Received a land grant in
Beckwith, Upper Canada, on
7 July 1817.
(PAO)

BOGLE ROBERT
Third son of Robert Bogle,
merchant in Glasgow. Born
c1801. Died 21 December
1819. Buried in Kingston
Cathedral, Jamaica.
(MIBWI)

BORLAND JOHN
Scottish merchant in
Boston, Massachusetts
c1699.
(DP)

BORTHWICK JAMES
Sailor. Died at Darien
on 3 December 1698.
(NLS)

BOSS ANDREW
Emigrated from Scotland,
with wife, to Canada on
the Brock during 1820.
Received a land grant in
Lanark, Upper Canada, on
25 October 1821.
(PAO)

BOSTON HENRY
Ettrick, Selkirkshire.
Emigrated from Scotland
to America c1640. Married
Anne... Father of Isaac.
Died c1670.
(BAF)

BOTHWELL ROBERT
Born at Glencorse on
18 March 1705, sixth son
of Henry Bothwell and
Mary Campbell. Surgeon
in Edinburgh. Emigrated
from Scotland to Jamaica.
Married Margaret Preston.
Father of Margaret.
(SP.4.438)

BOWEN DAVID
Emigrated from Scotland,
with wife, two sons and
two daughters, to Canada
on the Commerce during
June 1820. Received a
land grant in Lanark,
Upper Canada, on
1 October 1820.
(PAO)

BOWES JAMES sr.
Glamis, Angus. Emigrated
from Greenock, Renfrewshire,
with wife, three sons and
four daughters, to Canada
on the David of London
during May 1821. Received
a land grant in Ramsay,
Upper Canada, on
25 August 1821.
(PAO)

BOWES JOHN
Emigrated from Scotland
to Canada on the
Commerce. Received a
land grant in Lanark,
Upper Canada, on
29 July 1822.
(PAO)

BOWES THOMAS
Emigrated from Scotland
to Canada on the David
of London during May
1821. Settled in Upper
Canada.
(PAO)

BOWIE JOHN
Born 1688. Emigrated
from Scotland to
America during 1705.
Settled in Prince
George County, Mary-
land. Married Mary,
daughter of James
Milliken, during 1707.
Father of Allan born
in 1719. Died during
April 1759.
(BAF)

BOWIE THOMAS
Emigrated from Scotland
to Canada on the David
of London during June
1821. Received a land
grant in Ramsay, Upper
Canada, on 25 August
1821.
(PAO)

BOWMAN ALEXANDER
Born c1736, eldest son
of John Bowman and ....
Houghton, Kilwinning,
Ayrshire. Emigrated
from Scotland to
America c1775.
(HCA)

BOYD ALEXANDER
Son of Robert Boyd,
Dunlop, Ayrshire.
Emigrated from Scotland
to America. Settled in
Mecklenburg, Virginia,
during 1765. Married
Anne Simpson. Merchant
and planter.
(VMHB.1942)

BOYD JOHN
Indentured servant
imported from Scotland
to East New Jersey by
Lord Neil Campbell in
December 1685.
(EJD/A225)

BOYD JOHN
Born in Scotland.
Educated at University
of Glasgow c1701. Emigrated
from Scotland to America.
Ordained at Freehold, New
Jersey on 29 December 1706.
Presbyterian minister.
Died during 1708.
(AP)

BOYD JOHN
Born in Glasgow, son
of a minister.
Emigrated from Scotland
to America. Merchant
in Richmond, Virginia,
c1790.
(DU.23G/11.5.33)

BOYLE of INVERKIP STAIR
Merchant in St Kitts
c1761.
(SRA/B10/12/2)

BOYD THOMAS
Pitcon, Ayrshire.
Settled in Georgia
during 1736.
(HGP)

BRAIDWOOD JAMES
Emigrated from Greenock,
Renfrewshire, with wife,
three sons and a daughter,
to Canada on the George
Canning during May 1821.
Received a land grant in
Lanark, Upper Canada, on
25 July 1821.
(PAO)

BREBNER JAMES
(later J B Gordon of
 Knockespock)
Educated at Aberdeen
Grammar School and
Marischal College,
Aberdeen, c1725.
Chief Justice of
Grenada.
(MCA)

BREMNER CHARLES
Emigrated from Scotland,
with wife, to Canada on
the David of London
during June 1821.
Received a land grant
in Lanark, Upper Canada,
on 6 August 1821.
(PAO)

BREMNER GEORGE sr.
Emigrated from Greenock,
Renfrewshire, with four
sons and two daughters,
to Canada on the David
of London during May
1821. Received a land
grant in Lanark, Upper
Canada, on 6 August 1821.
(PAO)

BREMNER GEORGE jr.
Emigrated from Greenock,
Renfrewshire, with wife,
son and daughter, to
Canada on the David of
London during May 1821.
Received a land grant in
Lanark, Upper Canada, on
6 August 1821.
(PAO)

BREMNER JOHN
Born 1792, son of Joseph
Bremner, feuar in Fochabers,
Morayshire, and Mary Allan.
Settled in the Bahamas
after the wreck of the war-
ship Laurustinus. Merchant
in Nassau, New Providence.
Died on 30 August 1818.
(Bellie GS)

23

BREWER(?) THOMAS
Royalist soldier
captured after the
Battle of Worcester.
Transported from
Gravesend, Kent, to
Boston, Massachusetts,
on the John and Sarah,
master John Greene, on
13 May 1652.
(NER)

BRICHAN JAMES
Born c1767, son of
George Brichan, 1726-
1786, and Jean Anders,
1727-1772, Gallowhill.
Died in Demerara on
9 August 1802.
(Cargill GS)

BRIDGEMAN ROBERT
Merchant. Emigrated
from Scotland to East
New Jersey during
February 1685.
(EJD/A236)

BRODIE D.
Old Kilpatrick,
Dumbartonshire.
Applied to settle
in Canada on 3 March
1815.
(SRO/RH9)

BRODIE JOHN
Doctor, possibly from
Scotland, settled in
Virginia during 1700s.
(SA)

BRODIE JOHN PRINGLE
Born during 1806, son
of William Brodie,
schoolmaster, 1780-
1846, and Isabella
Plowman, 1784-1858,
Alloa. Died in San
Francisco, California, on
30 October 1868.
(Alloa GS)

BRODIE WILLIAM
Indentured servant
imported from Scotland
to East New Jersey by
David Mudie during
November 1684.
(EJD/A197)

BROOKS JAMES
Emigrated from Scotland,
with wife, four sons and
two daughters, to Canada
on the Earl of Buckingham,
during June 1821.
Received a land grant in
Dalhousie, Upper Canada,
on 20 July 1821.
(PAO)

BROWN ADAM
Workfieldbank. Applied
to settle in Canada on
5 March 1815.
(SRO/RH9)

BROWN ANDREW
'A boy aboard a French
ship'. Died at Darien on
24 December 1698.
(NLS)

BROWN ANDREW
Emigrated from Greenock,
Renfrewshire, with wife,
two sons and two daughters,
to Canada on the George
Canning during May 1821.
Received a land grant in
Ramsay, Upper Canada, on
25 July 1821.
(PAO)

BROWN CHARLES
Emigrated from Scotland,
with three sons and six
daughters, to Canada on
the Prompt. Received a
land grant in Dalhousie,
Upper Canada, on
11 November 1821.
(PAO)

BROWN GEORGE
Married Annabel Gordon
or Knox. Emigrated
from Scotland to
New Jersey during 1680s.
Settled Woodbridge, New
Jersey. Father of James.
('The NJ Browns', 1931)

BROWN GEORGE
Emigrated from Scotland
to Canada on the Prompt.
Received a land grant in
Dalhousie, Upper Canada,
on 21 November 1821.
(PAO)

BROWN GORDON
Son of Alexander Brown,
minister of New Spynie,
Elgin, Morayshire.
Student in Aberdeen 1799-
1802. Doctor in Demerara.
(MCA)

BROWN JAMES
Born in Angus during
1790. Emigrated from
Scotland to New
Brunswick during 1808.
Politician and surveyor.
Died during 1870.
(SO)

BROWN JAMES
Born c1752. Mason.
Emigrated from Scotland
to Canada. Settled in
Pictou Town, Nova Scotia,
during 1815.
(PANS/RG1)

BROWN JAMES
Emigrated from Scotland,
with wife and two sons, to
Canada on the Earl of
Buckingham. Received a
land grant in Dalhousie,
Upper Canada, on
3 September 1821.
(PAO)

BROWN JOHN
Royalist soldier captured
after Battle of Worcester.
Transported from Gravesend,
Kent, to Boston, Massachusetts
on the John and Sarah, master
John Greene, 13 May 1652.
(NER)

BROWN JOHN
Indentured servant
imported from Scotland to
East New Jersey by John
Laing in Middlesex County.
Land grant 17 January 1693.
(EJD/D)

BROWN JOHN
Coldstream, Berwickshire.
Doctor. Settled in
Virginia. Died in 1726.
(SA)

BROWN JOHN MURRAY
Galloway. Doctor.
Settled in Virginia
during eighteenth
century.
(SA)

BROWN Rev JOHN
Born in 1766 at
Common of Fossaway,
Perthshire. Educated
at University of
Glasgow. Ordained
as a missionary in
1795. Emigrated
from Scotland to Nova
Scotia via New York
during 1795. Minister
in Londonderry, Nova
Scotia, from 1795 to
1848. Died in 1848.
(HPC)

BROWN JOHN
Born in Dunsyre,
Lanarkshire during 1776,
son of William Brown,
1750-1816, and Margaret
.... 1753-1823. Died
in Jamaica on
19 October 1804.
(Dunsyre GS)

BROWN JOHN
Glasgow. Applied to
settle in Canada on
4 March 1815.
(SRO/RH9)

BROWN ROBERT
Emigrated from Scotland,
with wife and four
daughters, to Canada on
the Prompt. Received a
land grant in Dalhousie,
Upper Canada, on
11 November 1821.
(PAO)

BROWN WILLIAM
Kilmarnock, Ayrshire.
Covenanter - captured
at the Battle of Bothwell
Bridge on 22 June 1679.
Banished to the Plantations.
Drowned off Orkney.
(HCA)

BROWN WILLIAM
Glasgow (?) Merchant and
planter in St Kitts. Later
at Lower Quarter Plantation,
St David's parish, Courland,
Tobago. Died in 1767.
(SRA/B10/15/7493)

BROWN WILLIAM
Born in Haddington, East
Lothian, during 1752.
Educated in Edinburgh
c1770. Doctor. Settled
in Virginia.
(SA)

BROWN WILLIAM
Son of George Brown. Settled
in Norfolk, Virginia, c1740.
Married Janette, daughter
of Dr Joseph MacAdam,
Northumberland County,
Virginia on 20 October 1771.
Father of Edwin Conway
Brown etc. Died in 1797.
(BAF)

26

BROWN WILLIAM
Born in Scotland.
Former sergeant in the
70th Regiment. Wife.
Military settler.
Received a land grant
in Bathurst, Upper
Canada, on 2 September
1819.
(PAO)

BROWN WILLIAM
Emigrated from Scotland,
with wife, to Canada on
the Commerce during June
1820. Received a land
grant in Lanark, Upper
Canada, on 8 September
1820.
(PAO)

BROWNHILL HENRY
Royalist soldier
captured at the Battle
of Worcester. Transported
from Gravesend, Kent, to
Boston, Massachusetts, on
the John and Sarah,
master John Greene,
13 May 1652.
(NER)

BROWNING ARCHIBALD
Emigrated from Scotland,
with wife, two sons and a
daughter, to Canada on
the Commerce in June
1821. Received a land
grant in Lanark, Upper
Canada, on 1 August 1821.
(PAO)

BROWNLIE DAVID
Emigrated from Scotland
to Canada on the Commerce
during June 1821.
Received a land grant in
Dalhousie, Upper Canada,
on 15 July 1821.
(PAO)

BROWNLEE JAMES
Born near Glasgow in 1801.
Emigrated from Scotland
to America during 1827.
Settled in Mahony County,
Ohio. Politician and
abolutionist. Died in
Poland, Ohio, on
20 January 1879.
(TSA)

BROWNLIE JOHN
Emigrated from Scotland
to Canada on the Commerce
during June 1821.
Received a land grant in
Dalhousie, Upper Canada,
on 15 July 1821.
(PAO)

BROWNLEE WILLIAM CRAIG
Born in Lanarkshire 1784.
Graduated Glasgow University
M.A.1803, D.D. 1824. Pastor
of Associate Churches in
Washington County, Penn.
and Philadelphia in 1813.
Presbyterian pastor in
Baskingridge, NJ, 1817.
Professor at Rutgers 1825.
Dutch Reformed minister in
New York 1826. Died in New
York 10 February 1860.
(GG)

27

BROWNLIE WILLIAM
Emigrated from Scotland
to Canada on the Commerce
during June 1821.
Received a land grant in
Dalhousie, Upper Canada,
on 15 July 1821.
(PAO)

BRUCE CHARLES
Trooper. Emigrated
from Scotland to America.
Settled in Frederick
County, Virginia, 1756.
(OD)

BRUCE DAVID
Born in Edinburgh.
Emigrated from Scotland
to America during 1793.
Publisher in New York.
Died in Brooklyn 1857.
(TSA)

BRUCE GEORGE
Born in Edinburgh.
Emigrated from Scotland
to America during 1795.
Publisher in New York.
Died during 1866.
(TSA)

BRUCE JOHN
Emigrated from Scotland,
with wife, son and a
daughter, to Canada on
the George Canning during
June 1821. Received a
land grant in Ramsay,
Upper Canada, on
10 July 1821.
(PAO)

BRUCE ROBERT
Emigrated from Scotland,
with wife, three sons and
four daughters, to
Canada on the George
Canning during June 1821.
Received a land grant in
Lanark, Upper Canada, on
10 July 1821.
(PAO)

BRUNTON Rev WILLIAM
Born in Scotland. Educated
at University of Aberdeen.
Minister of Lachine,
Canada, 1820-1822.
(HPC)

BRYCE ARCHIBALD
Glasgow. Factor in
Richmond, Virginia, for
Thomson and Snodgrass,
tobacco importers in
Glasgow, c1776.
(SRA/B10/12/4)

BRYCE JAMES jr
Born during 1800 at West
Calder, West Lothian.
Emigrated from Greenock,
Renfrewshire, to Canada on
the Atlas during 1815.
Received a land grant in
Sherbrook, Upper Canada, on
8 December 1820.
(PAO)

28

BRYCE JOHN
Emigrated from Scotland
to Canada on the Phillip
during 1820. Received a
land grant in Sherbrook,
Upper Canada, 30 March
1821.
(PAO)

BRYCE WILLIAM sr.
Emigrated from Scotland,
with wife, four sons and
two daughters, to
Canada on the Commerce
during June 1821.
Received a land grant in
Sherbrook, Upper Canada,
on 1 August 1821.
(PAO)

BRYCE WILLIAM jr.
Emigrated from Scotland
to Canada on the Commerce
during June 1821.
Received a land grant in
Sherbrook, Upper Canada,
on 1 August 1821.
(PAO)

BRYSON JAMES
Emigrated from Scotland,
with wife, four sons and
three daughters, to
Canada on the Earl of
Buckingham in June 1821.
Received a land grant in
Ramsay, Upper Canada, on
25 July 1821.
(PAO)

BUCHAN ALEXANDER
Indentured servant
imported from Scotland
to East New Jersey in
October 1684 by George
Willocks. Land grant
1 May 1690.
(EJD/A267/D167)

BUCHAN JOHN
Third son of Thomas Buchan
of Auchmacoy, Aberdeenshire.
Apprenticed to Andrew
Stuart jr. Admitted to
the Society of Writers
to the Signet on
19 November 1782. Died
in Jamaica during 1793.
(WS)

BUCHANAN ARCHIBALD
Emigrated from Scotland,
with wife, two sons and
two daughters, to Canada
on the Commerce. Received
a land grant in Lanark,
Upper Canada, 9 September
1821.
(PAO)

BUCHANAN DANIEL
Born in Scotland. Former
sergeant in the Canadian
Fencibles. Military
settler. Wife. Received
a land grant in Kitley,
Upper Canada on 31 July
1817.
(PAO)

29

BUCHANAN DAVID
Born in Scotland.
Military settler.
Received a land grant
in Bathurst, Upper
Canada, on
20 September 1816.
(PAO)

BUCHANAN JAMES
Emigrated from Scotland
to Virginia before 1755.
Shoemaker.
(OD)

BUCHANAN JAMES
Emigrated from Scotland
to Canada on the Commerce
Received a land grant in
Lanark, Upper Canada, on
9 September 1821.
(PAO)

BUCHANAN JOHN
Emigrated from Scotland,
with wife, two sons and
two daughters, to Canada
on the Earl of Buckingham
during June 1821.
Received a land grant in
Ramsay, Upper Canada, on
24 July 1821.
(PAO)

BUCHANAN MARGARET
Daughter of John Buchanan
of Glens, married Thomas
Peters, son of John Peters,
merchant in Virginia.
Process of declarator of
marriage 4 November 1768.
(CPD)

BUCHANAN PETER
Cragon, Perthshire(?)
Emigrated from Greenock,
Renfrewshire, to Montreal
with wife Janet McLaren and
children John and Duncan,
on the brig Niagara in 1825.
Settled in McNab, Bathurst,
Upper Canada, during 1825.
(SG)

BUCHANAN THOMAS
Emigrated from Scotland
to Canada on the Earl of
Buckingham in June 1821.
Received a land grant in
Ramsay, Upper Canada, on
26 July 1821.
(PAO)

BUCHANAN WILLIAM
Emigrated from Scotland
to Canada on the
Trafalgar on 31 July 1817.
Received a land grant in
South Gower, Upper Canada,
on 13 October 1817.
(PAO)

BULLOCH JAMES
Emigrated from Scotland
to Canada on the Commerce
during June 1820.
Received a land grant in
Lanark, Upper Canada, on
8 September 1820.
(PAO)

30

BULLOCK THOMAS
Emigrated from Scotland,
with wife, five sons and
two daughters, to
Canada on the Commerce
during June 1820.
Received a land grant
in Lanark, Upper Canada,
on 8 September 1820.
(PAO)

BURGESS JOSEPH
Scottish settler in
Darien, Georgia, c1739.
(HGP)

BURGESS JOHN
Emigrated from Scotland,
with wife and son, to
Canada on the Commerce
during August 1820.
Received a land grant in
Lanark, Upper Canada, on
5 September 1820.
(PAO)

BURNETT ANDREW
Indentured servant
imported from Scotland
to East New Jersey in
1684.
(EJD/A)

BURNETT ELIZABETH
Indentured servant
imported from Scotland
to East New Jersey by
David Mudie during
November 1684. Land
grant on 1 May 1690.
(EJD/D167/A197)

BURNET Dr ICHABOD
Born in Scotland in 1693.
Educated in Edinburgh -
graduated M.D. Emigrated
from Scotland to America.
Settled Elisabethtown,
New Jersey. Father of
William, born 1730. Died
during 1773.
(NJHSP.111.2.80)

BURNET of LETHENTIE ROBERT
One of the Proprietors of
East New Jersey. Married
Ann ... Father of Patrick,
John, Robert, Mesdie,
Allen and Isabel. Settled
at Milston Brook, Freehold,
Monmouth County, New Jersey,
on 13 May 1702. Will dated
24 November 1712. Probate
16 November 1714.
(EJD/Liber I, 526)

BURNETT WILLIAM
Indentured servant
imported from Scotland to
East New Jersey by David
Mudie during November
1684. Land grantdated
1 May 1690.
(EJD/A197/D167)

BURNS JOHN
Emigrated from Scotland,
with wife and son, to
Canada on the Earl of
Buckingham during June
1821. Received a land
grant in Dalhousie,
Upper Canada, on
4 August 1821.
(PAO)

BURNS THOMAS
Emigrated from Scotland
to America. Settled in
Franklin County,
Pennsylvania. Father
of James. Died during
1816 in Bedford County,
Pennsylvania.
(H)

BURNS WALTER
Emigrated from Scotland,
with wife and son, to
Canada on the Commerce
during August 1820.
Received a land grant
in Dalhousie, Upper
Canada, on 5 September
1820.
(PAO)

BURROL JOHN
Sailor. Died at Darien
29 November 1698.
(NLS)

BURROWES THOMAS
Emigrated from Scotland,
with wife, five sons and
two daughters, to Canada
on the Commerce. Received
a land grant in Lanark,
Upper Canada, on
9 September 1821.
(PAO)

BURTT JOHN
Born during 1790 in
Knockmarlock, Kilmarnock,
Ayrshire. Served in the
Royal Navy from 1806 to
1811. Weaver in
Kilmarnock. Teacher in
Paisley, Renfrewshire.
Poet. Political radical.
Emigrated from Scotland
to America during 1817.
Educated at Princeton
University, New Jersey.
Presbyterian minister in
Salem, New Jersey, and
later in Blackwoodtown.
Died in Salem 1866.
(TSA)

CAINE JOHN
Yeoman. Emigrated from
Scotland to Canada.
Received a land grant
in Thorak, Home, Upper
Canada, on 8 March 1826.
(PAO)

CAIRNS ALEXANDER
Emigrated from Scotland,
with wife, two sons and a
daughter, to Canada on the
Commerce during August 1820.
Received a land grant in
Lanark, Upper Canada, on
5 September 1820.
(PAO)

CALDER JAMES
Emigrated from Scotland,
with wife and two sons,
to Canada on the George
Canning during June 1821.
Received a land grant in
Lanark, Upper Canada, on
30 June 1821.
(PAO)

CALDWELL DAVID
Emigrated from Scotland,
with wife, two sons and
three daughters, to
Canada on the Commerce
during August 1820.
Received a land grant in
Lanark, Upper Canada, on
5 September 1820.
(PAO)

CALDWELL JOHN
Emigrated from Scotland
on the Earl of Buckingham
during June 1821.
Received a land grant in
Lanark, Upper Canada, on
19 July 1821.
(PAO)

CALDWELL WILLIAM
Emigrated from Scotland,
with wife, two sons and
two daughters, to
Canada on the Earl of
Buckingham during June
1821. Received a
land grant in Lanark,
Upper Canada, on
16 July 1821.
(PAO)

CALLENDAR ALEXANDER
Emigrated from Scotland,
with wife, two sons and
four daughters, to Canada
on the Prompt. Received a
land grant in Dalhousie,
Upper Canada, on
13 November 1821.
(PAO)

CALLENDAR THOMAS
Born in Stirling during
1758. Political radical.
Emigrated from Scotland
to America during 1793.
Settled in Philadelphia,
Pennsylvania. Journalist
and author. Drowned in
James River, Richmond,
Virginia, during 1813.
(TSA)

CAMERON ALEXANDER
Born in Scotland. British
Army Engign at Fort Prince
George, South Carolina, in
1763. Married a Cherokee.
Deputy Superintendent for
Indian Department in the
South. Died in Savannah,
Georgia, on 27 December
1781.
(C)

CAMERON ALEXANDER
Emigrated from Scotland,
with wife, three sons and
four daughters, to Canada
on the Morning Field on
19 September 1816. Received
land grant in Burgess, Upper
Canada, 23 October 1816.
(PAO)

CAMERON ALEXANDER
Emigrated from Scotland
to Canada. Received a
land grant in Lanark,
Upper Canada, on
27 July 1821.
(PAO)

CAMERON ALEXANDER
Born in Scotland. Former
sergeant in the 103rd
Regiment. Military
settler. Received a
land grant in Upper
Canada during November
1818.
(PAO)

CAMERON ALLAN
Yeoman. Emigrated from
Scotland to Canada.
Received a land grant
in Eldon, Newcastle,
Upper Canada, on
8 March 1826.
(PAO)

CAMERON ANGUS
Born in Argyllshire,
Scotland. Wife, two
sons and two daughters.
Former sergeant in the
Canadian Fencibles.
Military settler.
Received a land grant
in Burgess, Upper Canada,
22 August 1816, and in
Leeds, Upper Canada, on
31 July 1817.
(PAO)

CAMERON ANGUS
Born in Scotland. Former
Quartermaster in the
Prince of York's Chasseurs.
Military settler. Received
a land grant in Bathurst,
Upper Canada, 12 October
1819.
(PAO)

CAMERON ANGUS
Born in Scotland c1784.
Labourer. Emigrated
from Scotland to Canada.
Settled in Pictou, Nova
Scotia during 1815.
(PANS/RG1)

CAMERON ANGUS
Born in Scotland c1785.
Labourer. Emigrated
from Scotland, with wife
and three children, to
Canada. Settled in
Pictou, Nova Scotia 1815.
(PANS/RG1)

CAMERON ANGUS
Yeoman. Emigrated from
Scotland to Canada.
Received a land grant in
Mora, Newcastle, Upper
Canada, on 8 March 1826.
(PAO)

CAMERON ANN
Born in Scotland c1755.
Widow. Emigrated from
Scotland to Canada.
Settled in Pictou, Nova
Scotia, during 1815.
(PANS/RG1)

CAMERON ARCHIBALD
Yeoman. Emigrated from
Scotland to Canada.
Received a land grant in
Thorak, Home, Upper Canada,
on 8 March 1826.
(PAO)

CAMERON CHARLES
Born Inverness on
16 May 1783.
Emigrated from Scotland
to Canada. Married
Sarah Houghton in
Toronto during 1808.
Died in Ontario on
1 August 1867.
(HFH)

CAMERON DONALD
Emigrated from Scotland
to Canada. Received a
land grant in
Charlotteburg, St Raphael,
Province of Quebec,
during 1787.
(PAO)

CAMERON Captain DONALD
Kinlocheil, Inverness-
shire. Emigrated from
Scotland to Canada.
Settled at La Chine,
near Montreal, c1805.
(GD202/70/12)

CAMERON DONALD
Yeoman. Emigrated from
Scotland to Canada.
Received a land grant
in Eldon, Newcastle,
Upper Canada, on
8 March 1826.
(PAO)

CAMERON DONALD
Emigrated from Scotland
to Canada. Received a
land grant in Thorak,
Home, Upper Canada, on
8 March 1826.
(PAO)

CAMERON DOUGALD
Born in Scotland. Former
soldier in the Glengarry
Fencibles. Military
settler. Received a land
grant in Upper Canada on
18 July 1816.
(PAO)

CAMERON DUGALD
Corpach, Fort William,
Inverness-shire. Applied
to emigrate to Canada 1818.
(CO384/3)

CAMERON DOUGALD
Yeoman. Emigrated from
Scotland to Canada.
Received a land grant in
Thorak, Home, Upper Canada
on 8 March 1826.
(PAO)

CAMERON DUNCAN
Born during 1764, son of
Alexander Cameron and
Margaret McDonell, Glen-
moriston, Inverness-shire.
Married Margaret McLeod of
Hamer c1821. Emigrated
from Scotland to Canada.
Settled in Williamstown,
Glengarry, Upper Canada.
Father of Duncan and
Roderick William. Politician.
(TML)

CAMERON DUNCAN
Emigrated from Scotland,
with wife and daughter, to
Canada on the Morning Field
19 September 1816.
Received a land grant in
Drummond, Upper Canada, on
9 December 1816.
(PAO)

CAMERON EWEN
Born 23 February 1768
at Gilhan, Ferintosh,
Ross and Cromarty, son
of Duncan Cameron and
Margaret Bain.
Emigrated from Scotland
to America in 1785.
Settled in Virginia.
Married Mary Frances
Buford during 1797.
Resettled in Tennessee
during 1798. Father of
Elizabeth, Margaret, John,
Duncan, Granville, William,
and Donald. Died in
Franklin, Tennessee, on
28 February 1846.
(CCAI)

CAMERON FRANCIS
Aberdeen. Graduated M.A.
at Aberdeen on 30 March
1821. Possibly an
Episcopalian minister in
America.
(UKA)

CAMERON HUGH
Emigrated from Scotland
to Canada on the Prompt
during September 1819.
Received a land grant in
Drummond, Upper Canada,
on 19 April 1820.
(PAO)

CAMERON JAMES
Born in Scotland on
18 May 1754. Married Jane
Craig, 1754-1829.
Emigrated from Scotland to
America. Settled in
Virginia. Father of Ann,
James, Rebekah, Jane, Mary,
and Lettice. Died in
Virginia 9 October 1799.
(CCAI)

CAMERON JAMES
Born in Scotland c1792.
Sawmiller. Emigrated
from Scotland, with wife
and two children, to
Canada. Settled Mount Tom,
Pictou, Nova Scotia, 1815.
(PANS/RG1)

CAMERON JAMES
Yeoman. Emigrated from
Scotland to Canada.
Received a land grant in
Eldon, Newcastle, Upper
Canada, on 8 March 1826.
(PAO)

CAMERON JEAN
Born c1780. Rhum,
Inverness-shire.
Emigrated from Leith to
Port Hawkesby, Cape Breton,
on the St Lawrence of
Newcastle, master Jon Cram,
during 1828.
(PANS/M6-100)

CAMERON JOHN
Emigrated from Scotland to
Canada. Received a land
grant in Charlotteburg,
St Raphael, Province of
Quebec, on 24 November 1787.
(PAO)

CAMERON JOHN
Emigrated from Scotland,
with his family, to
Canada. Landed at
Quebec 4 September 1804.
Settled at La Chine, near
Montreal. Farmer.
(GD202/70/12)

CAMERON JOHN
Born c1797. Labourer.
Emigrated from Scotland
to Canada. Settled in
Lower Settlement, East
Pictou, Nova Scotia,
during 1815.
(PANS/RG1)

CAMERON JOHN
Emigrated from Scotland
to Canada on the
Morning Field on
19 September 1816.
Received a land grant
in Drummond, Upper
Canada, on 23 October
1816.
(PAO)

CAMERON JOHN sr.
Emigrated from Scotland,
with wife and son, to
Canada on the
Speculation during
September 1819.
Received a land grant in
Beckwith, Upper Canada,
on 20 May 1820.
(PAO)

CAMERON JOHN
Yeoman. Emigrated from
Scotland to Canada.
Received a land grant
in Eldon, Newcastle,
Upper Canada, on
8 March 1826.
(PAO)

CAMERON KENNETH
Edinburgh. Applied to
settle in Canada on
4 March 1815.
(SRO/RH9)

CAMERON LACHLAN
Yeoman. Emigrated from
Scotland to Canada.
Received a land grant
in Thorak, Home, Upper
Canada, on 8 March 1826.
(PAO)

CAMERON Mrs MARGARET
Widow. Emigrated from
Scotland, with son John,
to America during 1740s.
(CCAI)

CAMERON ROBERT
Emigrated from Scotland,
with wife, four sons and
four daughters, to Canada
on the George Canning in
June 1821. Received a
land grant in Dalhousie,
Upper Canada, on 15 July
1821.
(PAO)

CAMERON WILLIAM
Born 1790. Labourer.
Emigrated from Scotland
to Canada. Settled in
Pictou, Nova Scotia,
during 1815.
(PANS/RG1)

CAMPBELL A.
Glasgow. Applied to
settle in Canada on
27 February 1815.
(SRO/RH9)

37

CAMPBELL ALEXANDER
Born during November 1734
at Killin, Perthshire,
son of James Campbell and
Elizabeth Buchanan.
Captain in the 84th
Regiment. Settled in
Johnstown, Upper Canada.
Married Magdalen Van Sice
at Schenectady, New York,
during May 1768. Father
of John and James. Died
during October 1800.
(JRC)

CAMPBELL ALEXANDER
Emigrated from Scotland,
with wife, son and
daughter, to Canada on
the Morning Field on
19 September 1816.
Received a land grant
in Beckwith, Upper
Canada, on
9 December 1816.
(PAO)

CAMPBELL ALEXANDER
Yeoman. Emigrated from
Scotland to Canada.
Received a land grant
in Eldon, Newcastle,
Upper Canada, on
8 March 1826.
(PAO)

CAMPBELL ANGUS
Born in Scotland.
Received a land grant
in Bathurst, Upper
Canada, on 31 August
1816.
(PAO)

CAMPBELL ARCHIBALD
Indentured servant
imported from Scotland
to East New Jersey in
October 1684 by John
Dobie.
(EJD/A)

CAMPBELL ARCHIBALD
Indentured servant
imported from Scotland
to East New Jersey by
Lord Neil Campbell in
December 1685.
(EJD/A225)

CAMPBELL ARCHIBALD
Eldest son of Ronald
Campbell, merchant in
Campbelltown, Argyllshire,
and Jean, daughter of
James Campbell of Duntroon.
Emigrated from Scotland to
the West Indies during
May 1790.
(CC)

CAMPBELL ARCHIBALD
Emigrated from Scotland
to Canada via the United
States. Received a land
grant in Bathurst, Upper
Canada, on 8 March 1818.
(PAO)

CAMPBELL CHRISTIAN
Born c1777. Emigrated
from Scotland to Canada.
Settled at Moole River,
Pictou, Nova Scotia, 1815.
(PANS/RG1)

CAMPBELL COLIN
Indentured servant
imported from Scotland
to East New Jersey in
October 1684 by John
Campbell. Land grant
1 May 1690.
(EJD/A/D325)

CAMPBELL COLIN
Born during June 1752
in Inveraray, Argyll-
shire, second son of
David Campbell of
Belmont, Corstorphine,
and Jean Campbell.
Studied law in
Edinburgh. Possibly a
Notary Public in New
York cMay 1782.
Loyalist. Settled in
Shelbourne, Nova Scotia,
during 1783. Lawyer 1791.
Married (1) widow of Col.
Samuel Campbell,
Wilmington, North Carolina,
(2) Elizabeth, daughter of
Richard Hardy on
15 November 1796. Father
of John and Colin.
(CC)

CAMPBELL COLIN
Son of Archibald Campbell
of Barnacary. Merchant
in Jamaica. Died c1789.
(CC)

CAMPBELL COLIN
Merchant in Greenock,
married Henrietta, daughter
of Duncan Campbell, Glasgow,
during August 1776. Settled
Holland Estate, St Elizabeth,
Cornwall, Jamaica. Process of
Divorce in 1790.
(CPD)

CAMPBELL COLIN
Born during 1785 in
Mulindry, Islay, Argyll-
shire, son of George
Campbell, tenant, and
Elizabeth Graham. Married
(1) Isabella Carmichael,
died 1832, parents of
Christina born in Islay
10 January 1818.
Emigrated from Scotland
to North Carolina during
1818. Settled during
1828 in Upper Canada.
Moved to Woodville,
Victoria County, 1832.
Married (2) Mary
Carmichael.
(SG)

CAMPBELL DANIEL
Son of Alexander Campbell
of Kilbride. Indentured
to John Glassford,
merchant in Glasgow, for
four years in Maryland on
28 September 1769.
Possibly settled in
Portobacco, Maryland.
(SRA/TD180/20)

CAMPBELL DANIEL
Emigrated from Scotland,
with wife and son, to
Canada on the David of
London during June 1821.
Received a land grant in
Lanark, Upper Canada, on
17 August 1821.
(PAO)

CAMPBELL DAVID
Argyllshire(?) Settler in
St Thomas in the Vale,
Jamaica, c1762.
(CC)

CAMPBELL of BELMONT
CORSTORPHINE DAVID
Born c1730. Writer to
the Signet. Married
(2) Jean Campbell in
March 1756. Emigrated
from Scotland to New
York during 1776.
Notary Public in New
York 15 March 1777.
Attorney-at-Law 1778.
May have returned to
Scotland.
(CC)

CAMPBELL DAVID
Emigrated from Scotland
to Canada on the Prompt.
Received a land grant in
Dalhousie, Upper Canada,
on 11 November 1821.
(PAO)

CAMPBELL DONALD
Argyllshire(?) Planter
in St Mary's parish,
Jamaica, c1777.
(CC)

CAMPBELL DONALD
Emigrated from Scotland,
with wife, to Canada on
the Lady of the Lake.
Received a land grant in
Drummond, Upper Canada,
on 30 November 1816.
(PAO)

CAMPBELL DUGALD
Born c1759. Officer in
the 42nd (Black Watch)
Regiment, 1777-1783.
Married Jacobina
Drummond, Poughkeepsie,
New York. Settled in
New Brunswick during
1784. Soldier and
surveyor. Died 12 April
1810 in Fredericton, New
Brunswick.
(DCB)

CAMPBELL DUGALD
North Knapdale, Argyll-
shire. Emigrated from
Scotland to Canada on the
Mars of Glasgow in 1818.
(CO384/3)

CAMPBELL DUNCAN
Eldest son of William
Campbell of Ormsary,
Argyllshire. Settled
in St Vincent pre 1775.
(CC)

CAMPBELL DUNCAN
Emigrated from Scotland
to Canada on the Lady of
the Lake. Received a land
grant in Drummond, Upper
Canada, on 30 November 1816.
(PAO)

CAMPBELL DUNCAN
Emigrated from Scotland
to Canada on the Fancy
18 August 1816. Received
a land grant in Beckwith,
Upper Canada, 9 December
1816.
(PAO)

CAMPBELL DUNCAN
Emigrated from Scotland,
with wife and two daughters,
to Canada on the Commerce
during June 1821.
Received a land grant in
Sherbrook, Upper Canada,
on 7 August 1821.
(PAO)

CAMPBELL DUNCAN
Lochearnhead, Perthshire.
Emigrated from Scotland,
with wife Helen Watt, to
Canada on the brig
Niagara from Greenock,
Renfrewshire, to Montreal
during 1825. Settled in
McNab, Bathurst, Upper
Canada, in 1825. Father
of Isabel, Catherine,
Alexander, Margaret, Anne
and Mary.
(SG)

CAMPBELL D.
Fort William, Inverness-
shire. Applied to
emigrate to Canada
during 1818.
(CO384/3)

CAMPBELL HUGH
Emigrated from Scotland
to America. Merchant in
Boston, Massachusetts,
in 1679.
(INSH)

CAMPBELL HUGH
Emigrated from Scotland,
with wife and two sons, to
Canada on the Commerce.
Received a land grant in
Dalhousie, Upper Canada,
on 3 September 1821.
(PAO)

CAMPBELL HUGH
Dalbrig, Perthshire(?)
Emigrated from Greenock,
Renfrewshire, to Montreal
on the brig Niagara in
1825. Settled in MacNab,
Bathurst, Upper Canada,
during 1825.
(SG)

CAMPBELL of ORMAIG JAMES
Settled at Marian Estate,
Grenada, pre 1788.
(CC)

CAMPBELL JAMES
Ardesier, Nairnshire.
Educated at King's
College, Aberdeen, -
graduated M.A. on
28 March 1794.
Merchant in Baltimore,
Maryland.
(KCA)

CAMPBELL JAMES
Emigrated from Scotland
to Canada during 1806.
Settled in Quebec.
Hemp producer.
(DCB)

CAMPBELL JAMES
Born in Scotland. Former
soldier in the 20th
Regiment. Wife and son.
Military settler. Received
a land grant in Lanark,
Upper Canada, 11 November
1820.
(PAO)

41

CAMPBELL JAMES
Born in Scotland.
Received a land grant
in Huntly, Upper Canada,
on 20 November 1821.
(PAO)

CAMPBELL JAMES
Emigrated from Scotland
to Canada on the Fancy
18 August 1816.
Received a land grant in
Beckwith, Upper Canada,
on 9 December 1816.
(PAO)

CAMPBELL JAMES
Son of Alexander Campbell,
tenant in Loderoir,
Perthshire(?), 1740-1791.
Died in Canada in 1828.
(Kenmore Shian GS)

CAMPBELL JOHN
Emigrated from Scotland,
with wife and three
children, to East New
Jersey during
October 1684.
(EJD/A)

CAMPBELL JOHN
Indentured servant
imported from Scotland
to East New Jersey by
Lord Neil Campbell in
December 1685.
(EJD/A225)

CAMPBELL JOHN
Born during 1674 in
Inveraray, Argyllshire.
Emigrated from Scotland
to Darien during 1699.
Settled in Jamaica in
1700. Married (1)
Katherine Clayborn, died
during 1715, (2) Mrs
Elizabeth Gaines.
Assemblyman, militia
officer and Custos of the
parish of St Elizabeth.
Member of H.M.Council.
Father of Colin etc.
Died on 29 January 1740.
Buried at Black River
Church, Jamaica.
(MIBWI)

CAMPBELL JOHN
Scottish merchant in
New England c1699.
(DP)

CAMPBELL JOHN jr
Emigrated from Scotland
to East New Jersey.
Settled in Freehold,
Monmouth County, New
Jersey, c1699.
(Monmouth Court Book)

CAMPBELL JOHN
Second son of Robert
Campbell of Torrie,
physician, and Anne
Burden, born on
17 February 1743.
Died in Jamaica.
(NHP)

CAMPBELL JOHN
Emigrated from Scotland
to Virginia before 1756.
Trooper.
(OD)

CAMPBELL JOHN
Glasgow(?) Emigrated from
Scotland to Virginia in
1760. Assistant factor
at Occoquan, Virginia, for
John Glassford, merchant in
Glasgow. Merchant in
Bladenburg, Virginia, 1784.
(SRA)(Letterbook of Alex
Henderson, Alexandria,
Virginia)

CAMPBELL JOHN
Born in Scotland. Wife,
five sons and a daughter.
Military settler.
Received a land grant in
Elmsley, Upper Canada, on
8 November 1815.
(PAO)

CAMPBELL JOHN jr
Emigrated from Scotland,
with his son, to Canada
on the Lady of the Lake
7 September 1816.
Received a land grant in
Drummond, Upper Canada, on
9 December 1816.
(PAO)

CAMPBELL JOHN
Born in Scotland. Military
settler. Received a land
grant in Chiesley, Upper
Canada, during October 1816.
(PAO)

CAMPBELL JOHN jr.
Emigrated from Scotland
via U.S.A. to Canada.
Received a land grant
in Drummond, Upper
Canada, on 8 April 1817.
(PAO)

CAMPBELL JOHN sr.
Emigrated from Scotland,
with wife, five sons and
three daughters, via U.S.A.
to Canada. Received land
grant in Bathurst, Upper
Canada, on 30 December 1816.
(PAO)

CAMPBELL JOHN
Born in Scotland. Ex York
Depot. Military settler.
Received a land grant in
Walford, Upper Canada, on
31 July 1817, and at
Drummond, Upper Canada,
in December 1819.
(PAO)

CAMPBELL JOHN
Edinburgh. Applied to
settle in Canada during
1818.
(CO384/3)

CAMPBELL JOHN
Emigrated from Scotland,
with wife, four sons and
three daughters, on the
Sophia 6 September 1818.
Received a land grant in
Drummond, Upper Canada, on
9 April 1819.
(PAO)

CAMPBELL JOHN
Born in Raag, Skye,
Inverness-shire c1808.
Stonemason. Married
Ann McLean. Emigrated
from Scotland to
Canada before 1832.
(SG)

CAMPBELL JOHN
Emigrated from Scotland,
with wife, four sons and
three daughters, to
Canada on the Commerce.
Received a land grant in
Lanark, Upper Canada, on
6 September 1821.
(PAO)

CAMPBELL JOSEPH
Emigrated from Scotland,
with wife, to Canada on
the Commerce in June
1821. Received a land
grant in Dalhousie,
Upper Canada, on
8 August 1821.
(PAO)

CAMPBELL KENNETH
Yeoman. Emigrated
from Scotland to Canada.
Received a land grant in
Thorak, Home, Upper
Canada, on 8 March 1826.
(PAO)

CAMPBELL LAUCHLIN
Islay, Argyllshire.
Emigrated from Scotland
to New York in 1736.
(HSNC)

CAMPBELL LACHLAN
Glasgow(?). Merchant.
Emigrated from Scotland
to Virginia in 1764.
Agent for John Glassford
and Company, merchants in
Glasgow. Merchant in
Fredericksburg, Virginia.
(SRA/A013/28)

CAMPBELL MOSES
Born at Killin, Perth-
shire during January
1733, son of James
Campbell and Elizabeth
Buchanan. Soldier in the
42nd(Black Watch) Regiment.
Married Elizabeth Coombs
in Schenectady, New York,
during 1758. Died in
Montreal during 1782.
(JRC)

CAMPBELL NEIL
Emigrated from Scotland,
with wife, four sons and
a daughter, to Canada on
the Brock during 1820.
Received land grants in
Lanark and Dalhousie,
Upper Canada, 25 October
1821.
(PAO)

CAMPBELL PETER
Glasgow(?) Tobacco factor
in Prince George County,
Virginia, until 1775 for
John Glassford and Company,
merchants in Glasgow.
(SRA

CAMPBELL PETER sr
Emigrated from Scotland,
with his wife, to Canada
on the Lady of the Lake
7 September 1816.
Received a land grant in
Drummond, Upper Canada,
on 9 December 1816.
(PAO)

CAMPBELL PETER jr
Emigrated from Scotland
via U.S.A. to Canada.
Received aland grant
in Bathurst, Upper
Canada, on
31 December 1816.
(PAO)

CAMPBELL PETER
Emigrated from Scotland,
with wife and two
daughters, to Canada
on the Prompt 8 July
1817. Received a land
grant in Drummond, Upper
Canada, on 29 July 1817.
(PAO)

CAMPBELL PETER
Emigrated from Scotland,
Received a land grant in
Bathurst, Upper Canada,
on 31 March 1817.
(PAO)

CAMPBELL PETER
Born in Scotland.
Received a land grant
in Beckwith, Upper
Canada, on 30 August
1821.
(PAO)

CAMPBELL PETER
Killin, Perthshire.
Emigrated from Greenock,
Renfrewshire, to Montreal
on the brig Niagara,
Hamilton, with wife
Christian and children
Hugh, Christian, Duncan
and Margaret. Settled
McNab, Bathurst, Upper
Canada, during 1825.
(SG)

CAMPBELL ROBERT
Indentured servant
imported from Scotland
to East New Jersey by
John Campbell during
October 1684.
(EJD/A)

CAMPBELL ROBERT
Indentured servant
imported from Scotland
to East New Jersey by
Lord Neil Campbell in
December 1685.
(EJD/A225)

CAMPBELL ROBERT
Emigrated from Scotland,
with wife, son and three
daughters, to Canada on
the Commerce. Received a
land grant in Dalhousie,
Upper Canada, on
3 September 1821.
(PAO)

CAMPBELL RONALD
Merchant in Campbell-
town, Argyllshire.
Married Jean Campbell.
Father of Archibald,
James, John, Jean and
Elizabeth. Merchant
in Jamaica c1777.
(CC)

CAMPBELL WHITAKER
Emigrated from Scotland
to America. Soldier.
Settled in King and
Queen County, Virginia,
before 1814.
(OD)

CAMPBELL WILLIAM
Merchant in Montrose,
Angus. Emigrated to
Georgia - possibly
on the Mary Anne from
Gravesend, Kent,
during 1737.
(HGP)

CAMPBELL WILLIAM
Born in Struckchaple on
16 November 1760.
Emigrated from Scotland
to Jamaica during 1778.
Planter in Hanover
parish. Died in Jamaica
during 1791.
(SP.V2.195)

CAMPBELL WILLIAM
Yeoman. Emigrated from
Scotland to Canada.
Received a land grant
in Thorak, Home, Upper
Canada, on 8 March 1826.
(PAO)

CAMPBELL ...
Emigrated from Scotland
to Canada. Landed in
Quebec on 4 September
1804. Settled at La Chine,
near Montreal, during 1805.
(GD202.70.12)

CAMPBELL ZACHARIAH
Born during 1742, second
son of James Campbell,
merchant in Glasgow.
Emigrated from Scotland
to America. Settled in
Vienna, Maryland, 1763.
Later a merchant in
Fredericksburg, Virginia.
(SRA/B10/15/6863)

CAMPSLIE WILLIAM
Blantyre, Lanarkshire.
Applied to settle in
Canada on 28 February
1815.
(SRO/RH9)

CANNIE JOHN
Sailor. Died at Darien
on 16 November 1698.
(NLS)

CANNON ROBERT
Emigrated from Scotland,
with wife and two sons,
to Canada on the Commerce
during June 1820.
Received a land grant in
Lanark, Upper Canada, on
1 October 1820.
(PAO)

CANNING ROBERT
Emigrated from Scotland,
with wife and son, to
Canada. Received a
land grant in
Dalhousie, Upper Canada,
on 24 March 1822.
(PAO)

CARGILL JOHN
Born in Scotland during
1745. Merchant. Died
September 1780. Buried
Kingston Cathedral,
Jamaica.
(MIBWI)

CARGILL RICHARD
Born in Scotland during
1744. Assemblyman and
militia officer in
St Thomas in the East,
Jamaica. Died during
March 1781. Buried in
Kingston Cathedral,
Jamaica.
(MIBWI)

CARLYLE JOHN
Emigrated from Scotland
to America. Settled in
Dumfries, Virginia, pre
1740. Merchant.
(OD)

CARMICHAEL DONALD
Emigrated from Scotland,
with wife, son and three
daughters, to Canada.
Received a land grant in
Dalhousie, Upper Canada,
on 21 February 1821.
(PAO)

CARMICHAEL JAMES
Emigrated from Scotland
to America. Joiner.
Settled in Prince George
County, Virginia, before
1756.
(OD)

CARMICHAEL JAMES
Doctor of medicine.
Educated in Edinburgh and
Glasgow c1798. Settled in
Virginia.
(SA)

CARMICHAEL JAMES
Born in Scotland.
Received a land grant in
Beckwith, Upper Canada, on
23 August 1820.
(PAO)

CARMICHAEL JAMES
Edinburgh. Emigrated from
Greenock, Renfrewshire, to
Montreal on the Niagara,
Hamilton, during 1825.
Settled in MacNab, Bathurst,
Upper Canada, in 1825.
Emigrated with wife Mary
Sinclair and children John,
Duncan, James and Donald.
(SG)

CARMICHAEL PETER
Born in Scotland 1782.
Emigrated from Scotland
to South Carolina c1800.
Settled in Marion County,
South Carolina. Later
moved to Clark County,
Mississippi.
(SHC)

CARMICHAEL PETER
Born in Scotland.
Received a land grant
in Beckwith, Upper
Canada, 23 August 1820.
(PAO)

CARMICHAEL ROBERT
Glasgow. Merchant in
Virginia c1765.
(SRA)

CARMICHAEL ROBERT
Emigrated from Ayr,
with wife and three
children, to America
c1800. Settled in
Pennsylvania. All
killed by Indians
except son Daniel,
who later settled in
Virginia in 1825.
(BAF)

CARMONT JOHN
Emigrated from Scotland
to America pre 1770.
Shop-keeper in Norfolk,
Virginia.
(OD)

CARNEGIE DAVID
Seventh son of Sir
David Carnegie of Pit-
arrow, and Catherine
Primrose. Baptised on
24 January 1697.
Merchant in the West
Indies. Died there.
(SP.VIII)

CARNOCHAN JOHN
Son of John Carnochan, 1737-
1790, and Mary Murray.
Born during 1778 in
Dumfries. Emigrated from
Scotland to Nassau,
Bahamas. Later settled in
Georgia. Married Harriet
Frances Putnam. Father
of John Murray Carnochan,
born 1812. Died 1845.
(BAF)

CARR ANDREW
Brother of Thomas Carr.
Emigrated from Scotland
to the West Indies. Later
moved to Canada and
settled in Otonabee,
Upper Canada, in 1819.
Died c1821.
(VT)

CARR THOMAS
Piper. Emigrated from
Scotland to Virginia
before 1755.
(OD)

CARR THOMAS
Born 1780. Emigrated from
Scotland to the West Indies.
Later moved to Canada and
settled in Otanabee, Upper
Canada, in 1819. Poet.
Died 1 November 1860.
(VT)

CARSTAIRS THOMAS
Born Largo, Fife, in 1759.
Architect and builder.
Emigrated from Scotland
to Pennsylvania in 1784.
(SO)

CARSWELL ROBERT
 Emigrated from Scotland
 to Canada on the George
 Canning during June 1821.
 Received a land grant in
 Ramsay, Upper Canada, on
 16 July 1821.
 (PAO)

CASSELS Rev. JOHN
 Born in Fife. Educated at
 the University of
 St Andrews, Fife.
 Emigrated from Scotland to
 Canada. Ordained in
 Pictou, Nova Scotia,
 during 1816. Minister in
 Windsor and Newport 1816-
 1817. Minister in
 St Andrews, New Brunswick,
 1817-1850. Died 18 July
 1850.
 (HPC)

CATHCART WILLIAM
 Son of Hugh Cathcart,
 merchant, and Helen
 Woodrup. Merchant in
 Kingston, Jamaica, pre
 1772.
 (SRA/B10/15/7551)

CHALMERS JAMES
 Son of James Chalmers of
 Balnellan, Boharm, Banff-
 shire. Planter in
 St Thomas in the Vale,
 Surrey, Jamaica, c1766.
 (CPD)

CHALMERS JAMES
 Aberdeen. Graduated M.A.,
 King's College, Aberdeen,
 on 31 March 1806.
 Minister in the West Indies.
 (UKA)(KCA)

CHALMERS ROBERT
 Emigrated from Scotland,
 with wife, two sons and
 four daughters, to
 Canada on the Commerce
 during June 1821.
 Received a land grant in
 Dalhousie, Upper Canada,
 on 15 July 1821.
 (PAO)

CHALMERS WILLIAM
 Born in Scotland. Former
 gunner in the Royal
 Artillery. Military
 settler. Received a land
 grant in Drummond, Upper
 Canada, 14 October 1816.
 (PAO)

CHAMBERS JOHN
 Indentured servant
 imported from Scotland to
 East New Jersey by Lord
 Neil Campbell during
 December 1685.
 (EJD/A225)

CHAMBERS ROBERT
 Indentured servant
 imported from Scotland to
 East New Jersey by Lord
 Neil Campbell during
 December 1685.
 (EJD/A225)

CHARTERS GEORGE
 Emigrated from Scotland,
 with wife and son, to
 Canada on the George Canning
 in June 1821. Received a
 land grant in Ramsay,
 Upper Canada, on
 14 August 1821.
 (PAO)

CHARTERIS HENRY
Volunteer. Died of
flux on voyage from
Scotland to Darien
16 October 1698.
(NLS)

CHERRY HUGH
Emigrated from Scotland,
with wife and three sons,
to Canada on the Earl of
Buckingham in June 1821.
Received a land grant in
Ramsay, Upper Canada, on
24 July 1821.
(PAO)

CHEYNE CHRISTIAN
Indentured servant
imported from Scotland
to East New Jersey by
George Keith during
February 1685. Married
Archibald Silver in
Matacopine, West New
Jersey.
(EJD/A226/D)

CHEYNE GEORGE
Born c1800 son of
William Cheyne, farmer,
Auchterless, Aberdeen-
shire. Educated at
Marischal College,
Aberdeen, 1818-1821, -
graduated M.A. Emigrated
from Scotland to Quebec
1831. Presbyterian
minister in Amherstberg,
1831-1843, and in
Binbrook and Saltfleet,
1843-1878. Died on
1 April 1878.
(HPC)(MCA)

CHEYNE JOHN
Edinburgh. Indentured
as a servant to John
Hancock, indweller in
Horsewynd, Abbey, Edin-
burgh, on 12 August 1685
for four years service in
East New Jersey.
(EJD/A253)

CHILD WILLIAM ARUNDALE
Son of William Child of
Glencorse, merchant in
Edinburgh. Apprenticed
to (1) Archibald Crawford
(2) James Dunlop.
Admitted to the Society
of Writers to the Signet
on 18 November 1825.
Stipendiary Magistrate of
Tobago. Married Amelia
White on 21 February 1856.
Died in Tobago on
20 October 1861.
(WS)

CHISHOLM ALEXANDER
Born during 1752, second
son of Colin Chisholm of
Knockfin, and Margaret
MacKenzie. Emigrated from
Scotland to America c1782.
(MB)

CHISHOLM ANGUS
Yeoman. Emigrated from
Scotland to Canada.
Received a land grant in
Eldon, Newcastle, Upper
Canada, on 8 March 1826.
(PAO)

CHISHOLM ARCHIBALD
Yeoman. Emigrated
from Scotland to
Canada. Received
a land grant in
Eldon, Newcastle,
Upper Canada, on
8 March 1826.
(PAO)

CHISHOLM COLIN
Inverness. Educated
at King's College,
Aberdeen, - graduated
M.D. on 22 May 1793.
Doctor in Grenada.
(KCA)

CHISHOLM COLIN
Yeoman. Emigrated
from Scotland to
Canada. Received a
land grant in Eldon,
Newcastle, Upper
Canada, on 8 March
1826.
(PAO)

CHISHOLM DONALD
Yeoman. Emigrated
from Scotland to
Canada. Received a
land grant in Eldon,
Newcastle, Upper
Canada, on 9 March
1826.
(PAO)

CHISHOLM DONALD
Yeoman. Emigrated
from Scotland to
Canada. Received a
land grant in Thorak,
Home, Upper Canada,
on 8 March 1826.
(PAO)

CHISHOLM DUNCAN
Yeoman. Emigrated from
Scotland to Canada.
Received a land grant
in Eldon, Newcastle,
Upper Canada, on
8 March 1826.
(PAO)

CHISHOLM JOHN
Yeoman. Emigrated from
Scotland to Canada.
Received a land grant
in Eldon, Newcastle,
Upper Canada, on
8 March 1826.
(PAO)

CHISHOLM WILLIAM
Born in Scotland. Military
settler. Received a land
grant in Bathurst, Upper
Canada, on 14 October 1816.
(PAO)

CHRISTIE ALEXANDER
Son of Alexander Christie,
merchant in Aberdeen.
Educated at Marischal
College, Aberdeen, c1813.
Hudson Bay Company employee.
(MCA)

CHRISTIE DUNCAN
Emigrated from Scotland,
with wife and nine
children, to Canada in
1817. From Tillicoutry,
Clackmannanshire.
(CO384/1)

51

CHRISTIE JOHN
Indentured servant
imported from Scotland
to East New Jersey in
1684 by Thomas
Yallerton.
(EJD/A)

CHRISTIE JOHN
Born 11 December 1772,
son of Peter Christie,
tenant (farmer?) on the
Island of Inchbraoch,
Montrose, Angus, 1743-
1809, and Isabel Nicol,
1738-1808. Died in
Jamaica on 6 May 1827.
(Craig Inchbraoch GS)

CHRISTIE JOHN
Farmer in Primrose,
Lothian. Applied to
settle in Canada on
9 March 1815.
(SRO/RH9)

CHRISTIE JOHN
Emigrated from Scotland,
with wife and son, to
Canada, on the James
Baillie on 3 June 1817.
Received a land grant in
South Gower, Upper Canada,
on 13 November 1817.
(PAO)

CHRISTIE MARGARET
Daughter of William
Christie, Stirling. Married
James Bell. Settled in
Quebec c1770. Mother of
William and Margaret. Died
10 September 1831.
(DCB)

CHRISTIE PETER
Born c1798. Died in
Jamaica on 10 March 1825.
(Craig Inchbraoch GS)

CHRISTIE ROBERT
Husband of Margaret Napier.
Formerly of Parish of
Glass, Aberdeenshire.
Wharfinger in St Catherine,
Middlesex County, Jamaica.
Process of Divorce 1782.
(CPD)

CHRISTISON WILLIAM
Emigrated from Scotland,
with wife, two sons and
two daughters, to
Canada on the Earl of
Buckingham in June 1821.
Received a land grant in
Sherbrook, Upper Canada,
on 20 July 1821.
(PAO)

CHIESLY JOHN
Volunteer. Died of flux
on voyage from Scotland
to Darien on 27 October
1698.
(NLS)

CLARK ALEXANDER
Son of Donald Clark.
Emigrated from Scotland
to America. Settled in
Darien, Georgia, c1739.
(HGP)

CLERK ANDREW
Emigrated from Scotland
to Canada. Received a
land grant in Cavan, New-
castle, Upper Canada, on
24 September 1817.
(PAO)

CLARK DANIEL
Emigrated from Scotland
to America. Settled in
Darien, Georgia, c1739.
(HGP)

CLARK DANIEL
Inverness-shire.
Educated at King's
College, Aberdeen, -
graduated M.A. during
March 1822. Minister
in Finch, Canada.
(KCA)

CLARK DONALD
Emigrated from Scotland
to America. Settled in
Darien, Georgia, c1739.
(HGP)

CLARK DUNCAN
Born in Scotland c1759.
Emigrated from Scotland
to Canada. Surgeon.
Married Justina Sophia
Boyer in Halifax, Nova
Scotia, on 7 February
1789. Died in Halifax
on 10 September 1808.
(DCB)

CLARK D.
Glasgow. Applied to
settle in Canada on
28 February 1815.
(SRO/RH9)

CLARKE JAMES
Indentured servant
imported from Scotland
to East New Jersey by
Robert Fullerton during
October 1684.
(EJD/A)

CLARK JAMES
Planter. Died at Darien
on 7 November 1698.
(NLS)

CLARK JAMES
Glasgow(?) Merchant in
Virginia during 1754.
(SRA/B10/15/6653)

CLARK JOHN
Born during 1758 at Petty,
Inverness-shire. Emigrated
from Scotland to South
Carolina. Teacher in South
Carolina and in Georgia.
Methodist and later a
Baptist missionary in
Georgia, 1789-1833. Died
in St Louis in 1833.
(TSA)

CLARKE JOHN
Graduated M.A. in 1764 at
University of Glasgow.
Possibly the John Clarke,
M.A., minister in Boston,
New England, created a
Doctor of Divinity by the
University of Edinburgh on
12 September 1795.
(GG)

CLARK JOHN
Born during 1761 in
Bowmore, Islay, Argyll-
shire. Married (1)
Rachel McNabb (2)
Betsy McNeil. Father of
John, Alexander and
Duncan. Died in Ore,
Ontario, 18 July 1845.
(CCAI)

CLARK RICHARD
Born 10 February 1663.
Emigrated from Scotland
to America. Died in New
Jersey on 16 May 1773.
Buried at Old Scots
cemetery, Freehold, New
Jersey.
(OSC)

CLARKE ROBERT
Emigrated from Scotland
to Canada on the brig
Ann 17 September 1816.
Received a land grant in
Beckwith, Upper Canada,
on 30 June 1817.
(PAO)

CLARKE WILLIAM
Born c1646. Indentured
servant imported from
Scotland to East New
Jersey in October 1684
by Robert Fullerton.
Married Elizabeth ...
born in Scotland 1651,
died in New Jersey 1693.
Died 25 December 1697.
Buried Topanemus cemetery,
Monmouth County, New
Jersey.
(HOT)(EJD/A)

CLARKSON JAMES
Baptised in Linlithgow,
West Lothian, on
8 November 1666. Settled
in New Jersey c1688.
Married Christian Spence
in Queensferry, West Lothian,
during 1687. Yeoman and
boatman. Died 30 December
1729. Buried Western
Presbyterian cemetery,
New Jersey.
(EJD/A)

CLAY WILLIAM
Emigrated from Scotland,
with wife, son and three
daughters, to Canada.
Received a land grant in
Lanark, Upper Canada, on
7 February 1821.
(PAO)

CLEGHORN ADAM
Scot in New York c1699.
(DP)

CLELAND WILLIAM
Son of Robert Cleland of
Pedinnes, writer in Edin-
burgh, and Jean, daughter
of Sir John Henderson of
Fordell. Settled in
Martinique c1733.
(IG)

CLEWSTON WILLIAM
Royalist soldier captured
at the Battle of Worcester.
Transported from Gravesend,
Kent, to Boston, New
England, on the John and
Sarah, master John Greene,
13 May 1652.
(NER)

CLINE GEORGE
Yeoman. Emigrated from
Scotland to Canada.
Received a land grant
in Eldon, Newcastle,
Upper Canada, on
8 March 1826.
(PAO)

CLOSS JOHN
Emigrated from Scotland
to Canada on the Earl of
Buckingham in June 1821.
Received a land grant in
Lanark, Upper Canada, on
21 July 1821.
(PAO)

CLOUSTON WILLIAM
Born during 1794 in the
Orkney Islands. Post-
master with the
Hudson Bay Company from
1812 to 1843.
(HBRS)

CLUNES ALLAN
Glen Pean. Emigrated
from Scotland to
Canada. Settled in
La Chine, near
Montreal, c1805.
(GD202/70/12)

CLYMIE ANDREW
Emigrated from Scotland,
with wife, five sons and
two daughters, to
Canada on the Commerce
in June 1821. Received a
land grant in Dalhousie,
Upper Canada, 1 August 1821.
(PAO)

CLYMIE DUNCAN
Emigrated from Scotland
to Canada on the Prompt
during June 1820.
Settled in Upper Canada.
(PAO)

CLYMIE JOHN
Emigrated from Scotland,
with wife, three sons and
four daughters, to Canada
on the Prompt in June 1820.
Received a land grant in
Dalhousie, Upper Canada,
on 11 November 1821.
(PAO)

COATS JAMES
Emigrated from Scotland
to America. Settled in
Port Royal, Virginia,
before 1791.
(OD)

COBB JOHN
Emigrated from Scotland,
with wife, two sons and
two daughters, to Canada
on the Commerce.
Received a land grant in
Ramsay, Upper Canada, on
10 September 1821.
(PAO)

COBBAN JAMES
Son of James Cobban,
merchant in Aberdeen.
Educated at Marischal
College, Aberdeen, c1818,
graduated M.A. Surgeon in
Canada.
(MCA)

COCHRANE J.
Rutherglen, Lanark-
shire. Applied to
settle in Canada on
3 March 1815.
(SRO/RH9)

COCHRANE JAMES
Emigrated from Scotland,
with wife, three sons
and two daughters, to
Canada on the Commerce.
Received a land grant
in Lanark, Upper Canada,
on 10 September 1821.
(PAO)

COCHRANE Dr JOHN
Brother of Dr William
Cochrane in Edinburgh.
Settled in Kingston,
Jamaica, c1714.
(SRO/GD237)

COCK Rev DANIEL
Born in Clydesdale 1717.
Ordained minister of
Cartsdyke, Greenock,
in 1752. Emigrated from
Scotland to Nova Scotia
during 1770. Minister
in Truro, Nova Scotia,
from 1772 to 1798.
Died during 1805.
(HPC)

COCKBURN Dr ALEXANDER
Born in Duns, Berwickshire,
during August 1739, son of
William Cockburn and
Barbara Home. Married
Elizabeth Kennedy. Father
of Thomas, Helen, Walter
and Wilhelmina. Settled
in Grenada. Died November
1815.
(CFR)

COCKBURN JOHN
Indentured servant
imported from Scotland
to East New Jersey during
October 1684 by John
Campbell for Captain
Andrew Hamilton.
(EJD/A)

COCKBURN WILLIAM
Born in Duns, Berwickshire,
during July 1736, son of
William Cockburn and
Barbara Home. Emigrated
from Scotland to America.
Settled Kingston, Ulster
County, New York. Married
Catherine Tremper, 1744-
1820. Father of William,
Alexander, Catherine and
James. Died in April 1810.
(CFR)

CODD GEORGE
Emigrated from Scotland
to Canada on the Brock in
1820. Settled in Lanark,
Upper Canada, during 1821.
(PAO)

COLQUHOUN ANGUS
Emigrated from Scotland,
with wife, son and three
daughters, to Canada on the
George Canning in June 1821.
Received a land grant in
Lanark, Upper Canada, on
28 July 1821.
(PAO)

COLQUHOUN ARCHIBALD
Emigrated from Scotland,
with wife, son and two
daughters, to Canada.
Received a land grant in
Ramsay, Upper Canada, on
16 August 1822.
(PAO)

COLQUHOUN JAMES
Emigrated from Scotland.
with wife, two sons and
four daughters, to Canada
on the Commerce in June
1820. Received a land
grant in Lanark, Upper
Canada, 1 October 1820.
(PAO)

COLQUHOUN JAMES
Emigrated from Scotland,
with wife, son and two
daughters, to Canada on
the George Canning during
June 1821. Received a
land grant in Lanark,
Upper Canada, on 25 July
1821.
(PAO)

COLQUHOUN ROBERT
GLasgow(?) Merchant in
St Kitts during 1700s.
(SRA/B10/15/6183)

COLTBERT WILLIAM
Emigrated from Scotland
to America before 1756.
Planter in Virginia.
(OD)

CONDON JAMES
Emigrated from Scotland,
with son, to Canada on
the Prompt. Received a
land grant in Lanark,
Upper Canada, on
23 November 1821.
(PAO)

COOPER ANDREW
Born in Perth, Scotland.
Former corporal in the
37th Regiment. Military
settler. Received a land
grant in Upper Canada on
16 August 1816.
(PAO)

CORRIE GEORGE
Indentured servant
imported from Scotland
to East New Jersey by
Lord Neil Campbell in
December 1685.
(EJD/A225)

CORRIGAL JACOB
Orkney Islands. Hudson
Bay Company employee
from 1790 to 1840. Chief
Trader in charge of
Albany River district.
Died in 1844.
(HBRS)

CORSTORPHEN ROBERT
Jacobite surgeon. Emigrated
from Scotland to America
after 1746, with sons John,
Robert and James. Settled
in James River District,
Virginia.
(UNC/Corstorphen PP)

COUPER JOHN
Son of Rev John Coupar, 1706
-1787, Lochwinnoch, Renfrew-
shire, born during 1759.
Settled Hopeton, St Simon's
Island, Georgia 1804.
Father of James H. Coupar
and William A. Coupar. Died
during 1850.
(UNC/Couper PP)

COUPAR ROBERT
Educated in Glasgow
c1782. Doctor of
medicine. Tutor
in Virginia.
(SA)

COWAN JOHN
Royalist soldier
captured after the
Battle of Worcester.
Transported from
Gravesend, Kent, to
Boston, New England,
on the John and Sarah,
master John Greene,
13 May 1652.
(NER)

COWAN JOHN
Baker in Falkirk,
Stirlingshire.
Emigrated from Scotland
to America c1786.
(CPD)

COWEN JOSEPH
Emigrated from Scotland,
with wife, two sons and
a daughter, to Canada on
the Prompt. Received a
land grant in Dalhousie,
Upper Canada, on
13 November 1821.
(PAO)

COWAN ROBERT
Emigrated from Scotland
to America. Planter in
Bedford County,
Virginia, before 1790.
(OD)

COWIE GEORGE
Edinburgh. Former
sergeant in the 65th
Regiment. Out-pensioner
of the Royal Hospital
Chelsea. Applied to
emigrate to Canada with
his five children in 1818.
(CO384/3)

COWIE JAMES
Born 20 April 1794 in
Montrose(?), son of
James Cowie, 1758-1837,
and Catherine Gairdner,
1768-1818. Died in
St Salvador.
(Montrose GS)

COWIE WILLIAM
Born in Scotland. Hudson
Bay Company employee from
1822 to 1835. Drowned in
Mississague River during
April 1835.
(HBRS)

CRAIG ADAM
Emigrated from Scotland
to Canada. Received a
land grant in Lanark,
Upper Canada, on
21 September 1821.
(PAO)

CRAIGE ANDREW
Indentured servant
imported from Scotland
to East New Jersey during
October 1684 by John
Forbes.
(EJD/A266)

CRAIG ARCHIBALD
  Born during 1677 in
  Scotland, son of John
  and Ursula Craig.
  Emigrated from Leith,
  Midlothian, to East New
  Jersey in December 1685
  on the Henry and Francis.
  Married Mary.., 1683-1752.
  Father of Margaret,
  Ursula, Sarah, Mary,Kate,
  Elizabeth, William, Samuel,
  John, Hannah, William,
  Died on 6 March 1750.
  Buried at Old Scots
  cemetery, Monmouth
  County, New Jersey.
  (MNJ)

CRAIG ARCHIBALD
  Indentured servant
  imported from Scotland
  by Lord Neil Campbell
  in December 1685.
  (EJD/A225)

CRAIG GRISELDA
  Indentured servant
  imported from Scotland
  to East New Jersey by
  Lord Neil Campbell in
  December 1685.
  (EJD/A225)

CRAIG JAMES
  Indentured servant
  imported from Scotland
  to East New Jersey by
  Lord Neil Campbell in
  December 1685.
  (EJD/A225)

CRAIG JOHN
  Indentured servant
  imported from Scotland
  to East New Jersey, with
  wife Ursula and children
  Archibald, James and
  Ursula, on the Henry and
  Francis in December 1685
  by Lord Neil Campbell.
  Settled in Middlesex
  County, New Jersey,
  during 1690.
  (EJD/A225)(HOT)(MNJ)

CRAIG JOHN
  Born in Scotland during
  1733. Emigrated from
  Scotland to America in
  1753. Storekeeper. Married
  Jane...., 1734-1807. Father
  of Daniel, Charlotte, Mary,
  John and William. Lieutenant
  in the Revolutionary Army.
  Died 11 July 1821. Buried
  at Tennant cemetery,
  Monmouth County, New Jersey.
  (MNJ)

CRAIG JOHN
  Glasgow(?) Tobacco factor
  at Portobacco, Maryland,
  for Cunningham, Findlay
  and Company before 1776.
  (SRA)

CRAIG ROBERT
  Emigrated from Scotland,
  with wife, three sons and
  a daughter, to Canada on
  the Commerce in June 1821.
  Received a land grant in
  Lanark, Upper Canada, on
  1 August 1821.
  (PAO)

59

CRAIG THOMAS
 Emigrated from Scotland,
 with his son and
 daughter, to Canada on
 the Earl of Buckingham
 in June 1821. Received
 a land grant in
 Ramsay, Upper Canada,
 on 26 July 1821.
 (PAO)

CRAIG WILLIAM
 Emigrated from Scotland
 to Canada. Received a
 land grant in Lanark,
 Upper Canada, on
 4 October 1821.
 (PAO)

CRAIGIE JOHN
 Born c1757 in Kilgraston,
 Perthshire, third son of
 John Craigie. Emigrated
 from Scotland to Canada.
 Married Susannah Coffin,
 widow of James Grant, on
 13 November 1792. Public
 official and merchant.
 Died in Quebec on
 26 November 1813.
 (DCB)

CRAIGIE WILLIAM
 Aberdeen. Educated
 in Aberdeen - graduated
 M.A. on 25 March 1814.
 Doctor in Dundas,
 Canada.
 (UKA)

CRAIK JAMES
 Born in Scotland c1730.
 Physician to George
 Washington. Settled in
 Fairfax County, Virginia,
 Died during 1814.
 (DU)

CRAIK ROBERT
 Possibly brother of
 James Craik. Scottish
 doctor. Settled in
 Virginia. Died 1754.
 (SA)

CRAM JAMES
 Born in Scotland.
 Received a land grant
 in Beckwith, Upper
 Canada, 23 August 1820.
 (PAO)

CRAM PETER sr.
 Born in Scotland.
 Received a land grant
 in Beckwith, Upper
 Canada, 31 January 1821.
 (PAO)

CRAM PETER jr.
 Born in Scotland.
 Received a land grant
 in Beckwith, Upper
 Canada, 9 July 1821.
 (PAO)

CRANSTOUN JAMES EDMUND
 Son of Charles Cranstoun
 and Elizabeth Turner. Lord
 Cranstoun in 1796. Married
 Ann Linnington Macnamara,
 daughter of John Macnamara,
 St Kitts, at the Retreat,
 St Kitts on 25 August 1807.
 Father of James E., Charles
 F., Eliza L., and Anna C.
 Died on 5 September 1818.
 (S.P.2)

CRAWFORD JAMES
  Emigrated from Scotland,
  with wife, two sons and
  four daughters, to
  Canada on the Earl of
  Buckingham in June 1821.
  Received a land grant
  in Lanark, Upper Canada,
  18 July 1821.
  (PAO)

CRAWFORD JOHN
  Glasgow. Emigrated from
  Scotland to America in
  June 1755.
  (SRA/B10/15/6482)

CRAWFORD JOHN
  Emigrated from Scotland,
  with wife, two sons and
  two daughters, to Canada
  on the Commerce during
  June 1821. Received a
  land grant in Dalhousie,
  Upper Canada, 4 August
  1821.
  (PAO)

CRAWFORD PATRICK
  Scottish merchant in
  New York c1699.
  (DP)

CRAY JAMES
  Emigrated from Scotland
  to Canad on the Earl of
  Buckingham in June 1821.
  Received a land grant in
  Ramsay, Upper Canada, on
  26 July 1821.
  (PAO)

CRAY ROBERT
  Emigrated from Scotland,
  with wife, son and a
  daughter, to Canada on the
  Earl of Buckingham during
  June 1821. Received a
  land grant in Sherbrook,
  Upper Canada, 20 July 1821.
  (PAO)

CREEL CHARLES
  Emigrated from south-west
  Scotland(?) to America in
  1680. Settled in Richmond
  County, Virginia. Father
  of Charles, born 1721.
  (BAF)

CRICHTON ELIZABETH
  Born during 1798 daughter
  of Patrick Crichton,
  Edinburgh. Married
  William Lambie. Died in
  Kingston, Jamaica, on
  20 December 1821. Buried
  in Kingston Cathedral.
  (MIBWI)

CRICHTON ROBERT
  Doctor of medicine. Possibly
  educated in Edinburgh c1749.
  Settled in Virginia.
  (SA)

CREIGHTON WILLIAM
  Emigrated from Scotland,
  with wife, three sons and
  a daughter, to Canada on
  the George Canning in June
  1821. Received a land
  grant in Ramsay, Upper
  Canada, on 16 July 1821.
  (PAO)

CROOME JOHN
Royalist soldier
captured at Battle
of Worcester.
Transported from
Gravesend, Kent, to
Boston, New England,
on the John and Sarah,
master John Greene, on
13 May 1652.
(NER)

CROSBIE(?) THOMAS
Born in Scotland. Former
sergeant in the 70th
Regiment. Received a
land grant in Bathurst,
Upper Canada, on
18 March 1820.
(PAO)

CROSS JAMES
Glasgow(?) Tobacco factor
for Speirs, French and Co.
in Virginia during 1782.
(SRA/TD/131/13)

CROSSTONE PATRICK
Royalist soldier captured
at Battle of Worcester.
Transported from Graves-
end, Kent, to Boston, New
England, on the John and
Sarah, master John Green,
13 May 1652.
(NER)

CROWLEY OLIVER
Emigrated from Scotland,
with wife and daughter, to
Canada on the Earl of
Buckingham in June 1821.
Received a land grant in
Sherbrook, Upper Canada,
on 20 July 1821.
(PAO)

CRUDEN ALEXANDER
Son of Alexander Cruden,
maltster in Aberdeen.
Educated at Aberdeen
Grammar School, and at
Marischal College, Aber-
deen, from 1736 to 1740,
graduated M.A. Rector
of Farnham, Virginia.
(MCA)

CRUIKSHANKS CHARLES
Glasgow(?) Merchant and
principal factor in Mary-
land for Speirs, French
and Company c1775.
(SRA)

CRUIKSHANK ROBERT
Born c1748 in Aberdeen(?)
Silversmith and merchant.
Settled in Montreal in
1773. Married Ann Kay in
August 1789. Died at sea
16 April 1809.
(DCB)

CRUIKSHANK RONALD
Yeoman. Emigrated from
Scotland to Canada.
Received a land grant in
Eldon, Newcastle, Upper
Canada, on 8 March 1826.
(PAO)

CULBERTSON ROBERT
Laggan Farm, Campbelltown,
Argyllshire. Emigrated
from Kintyre, Argyllshire,
to America in early eighteenth century. Father of
Thomas, 1754-1823. Died
c1767.
(BAF)

CUMMING ALEXANDER
Educated at Marischal
College, Aberdee,
graduated M.A. 1731.
Doctor of Divinity in
1785. Vicar of
Kingston, Jamaica.
(MCA)

CUMMING ARCHIBALD
Emigrated from Scotland
to Canada on the
Commerce in June 1820.
Received a land grant in
Lanark, Upper Canada, on
1 October 1820.
(PAO)

CUMMING ARCHIBALD
Emigrated from Scotland
to Canada on the George
Canning in June 1821.
Received a land grant in
Lanark, Upper Canada, on
30 June 1821.
(PAO)

CUMMING CUTHBERT
Born in Scotland 1787.
North West Company
employee from 1804 to
1821. Hudson Bay
Company employee 1821
to 1846. Chief Trader
1827. Died 5 April
1870.
(HBRS)

CUMMING DANIEL
Emigrated from Scotland
to Canada on the Commerce
in June 1820. Received a
land grant in Lanark,
Upper Canada, 1 October
1820.
(PAO)

CUMMING FRANCIS H.
Born in Scotland. Former
lieutenant in the 104th
Regiment. Received a
land grant in Drummond,
Upper Canada, on 15 April
1820.
(PAO)

CUMMING GEORGE
Emigrated from Scotland,
with wife, to Canada on
the George Canning in
June 1821. Received a
land grant in Lanark,
Upper Canada, on 30 June
1821.
(PAO)

CUMMING JOHN sr
Emigrated from Scotland,
with wife and two sons, to
Canada on the Commerce in
June 1820. Received a
land grant in Dalhousie,
Upper Canada, on
5 September 1820.
(PAO)

CUMMING JOHN sr.
Emigrated from Scotland,
with wife, son and four
daughters, to Canada on the
Commerce during June 1820.
Received a land grant in
Lanark, Upper Canada, on
1 October 1820.
(PAO)

CUMMING JOHN
Emigrated from Scotland,
with wife, son and daughter,
to Canada on the Commerce
in August 1820. Received
a land grant in Dalhousie,
Upper Canada, 5 September
1820.
(PAO)

CUMMING PAUL
Emigrated from Scotland,
with three daughters, to
Canada on the Commerce
in June 1820. Received
land grants in Lanark,
Upper Canada, on
1 October 1820, and on
30 July 1822.
(PAO)

CUMMING ROBERT
Born c1787 in the Orkney
Islands. Hudson Bay Co.
employee from 1812 to
1856. Postmaster. Died
21 June 1863.
(HBRS)

CUNNINGHAM ADAM
Midshipman. Died of
fever on the voyage
from Scotland to Darien
on 22 October 1698.
(NLS)

CUNNINGHAM ADAM
Scottish doctor. Settled
in Virginia 1728-1735.
(SA)

CUNNINGHAM ARCHIBALD
Born 1795. Emigrated
from Linlithgow, West
Lothian, to America
during 1818. Father of
George Francis
Cunningham, born 1826.
(BAF)

CUNNINGHAM JANET
Indentured servant
imported from Scotland
to East New Jersey by
Lord Neil Campbell in
December 1685.
(EJD/A225)

CUNNINGHAM JOHN
Born during 1738 at
Kirknewton, Midlothian(?)
Married Elizabeth, widow
of Robert Westland.
Father of James, Samuel and
George. Died during 1812.
Buried at Montego Bay
Jamaica.
(MIBWI)

CUNNINGHAM JOHN
Emigrated from Scotland
to America. Merchant
and shipmaster in Norfolk,
Virginia, pre 1793.
(OD)

CUNNINGHAM ROBERT
Born during 1669 in Glen
Garnock, Ayrshire, son of
Richard Cunningham and
Elizabeth Heriot.
Emigrated from Scotland to
America or the West Indies
before 1687. Settled in
Cayen, St Kitts. Married
(1) Judith E. de Bonnison
in 1693, (2) Mary Garnier.
Father of Daniel, Susanna,
and others.
(HCA)

CUNNINGHAM ROBERT
Third son of Rev Richard
Cunningham, minister of
Symington, Lanarkshire, and
Ann Murray. Emigrated from
Scotland to America.
Settled in Blandford, Virginia.
Married Martha Baird. Father
of Alex, Richard etc. Died
during 1796.
(HCA)

CURRY DAVID
Emigrated from Scotland,
with wife and son, to
Canada on the Earl of
Buckingham in June 1821.
Received a land grant in
Lanark, Upper Canada, on
26 July 1821.
(PAO)

CURRIE DUNCAN
Emigrated from Scotland,
with wife, three sons and
four daughters, to
Canada. Received a land
grant in Lanark, Upper
Canada, on 20 September
1821.
(PAO)

CURRY EDWARD
Emigrated from Scotland,
with wife, two sons and
three daughters, to
Canada, on the Prompt.
Received a land grant in
Dalhousie, Upper Canada,
23 November 1821.
(PAO)

CURRIE MALCOLM
Emigrated from Scotland
to Canada on the Commerce.
Received a land grant in
Lanark, Upper Canada, on
20 September 1821.
(PAO)

CURRY W.
Emigrated from Scotland,
with wife, son and two
daughters, on the George
Canning during June 1821.
Received a land grant in
Ramsay, Upper Canada, on
16 July 1821.
(PAO)

CUSHNIE ARTHUR
Son of Alexander Cushnie,
minister of Oyne, Aberdeen-
shire. Educated at
Marischal College, Aberdeen,
from 1801 to 1805, graduated
M.A. Merchant in Trinidad.
(MCA)

CUTHBERT GEORGE
Inverness. Emigrated
from Scotland to America.
Signed a treaty with the
Creek Indians in Georgia
on 11 August 1739.
(HGP)

CUTHBERT JOHN
Emigrated from Inverness,
Scotland, to Georgia on
the Prince of Wales during
October 1735. Settled in
Josephstown, Georgia, 1735.
Trader. Presumably the
John Cuthbert of Drackes,
who signed a treaty with
the Creek Indians in
Georgia on 11 August 1739.
(HGP)

CUTHBERTSON JAMES
Emigrated from Scotland
to Canada on the Prompt.
Received aland grant in
Dalhousie, Upper Canada,
on 23 November 1821.
(PAO)

CUTHBERTSON JOHN
Kilmarnock, Ayrshire.
Covenanter - captured at
the Battle of Bothwell Bridge
22 June 1679. Banished to
the Plantations. Drowned
off the Orkney Islands.
(HCA)

CUTHBERTSON WILLIAM
Covenanter and rebel
in 1666. Prisoner in
Edinburgh Tolbooth.
Banished to the
Plantations on
10 June 1669.
(PC)

DALGETTY ALEXANDER
Born in Scotland. Former
Royal Navyman. Military
settler. Received a
land grant in Beckwith,
Upper Canada, on
16 September 1817.
(PAO)

DALGLEISH Rev ALEXANDER
Probationer minister. Died
during November 1699 near
Montserrat, on voyage
from Scotland to Darien.
(SHR)

DALRYMPLE JOHN HAMILTON
Born in Scotland 1776.
Collector of Customs.
Died 7 August 1804.
Buried at Montego Bay,
Jamaica.
(MIBWI)

DALRYMPLE THOMAS
Planter. Died of fever
on voyage from Scotland
to Darien 5 October 1698.
(NLS)

DALRYMPLE WILLIAM
Son of James Dalrymple,
merchant in Fraserburgh,
Aberdeenshire. Educated
Marischal College, Aber-
deen c1821. Surgeon in
Jamaica.
(MCA)

DANIEL JOHN
Planter. Died of flux on
the voyage from Scotland
to Darien 24 October 1698.
(NLS)

DAVIDSON ...
Son of .. Davidson, farmer
in Pityoulish, died March
1767, and Mary Grant,
died in December 1779.
Merchant in Washington,
North America.
(Garten/Kincardine GS)

DAVIDSON ARTHUR
Born 12 November 1743,
eldest son of Walter
Davidson, Kinnethmont.
Educated at King's College,
Aberdeen. Emigrated from
Scotland to Quebec 10 July
1766. Married (1) Jane
Fraser 3 March 1785 (2)
Eleanor Birnie 9 March 1799.
Advocate and judge. Died
in Montreal on 4 May 1807.
(DCB)

DAVIDSON CHARLES
Son of John Davidson of
Tilchetlly, Aberdeenshire.
Educated at Marischal
College, Aberdeen, from
1790 to 1794 - graduated
M.A. Physician in Grenada.
(MCA)

DAVIDSON JAMES
Planter. Died of flux on
voyage from Scotland to
Darien on 15 October 1698.
(NLS)

DAVIDSON JAMES
Edinburgh. School
master. Settled in
Philadelphia, Nova
Scotia, in 1769.
(SF)

DAVIDSON JOHN
Perthshire. Soldier.
Emigrated from Scotland
to Canada during 1817.
Storekeeper in Dundee,
Quebec.
(SO)

DAVIDSON PETER
Emigrated from Scotland,
with wife, two sons and
two daughters, to
Canada on the Earl of
Buckingham during June
1821. Received a land
grant in Dalhousie,
Upper Canada, on
6 July 1821.
(PAO)

DAVIDSON THOMAS
Born c1706. Distiller
in Berwick. Indentured
servant for Jamaica
30 April 1731.
(LGR)

DAVIDSON THOMAS
Emigrated from Scotland
to Canada on the Commerce
during June 1820. Received
a land grant in Lanark,
Upper Canada, on
5 September 1820.
(PAO)

DAVIDSON WILLIAM
Indentured servant
imported from Scotland
to East New Jersey by
Thomas Yallerton in 1684.
Employed by John Laing in
Middlesex County, New
Jersey. Land grant on
17 January 1693.
(EJD/A/D)

DAVISON WILLIAM
Indentured servant
imported from Scotland
to East New Jersey by
Dr John Gordon during
1685.
(EJD/A302)

DAVIDSON WILLIAM
Inverness. Emigrated
from Scotland to Canada.
Settled at Wilson's Point,
New Brunswick, c1765.
Timber merchant.
(SO)

DAVIE WILLIAM
Emigrated from Scotland,
with wife, son and five
daughters, to Canada on
the Earl of Buckingham
Received a land grant
in Ramsay, Upper Canada,
on 30 August 1821.
(PAO)

DAVIES JOSIAH
Emigrated from Scotland,
with wife, seven sons and
two daughters, to Canada
on the Earl of Buckingham
in June 1821. Received a
land grant in Sherbrook,
Upper Canada, 24 July 1821.
(PAO)

DEANS JOHN
Glasgow(?) Merchant
in Tapahannock,
Virginia. Overseas
factor for John Barnes
and Company pre 1776.
(SRA)

DEBEARE JAMES
Berwick. Tailor.
Indentured servant for
Jamaica 12 November 1685.
(LGR)

DEMPSTER DANIEL
Emigrated from Scotland
to Canada on the Commerce
in June 1820. Received a
land grant in Lanark,
Upper Canada, on
8 September 1820.
(PAO)

DENOON HUGH
Born during 1762, son
of Rev David Denoon,
Killearran, Ross-shire.
Served in British Army
in American Revolution.
Settled in Merigomish,
Pictou, Nova Scotia.
Merchant. Emigrant
recruiter c1801.
(PNS)

DEWAR PETER
Emigrated from Greenock,
Renfrewshire, with wife
and family, to Quebec
during July 1804.
Settled in St Andrews,
Quebec.
(CP)

DICK ARCHIBALD
Born during 1715, son
of Thomas Dick, Edinburgh,
and Jean Harvie. Emigrated
from Scotland to America.
Married Mrs Mary Barnard
or Hewes c1760. Settled in
Chichester, near Marcus
Hook, Pennsylvania, in 1771.
Revolutionary officer.
Father of Elisha Cullen Dick,
1762-1825, and Thomas
Barnard Dick, 1766-1811.
Died during 1782.
(BAF)

DICK JAMES
Son of Thomas Dick,
merchant, baillie and Dean
of Guild of Edinburgh.
Merchant burgess and guild
brother of Edinburgh.
Emigrated from Scotland
to America. Settled in
London Town, South River,
Maryland, on 1 June 1734.
Married Margaret ..., 1701-
1766. Buried in Anne
Arundel County, Maryland.
(MHR)(HGM)

DICK JOHN
Emigrated from Scotland,
with wife, four sons and
six daughters, to Canada
on the David of London
in June 1821. Received a
land grant in Lanark,
Upper Canada on 6 August
1821.
(PAO)

DICKSON MARGARET
Indentured servant
imported from Scotland
to East New Jersey by
John Campbell for
Captain Andrew Hamilton
during October 1684.
(EJD/A)

DICKSON WILLIAM
Born during 1719 at
Whitslaid, Berwickshire.
Emigrated to Jamaica.
during 1748. Settled
in Philadelphia,
Pennsylvania, in 1763.
Father of Samuel, born
in Pennsylvania.
(BAF)

DICKSON WILLIAM
Born during 1769 in
Dumfries. Emigrated
from Scotland to Canada
in 1792. Settled in
Niagara, Upper Canada.
Lawyer and politician.
Died on 19 February 1846.
(CP)

DINGWALL ARTHUR
Born on 25 February 1752,
son of Baillie John Ding-
wall of Rannieston, and
Mary Lumsden. Emigrated
from Scotland to America.
Merchant in New York.
Settled in St John, New
Brunswick. Married Mrs
Elizabeth Stuart or Evans.
(DF)

DINGWALL EDWARD
Royalist soldier captured
at the Battle of Worcester.
Transported from Gravesend,
Kent, to Boston, New
England, on the John and
Sarah, master John Greene
13 May 1652.
(NER)

DINGWALL WILLIAM
Royalist soldier captured
at the Battle of Worcester.
Transported from Gravesend,
Kent, to Boston, New
England, on the John and
Sarah, master John Greene
13 May 1652.
(NER)

DINWIDDIE ROBERT
Born in Glasgow during 1692.
Matriculated at Glasgow
University in 1707.
Collector of Customs in
Bermuda. Lieutenant
Governor of Virginia.
Granted a LL.D. by Glasgow
University in 1754. Died
Clifton, England, on
1 August 1770.
(GG)

DOBIE JAMES
Emigrated from Scotland,
with wife, son and two
daughters, to Canada on the
Commerce during June 1820.
Received a land grant in
Lanark, Upper Canada, on
8 September 1820.
(PAO)

DOBIE JOHN
Emigrated from Scotland
to Canada on the Phillip
during 1820. Received a land
land grant in Sherbrook,
Upper Canada on 30 March
1821.
(PAO)

DOBIE RICHARD
Born c1731 in Liberton.
Emigrated from Scotland
to Canada. Fur-trader
and merchant. Died in
Montreal on 23 March 1805.
(DCB)

DOBIE THOMAS
Emigrated from Scotland,
with wife, two sons and
three daughters, to
Canada on the George
Canning during June 1821.
Received a land grant in
Dalhousie, Upper Canada,
on 19 July 1821.
(PAO)

DODDS THOMAS
Emigrated from Scotland,
with wife and eight sons,
to Canada on the David of
London. Received a land
grant in Lanark, Upper
Canada, on 14 August 1821.
(PAO)

DONALD GEORGE
Emigrated from Scotland,
with wife, son and two
daughters, to Canada on
the Commerce during
August 1820. Received
a land grant in Lanark,
Upper Canada, on
5 September 1820.
(PAO)

DONALD JOHN
Emigrated from Scotland,
with wife, to Canada.
Received a land grant in
Dalhousie, Upper Canada,
on 29 November 1821.
(PAO)

DONALD ROBERT
Emigrated from Scotland
to America. Merchant in
Chesterfield County,
Virginia, c1775.
(OD)

DONALDSON ANDREW sr.
Emigrated from Scotland,
with wife, to Canada on
the Eliza 1 October 1815.
Received a land grant in
Elmsley, Upper Canada, on
30 June 1817.
(PAO)

DONALDSON JAMES
Emigrated from Scotland
to Virginia pre 1755.
Planter.
(OD)

DONALDSON JAMES
Emigrated from Scotland,
with wife, two sons and
two daughters, to Canada
on the Commerce in June
1821. Received a land gr
grant in Lanark, Upper
Canada, on 26 July 1821.
(PAO)

DONALDSON ROBERT
Planter. Died of flux on
voyage from Scotland to
Darien 22 August 1698.
(NLS)

DONALDSON ROBERT
Greenock, Renfrewshire.
Applied to settle in
Canada on 4 March 1815.
(SRO/RH9)

DONALDSON THOMAS
Emigrated from Scotland,
with his wife, to
Canada on the Commerce
in June 1821. Received
a land grant in
Dalhousie, Upper Canada,
on 16 July 1821.
(PAO)

DONALDSON WILLIAM
Master cooper. Emigrated
from Scotland to Portsmouth,
Virginia, during 1763.
(OD)

DOUGLAS ANNE
Born in Scotland c1735.
Widow. Emigrated from
Scotland, with four
children, to Canada.
Settled at Roger's Hill,
Pictou, Nova Scotia, in
1815,
(PANS/RG1)

DOUGLAS CHARLES J.S.
Second son of Sir John
Douglas of Kelhead, 1706-
1778, and Christian
Cunningham, 1710-1741.
Collector of Customs in
Jamaica. Married (1)
Basilia, daughter of
James Dawes of Rockspring,
Jamaica, (2) Mary, daughter
of Rev Richard Bullock.
(SP.V.150)

DOUGLAS DAVID
Born during 1798 in
Scone, Perthshire.
Botanist and explorer
in Canada and the United
States. Murdered in
Hawaii during 1834.
(TSA)

DOUGLAS DONALD
Born c1791. Blacksmith.
Emigrated from Scotland
to Canada. Settled at
Roger's Hill, Pictou,
Nova Scotia, in 1815.
(PANS/RG1)

DOUGLAS DONALD
Born c1793. Emigrated
from Scotland, with his
mother, two sons and two
daughters, to Canada.
Received a land grant in
Halifax, Nova Scotia, 1815.
(PANS/RG20)

DOUGLAS GEORGE
Emigrated from Scotland
to Canada on the Commerce
in June 1820. Settled
in Upper Canada.
(PAO)

DOUGLAS JAMES
Emigrated from Scotland
to America. Merchant in
Dumfries, Virginia.
Married Catherine, daughter
of Robert Brent. Died c1767.
(VMHB.1911)

DOUGLAS JAMES
Born in Edinburgh during
1757, son of John Douglas.
Public official. Died in
Prince Edward Island on
26 September 1803.
(DCB)

DOUGLAS JOHN
Emigrated from Scotland
to Canada on the
Commerce in June 1820.
Settled in Upper Canada.
(PAO)

DOUGLAS JOHN
Born c1796 at Castle
Stewart(?), Wigtownshire.
Emigrated from Scotland
to America. Died on
2 November 1832. Buried
at Monacacy cemetery,
Montgomery County,
Maryland.
(HGM)

DOUGLAS Rev ROBERT
Born during 1781 in
Roxburghshire. Ordained
by Presbytry of Kilmarnock,
Ayrshire. Emigrated from
Scotland to Nova Scotia
during 1816. Minister in
Onslow, Nova Scotia, 1816-
1821. Minister of St Peter's,
Bay Fortune, and Cove Head,
Prince Edward Island, 1821 -
1846. Died 17 September 1846.
(HPC)

DOUGLAS THOMAS
Emigrated from Scotland
to America pre 1755. Baker
in Fredericksburg, Virginia.
(OD)

DOUGLAS WILLIAM
Born in Scotland during
1610. Emigrated from Scot-
land to America in 1640.
Town Clerk of New London.
Married Ann Mattle. Father
of Robert, born in 1639.
Died during 1682.
(BAF)

DOUGLAS WILLIAM
Born c1789. Emigrated
from Scotland, with
wife and two children,
to Canada. Settled at
Roger's Hill, Pictou,
Nova Scotia, in 1815.
(PANS/RG1)

DOUGLAS WILLIAM
Born c1785. Emigrated
from Scotland, with wife
and child, to Canada.
Received a land grant in
Halifax, Nova Scotia,
during 1815.
(PANS/RG20)

DOURIE JOHN
Emigrated from Scotland
to Canada on the Earl of
Buckingham in June 1821.
Received a land grant in
Ramsay, Upper Canada, on
26 July 1821.
(PAO)

DOW ALEXANDER
Indentured servant
imported from Scotland
to East New Jersey. Head-
right land grant in 1689.
(EJD/B159)

DOW JAMES
Emigrated from Scotland,
with wife, three sons and
four daughters, to Canada
on the David of London in
June 1821. Received a
land grant in Lanark,
Upper Canada, on 14 August
1821.
(PAO)

DRUMMOND Miss
  Daughter of Gregor
  McGregor of Inverardran.
  Married Colin Campbell
  during 1776. Died in
  New York c1778.
  (SP.II)

DRUMMOND JAMES
  Born in Scotland. Land
  grant in Beckwith,
  Upper Canada, on
  27 February 1821.
  (PAO)

DRUMMOND PETER
  Emigrated from Greenock,
  Renfrewshire to Montreal
  on the brig Niagara,
  Hamilton, during 1825.
  Settled in McNab,
  Bathurst, Upper Canada,
  in 1825.
  (SG)

DRUMMOND ROBERT
  Son of James Drummond,
  merchant in Prestonpans,
  East Lothian. Yeoman in
  Shrewsbury, Monmouth
  County, New Jersey, Will
  6 February 1709. Probate
  8 September 1710.
  (WM)

DRUMMOND THOMAS
  Born during 1742, second
  son of James Drummond of
  Lundin, Fife, 1707-1781,
  and Rachel Bruce, died 1769.
  Baptised at Largo, Fife, on
  21 July 1742. Emigrated from
  Scotland to America in 1768.
  Member of the St Andrews
  Society of New York. American
  prisoner. Died in Bermuda in
  November 1780.
  (NHP)(SP.V)

DRYDEN ROBERT
  Born 11 January 1784 at
  St Boswells(?), Roxburgh-
  shire, son of Thomas
  Dryden and Jean Thomson.
  Married Alison Young in
  1814. Emigrated from
  Scotland to Canada in 1818.
  (SG)

DRYNON WILLIAM
  Emigrated from Greenock,
  Renfrewshire, to Canada
  on the David of London.
  Settled in Upper Canada.
  (PAO)

DRYSDALE JAMES
  Emigrated from Scotland
  to Canada on the Commerce
  in June 1820. Received a
  land grant in Dalhousie,
  Upper Canada, on
  5 September 1820.
  (PAO)

DRYSDALE ROBERT
  Emigrated from Scotland,
  with wife and son, to
  Canada on the Commerce in
  June 1820. Received a
  land grants in Lanark,
  Upper Canada, on
  5 September 1820, and on
  1 June 1821.
  (PAO)

DUFFUS JOHN
  Sailor. Died of fever on
  voyage from Scotland to
  Darien 1 October 1698.
  (NLS)

DULEN EDWARD
Royalist soldier captured
at Battle of Worcester.
Transported from Graves-
end, Kent, to Boston, New
England, on the John and
Sarah, John Greene
13 May 1652.
(NER)

DUNBAR GEORGE
Inverness(?) Emigrated
from Scotland to America.
Settled in Josephstown,
Georgia, in 1735. Trader.
Possibly the Lieutenant
George Dunbar who signed
a treaty with the Creek
Indians on 11 August 1739.
(HGP)

DUNBAR JAMES
A Scot, late of Jamaica,
graduated M.D. at King's
College, Aberdeen, on
8 November 1742.
(KCA)

DUNBAR THOMAS
Indentured servant
imported from Scotland
to East New Jersey by
James Dobie during
October 1684.
(EJD/A)

DUNBAR WILLIAM
Born in 1749, son of
Sir Archibald Dunbar,
1693-1769, and Anne Bain.
Emigrated from Scotland
to Philadelphia in 1771.
Partner of John Ross, a
Scot, there. Indian trader
at Fort Pitt. Planter in
Florida, Louisiana and in
Natchez, Adams County,
Mississippi 1773. Married
Dinah Clark. Died 1810.
(PWD)(UNC/Dunbar PP)

DUNBAR WILLIAM
Inverness. Graduated M.A.
Aberdeen, 26 April 1813.
Minister in Nova Scotia.
(UKA)(KCA)

DUNCAN ALEXANDER
Born in Scotland. Former
soldier in the 104th
Regiment. Military
settler. Received a land
grant in Bathurst, Upper
Canada, on 30 June 1817.
(PAO)

DUNCAN ALEXANDER
Emigrated from Scotland
to Canada. Received a
land grant in Toronto,
Home, Upper Canada, on
22 April 1819.
(PAO)

DUNCAN ALEXANDER
Emigrated from Scotland,
with wife, four sons and
three daughters, to
Canada on the Earl of
Buckingham in June 1821.
Received a land grant in
Ramsay, Upper Canada, on
25 July 1821.
(PAO)

DUNCAN ARCHIBALD
Emigrated from Scotland
to Canada on the Prompt.
Received a land grant in
Dalhousie, Upper Canada,
on 13 November 1821.
(PAO)

DUNCAN CHARLES
Born in Scotland. Former
soldier in the 104th
Regiment. Received
a land grant in
Bathurst, Upper
Canada, on 30 June 1817.
(PAO)

DUNCAN GEORGE
Emigrated from Scotland
to America. Settled in
Stirling, Ohio, in 1824.
(SHR)

DUNCAN GYLES
Indentured servant
imported from Scotland
to East New Jersey by
Lord Neil Campbell in
December 1685.
(EJD/A225)

DUNCAN JOHN
Indentured servant
imported from Scotland
to East New Jersey by
Lord Neil Campbell in
December 1685.
(EJD/A225)

DUNCAN JOHN
Emigrated from Scotland,
with wife, son and a
daughter, to Canada on
the Prompt. Received a
land grant in Dalhousie,
Upper Canada, on
15 November 1821.
(PAO)

DUNCAN JOHN
Emigrated from Scotland,
with two sons and two
daughters, to Canada on
the Prompt. Received a
land grant in Dalhousie,
Upper Canada, on
23 November 1821.
(PAO)

DUNCAN NICHOLAS
Born 25 May 1764, son of
Robert Duncan and Mary
Hutcheon, in Aberdeen.
Educated at Aberdeen
Grammar School.
Apprenticed to a wright
in 1778. Absconded to
the West Indies.
(FF)

DUNCAN PETER
Born 1624 in Edinburgh(?)
Married Bessie Caldwell
in the Canongate during
1646. Father of John,
born 1648. Transported
to Nomini Creek, Virginia,
1650. Landowner there in
1655, Died c1676.
(BAF)

DUNCAN ROBERT
Emigrated from Scotland,
with wife, four sons and
three daughters, to
Canada on the Earl of
Buckingham in June 1821.
Received a land grant in
Ramsay, Upper Canada, on
25 July 1821.
(PAO)

DUNCAN THOMAS
Emigrated from Scotland,
with wife and son, to
Canada on the David of
London on June 1821.
Received a land grant
in Lanark, Upper Canada,
on 25 August 1821.
(PAO)

DUNCAN WILLIAM
Emigrated from Scotland
to Canada. Received a
land grant in Westminster,
London, Upper Canada, on
6 June 1818.
(PAO)

DUNCAN WILLIAM
Emigrated from Scotland,
with wife, to Canada on
the David of London in
June 1821. Received a
land grant in Ramsay,
Upper Canada, on
17 August 1821.
(PAO)

DUNCAN WILLIAM
Emigrated from Scotland,
with wife, three sons and
a daughter, to Canada on
the Prompt. Received a
land grant in Dalhousie,
Upper Canada, on
13 November 1821.
(PAO)

DUNCAN Widow
Emigrated from Scotland,
with four sons and four
daughters, to Canada on
the Prompt. Received a
land grant in Dalhousie,
Upper Canada, on
15 November 1821.
(PAO)

DUNLOP AGNES
Indentured servant
imported from Scotland
to East New Jersey by
Lord Neil Campbell in
December 1685.
(EJD/A225)

DUNLOP ARCHIBALD
Glasgow. Merchant at
Cabin Point, James River,
Virginia, c1762.
(SRA)

DUNLOP JAMES
Born in 1754, son of
James Dunlop of Garnkirk,
Lanarkshire. Merchant.
Died in America.
(SRA)

DUNLOP JAMES
Born during November 1757
in Glasgow, third son of
David Dunlop, merchant.
Emigrated from Scotland
to Virginia in 1773.
Loyalist. Settled in
Quebec during 1779.
Merchant. Died in Montreal
on 28 August 1815.
(DCB)

DUNLOP JAMES
Son of David Dunlop of
Clober, Stirlingshire.
Settled in Canada during
1773. Died in Montreal.
(CFG)

DUNLOP JOHN
Indentured servant
imported from Scotland
to East New Jersey by Lord
Neil Campbell during
December 1685.
(EJD/A225)

DUNLOP JOHN
Eldest son of
Alexander Dunlop and
Antonia Brown. Died
in Darien in 1699.
(DD)

DUNLOP JOHN
Dolphinton, Lanarkshire.
Emigrated from Scotland,
with father, to America
during 1774. Minister
in Cambridge.
(Dolphinton GS)

DUNLAP JOHN
Emigrated from Campbell-
town, Argyllshire, to
America during 1775.
Settled in Chambersburg,
Pennsylvania. Married
Nancy Collins. Father
of Robert.
(BAF)

DUNLOP JOHN
Emigrated from Scotland,
with wife, three sons and
three daughters, to
Canada on the Commerce in
June 1821. Received a
land grant in Dalhousie,
Upper Canada, on
15 July 1821.
(PAO)

DUNLOP JOHN
Emigrated from Scotland,
with wife and two sons,
to Canada on the George
Canning during June 1821.
Received a land grant in
Ramsay, Upper Canada, on
24 July 1821.
(PAO)

DUNLOP WILLIAM
Indentured servant
imported from Scotland
to East New Jersey by
Lord Neil Campbell in
December 1685.
(EJD/A225)

DUNLOP WILLIAM
Born 29 August 1708,
son of Alexander Dunlop,
Professor of Greek at the
University of Glasgow.
Merchant in Rotterdam,
the Netherlands, before
1728. Emigrated to
America. Settled in
Dumfries, Williamsburg
County, Virginia.
Married Mary Pope in 1737.
Father of Alexander,
Died during 1739.
(DD)

DUNLOP WILLIAM
Born in Scotland in 1792.
Emigrated from Scotland
to Upper Canada in 1813
and again during 1826.
Surgeon and politician.
Died in 1848.
(TO)

DUNLOP WILLIAM
Emigrated from Scotland,
with wife, three sons and
three daughters, to
Canada on the Earl of
Buckingham during June
1821. Received a land
grant in Sherbrook, Upper
Canada, on 1 August 1821.
(PAO)

DUNN ALEXANDER
Indentured servant
imported from Scotland
to East New Jersey by
Thomas Gordon during
October 1684.
(EJD/A)

DUNN JOHN
Indentured servant
imported from Scotland
to East New Jersey by
Robert Fullerton in
October 1684.
(EJD/A)

DUNN JOHN
Emigrated from Scotland,
with wife and daughter,
to Canada on the
Commerce. Received a
land grant in Dalhousie,
Upper Canada, on
3 September 1821.
(PAO)

DUNN WILLIAM
Emigrated from Scotland,
with wife and son, to
Canada on the David of
London in June 1821.
Received a land grant
in Lanark, Upper Canada,
on 14 August 1821.
(PAO)

DUNNIE JAMES
Planter. Died on the
voyage from Scotland
to Darien, of flux on
16 September 1698.
(NLS)

EASTON GEORGE
Emigrated from Scotland,
with wife and three
daughters, to Canada on
the Prompt. Received a
land grant in Dalhousie,
Upper Canada, on
23 November 1821.
(PAO)

EASTON THOMAS
Emigrated from Scotland,
with wife, son and a
daughter, to Canada on
the Prompt. Received a
land grant in Dalhousie,
Upper Canada, on
23 November 1821.
(PAO)

EATON GEORGE
Emigrated from Scotland
to Canada on the Earl of
Buckingham in June 1821.
Received a land grant in
Sherbrooke, Upper
Canada, on 25 July 1821.
(PAO)

EDABURN BENJAMIN
Emigrated from Scotland
to America during 1738.
Settled in Illinois, and
later in Iowa.
(SG)

EDABURN DAVID
Emigrated from Scotland
to America during 1738.
Settled in Illinois, and
later in Iowa.
(SG)

EDABURN HUGH
 Emigrated from Scotland
 to America during 1738.
 Settled in Illinois,
 and later in Iowa.
 (SG)

EDGAR MARGARET
 Indentured servant
 imported from Scotland
 to East New Jersey by
 Lord Neil Campbell in
 December 1685.
 (EJD/A225)

EDGAR THOMAS
 Born on 19 October 1681
 at Keithock, Angus,
 second son of David
 Edgar of Keithock, and
 Katherine Forrester.
 Married Janet Knox.
 Emigrated from Scotland
 to America in 1703.
 Bought land near
 Elizabeth and Rathway,
 New Jersey. Father of
 David, born in Woodbridge,
 New Jersey, during 1720.
 Died on 16 June 1759.
 (BAF)

EDMINSTEIRE JOHN
 Royalist soldier captured
 at Battle of Worcester.
 Transported from Graves-
 end, Kent, to Boston, New
 England, on the John and
 Sarah, master John Greene
 13 May 1652.
 (NER)

EDMONSTONE BETHIA
 Born c1798, daughter of
 Archibald Edmonstone of
 Spittal, 1754-1821, and
 Elizabeth Aitken, 1762-
 1828. Married John
 Montgomerie. Died in
 Trinidad on 27 August 1821.
 (Stirling GS)

EDMONSTONE CHARLES
 Born c1793, son of
 Archibald Edmonstone of
 Spittal, 1754-1821, and
 Elizabeth Aitken, 1762-
 1828. Died in Demerara
 on 1 September 1822.
 (Stirling GS)

EDMONSTONE GEORGE
 Born during 1795, son of
 Archibald Edmonstone of
 Spittal, 1754-1821, and
 Elizabeth Aitken, 1762-
 1828. Died in Demerara
 on 12 January 1818.
 (Stirling GS)

EDWARDS ANDREW
 Emigrated from Scotland,
 with wife, son and daughter,
 to Canada on the Earl of
 Buckingham in June 1821.
 Received a land grant in
 Sherbrook, Upper Canada,
 on 1 August 1821.
 (PAO)

EDWARD JAMES
 Married Alison Neil in
 Stevenston, Ayrshire(?)
 Emigrated from Scotland
 to America in 1680s.
 Settled in Morganville,
 New Jersey. Father of
 Elizabeth, Jane and Elsie.
 (MNJ)

ELDER ALEXANDER
Sailor. Died of fever
on voyage from Scotland
to Darien on
25 September 1698.
(NLS)

ELLIOT WALTER
Midshipman. Died of fever
on voyage from Scotland to
Darien on 20 October 1698.
(NLS)

ELLIOT WILLIAM
Emigrated from Scotland to
Canada on the Lord Middleton
20 July 1818. Received land
grants in Burgess, Upper
Canada, 30 November 1818, and
in Drummond, Upper Canada, on
17 July 1820.
(PAO)

ENGLISH (INGLIS?) JOHN
Indentured servant
imported from Scotland
to East New Jersey by
James Johnston during
October 1685.
(EJD/A226)

ERSKINE EBENEZER
Born during 1750, second
son of Rev Henry Erskine
and Agnes Kay, in Falkirk,
Stirlingshire. Emigrated
from Scotland to America.
Died in 1785.
(EHG)

ERSKINE WILLIAM
Planter. Died at Darien
on 7 December 1698.
(NLS)

ESDALE CHARLES
Emigrated from Scotland
to Canada on the Commerce
in June 1820. Settled in
Upper Canada.
(PAO)

ESSON HENRY
Son of Robert Esson,
Balnacraig, Aboyne,
Aberdeenshire. Educated
at Marischal College,
Aberdeen, from 1807 to
1811, graduated M.A.
Minister of the Scots
Church in Montreal.
(MCA)

EVANS EDWARD
Drummer. Emigrated from
Scotland to Fredericksburg,
Virginia, before 1754.
(OD)

EWART JOHN
Born during 1788.
Emigrated from Scotland
to Canada. Building
contractor in York,
Ontario. Died in 1867.
(TO)

EWING JOHN
Baker. Emigrated from
Scotland to Portsmouth,
Virginia, during 1766.
(OD)

EWING ROBERT
Emigrated from Scotland
via County Londonderry,
Ireland, to America.
Settled in Bedford County,
Virginia, c1740. Married
Mary Baker in Virginia
c1748. Father of Robert.
Died in 1787.
(BAF)

EYRES THOMAS
Inverness(?) Signed
a treaty with the
Creek Indians in
Georgia on
11 August 1739.
(HGP)

FAIR GEORGE
Emigrated from Scotland
to Canada on the Commerce
in June 1820. Received a
land grant in Dalhousie,
Upper Canada, on
5 September 1820.
(PAO)

FAIR JAMES
Emigrated from Scotland
to Canada on the Brock.
Received a land grant
in Dalhousie, Upper
Canada, on
27 October 1821.
(PAO)

FAIR JOHN
Emigrated from Scotland
to Canada on the Brock
during 1820. Received
a land grant in
Dalhousie, Upper Canada,
on 11 November 1821.
(PAO)

FALCONER DAVID
Merchant in Edinburgh.
Leased 500 acres in
East New Jersey on
20 February 1683.
(EJD/A)

FALCONER JOHN
Son of David Falconer,
Edinburgh. Landowner at
Amboy Point, East New
Jersey, 23 November 1682.
(EJD/A)

FALCONER J.
Emigrated from Scotland to
Portsmouth, Virginia, pre
1766.
(OD)

FALCONER PATRICK
Son of William Falconer,
1720-1793, farmer in
Kinnermony, Inveravon,
and Anna Rose, 1743-1821.
Merchant in firm of
MacAdam and Falconer, New
York. Died in 1837.
(Inveravon GS)

FALCONER ROBERT
Son of William Falconer,
1720-1793, farmer in
Kinnermony, Inveravon,
and Anna Rose, 1743-1821.
Merchant in New York.
Died during 1851.
(Inveravon GS)

FALCONEY ROBERT
Born 22 December 1780, at
Pitchash, Inveravon.
Educated at the University
of Aberdeen. Emigrated
from Aberdeen to America
c1800. Settled in Sugar
Grove, Pennsylvania. Father
of Robert James Falconer,
1809-1876.
(BAF)

FALCONER THOMAS
Emigrated from Scotland,
with wife, two sons and
two daughters, to
Canada on the George
Canning during June
1821. Received a land
grant in Ramsay, Upper
Canada, 10 July 1821.
(PAO)

FALCONER WILLIAM
Born c1765, son of
William Falconer, 1720-
1793, farmer, Kinnermony,
Inveravon, and Anna Rose,
1743-1821. Merchant in
New York. Died in 1818.
(Inveravon GS)

FARLEY EDWARD
Glasgow. Emigrated from
Scotland to America 1826.
(BAF)

FARQUHAR ALEXANDER
Son of Alexander Farquhar,
Kintore, Aberdeenshire.
Educated at Marischal
College, Aberdeen, c1781.
Settled in Antigua.
(MCA)

FARQUHARSON CHARLES
Born c1759, son of
James Farquharson and Ann
Stuart, Ballintruan, Kirk-
michael, Morayshire. Died
in Baltimore, Maryland,
on 2 June 1860.
(Kirkmichael GS)

FARQUHARSON DANIEL
Married Margaret...
Father of John, Finley
and Donald. Emigrated
from Scotland to America.
Died during 1803 in
Genesee County, New York.
(H)

FARQUHARSON DONALD
Son of Daniel and Margaret
Farquharson. Emigrated from
Scotland to America in 1800
with his second wife.
Settled in Ohio.
(H)

FARQUHARSON FINLEY
Son of Daniel and Margaret
Finley. Emigrated from
Scotland to America c1802.
Settled in Genesee County,
New York. Father of
Patrick.
(H)

FARQUHARSON PATRICK
Son of Finley Farquharson.
Emigrated from Scotland
to America c1802. School-
master in Johnstown, New
York, c1810.
(H)

FARQUHARSON ROBERT
Born during 1777, fourth
son of James Farquharson
and Ann Stuart, Ballintruan,
Kirkmichael, Morayshire.
Died in Nashville,
Tennessee, on 28 June 1856.
(Kirkmichael GS)

FARQUHARSON WILLIAM
Achnagoneen. Jacobite
in MacDonell of Glen-
garry's Regiment 1745.
Prisoner 5 May 1746.
Transported to the
Plantations.
(MR)

FAUBES WILLIAM
Born in Scotland in 1730.
Emigrated from Scotland
to Virginia pre 1756.
Planter in Virginia.
(OD)

FENNER THOMAS
Clerk to Mr Patterson.
Died of fever on the
voyage from Scotland
to Darien on
2 November 1698.
(NLS)

FERGUSON ALEXANDER
Born in Edinburgh.
Emigrated from Scotland
to Halifax, Nova Scotia,
before 1808. Cattle
dealer. Father of George
Lester Ferguson.
(RCF)

FERGUSON A.
Johnstone, Renfrewshire.
Applied to settle in
Canada on 28 February
1815.
(SRO/RH9)

FERGUSON ALEXANDER
Emigrated from Scotland
to Canada on the Commerce
in June 1860. Received
a land grant in Lanark,
Upper Canada, on
5 September 1820.
(PAO)

FERGUSON DONALD
Emigrated from Scotland,
with wife and two sons,
to Canada on the Commerce.
Received a land grant in
Ramsay, Upper Canada, on
31 July 1821.
(PAO)

FERGUSON DONALD
Ruskachon, Perthshire(?)
Emigrated from Greenock,
Renfrewshire, to Montreal
during 1825 on the brig
Niagara, Hamilton.
Settled in MacNab,
Bathurst, Upper Canada,
in 1825.
(SG)

FERGUSON DUNCAN
Born in Scotland c1735.
Emigrated from Scotland
to Virginia pre 1756.
Drummer.
(OD)

FERGUSON DUNCAN
Emigrated from Scotland
to Canada on the Eliza Ann
in 1819. Received a land
grant in Drummond, Upper
Canada, 9 September 1820.
(PAO)

FERGUSON DUNCAN
 Emigrated from Scotland,
 with three daughters,
 to Canada on the David
 of London in June 1821.
 Received a land grant
 in Ramsay, Upper Canada,
 on 7 August 1821.
 (PAO)

FERGUSON FRANCIS
 Born in Dunlop, Ayrshire.
 Emigrated from Scotland
 to Canada in 1826.
 Settled in Bathurst, New
 Brunswick. Married Ann
 Munro.
 (RCF)

FERGUSON GEORGE
 Born in Scotland. Former
 Captain of the Canadian
 Fencibles. Military
 settler. Received land
 grants in Drummond, Upper
 Canada, 6 November 1815,
 and in Beckwith, Upper
 Canada, on 14 June 1817.
 (PAO)

FERGUSON GEORGE
 Youngest son of James
 Ferguson and Ann Murray,
 Aberdeenshire. Governor
 of Tobago. Died in 1820.
 (FF)

FERGUSON JAMES
 Aberdeen. Planter in
 Bellfield Estate, St Mary,
 Anota Bay, Jamaica, c1812.
 (FF)

FERGUSON JAMES
 Born in Perthshire during
 1797. Surveyor in Canada
 and United States. U.S.
 Naval Observatory
 Astronomer. Died during
 1867 in Washington.
 (TSA)

FERGUSON JAMES
 Emigrated from Oban, Argyll-
 shire, to Canada in 1818.
 Settled Kenyon township,
 Ontario. Father of John,
 Mary, Christian, Catherine,
 Annie, Duncan, Colin, Donald,
 and James.
 (RCF)

FERGUSON JAMES
 Emigrated from Scotland
 to Canada on the Trafalgar
 19 July 1817. Received a
 land grant in Bathurst,
 Upper Canada, 15 January
 1818.
 (PAO)

FERGUSON JAMES
 Emigrated from Scotland,
 with three daughters, to
 Canada on the David of
 London. Received a land
 grant in Lanark, Upper
 Canada, 4 October 1821.
 (PAO)

FERGUSON JAMES
 Son of Andrew Ferguson,
 surgeon in Aberdeen.
 Educated at Marischal
 College, Aberdeen, 1816-
 1820 - graduated M.A.
 Rector of Rutgers College,
 New Jersey. Superintendant
 of Schools, Lockport, New
 York. (MCA)

FERGUSON JOHN
 Emigrated from Scotland,
 with wife, son and two
 daughters, to Canada on
 the Caledonian 10 July
 1816. Received land
 grants in Upper Canada
 on 24 September 1816,
 on 27 August 1816, and in
 Bathurst, Upper Canada, on
 22 January 1819.
 (PAO)

FERGUSON JOHN jr.
 Emigrated from Scotland
 to Canada on the brig Ann
 1 September 1816.
 Received a land grant in
 Drummond, Upper Canada,
 8 October 1816.
 (PAO)

FERGUSON JOHN
 Born in Scotland. Former
 sergeant in the 104th
 Regiment. Military
 settler. Received land
 grants in Landsdowne,
 Upper Canada, 31 July
 1817, in Drummond, Upper
 Canada on 17 June 1817 and
 on 19 January 1819.
 (PAO)

FERGUSON JOHN
 Born during 1813 in
 Dunlop, Ayrshire.
 Emigrated from Scotland
 to Canada during 1826.
 Settled in Bathurst,
 New Brunswick. Married
 Mary Munro.
 (RCF)

FERGUSON PETER
 Emigrated from Scotland,
 with wife, two sons and
 three daughters, to
 Canada on the Jane
 24 August 1818.
 Received a land grant in
 Drummond, Upper Canada,
 15 October 1818.
 (PAO)

FERGUSON ROBERT
 Emigrated from Scotland,
 with wife, two sons and
 two daughters, to
 Canada on the Caledonian
 10 July 1816. Received
 a land grant in
 Bathurst, Upper Canada,
 on 24 September 1816.
 (PAO)

FERGUSON ROBERT
 Emigrated from Scotland,
 with wife and son, to
 Canada on the Commerce
 in June 1820. Received a
 land grant in Lanark,
 Upper Canada, on
 1 October 1820.
 (PAO)

FERGUSON ROBERT
 Born in Dunlop, Ayrshire.
 Emigrated from Scotland
 to Canada in 1826.
 Settled in Bathurst, New
 Brunswick. Married Belle
 Willis.
 (RCF)

FERGUSON THOMAS
 Johnstone, Renfrewshire.
 Applied to settle in
 Canada 28 February 1815.
 (SRO/RH9)

FERGUSON THOMAS
Emigrated from Scotland.
with wife, four sons and
two daughters, to
Canada on the Earl of
Buckingham in June 1821.
Received a land grant in
Dalhousie, Upper Canada,
on 20 July 1821.
(PAO)

FERGUSON WILLIAM ERSKINE
Son of John Ferguson,
Aberdeen Educated at
Marischal College,
Aberdeen, c1817, and at
University of St Andrews,
Fife. Inspector of
Schools in Dundas County,
Canada.
(MCA)

FERGUSON WILLIAM
Emigrated from Scotland
to Canada on the Commerce
during June 1820.
Settled in Upper Canada.
(PAO)

FERRIER DAVID
Merchant in Montrose,
Angus. Emigrated to
Georgia - possibly on
the Mary Anne from
Gravesend, Kent, in
1737.
(HGP)

FERRIER WILLIAM
Dumbarton. Applied to
settle in Canada on
27 February 1815.
(SRO/RH9)

FINLAY HUGH
Born c1730 in Glasgow(?),
third son of Robert Finlay,
tanner and cordwainer, and
Susanna Parkins. Emigrated
from Glasgow to Quebec in
1763. Married Mary
Phillips in Quebec during
1769. Merchant and
politician. Died in
Quebec on 26 December 1801.
(DCB)

FINLAY JOHN
Emigrated from Scotland,
with wife, two sons and
three daughters, to
Canada on the David of
London. Received a land
grant in Lanark, Upper
Canada, on 24 January 1822.
(PAO)

FINLAY ROBERT
Emigrated from Scotland,
with wife, son and four
daughters, to Canada on the
Earl of Buckingham.
Received a land grant in
Dalhousie, Upper Canada,
on 6 August 1821.
(PAO)

FINLAY THOMAS
Kilmarnock, Ayrshire.
Covenanter. Captured at
Battle of Bothwell Bridge
on 22 June 1679.
Banished to the Plantations.
Drowned off the Orkney
Islands.
(HCA)

FINLAY THOMAS
Son of James Finlay of
Balchrystie, Fife.
Apprenticed to John
McFarlane. Admitted to
the Society of Writers
to the Signet on
24 May 1720. Attorney
at Law in Barbados. Died
during June 1760.
(WS)

FINLAYSON WALTER
Born c1781, son of
William Finlayson,
Deputy Clerk of the Bills.
Apprenticed to Charles
Bremner. Admitted to
the Society of Writers to
the Signet on 10 March
1813. Stipeniary
Magistrate for Montego
Bay, Jamaica. Died on
21 December 1841 in
Jamaica.
(WS)

FISHER ARCHIBALD
Emigrated from Scotland
to America. Settled in
Stirling, Ohio, in 1824.
(SHR)

FISHER DONALD
Emigrated from Scotland
to Canada on the Agincourt
on 12 August 1817.
Received a land grant in
Bathurst, Upper Canada, on
4 December 1817.
(PAO)

FISHER DONALD
Lochearnhead, Perthshire.
Emigrated from Greenock,
Renfrewshire, with wife
Margaret MacEwan and
children Catherine, Mary,
Margaret, Christian and
Janet, to Montreal on the
brig Niagara, Hamilton,
during 1825. Settled in
McNab, Bathurst, Upper
Canada, in 1825.
Drowned in July 1826.
(SG)

FISHER DUNCAN
Born c1753 in Dunkeld,
Perthshire, son of
Duncan Fisher, a farmer,
and Christian Creighton.
Shoemaker. Emigrated
from Scotland to
America. Settled in
Argyll, New York, during
1773. Moved to Montreal
during 1777. Married
Catherine Embury in
Montreal on 27 February
1783.
(DCB)

FISHER DUNCAN
Emigrated from Scotland
to Canada on the
Swiftsure in March 1820.
Received a land grant in
Beckwith, Upper Canada,
on 31 July 1821.
(PAO)

FISHER FINLAY
Born c1756 in Dunkeld,
Perthshire. Emigrated
from Scotland to New York
in June 1775. Farmer in
Washington County, New York.
Settled in Montreal. Died
there 14 January 1819.
(DCB)

FISHER JAMES
Born in Killin,
Perthshire.
Emigrated from Scotland
to America during 1784.
Settled in Hemingford,
Quebec, in 1800.
(CP)(SO)

FISHER JAMES
Johnstone, Renfrewshire.
Applied to settle in
Canada on 28 February
1815.
(SRO/RH9)

FISHER JOHN
Emigrated from Scotland
to Canada on the brig John
19 August 1817. Received
a land grant in Lancaster,
Upper Canada, on
12 November 1817.
(PAO)

FITCHETT JAMES
Emigrated from Scotland
to East New Jersey in
February 1685.
(EJD/A196)

FLEMING JAMES
Emigrated from Scotland,
with wife, two sons and
three daughters, to
Canada on the David of
London in June 1821.
Received a land grant in
Lanark, Upper Canada, on
10 September 1821.
(PAO)

FLEMING JOHN
Emigrated from Scotland
to Canada on the Earl of
Buckingham in June 1821.
Received a land grant in
Dalhousie, Upper Canada,
on 28 July 1821.
(PAO)

FLEMING ROBERT
Emigrated from Scotland,
with wife, two sons and
a daughter, to Canada on
the Commerce in June 1820.
Received a land grant in
Lanark, Upper Canada, on
1 October 1820.
(PAO)

FLEMING THOMAS
Son of Rev James Fleming
and Magdalene Way. Rector
of St John, Jamaica. Died
on 2 December 1741.
(SP.VIII)

FLEMING WILLIAM
Emigrated from Scotland,
with wife and son, to
Canada on the George Canning
in June 1821. Received a
land grant in Ramsay, Upper
Canada, on 24 July 1821.
(PAO)

FLETCHER JOHN
Planter. Died in Darien
on 11 November 1698.
(NLS)

FLINN JOHN
Emigrated from Scotland,
to Canada on the Brock
during 1820. Settled
in Upper Canada 1821.
(PAO)

FLOOD JOHN
Anderston. Applied to
settle in Canada on
4 March 1815.
(SRO/RH9)

FOGO JAMES
Son of James Fogo,
writer in Glasgow.
Merchant in Clarendon,
Jamaica, c1771.
(SRA/B10/15/7435)

FORBES ALEXANDER
Born in Edinburgh on
27 July 1689, second
son of Sir David Forbes
of Newhall. Provost
Marshal General, and
a member of H.M.Council
of Jamaica. Died in
Jamaica on 13 November
1729. Buried at
St Catherine's,
Spanish Town, Jamaica.
(MIBWI)

FORBES FRANCIS
Aberdeenshire. Educated
at King's College,
Aberdeen, - graduated
M.A. on 30 March 1821.
Minister of St Luke's,
British Guiana.
(KCA)

FORBES GEORGE
Son of Lachlan Forbes
of Edenglassie. M.D.
Settled in Bermuda
pre 1784.
(BCG)

FORBES JANET
Born in 1735, daughter
of Thomas Forbes of
Waterton, and Margaret
Montgomerie. Died in
Antigua during 1775.
(HF)

FORBES JOHN
Son of Rev John Forbes,
Moderator of the Church
of Scotland. Emigrated
to America, with his wife
Constance Mitchell and her
sister, on the Little Ann
during 1623. Settled in
Duxbury, Massachusetts,
and later, during 1645, in
Bridgewater, Massachusetts.
Father of Edward. Died in
1661.
(BAF)

FORBES JOHN
Born during 1700 in
Aberdeenshire(?).
Emigrated from Scotland
to America between 1715
and 1729. Married Dryden,
daughter of Kenelm
Cheseldyne, on 1 July 1729.
Father of James, 1731-1780.
Died on 26 January 1737.
(BAF)

FORBES JOHN·
Born during 1728, son
of William Forbes,
Chamberlain to the
Earl of Kintore,and
Anna Forbes. Merchant
in Aberdeen. Emigrated
from Scotland to
America during 1747.
Died in Virginia in
1757.
(HF)

FORBES JOHN
Eldest son of Archibald
Forbes of Deskrie.
Emigrated from Scotland
to America. Rector of
St Augustine, Florida.
Married Dorothy Murray
in America on
2 February 1769. Father
of James Grant Forbes,
John Murray Forbes, and
Ralph Bennett Forbes.
Died on 17 September
1783.
(HF)

FORBES WILLIAM
Eldest son of George
Forbes, 1741-1791,
coppersmith in Aberdeen,
and Jean Lumsden. M.D.
in Jamaica. Married
... Tamplin. Father
of Ellen.
(HF)

FORD GEORGE
Indentured servant
imported from Scotland
to East New Jersey by
James Johnston during
October 1685.
(EJD/A226)

FORDYCE JOHN
Born in June 1796, son
of Charles Fordyce, 1755
-1836, and Mary Whitton,
1762-1825. Died in
Trinidad.
(Arbroath Abbey GS)

FORGIE GILBERT
Emigrated from Scotland,
with wife, three sons and
nine daughters, to Canada
on the Commerce in June
1820. Received a land grant
in Lanark, Upper Canada, on
1 October 1820, and there
also on 15 June 1822.
(PAO)

FOREST ROBERT
Emigrated from Scotland,
with wife, three sons and
three daughters, to
Canada on the Prompt.
Received a land grant in
Lanark, Upper Canada, on
27 November 1821.
(PAO)

FORRESTER JOHN
Planter. Died of flux on
the voyage from Scotland
to Darien on 11 September
1698.
(NLS)

FORSTER THOMAS
Emigrated from Scotland
to Canada. Received a
land grant in Ramsay,
Upper Canada, on 9 April
1821.
(PAO)

FORSYTH ALEXANDER
  Educated at Marischal
  College, Aberdeen, c1814,
  and at King's College,
  Aberdeen, in 1817.
  Graduated M.A.
  Settled in Halifax,
  Nova Scotia.
  (MCA)

FORSYTH JOSEPH
  Born c1760 in Huntly,
  Aberdeenshire, son of
  William Forsyth and
  Jean Phyn. Emigrated
  from Scotland to Canada.
  Married (1) Ann Bell, in
  Kingston, Upper Canada,
  c1797, (2) Alice Robins
  c1803. Merchant. Died
  on 20 September 1813.
  (DCB)

FORSYTH MATTHEW
  Born during 1700 in
  Tailzerton, Ayrshire,
  second son of James
  Forsyth and Margaret
  Montgomerie. Married
  Esther Graham in
  Ireland. Emigrated to
  America during 1742.
  Settled in Chester, New
  Hampshire. Died in 1791.
  (BCG)

FORSYTH THOMAS
  Emigrated from Scotland,
  with wife, three sons and
  four daughters, to
  Canada on the Commerce
  in August 1820. Received
  a land grant in Lanark,
  Upper Canada, 5 September
  1820.
  (PAO)

FORSYTH Rev
  Born in Ecclefechan,
  Dumfries-shire.
  Emigrated from Scotland
  to Prince Edward Island.
  Minister in Cornwallis,
  Prince Edward Island,
  from 1800 to 1835. Died
  there 9 August 1840.
  (HPC)

FOSSEM MICHAEL
  Royalist soldier captured
  at the Battle of Worcester.
  Transported from Gravesend,
  Kent, to Boston, New
  England, on the John and
  Sarah, master John Greene
  13 May 1652.
  (NER)

FOWLER ANDREW
  Born in Scotland c1730.
  Settled in Virginia pre
  1756. Farmer.
  (OD)

FOWLER JAMES
  Yeoman. Emigrated from
  Scotland to Canada.
  Received a land grant in
  Newcastle, Upper Canada,
  on 15 September 1818.
  (PAO)

FOWLER WILLIAM
  Emigrated from Scotland
  to Canada. Yeoman.
  Received a land grant in
  Newcastle, Upper Canada,
  on 15 September 1818.
  (PAO)

FRAME JAMES
Born in Alloa,
Clackmannanshire, c1766.
Emigrated from Scotland
to America. Settled in
Blandford, Virginia,died
during 1803.
(OD)

FRAME JOHN
Born in Scotland.
Military settler.
Received a land grant
in Upper Canada on
25 November 1816.
(PAO)

FRAME NINIAN
Emigrated from Scotland,
with wife, son and two
daughters, to Canada on
the George Canning during
June 1821. Received a
land grant in Ramsay,
Upper Canada, on
16 July 1821.
(PAO)

FRASER ALEXANDER
Born in Scotland. Former
corporal in the 49th
Regiment. Military
settler. Wife.
Received a land grant
in Drummond, Upper Canada,
on 29 October 1816.
(PAO)

FRASER ALEXANDER
Born in Scotland. Former
lieutenant in the New
Brunswick Fencibles.
Wife and daughter. Military
settler. Received land
grants in Elmsley and
Drummond on 1 November 1815,
in Elizabethtown 31 July
1817, and in Drummond on
18 March 1820.
(PAO)

FRASER DONALD
Born in Scotland. Former
lieutenant in the Royal
Regiment. Wife, son and
daughter. Military settler.
Received land grants in
Upper Canada - in Lanark
on 6 November 1820, and
in Bathurst on 2 August 1820.
(PAO)

FRASER Rev DONALD ALLAN
Born during 1793 in Mull,
Argyllshire. Emigrated
from Scotland to Pictou,
Nova Scotia, 1817.
Minister in Pictou from
1817 to 1837, in Lunenburg,
Nova Scotia, from 1837 to
1842, and in St John's,
Newfoundland from 1842 to
1845. Died in 1845.
(HPC)

FRAZIER JAMES
Born in Scotland in 1730.
Emigrated from Scotland
to Virginia pre 1756.
Waterman.
(OD)

FRAZIER JOHN
Born in Aberdeen c1678.
Settled in Darien.
Deserted to the Spanish
during 1700.
(Darien Disaster)

FRASER JOHN
Born c1734 in Scotland(?)
Soldier and teacher. Died
in Quebec 13 February 1803.
(DCB)

FRASER JOHN
Born c1775. Emigrated
from Scotland, with
wife and six children,
to Canada. Weaver.
Settled at Roger's
Hill, Pictou, Nova
Scotia, in 1815.
(PANS/RG1)

FRASER JOHN
Born c1771. Emigrated
from Scotland, with
wife and five children,
to Canada. Weaver.
Settled at West River,
Pictou, Nova Scotia,
during 1815.
(PANS/RG1)

FRASER JOHN
Born in Scotland. Army
conductor. Military
settler. Wife and a
daughter. Received a
land grant in Drummond,
Upper Canada, on
26 November 1815.
(PAO)

FRASER JOHN
Born c1789, son of Rev
John Fraser, 1753-1812,
and Jane Smith, 1765-
1831, Libberton. Died
in Jamaica at the residence
of his uncle Dr Patrick
Smith, on 6 November 1821.
(Libberton GS)

FRASER JOSEPH
Born c1780. Copper
and iron plate worker.
Emigrated from Leith,
with wife aged 36 and
children Francis 7, Jean
4, and John1, to Halifax,
Nova Scotia during 1817.
(CO384/1/116.237)

FRASER MALCOLM
Born in Abernethy on
26 May 1733, son of
Donald Fraser and Janet
McIntosh. Lieutenant in
a Highland Regiment.
Settled at Murray Bay,
Quebec, in 1762. Died
in Quebec on 14 June 1815.
(CP)(DCB)(PRSC)

FRASER PAUL
Glasgow. Applied to
settle in Canada on
4 March 1815.
(SRO/RH9)

FRASER SIMON
Born in Kirkhill, Inverness.
Married Lydia Fraser.
Father of Thomas, John,
Donald, William and two
daughters. Emigrated
from Scotland to Canada in
1784. Settled at East River,
Pictou, Nova Scotia. Died
in June 1787.
(DF)

FRASER of FORD SIMON
Son of William Fraser of
Ford. Admitted to Society
of Writers to the Signet
19 December 1767. Married
Janet Cruikshank, daughter
of Charles Douglas, Clifton-
hall, Philadelphia,2 March
1784. Died 25 September
1819.
(WS)

FRASER THOMAS
Educated at University
of Glasgow - graduated
M.D. in 1749.
'practioner of Physick
in the Island of Antigua'
8 December 1749.
(GG)

FRASER THOMAS
Born in Scotland c1780.
Emigrated to Canada.
Employed by the North
West Company from 1800
until 1821, and then by
the Hudson Bay Company
until 1849. Appointed
Chief Trader in 1836.
Died 31 January 1849.
(HBRS)

FRASER WILLIAM
Born c1786. Emigrated
from Scotland to Canada.
Settled in Pictou Town,
Nova Scotia, during
1815. Schoolteacher.
(PANS/RG1)

FRASER Rev WILLIAM
Born 22 December 1763,
second son of Francis
Fraser of Findrack,
Aberdeenshire.
Educated in Aberdeen and
in Cambridge. Married
Elizabeth Lucy James.
Rector of Trelawny parish,
Jamaica. Died on 1 April
1844 in Falmouth, Jamaica.
Buried in Falmouth cemetery.
(MIBWI)

FRASER WILLIAM
Born 27 July 1799 in
Forfar, Angus. Merchant
in Kingston, Jamaica.
Died on 12 June 1839.
Buried in the Scots
cemetery.
(MIBWI)

FRASER WILLIAM
Emigrated from Scotland
to Canada on the Morning
Field on 19 September
1816. Received a land
grant in Drummond, Upper
Canada, on 18 November
1816.
(PAO)

FREELAND DAVID
Emigrated from Scotland,
with wife, son and four
daughters, to Canada on
the David of London in
June 1821. Received a
land grant in Lanark,
Upper Canada, on
30 August 1821.
(PAO)

FRENCH(?) DAVID
Emigrated from Scotland,
with wife, two sons and
a daughter, to Canada on
the David of London in
June 1821. Received a
land grant in Ramsay,
Upper Canada, 7 August 1821.
(PAO)

FROST ROBERT
Indentured servant
imported from Scotland
to East New Jersey in
October 1684 by Robert
Fullerton.
(EJD/A)

FROST THOMAS
Indentured servant
imported from Scotland
to East New Jersey in
October 1684 by
Robert Fullerton.
(EJD/A)

FROST WILLIAM
Indentured servant
imported from Scotland
to East New Jersey in
October 1684 by
Robert Fullerton.
(EJD/A)

FULLARTON JOHN
Edinburgh. Tradesman.
Hudson Bay Company
employee from 1683 to
1711. Sailed to Hudson
Bay on the Diligence
during 1683. Died in
England during 1738.
(HBRS)

FULLERTON ROBERT
Brother of John
Fullerton in Angus.
Emigrated from Scotland
to America. Settled in
New York. Died during
January 1687. Power of
Attorney 13 October 1691.
(EJD/D)

FULLERTON THOMAS
Brother of John Fullerton
in Angus. Emigrated from
Scotland to America.
Settled in New York. Later
c1691 settled in
Barbados.
(EJD/D)

FULLARTON Captain THOMAS
Commander of the Dolphin.
Died in Darien on
25 December 1698.
(NLS)

FULTON GEORGE
Born in Perth, Scotland.
Former soldier in the
37th Regiment. Military
settler. Received a land
grant in Bathurst, Upper
Canada, on 17 July 1816.
(PAO)

FULTON JOHN
Emigrated from Scotland,
with wife, two sons and
two daughters, to Canada
on the Commerce in June
1820. Received a land
grant in Lanark, Upper
Canada, on 8 September
1820.
(PAO)

FULTON WILLIAM
Scottish merchant in
Bristol, New England c1699.
Joint-owner of the Society.
(SPAWI)

FYFE MACDUFF
Son of John Fyfe, Cabrach,
Banffshire. Educated at
Marischal College, Aberdeen,
from 1785 to 1789, graduated
M.A. Planter in St Vincent.
(MCA)

FYFE ROBERT
Born c1775, son of Barclay
Fyfe, merchant in Leith.
Died 1 August 1794. Buried
in Kingston Cathedral,
Jamaica.
(MIBWI)

GAIRDNER JAMES
Born during 1761, son of
Andrew Gairdner and
Rebecca Penman, Edinburgh.
Emigrated from Scotland to
America. Landed in
Charleston, South Carolina.
Married Mary Gordon from
Edinburgh. Cotton planter
in Georgia. Father of
James Penman Gairdner,
1792-1862. Died during
1830.
(BAF)

GALBRAITH ALEXANDER
Emigrated from Scotland,
with wife, two sons and
two daughters, to Canada
on the George Canning in
June 1821. Received a
land grant in Ramsay,
Upper Canada, on
16 July 1821.
(PAO)

GALBRAITH DAVID
Born c1770, son of John
Galbraith, tenant farmer
in Anniston, Symington,
Lanarkshire. Surgeon.
Died in Jamaica on
13 October 1793.
(Symington GS)

GALBREATH JOHN
Edinburgh. Indentured as
a servant to John Hancock
in Edinburgh for four years
service in East New Jersey
on 12 August 1685.
(EJD/A252)

GALBREATH JOHN
Emigrated from Scotland
to Canada on the Commerce
with his wife, son and
daughter in June 1820.
Received a land grant in
Lanark, Upper Canada, on
8 September 1820.
(PAO)

GALBREATH THOMAS
Glasgow(?) Merchant in
New York c1777.
(SRA/B10/12/4)

GALE ALEXANDER
Son of Alexander Gale,
farmer, Coldstone,
Aberdeenshire. Educated
at Marischal College,
Aberdeen, from 1815 to
1819, graduated M.A.
Presbyterian minister
in Hamilton, Ontario.
(MCA)

GALLOWAY SAMUEL
Born during 1645 in
Galloway. Emigrated to
America. Settled in
Arundel County, Maryland,
c1690. Father of William.
Died on 17 April 1719.
(BAF)

GALT WILLIAM
Born in Scotland c1755
(Dundonald, Ayrshire?)
Emigrated from Scotland
to America. Settled in
Virginia c1775. Merchant.
Presbyterian. Died in
Richmond, Virginia, on
26 March 1825.
(Raleigh Register Weekly)

GARDINER JAMES
Emigrated from Scotland,
with wife and son, to
Canada. Received a
land grant in Ramsay,
Upper Canada, on
24 January 1822.
(PAO)

GARDNER JOHN
Eldest son of Alexander
Gardner, jeweller in
Edinburgh. Apprentice
to Isaac Grant.
Admitted to the Society
of Writers to the
Signet on 21 December
1786. Attorney at Law
in Jamaica. Died 1794.
(WS)

GARDINER ROBERT
Emigrated from Scotland,
with son and daughter,
to Canada on the Commerce
in June 1821. Received a
land grant in Dalhousie,
Upper Canada, on
15 July 1821.
(PAO)

GARDNER WALTER
Emigrated from Greenock,
Renfrewshire, to Canada,
with his wife and
daughter, on the David
of London in May 1821.
Received a land grant
in Ramsay, Upper Canada,
on 22 August 1821.
(PAO)

GARNOCH DUNCAN
With wife Margaret
indentured as servants to
Andrew Alexander for
four years service in
East New Jersey, in
Edinburgh on 29 May 1684.
Emigrated from Scotland
to East New Jersey in
November 1684. Assigned
to Andrew Winton in
Fairfield, Connecticut.
Settled in Boston,
Massachusetts.
(EJD/D325)(Stratford TR2)
(Boston Rec. Com. Rep.9)

GARNOCH ELIZABETH
Indentured as a servant
to Andrew Alexander for
four years service in
East New Jersey, in
Edinburgh on 29 May 1684.
Emigrated from Scotland
to East New Jersey during
November 1684. Assigned
to Andrew Winton in
Fairfield, Connecticut.
Settled in Boston,
Massachusetts.
(EJD/D325)(Stratford TR2)
(Boston Rec. Com. Rep.9)

GAUDIE ROBERT
Planter. Died of flux on
the voyage from Scotland
to Darien on 28 October
1698.
(NLS)

GEDDES JOHN
Indentured servant
imported from Scotland to
East New Jersey by David
Mudie in November 1684.
(EJD/A197)

GEILLS ANDREW
Glasgow(?) Tobacco
merchant and shipmaster
in Virginia c1744.
(SRA/B10/15/5959)

GEMMEL JAMES
Emigrated from Scotland,
with wife, son and
daughter, to Canada on
the Earl of Buckingham
in June 1821. Received
a land grant in Ramsay,
Upper Canada, on
26 July 1821.
(PAO)

GEMMEL JOHN
Emigrated from Scotland,
with wife, three sons and
two daughters, to Canada
on the David of London
in May 1821. Received a
land grant in Lanark,
Upper Canada, on
4 October 1821.
(PAO)

GEMMEL JOHN
Emigrated from Scotland,
with wife, son and
daughter, to Canada
on the David of London
in June 1821. Received
a land grant in Ramsay,
Upper Canada, on
3 September 1821.
(PAO)

GEMMEL JOHN
Glasgow. Settled in
Lanark, Upper Canada,
pre 1822.
(SRA/NRAS0396)

GEMMEL SAMUEL
Emigrated from Scotland
to Canada on the Commerce
in June 1821. Received
a land grant in Lanark,
Upper Canada, on
6 August 1821.
(PAO)

GEMMEL THOMAS
Emigrated from Scotland
to Canada on the Commerce
in June 1820. Received
a land grant in Lanark,
Upper Canada, on
1 October 1820.
(PAO)

GENTLEMAN MARGARET
Indentured servant
imported from Scotland
to East New Jersey by
David Mudie during
November 1684. Head-
right land grant 1689.
(EJD/A196/B159)

GIBB JAMES
Son of John Gibb, 1760-
1802, farmer, Hillhead,
Carluke, Lanarkshire, and
Agnes Watson, 1765-1845.
Emigrated from Scotland
to Quebec pre 1826.
Father of James Lawson
Gibb. Died in Quebec 1833.
(Carluke GS)

GIBB JOHN
Indentured servant
imported from Scotland
to East New Jersey by
James Johnston during
October 1685.
(EJD/A226)

98

GIBB JOHN
Son of John Gibb, 1760-
1802, farmer, Hillhead,
Carluke, Lanarkshire,
and Jean Lawson, 1756-
1839. Emigrated from
Scotland to Canada.
Settled in Quebec or
Montreal pre 1826.
(Carluke GS)

GIBB MARGARET
Indentured servant
imported from Scotland
to East New Jersey by
James Johnston during
October 1685.
(EJD/A226)

GIBB THOMAS
Son of John Gibb, 1760-
1802, farmer, Hillhead,
Carluke, Lanarkshire,
and Jean Lawson, 1756-
1839. Emigrated from
Scotland to Quebec
before 1826.
(Carluke GS)

GIBBON JOHN
Son of Alexander Gibbon,
sailor in Aberdeen.
Educated at Marischal
College, Aberdeen, from
1798 to 1802, graduated
M.A. Settled in Canada.
(MCA)

GIBBONS WILLIAM
Emigrated from Scotland
to Canada on the Commerce
in June 1820. Settled in
Upper Canada.
(PAO)

GIBSON BARTHOLEMEW
Edinburgh. H.M.Forger.
Leased 10 acres in
East New Jersey at
Amboy Point on
23 November 1682.
(EJD/A)

GIBSON JAMES
Emigrated from Scotland
to America. Settled in
Suffolk, Virginia, before
19 February 1765.
(OD)

GIBSON JAMES
Emigrated from Scotland,
with wife, two sons and
three daughters, to
Canada on Baltic Merchant
during 1815. Received a
land grant in Younge,
Upper Canada, on
16 October 1817.
(PAO)

GIBSON JAMES
Emigrated from Scotland,
with wife, three sons
and three daughters, to
Canada on the Prompt.
Received a land grant in
Dalhousie, Upper Canada,
on 17 November 1821.
(PAO)

GIBSON JOHN
Emigrated from Scotland
to America. Settled in
Cambridge, Massachusetts,
during 1634. Freeman
there 17 May 1637. Land-
owner. Married (1)
Rebecca Thompson, Duddings-
ton, Midlothian (2) Mrs
Joan Prentice in 1662.
Father of John, 1641-1679.
Died during 1694.
(BAF)

GIBSON JOHN
Glasgow. Factor at
Colchester, Virginia,
for Oswald, Dennistoun
and Company, tobacco
merchants in Glasgow,
c1770.
(SRA/779/21)

GIBSON ROBERT
Covenanter and rebel in
1666. Prisoner in
Tolbooth of Edinburgh.
Banished to Virginia
on 10 June 1669.
(PC)

GIBSON RYDER
Born mid eighteenth
century in Kelso(?),
Roxburghshire, son of
John Gibson, captain
of the 4th Foot, and
Elizabeth Duff.
Emigrated from Scotland
to Jamaica, pre 1802.
(FC)

GIBSON THOMAS
Born before 1706,
eldest son of
Dr John Gibson,
physician in Kelso,
Roxburghshire, and
Catherine Home.
Surgeon. Emigrated
from Scotland to
America.
(FC)

GIBSON WILLIAM
Emigrated from Scotland,
with wife, four sons and
two daughters, to Canada
on the Commerce during
August 1820. Received
a land grant in
Dalhousie, Upper Canada,
on 3 September 1820.
(PAO)

GILL HENRY
Emigrated from Scotland
via Ulster to America.
Settled in Chester County,
Pennsylvania, pre 1785.
(SG)

GILLEN JOHN
Emigrated from Scotland
to America on the David
of London, in May 1821.
Settled in Upper Canada.
(PAO)

GILLESPIE GEORGE LEWIS
Emigrated from Scotland
to America during 1720.
Landed at Leesburg,
Virginia. Settled in
Tennessee.
(BAF)

GILLESPIE JAMES
Born in Greenock, Renfrew-
shire c1796. Shipmaster.
Died on 19 October 1827.
Buried in Kingston
Cathedral, Jamaica.
(MIBWI)

GILLESPIE THOMAS
Born c1765 at Wiston,
Lanarkshire(?) Died in
Jamaica on 29 April 1799.
(Wiston GS)

GILLIES HUGH
Emigrated from Scotland
to Canada. Received a
land grant in Charlotten-
burg, St Raphael, Quebec,
on 24 November 1787.
(PAO)

GILLICE JOHN
 Son of John Gillice,
 writer, Keith, Banff-
 shire. Educated at
 Marischal College, Aberdeen,
 from 1818 to 1821, - M.A.
 Medical practitioner in
 America.
 (MCA)

GILLIES WILLIAM
 Emigrated from Scotland
 to Canada. Settled in
 Charlottenburg,
 St Raphael, Quebec, on
 23 November 1787.
 (PAO)

GILLON JOHN
 Emigrated from Scotland
 to Canada on the David
 of London in June 1821.
 Received a land grant
 in Ramsay, Upper Canada,
 on 25 August 1821.
 (PAO)

GILMOUR ALLAN
 Emigrated from Scotland,
 with wife, son and daughter,
 to Canada on the David of
 London in June 1821.
 Received a land grant in
 Ramsay, Upper Canada, on
 31 July 1821.
 (PAO)

GILMOUR HUGH
 Emigrated from Scotland,
 with wife and two daughters,
 to Canada on the David of
 London in June 1821.
 Received a land grant in
 Ramsay, Upper Canada, on
 31 July 1821.
 (PAO)

GILMOUR JAMES
 Glasgow(?) Emigrated from
 Scotland, with wife two
 sons and two daughters,
 to Canada on the Earl of
 Buckingham in June 1821.
 Received a land grant in
 Sherbrook, Upper Canada,
 on 31 July 1821.
 (PAO)

GILMOUR JAMES
 Emigrated from Scotland
 to Canada on the David of
 London in June 1821.
 Received a land grant in
 Ramsay, Upper Canada, on
 31 July 1821.
 (PAO)

GILMOUR JOHN
 Emigrated from Scotland,
 with wife and daughter,
 to Canada on the David of
 London in June 1821.
 Received a land grant in
 Ramsay, Upper Canada, on
 31 July 1821.
 (PAO)

GILMOR ROBERT
 Born in Paisley, Renfrew-
 shire, on 10 November 1748,
 son of John Gilmor, a
 manufacturer. Emigrated
 from Scotland to Oxford,
 Maryland, during 1767.
 Married Louisa, daughter
 of Rev Thomas Airey,
 Dorchester County, Maryland,
 25 September 1771.
 Tobacco merchant in
 Amsterdam, Holland, and
 Baltimore, Maryland.
 Father of Robert and William.
 (TSA)

GILMOUR WILLIAM
Emigrated from Scotland
to Canada on the Earl of
Buckingham in June 1821.
Received a land grant in
Sherbrook, Upper Canada,
on 31 July 1821.
(PAO)

GLASS HENRY
Emigrated from Scotland
to Canada on the Commerce
in June 1820. Received
land grants in Lanark,
Upper Canada, on
8 September 1820, and
on 4 October 1821.
(PAO)

GLASSFORD JAMES
Brother of John Glassford,
1715-1783, merchant and
tobacco importer in Glasgow.
Emigrated from Scotland to
Quebec c1760. Moved to
Boston, Massachusetts.
Later a partner of Neil
Jamieson in Norfolk,
Virginia, c1765.
(SRA)

GLASSFORD ROBERT
Glasgow. Merchant in
St Kitts, and later in
Grenada c1764.
(SRA/T-MJ)

GLEN ANDREW
Lochwinnoch, Renfrew-
shire. Emigrated from
Scotland to Canada 1818.
Minister - ordained in
Montreal 14 July 1818.
Minister at River du Chene,
and later at Richmond.
(HPC)

GLENN DAVID
Emigrated from Ayrshire
to America during 1819.
Settled in Vevay,
Switzerland County,
Indiana. Married Ann
Boyle in Ayrshire on
25 February 1795. Father
of William, 1806-1888.
Died during 1822.
(BAF)

GLENN JAMES ANDERSON
Born in Paisley, Renfrew-
shire. Tobacco merchant.
Settled in Petersburg,
Virginia, pre 1822.
Married Isabella Wilson.
(UNC/Glenn PP)

GLENDINNING CHARLES
Born in Dumfries in
early 1700s.
Emigrated from Scotland
to America pre 1750.
(SG)

GLENDENING DAVID
Soldier. Emigrated from
Scotland to Virginia pre
1756.
(OD)

GLENDINNING JAMES
Born in Dumfries in
early 1700s.
Emigrated from Scotland
to America. Settled in
Pennsylvania.
(SG)

GLENDINNING JOHN
Born in Dumfries 1704.
Emigrated from Scotland
to America. Settled in
Pennsylvania.
(SG)

GLENIE JAMES
  Born in Scotland.
  Officer in the Royal
  Engineers. Member of
  Colonial Assembly of
  New Brunswick 1791.
  (SO)

GOLD GEORGE
  Emigrated from Scotland
  to Canada on the Commerce
  in June 1820. Received
  a land grant in Lanark,
  Upper Canada, on
  5 September 1820.
  (PAO)

GOLD HENRY
  Emigrated from Scotland
  to Canada on the Commerce
  in June 1820. Received a
  land grant in Lanark,
  Upper Canada, on
  5 September 1820.
  (PAO)

GOLIGHTLY ADAM
  Emigrated from Scotland,
  with wife and two
  daughters, to Canada
  on the Diana 29 May 1817.
  Received land grants in
  Drummond, Upper Canada,
  17 October 1817, and in
  Burgess, Upper Canada,
  on 14 March 1818.
  (PAO)

GOODLETT ROBERT
  Born during 1720 in
  Glasgow(?) Emigrated to
  Philadelphia in 1730s
  Cabinet maker. Settled
  in Westmoreland County,
  Virginia. Married
  Nancy Middleton in 1750.
  (H)

GOODWIN ALEXANDER
  Emigrated from Scotland,
  with wife, three sons and
  three daughters, to
  Canada on the George
  Canning in June 1821.
  Received a land grant in
  Dalhousie, Upper Canada,
  on 12 July 1821.
  (PAO)

GORDON ALEXANDER
  Emigrated from Scotland
  to America pre 1734.
  Settled in Cumberland
  County, Pennsylvania.
  Died pre 1750.
  (HG)

GORDON ALEXANDER
  Born in Kirkcudbright.
  Merchant in Petersburg,
  Virginia, during
  eighteenth century.
  Married Mary...
  Father of Peggy.
  (HBV)

GORDON ALEXANDER
  Aberdeen student in 1749.
  Graduated M.D. in 1761.
  Chief surgeon in a West
  Indian hospital.
  (MCA)

GORDON ARCHIBALD
  Emigrated from Scotland
  to America. Colonel in
  Pittsylvania County
  Militia, Virginia, 1774.
  Died in Franklin County,
  Virginia.
  (HG)

GORDON BASIL
Born on 15 May 1768 in
Kirkcudbright, son of
Samuel Gordon. Emigrated
from Scotland to
America c1784. Married
Anne Campbell Knox,
Windsor Lodge, Culpepper
County, Virginia. Father
of Basil Gordon and
Douglas Hamilton Gordon.
(BAF)

GORDON CHARLES
Son of Robert Gordon of
Pitlurg, and Catherine
Burnett. Emigrated
from Scotland to East
New Jersey before
January 1685. Possibly
father of Charles and
Peter. Died during 1698
at Perth Amboy, New Jersey.
(MNJ)(EJD/A248)

GORDON GEORGE
Planter in East New Jersey.
Land owner in Perth Amboy
c1685.
(EJD/A248)

GORDON GEORGE
Educated at King's College,
Aberdeen. M.D. 18 August
1770. Surgeon in Santa
Cruz.
(KCA)

GORDON GEORGE
Born on 4 May 1763,
second son of Sir
Alexander Gordon of
Lesmoir, and Margaret
Scott. Died during
1780 in the West Indies.
(MGL)

GORDON JOHN
Minister in Wilmington
parish, James City,
Virginia. Brother of
Patrick Gordon, Rector
of Aberley, Worcester,
and of Alexander Gordon,
Professor of Humanity in
King's College, Aberdeen,
and of George Gordon,
Professor of Oriental
Languages in King's
College, Aberdeen, and of
Mary Gordon, and Helen
Gordon, wife of William
Baxter, baillie of
Aberdeen. Birth brief
dated 16 February 1705.
(APB)

GORDON JOHN GEORGE
Emigrated from Scotland
to America in 1724.
Settled in Spottsylvania
County, Virginia.
Father of George and
Charles.
(HG)

GORDON JOHN
Son of Thomas Gordon,
minister in Aboyne,
Aberdeenshire. Educated
at Marischal College,
Aberdeen, from 1795 to
1799, graduated M.A.
Settled in Jamaica.
(MCA)

GORDON LEWIS
Jacobite in 1745.
Emigrated from Scotland
to Philadelphia,
Pennsylvania. Married
Mary Jenkins in Phila-
delphia during 1750.
Died during 1778.
(HG)

GORDON Rev PETER
Born in Careston, Angus.
Educated at University
of Glasgow. Emigrated
from Scotland to Nova
Scotia during 1806.
Minister in Covehead,
St Peter's and Bay
Fortune, Prince Edward
Island, from 1807 to
1809. Died in 1809.
(HPC)

GORDON SAMUEL
Emigrated from Scotland
to Virginia before 1771.
Merchant.
(OD)

GORDON THOMAS
Born in Scotland in 1652,
son of Robert Gordon of
Pitlurg, and Catherine
Burnett. Emigrated from
Scotland to America during
1684. Settled at Scotch
Plains, New Jersey.
Married (1) Helen, died
1687, (2) Janet, daughter
of David Mudie, died 1744.
Father of Mary, Euphame,
Margaret, Andrew, John,
and Thomas. Died on
28 April 1722. Buried at
Perth Amboy, New Jersey.
(MNJ)(EJD/A248)

GORDON THOMAS
Born in Scotland c1727.
Escaped from Elizabeth
Borough Gaol on
11 May 1767.
(N.Y.Mercury.811)

GORDON WILLIAM
Emigrated from Scotland,
with wife, two sons and
two daughters, to Canada
on the Commerce during
June 1820. Received a
land grant in Lanark,
Upper Canada, on
8 September 1820.
(PAO)

GORRIE ROBERT
Indentured servant
imported from Scotland
to East New Jersey by
Lord Neil Campbell
in December 1685.
(EJD/A225)

GORTHY WILLIAM
Emigrated from Scotland
to Canada. Received a
land grant in Cavan,
Newcastle, Upper Canada,
on 15 August 1819.
(PAO)

GOURLAY WILLIAM
Emigrated from Scotland,
with wife, two sons and
a daughter, to Canada on
the George Canning during
June 1821. Received a
land grant in Lanark,
Upper Canada, on 12 July
1821.
(PAO)

GOURLAY WILLIAM
Emigrated from Scotland,
with wife, son and daughter,
to Canada on the Brock.
Received a land grant in
Lanark, Upper Canada, on
21 October 1821.
(PAO)

GOWANS WILLIAM
Born during 1803 in
Lesmahowgow, Lanark-
shire. Emigrated from
Scotland to America in
1821. Settled in
Philadelphia,
Pennsylvania. Book-
dealer.
(TSA)

GRAHAM ALEXANDER
Emigrated from Scotland,
with wife, two sons and
two daughters, to Canada
on the Commerce during
June 1821. Received a
land grant in
Dalhousie, Upper Canada,
on 10 July 1821.
(PAO)

GRAEME CAMERON
Glasgow. Applied to
settle in Canada on
25 February 1815.
(SRO/RH9)

GRAHAM COLIN
Born 31 August 1801,
eldest son of Colin
Dundas Graham, Scotland.
Died on 21 October 1814.
Buried at St Catherine's,
Spanish Town, Jamaica.
(MIBWI)

GRAHAM FRANCIS
Born on 17 October 1773,
son of Alexander Graham
of Drymie. Planter,
attorney and Assemblyman
in Jamaica. Died at
Tulloch Castle, St Thomas
in the Vale, Jamaica, on
1 February 1820. Buried
in St Catherine's.
(MIBWI)

GRAHAM Rev HUGH
Born during 1755 at
Slateheugh, West Calder,
West Lothian. Educated
at University of
Edinburgh, and at
Theological Hall,
Haddington, East Lothian.
Licenced as a minister in
1781. Emigrated from
Greenock, Renfrewshire,
to Halifax, Nova Scotia,
during 1785. Minister
in Cornwallis, Nova Scotia,
from 1785 until 1800.
Minister in Stewiacke,
Truro, Nova Scotia, from
1800 until 1829. Died
during 1829.
(HPC)

GRAHAM JAMES
Volunteer. Died of flux
on the voyage from Scotland
to Darien, 25 October 1698.
(NLS)

GRAHAM JAMES
Emigrated from Scotland,
with wife, to Canada on the
Caledonian on 10 July 1816.
Received a land grant in
Drummond, Upper Canada,
on 9 December 1816.
(PAO)

GRAHAM JAMES
Emigrated from Scotland
to Canada. Received a
land grant in Cavan,
Newcastle, Upper Canada,
on 14 May 1818.
(PAO)

GRAHAM JOHN
Born in Edinburgh
during 1694. Educated
at University of
Glasgow. Doctor.
Emigrated from Scotland
via Londonderry, Ulster,
to Exeter, New Hampshire,
during 1718. Minister
in Stafford, Connecticut,
and in Woodbury,
Connecticut. Died 1774.
(TSA)

GRAHAM JOHN
Son of Jean Luke, and
grandson of Henry Luke,
deceased, stationer in
Glasgow. Tailor in
Albemarle County, on
the James River,
Virginia, c1765.
(SRA)

GRAEM JOHN
Emigrated from Scotland,
with two brothers, to
Canada. Settled at
La Chene, near Montreal,
c1805.
(SRO/GD/202.70.12)

GRAHAM JOHN
Emigrated from Scotland,
with wife and daughter,
to Canada on the Commerce
in June 1820. Received a
land grant in Lanark,
Upper Canada, on
1 September 1820.
(PAO)

GRAHAM JOHN
Emigrated from Scotland,
with wife, two sons and
three daughters, to
Canada on the George
Canning in June 1821.
Received a land grant in
Ramsay, Upper Canada, on
25 July 1821.
(PAO)

GRAHAM WILLIAM
Born in 1765. Emigrated
from Scotland, with wife
and seven children, to
Canada. Settled at West
River, Pictou, Nova Scotia,
in 1815. Labourer.
(PANS/RG1)

GRANGER WILLIAM
Emigrated from Scotland
to Canada on the Prompt
in June 1820. Received
a land grant in
Dalhousie, Upper Canada,
on 17 November 1821.
(PAO)

GRANT ALEXANDER
Born in Glen Moriston,
Inverness-shire, on
20 May 1734, son of
Patrick Grant and Isabel
Grant. Army officer and
merchant. Married
Therese Barthe on
30 September 1774. Died
on 8 May 1813 at Castle
Grant, Gross Point,
Michigan. Buried at
Sandwich, Upper Canada.
(DCB)

GRANT ALEXANDER
 Emigrated from Scotland
 to Canada. Received a
 land grant in Charlottenburg, St Raphael,
 Quebec, on
 24 November 1787.
 (PAO)

GRANT ALEXANDER
 Born 27 April 1769, son
 of John Grant, merchant
 in Leith, MidLothian,
 and Elizabeth Whyte.
 Merchant in
 St Petersburg.
 (BAF)

GRANT ALLAN sr
 Yeoman. Emigrated from
 Scotland to Canada.
 Received a land grant
 in Thorak, Home, Upper
 Canada, on 8 March 1826.
 (PAO)

GRANT ANDREW
 Indentured servant
 imported from Scotland
 to East New Jersey by
 Lord Neil Campbell in
 December 1685.
 (EJD/A225)

GRANT CHARLES
 Born 13 March 1741, son
 of Alexander Grant of
 Sheuglie, and Isabel
 Grant. Soldier in the
 42nd(Black Watch) Regt.
 Prisoner amongst the
 Indians. Died in New York.
 (GC)

GRANT DONALD
 Grantown-on-Spey,
 Morayshire. Emigrated
 from Scotland to
 America c1814. Father
 of Donald Cameron Grant,
 born 1822.
 (BAF)

GRANT DONALD
 Yeoman. Emigrated from
 Scotland to Canada.
 Received a land grant
 in Thorak, Home, Upper
 Canada, on 8 March 1826.
 (PAO)

GRANT JAMES MCDOWAL
 Son of David Grant of
 Arndilly, Banffshire.
 Educated at Marischal
 College, Aberdeen, from
 1817 to 1820. Planter
 in Jamaica.
 (MCA)

GRANT LEWIS
 Born in July 1734, son of
 Alexander Grant of
 Sheuglie, and Isabel Grant.
 Soldier in the 42nd(Black
 Watch) Regiment. Died in
 America.
 (GC)

GRANT Dr N.
 Edinburgh. Applied to
 settle in Canada on
 2 March 1815.
 (SRO/RH9)

GRANT PETER
  Emigrated from Scotland
  to Canada. Received a
  land grant in
  Charlottenburg, St Raphael,
  Quebec, 24 November 1787.
  (PAO)

GRANT ROBERT
  Emigrated from Scotland,
  with wife and three sons,
  to Canada on the Commerce
  in June 1821. Received a
  land grant in Ramsay,
  Upper Canada, on
  1 August 1821.
  (PAO)

GRANT WALTER
  Educated at Marischal
  College, Aberdeen, c1738.
  Apprenticed to a surgeon
  and physician in Aberdeen.
  Physician and surgeon in
  Jamaica. Partner of
  Andrew Rose. Graduated
  M.D. Aberdeen, 21 August
  1753.
  (MCA)

GRANT WILLIAM
  Born during 1743 in
  Kirkmichael, son of
  John Grant and Genevieve
  Forbes. Emigrated from
  Scotland to Canada pre
  1767. Married Marguerite
  Fafard, dit La Framboise,
  in Trois Rivieres,
  Quebec. Merchant. Died
  20 November 1810 near
  William Henry/Sorel,
  Lower Canada.
  (DCB)

GRANT WILLIAM
  Born 15 June 1744 in
  Blairfindy, son of William
  Grant and Jean Tyrie.
  Emigrated from Scotland
  to Quebec during 1759.
  Merchant and public
  figure. Died in Quebec
  on 5 October 1805.
  (DCB)

GRANT WILLIAM
  Born in Scotland.
  Received a land grant in
  Huntley, Upper Canada,
  on 20 March 1821.
  (PAO)

GRANT ...
  Born c1792. Emigrated
  from Scotland to Canada.
  House-carpenter. Settled
  in Pictou Town, Nova Scotia,
  during 1815.
  (PANS/RG1)

GRAPES HENRY
  Trumpeter. Died at Darien
  on 5 November 1698.
  (NLS)

GRAY ALEXANDER
  Emigrated from Scotland
  to Canada. Yeoman.
  Received a land grant in
  Thorak, Home, Upper
  Canada, on 8 March 1826.
  (PAO)

GRAY ARCHIBALD
  Educated at King's College,
  Aberdeen, graduated D.D.
  15 August 1804. Minister
  in Halifax, Nova Scotia.
  (KCA)

GRAY GEORGE
Glasgow(?) Tobacco factor
for J. and J.Jamieson in
Portobacco, Charles County,
Maryland. Later, after 1784,
tobacco factor for
Glassford and Company in
Dumfries, Virginia.
(SRA)

GRAY GEORGE
Emigrated from Scotland
to Canada on the Earl of
Buckingham. Received a
land grant in Dalhousie,
Upper Canada, on
3 September 1821.
(PAO)

GRAY JAMES
Born in Edinburgh during
1776, third son of David
Gray and Anne Somerville.
Emigrated from Scotland
to Jamaica. Later moved
to Philadelphia,
Pennsylvania. Married
Elizabeth... Died 1838.
(BAF)

GRAY JAMES
Born in Scotland. Former
lieutenant in the 104th
Regiment. Military
settler. Received a
land grant in Drummond,
Upper Canada, 8 June 1817,
and in Bathurst, Upper
Canada, 31 July 1817.
(PAO)

GRAY RALPH
Born in Scotland c1738.
Emigrated from Scotland
to Canada as a regimental
tailor. Married Mary Ann
Scott. Settled in
Quebec. Merchant and
landowner. Died on
27 December 1813 in
Beauport, Lower Canada.
(DCB)

GRAY SIMON
Born in Scotland. Former
sergeant in the 4th Royal
Veteran Battalion.
Military settler. With
wife, four sons and two
daughters. Received a
land grant in Burgess,
Upper Canada, on 30 June
1817, and in Younge.
Upper Canada, on 3J July.
1817.
(PAO)

GRAY THOMAS
Merchant in Boston,
Massachusetts, executor
of the last will of
William Corbett, merchant
in Boston, and late of
Glasgow, 1766.
(SRA/B10.15.7234)

GRAY WILLIAM
Born in Scotland. Former
soldier in the 104th
Regiment. Military
settler. Received a
land grant in Beckwith,
Upper Canada, on
30 September 1817.
(PAO)

GRINLEY GEORGE
Yeoman. Emigrated from
Scotland to Canada.
Received a land grant
in Mora, Newcastle,
Upper Canada, on
8 March 1826.
(PAO)

GRUBB THOMAS
Indentured servant
imported from Scotland
to East New Jersey by
Thomas Yallerton in
1684. Married Jean..
Land grant 19 January
1689.
(EJD/A/D351)

GUACK MATTHEW
Born in Scotland. Former
lieutenant in the 10th
Stirlingshire Militia.
With wife, three sons and
two daughters. Military
settler. Received a land
grant in Ramsay, Upper
Canada, on 13 April 1821.
(PAO)

GUILD JOHN
Born during 1612.
Emigrated from Scotland
to America. Settled in
Dedham, Massachusetts,
during 1636. Married
Elizabeth Crooke, in
Roxbury during 1645.
Father of John,1649-1723.
Died in 1682.
(BAF)

GUNN ADAM
Caithness. Graduated M.A.
King's College, Aberdeen,
in March 1819. Settled
in America.
(UKA)

GUNN ARCHIBALD
Born c1794. Labourer.
Emigrated from Scotland
to Canada. Settled at
Mount Tom, Pictou, Nova
Scotia, 1815.
(PANS/RG1)

GUNN CHRISTIANA
Born c1762 in Scotland.
Indentured servant.
Absconded from Samuel
Robbins, Bibury,
Philadelphia County, on
24 February 1778.
(NJ Gaz.)

GUNN CRAWFORD
Emigrated from Scotland,
with wife, to Canada, on
the George Canning.
Received a land grant in
Ramsay, Upper Canada, on
6 August 1821.
(PAO)

GUNN ELIZABETH
Born c1791. Emigrated from
Scotland, with a child,
to Canada. A widow.
Settled at Mount Tom,
Pictou, Nova Scotia,
during 1815.
(PANS/RG1)

GUNN JOHN
Emigrated from Scotland,
with wife, son and daughter,
to Canada on the Brock 1820.
Settled in Lanark, Upper
Canada, 23 October 1821.
(PAO)

GUTHRIE DONALD
Yeoman. Emigrated from
Scotland to Canada.
Received a land grant
in Eldon, Newcastle,
Upper Canada, on
8 March 1826.
(PAO)

GUTHRIE DONALD
Emigrated from Scotland
to Canada. Received a
land grant in Thorak,
Home, Upper Canada, on
14 April 1826.
(PAO)

GUTHRIE JAMES
Emigrated from Scotland,
with wife, son and
daughter, to Canada on
the Commerce in August
1820. Received a land
grant in Lanark, Upper
Canada, on 5 September
1820.
(PAO)

HAGGART JAMES
'A Scotch boy' aged 12(?)
Sold by James Trent to
Martin Scott, Nottingham,
Burlington County, New
Jersey, on 21 July 1697.
(Burlington Court Book)

HAIG of BEMERSYDE WILLIAM
Son of David Haig of
Bemersyde, Berwickshire,
and Hibernia Schols,
born 28 March 1646.
Merchant in London.
Quaker. Emigrated to
America during 1683.
Married Mary, daughter of
Gavin Lawrie in 1673.
Father of Obadiah,
Lawrie and Rebekah.
Died in Burlington,
New Jersey during 1688.
(HB)

HAIG WILLIAM
Born 20 June 1670, son
of Anthony Haig of
Bemersyde and Jean Home.
Merchant in Antigua.
(HB)

HAIG WILLIAM
Third son of James
Anthony Haig of Bemersyde
and Barbara Robertson.
Died in Martinique on
1 May 1794.
(HB)

HAIR GEORGE
Born in 1789, son of
Ninian Hair, Dumfries(?)
Died in St Thomas, Jamaica
on 27 February 1812.
(Dumfries GS)

HALDANE GEORGE
Son of Patrick Haldane of
Gleneagles, advocate, and
Margaret Forester.
Governor of Jamaica. Died
in Jamaica during 1759.
(SP.IV)

HALIBURTON MARGARET
Indentured servant
imported from Scotland
to East New Jersey by
Robert Fullerton in
October 1684.
(EJD/A)

HALL FRANCIS
Clackmannan. Applied
to settle in Canada
during 1818.
(CO384/3)

HALL JAMES
Emigrated from Scotland,
with wife, three sons
and a daughter, to
Canada on the Commerce
in June 1820. Received
a land grant in Lanark,
Upper Canada, on
8 September 1820.
(PAO)

HALL JAMES jr
Emigrated from Scotland
to Canada on the
Commerce in June 1820.
Received a land grant
in Lanark, Upper Canada,
on 8 September 1820.
(PAO)

HALL JOHN
Clackmannan. Applied
to settle in Canada
during 1818.
(CO384/3)

HALL JOHN
Emigrated from Scotland
to Canada. Received a
land grant in Lanark,
Upper Canada, on
4 October 1821.
(PAO)

HALL THOMAS
Emigrated from Scotland
to Canada on the Earl of
Buckingham in June 1821.
Received a land grant in
Sherbrook, Upper Canada,
on 31 July 1821.
(PAO)

HAMASH(?) JAMES
Emigrated from Scotland,
with wife, son and four
daughters, to Canada on
the Brock in June 1820.
Received a land grant in
Lanark, Upper Canada, on
23 October 1821.
(PAO)

HAMILTON ALEXANDER
Glasgow. Factor at
Piscataway on the Potomac
River, Virginia, for
Simpson, Baird and Company,
tobacco importers in
Glasgow, c1766.
(SRA)

HAMILTON ANDREW
Midshipman. Died at
Darien 22 November 1698.
(NLS)

HAMILTON CHARLES
Midshipman. Died of
flux on the voyage
from Scotland to
Darien on
10 October 1698.
(NLS)

HAMILTON DAVID
Emigrated from Scotland
to Canada on the Commerce
in June 1820. Received a
land grant in Lanark,
Upper Canada, on
1 October 1820.
(PAO)

HAMILTON GAVIN
Glasgow(?) Merchant and
factor for the
Britannia Company in
Virginia c1750.
(SRA/B10.15.6087)

HAMILTON HENRY
Born after 1762, son of
John Hamilton and
Isabella Stirling.
Former ensign of the
71st Regiment.
Settled in Jamaica.
(SP.V)

HAMILTON JAMES
Born c1800, son of
James Hamilton, 1758-
1825, merchant in
Biggar, Lanarkshire,
and Agnes Watson, 1765-
1845. Died in Jamaica
on 3 January 1824.
(Biggar GS)

HAMILTON JOHN
Glasgow. Partner and
manager of Archibald
Hamilton and Company, of
Glasgow, merchants in
Norfolk, Virginia, and
North Carolina, c1770.
(SRA/T79.18)

HAMILTON JOHN
Emigrated from Scotland,
with wife and son, to
Canada on the Commerce
in June 1821. Received
a land grant in Lanark,
Upper Canada, on
27 July 1821.
(PAO)

HAMILTON JOHN
Emigrated from Scotland,
with wife and three
daughters, to Canada on
the Prompt. Received a
land grant in Dalhousie,
Upper Canada, on
23 November 1821.
(PAO)

HAMILTON MARY ANN
Widow, late of Edinburgh,
married EDward Marshall
alias Peter Fisher,
bachelor, at the Anglican
Cathedral of St John the
Baptist, St Johns,
Newfoundland, on
23 February 1815.
(Gents. Mag.3182)

HAMILTON ROBERT
  Son of John Hamilton
  and Jean Wight, born
  on 14 September 1753
  in Bolton, Scotland.
  Emigrated from Scotland
  to Canada. Married (1)
  Catherine Askin, widow
  of Samuel Robertson (2)
  Mary Herkimer, widow of
  Neil McLean. Entrepreneur.
  Died in Queenstown, Upper
  Canada, on 8 March 1809.
  (DCB)

HAMILTON WILLIAM
  Ensign. Died at Darien
  on 3 December 1698.
  (NLS)

HAMILTON WILLIAM
  Born after 1762, son of
  John Hamilton and
  Isabel Stirling. Settled
  in Jamaica.
  (SP.II)

HAMILTON WILLIAM
  Emigrated from Scotland,
  with wife, son and
  daughter, to Canada on
  the Earl of Buckingham in
  June 1821. Received a
  land grant in Ramsay,
  Upper Canada, on
  31 July 1821.
  (PAO)

HAMILTON WILLIAM
  Emigrated from Scotland
  to Canada on the David
  of London in June 1821.
  Received a land grant
  in Ramsay, Upper Canada,
  on 3 September 1821.
  (PAO)

HAMMOND HENRY
  Emigrated from Scotland
  to Canada on the Commerce
  in June 1820. Settled
  in Upper Canada.
  (PAO)

HAMMOND WILLIAM
  Emigrated from Scotland,
  with wife, son and
  daughter, to Canada on the
  Earl of Buckingham.
  Received a land grant in
  Dalhousie, Upper Canada,
  on 9 September 1821.
  (PAO)

HAMPTON JANET
  Indentured servant
  imported from Scotland
  to East New Jersey in 1684.
  (EJD/A)

HAMPTON JOHN
  Gardener. Elphinstone,
  East Lothian. Quaker.
  Joint overseer of East New
  Jersey. Emigrated from Leith
  to East New Jersey. Landed
  on Staten Island 19 March
  1683. Settled in Perth
  Amboy, New Jersey, on
  23 November 1683. Later in
  Freehold, New Jersey. Married
  (1) Katherine Cloudsley on
  7 December 1675 (2) Martha,
  daughter of Abraham Brown
  (3) Mrs Jane Curtis or
  Osborne. Father of John,
  Joseph, Andrew, David, Noah,
  Jonathan, Elizabeth, Lydia,
  and Jane. Died during
  January 1703. Will dated
  23 January 1702.
  (MNJ)(EJD/A256)

HANCOCK JOHN
Edinburgh. Emigrated
from Scotland to East
New Jersey. Died at
sea on the voyage.
Administration to
Peter Sonmans and John
Barclay, both of Perth
Amboy, East New Jersey,
18 January 1685.
(EJD/A234)

HANNAH JAMES
Emigrated from Scotland
to Canada on the Brock
during 1820. Settled
in Lanark, Upper Canada,
during 1821.
(PAO)

HARDY ALEXANDER
Indentured servant
imported from Scotland
to East New Jersey by
Governor Gavin Lawrie
during 1684.
(EJD/A)

HARDY HENRY
Born during 1767, son
of James Hardy in West
Craigs, and Susan Young.
Merchant in Quebec.
Drowned in the River
St Lawrence on
20 August 1805.
(SOF)

HARDIE JAMES
Born in Aberdeen 1750.
Educated at Marischal
College, Aberdeen.
Emigrated from Scotland
to America. Tutor at
Columbia College, New
York, 1787-1790. Author.
Died in New York 1832.
(TSA)

HARDY ROBERT
Volunteer. Died of
fever on the voyage from
Scotland to Darien on
19 September 1698.
(NLS)

HARDY WILLIAM
Indentured servant
imported from Scotland to
East New Jersey in 1684.
(EJD/A)

HARGRAVE JAMES
Born in Scotland during
1798. North West Company
employee from 1820 to 1821.
Hudson Bay Company employee
from 1821 to 1858. Chief
trader 1844. Died in 1865.
(HBRS)

HARKNESS EDWARD
Emigrated from Scotland to
Canada on the Brothers
14 August 1817. Received
a land grant in Burgess,
Upper Canada, 3 December
1817.
(PAO)

HARPER Rev ALEXANDER
Lanark. Applied to
settle in Canada on
1 March 1815.
(SRO/RH9)

HARPER JOHN
Kilmaurs, Ayrshire.
Hudson Bay Company
employee from 1818
to 1821(?)
(HBRS)

HARPER ROBERT
Covenanter and rebel
in 1666. Prisoner in
Edinburgh Tolbooth.
Banished to Virginia
10 June 1669.
(PC)

HARPER WILLIAM
Teacher. Orkney(?)
Settled at Albany Fort,
Canada, c1808.
(Orkney Library,Marwickpp)

HARROWER GEORGE
Emigrated from Scotland
to Canada. Received a
land grant in Sherbrook,
Upper Canada, on
10 August 1822.
(PAO)

HART JAMES
Emigrated from Scotland,
with wife and two
daughters, to Canada
on the Earl of Buckingham
in June 1821. Received a
land grant in Ramsay,
Upper Canada, on
25 July 1821.
(PAO)

HART JOHN
Emigrated from Scotland,
with wife, son and four
daughters, to Canada on
the Earl of Buckingham
in June 1821. Received
a land grant in Lanark,
Upper Canada, on
20 July 1821.
(PAO)

HARVEY ...
A Scottish soldier.
Settled at Murray Bay
or Mount Murray, Quebec,
after the Siege of
Quebec in 1762.
(PRSC.X)

HARVEY JOHN
Emigrated from Scotland to
Canada. Received a land
grant in Cavan, Newcastle,
Upper Canada, on
15 October 1818.
(PAO)

HARVEY WILLIAM
Born in Scotland 1727.
Emigrated from Scotland
to America. Settled in
Elkton, Cecil County,
Maryland, in 1763.
Married Rebecca
Carruthers, 1737-1797.
Father of Matthew,
William and Robert.
Died during 1767.
(BGC)

HATMAKER MAGDALENE
Indentured servant
imported from Scotland
to East New Jersey by
Lord Neil Campbell in
December 1685.
(EJD/A225)

HAY ALEXANDER
Emigrated from Scotland,
with wife and son, to
Canada on the Prompt.
Received a land grant in
Dalhousie, Upper Canada,
on 17 November 1821.
(PAO)

HAY DANIEL
Son of James Hay,1694-
after 1758, merchant in
Dundee, Angus. Married
Catherine... Emigrated
from Scotland to America.
Father of Catherine,
Mary and Peter,1789-1879.
Died in Philadelphia,
Pennsylvania, on
4 July 1797.
(BAF)

HAY DANIEL
Emigrated from Scotland,
with wife, two sons and
a daughter, to Canada
on the Earl of
Buckingham in June 1821.
Received a land grant in
Dalhousie, Upper Canada,
on 20 July 1821.
(PAO)

HAY DAVID
Volunteer. Died of flux
on the voyage from
Scotland to Darien on
1 November 1698.
(NLS)

HAY EDWARD
Born in 1722, son of
the Earl of Kinnoull.
Married (1) Mary Flower
in London during 1752, (2)
Mary Harbourne Barnwell
in Barbados on 24 January
1779. Governor of
Barbados from 1772 to
1779. Died in Barbados
on 21 October 1779.
(SP.V)

HAY Lieutenant HUGH
Died of fever on the
voyage from Scotland
to Darien 28 October
1698.
(NLS)

HAY JOHN
Emigrated from Scotland
to Canada on the Commerce
in June 1820. Settled
in Upper Canada.
(PAO)

HAY Mrs
Wife of Lieutenant John Hay
Died of flux on the voyage
from Scotland to Darien
on 19 October 1698.
(NLS)

HAY ROBERT
Cooper. Edinburgh.
Emigrated from Scotland
to Georgia - possibly on
the Two Brothers, Captain
Thomson, from Inverness
to Savannah. Received a
land grant of 500 acres
in Georgia on
5 October 1737.
(SPAWI)

HAY WILLIAM
Emigrated from Scotland,
with wife, son and a
daughter, to Canada on the
David of London. Received
a land grant in Dalhousie,
Upper Canada, 7 August 1821.
(PAO)

HAZEL DAVID
Emigrated from Scotland to
Virginia pre 1755. Planter.
(OD)

HEADRICK JAMES
Emigrated from Scotland,
with wife, five sons and
a daughter, to Canada on
George Canning in June 1821.
Received a land grant in
Lanark, Upper Canada, on
10 July 1821.
(PAO)

HEDDERWICK WILLIAM
Royalist soldier
captured at Worcester.
Transported on the John
and Sarah, master John
Greene, from Gravesend,
Kent, to Boston, New
England, 13 May 1652.
(NER)

HEMMINGS(?) WILLIAM
Born in Scotland.
Military settler.
Received a land grant
in Bathurst, Upper Canada,
on 16 July 1816.
(PAO)

HENDERSON ALEXANDER
Glasgow(?) Tobacco factor
at Colchester and Occoquan,
Virginia, c1760.
(Alexandria Library, Va.)

HENDERSON ARCHIBALD
Glasgow(?) Brother of
Alexander Henderson.
Merchant in Dumfries,
Virginia, c1760.
(Alexandria Library, Va.)

HENDERSON CHARLES
Servant. Rescobie, Angus.
Jacobite in the Forfar-
shire Regiment, 1745.
Prisoner at Carlisle.
Transported to the
Plantations.
(MR)

HENDERSON DAVID
Sailor. Died of flux on
the voyage from Scotland
to Darien, 25 October 1698.
(NLS)

HENDERSON GEORGE
Emigrated from Scotland,
with his wife, to Canada
on the Earl of Buckingham.
Received a land grant in
Dalhousie, Upper Canada,
on 17 August 1821.
(PAO)

HENDERSON JAMES
Born during 1763.
Educated in Edinburgh.
Emigrated from Scotland
to America. Doctor in
Virginia. Died 1829.
(SA)

HENDERSON JAMES
Merchant in Virginia.
Left a legacy of £400 to
Hutcheson's Hospital in
Glasgow, during 1814.
(HHG)

HENDERSON J.
Gorbals, Glasgow.
Applied to settle in
Canada on 3 March 1815.
(SRO/RH9)

HENDERSON JOHN
Emigrated from Scotland,
with wife, son and daughter,
to Canada on the Commerce
in June 1820. Received a
land grant in Lanark,
Upper Canada, on
1 October 1820.
(PAO)

HENDERSON JOHN
Emigrated from Scotland,
with wife, to Canada on
the Commerce in June 1821.
Received a land grant in
Ramsay, Upper Canada, on
1 August 1821.
(PAO)

HENDERSON THOMAS
Born in Scotland.
Settled in Virginia
before 1607.
(AEG)

HENDERSON WILLIAM
Aberdeenshire. Educated
at King's College,
Aberdeen, graduated M.A.
in March 1822. Minister
in Newcastle, New
Brunswick.
(KCA)

HENDERSON WILLIAM
Born in Scotland. Former
soldier in the 55th
Regiment. Military
settler. Received a land
grant in Beckwith, Upper
Canada, on 25 September
1817.
(PAO)

HENDRY FRANCIS
Born c1785. Shoemaker.
Emigrated from Scotland
to Canada with his wife
and two children.
Settled at West River,
Pictou, Nova Scotia, in
1815.
(PANS/RG1)

HENRY Rev GEORGE
Born in 1709. Emigrated
from Scotland to Canada
c1765. Presbyterian
minister in Quebec from
1765 to 1793. Died on
9 July 1795.
(HPC)

HEPBURN JOHN
Indentured servant
imported from Scotland
to East New Jersey 1684.
(EJD/A)

HEPBURN ROBERT
Born c1784, son of Henry
Hepburn, 1762-1832,
builder in Perth, and Jean
Forrester, 1760-1843.
Died in Tobago on
7 September 1801.
(Perth Greyfriars GS)

HERIOT DAVID
Indentured servant
imported from Scotland
to East New Jersey by
Lord Neil Campbell in
December 1685.
(EJD/A225)

HERRON GEORGE
Emigrated from Scotland,
with wife, two sons and
two daughters, to Canada
on the Earl of Buckingham
Received a land grant in
Lanark, Upper Canada, on
14 August 1821.
(PAO)

HERON SAMUEL
Born in Kirkcudbright
during 1770. Emigrated
from Scotland to New York.
Settled in Canada. Married
(1) Sarah Ashbridge (2)
Sarah Connott. Died in
York, Upper Canada, c1818.
(DCB)

HERON WILLIAM
Glasgow. Applied to
settle in Canada on
25 February 1815.
(SRO/RH9)

HETHERINGTON JOSEPH
Emigrated from Scotland
to Canada on the George
Canning in June 1821.
Received a land grant in
Dalhousie, Upper Canada,
on 2 July 1821.
(PAO)

HILL ADAM
Planter. Died of flux on
the voyage from Scotland
to Darien on 20 October
1698.
(NLS)

HILL ALEXANDER
Emigrated from Scotland,
with wife, four sons and
three daughters, to
Canada on the Earl of
Buckingham in June 1821.
Received a land grant in
Lanark, Upper Canada, on
26 July 1821.
(PAO)

HILL ANDREW
Emigrated from Scotland,
with wife, three sons and
two daughters, to Canada
on the Commerce in June
1821. Received a land
grant in Dalhousie, Upper
Canada, on 25 July 1821.
(PAO)

HINY WALTER
Emigrated from Scotland
to Canada. Received a
land grant in Cavan,
Newcastle, Upper Canada,
on 11 June 1818.
(PAO)

HODKINS RICHARD
Apprentice, imported
from Scotland to East
New Jersey by George
Keith in February 1685.
(EJD/A226)

HOGG GRISSELL
Indentured servant
imported from Scotland
to East New Jersey by
Lord Neil Campbell in
December 1685.
(EJD/A225)

HOGG JOHN
Indentured servant
imported from Scotland
to East New Jersey by
Lord Neil Campbell in
December 1685.
(EJD/A225)

HOGGAN JAMES
Glasgow(?) Tobacco factor
for James Brown and Company
at Bladensburg, Virginia,
from 1774 to 1777.
(SRA)

HOGUE THOMAS
Bridgeton. Applied to
settle in Canada on
4 March 1815.
(SRO/RH9)

HOLLAND GABRIEL
Indentured servant
imported from Scotland
to East New Jersey by
Governor Gavin Lawrie
during 1684. Headright
land grant in 1689.
(EJD/A/B159)

HOLLIDAY THOMAS
Indentured servant
imported from Scotland
to East New Jersey by
Charles Gordon during
October 1684.
(EJD/A255)

HOLLY ANDREW
Born in Scotland. Former
soldier in the 70th
Regiment. Military
settler. Received a
land grant in Bathurst,
Upper Canada, on
2 September 1820.
(PAO)

HOLMES JOHN
Emigrated from Scotland,
with wife, four sons and
two daughters, to Canada
on the Martha in August
1820. Received a land
grant in Sherbrook, Upper
Canada, on 3 December 1821.
(PAO)

HOLMES ROBERT
Born during 1744 in
Greenock, Renfrewshire.
Died during 1807 in
Falmouth, Jamaica.
(MIBWI)

HOME of ECCLES Sir GEORGE
Emigrated from Scotland
with his wife and family
to Canada. Settled at
Port Royal, Nova Scotia,
in summer of 1630.
(Insh)(PC)

HOME GEORGE
Billie, Berwickshire.
Emigrated from Scotland
to Virginia in 1723.
Storekeeper in Essex
County, Virginia. Merchant
in Rappahannock, Culpepper
County, Virginia.
(VMHB.1912)

HONEYMAN JAMES
Son of James Honeyman,
minister of Kinneff,
Kincardineshire.
Educated at Marischal
College, Aberdeen, from
1759 to 1763, graduated
M.A. Minister of Newport,
Rhode Island.
(MCA)

HONEYMAN ROBERT
Son of James Honeyman,
minister of Kinneff,
Kincardineshire.
Educated at Marischal
College, Aberdeen, from
1761 to 1765. Physician
in Virginia.
(MCA)

HOOD ALEXANDER
Son of James Hood, Excise
officer in Glasgow,
brother of Mary Hood,
Drygate, Glasgow. Died
in Montserrat pre 1817.
(HHG)

HOOD JAMES
Emigrated from Scotland,
with wife, two sons and
six daughters, to
Canada on the Prompt in
June 1820. Received a
land grant in Dalhousie,
Upper Canada, on
17 November 1821.
(PAO)

HOOD MATTHEW
Glasgow. Carpenter.
Settled in St Paul's,
Tobago, pre 1800.
(CPD)

HOOD WILLIAM
Emigrated from Scotland
to Canada on the Prompt
in June 1820. Settled
in Upper Canada.
(PAO)

HOOK CHARLES
Born before 1745, son
of Henry Hook, manufacturer
in Glasgow. Emigrated from
Scotland to Jamaica.
(VMHB.1926)

HOOKS JANE
Indentured servant
imported from Scotland
to East New Jersey by
Thomas Yallerton in 1684.
(EJD/A)

HOOK JOHN
Born during 1745, fourth
son of Henry Hook,
manufacturer in Glasgow.
Indentured servant to
William and James Donald,
merchants and shipowners
of Glasgow, trading in
Virginia. Emigrated from
Scotland to Virginia in
1758. Settled in Blandford,
Virginia. Merchant. Married
Elizabeth, daughter of Col.
John Smith, Goochland, 1772.
Settled in New London,
Bedford County, Virginia,
and later at Hale's Fort.
Died during 1808.
(VMHB.1926)

HOOKS ROBERT
Indentured servant
imported from Scotland
to East New Jersey by
Robert Fullerton during
October 1684.
(EJD/A)

HOOPER WILLIAM
Born in Ednam, Berwickshire.
Emigrated from Scotland to
America. Minister of West
Church, Boston, New England,
in 1737.
(SO)

HOPE HENRY
Fifth son of Charles Hope
of Craigiehall, and
Catherine Weir. Married
Sarah Jones. Lieutenant
Governor of Canada. Died
in Quebec 13 April 1789.
(SP.IV)

HOPE JOHN
Glasgow(?) Merchant.
Factor for Buchanan,
Hastie and Company
in Osborne and Halifax,
Virginia pre 1776.
(SRA/T79.25)

HORNE JAMES
Emigrated from Scotland,
with wife, two sons and
a daughter, to Canada on
the Brock. Received a
land grant in Lanark,
Upper Canada, 23 October
1821.
(PAO)

HORSBURGH ALEXANDER
Glasgow(?) Merchant and
factor for William
Cunningham and Company
at Brunswick and at
Petersburg, Virginia,
pre 1776.
(SRA/T79.1)

HOUSTON JAMES
Emigrated from Scotland
to America. Settled in
Georgia during 1734.
(HGP)

HOUSTON STEWART
Emigrated from Scotland,
with wife, two sons and
three daughters, to
Canada on the Earl of
Buckingham in June 1821.
Received a land grant in
Ramsay, Upper Canada, on
8 August 1821.
(PAO)

HOUSTON WILLIAM
Emigrated from Scotland
to Canada on the Earl of
Buckingham in June 1821.
Received a land grant in
Ramsay, Upper Canada, on
8 August 1821.
(PAO)

HUE THOMAS
Indentured servant
imported from Scotland
to East New Jersey by
John Campbell for
Captain Andrew Hamilton
in October 1684.
(EJD/A)

HUGHES JOHN
Emigrated from Greenock,
Renfreshire, to Canada
on the David of London
during May 1821. Settled
in Upper Canada.
(PAO)

HUME CATHERINE
Indentured servant
imported from Scotland
to East New Jersey by
John Campbell for
Captain Andrew Hamilton
in October 1684.
(EJD/A)

HUME JANE
Indentured servant
imported from Scotland
to East New Jersey by
John Campbell for Captain
Andrew Hamilton during
October 1684.
(EJD/A)

HUME JOHN
Indentured servant
imported from Scotland
to East New Jersey by
John Campbell for Captain
Andrew Hamilton during
October 1684.
(EJD/A)

HUME ROBERT
Indentured servant
imported from Scotland
to East New Jersey by
John Campbell for Captain
Andrew Hamilton during
October 1684.
(EJD/A)

HUNTER HUGH
Emigrated from Scotland,
with wife, son and daughter,
to Canada on the George
Canning in June 1821.
Received a land grant in
Dalhousie, Upper Canada,
on 10 July 1821.
(PAO)

HUNTER JOHN
Born in Ayr during 1746,
fourth son of James Hunter
of Thurston, 1698-1784, and
Janet ...,1699-1746.
Emigrated from Scotland to
America. Settled in
Virginia. Married Jane
Broadwater. Father of Ann,
James, Robert, George W.,
and John.
(HCA)(RAF)

HUNTER JOHN
Emigrated from Scotland,
with two sons and five
daughters, to Canada on
the Commerce in August
1820. Received a land
grant in Lanark, Upper
Canada, on 5 September
1820.
(PAO)

HUNTER PETER
Baptised 11 July 1746, at
Longforgan, Perthshire,
son of John Hunter of
Knap and Euphemia Jack.
Army officer and public
administrator. Died in
Quebec on 21 August 1805.
(DCB)

HUNTER General ROBERT
Son of James Hunter of
Hunterston, and Margaret
Spalding. Governor of
Jamaica. Died during 1734
in Jamaica.
(RAF)

HURST SAMUEL
Former officer. Lightburn.
Applied to settle in
Canada on 4 March 1815.
(SRO/RH9)

HUTCHESON ALEXANDER
Educated at the University
of Glasgow c1714. Emigrated
from Glasgow to Philadelphia,
Pennsylvania, in 1722.
Ordained at Bohemia Manor,
Maryland, on 6 June 1723.
(AP)

HUTCHISON JOHN
Emigrated from Scotland,
with wife and son, to
Canada on the Earl of
Buckingham in June 1821.
Received a land grant
in Ramsay, Upper Canada,
on 24 July 1821.
(PAO)

HUTCHISON Captain WILLIAM
A Scot settled near Port
Royal, Jamaica, c1700.
(DP)

HUTTON GEORGE
Emigrated from Scotland,
with wife, four sons and
two daughters, to Canada
on the Earl of Buckingham
in June 1821. Received a
land grant in Sherbrook,
Upper Canada, on
7 August 1821.
(PAO)

HYNDMAN ALEXANDER
Joppa, Mid Lothian.
Applied to settle in
Canada on 2 March 1815.
(SRO/RH9)

IMBRIE JAMES
Born c1780, son of Rev
James Imbrie and Janet
Pattison, Paisley,
Renfrewshire. Merchant.
Emigrated from Scotland
to America. Settled in
Philadelphia, Pennsylvania,
during 1805. Married
Margaretta Kisselman in
1809. Father of James.
Died on 29 March 1850.
(BAF)

INGLIS Lieutenant JAMES
Died on the voyage from
Scotland to Darien on
3 November 1698.
(NLS)

INGLIS JAMES
Glasgow. Applied to
settle in Canada on
25 February 1815.
(SRO/RH9)

INGRAM ARCHIBALD
Son of Archibald Ingram of
Cloberhill, East Kilpatrick,
Dunbartonshire,1699-1770.
Merchant in St Kitts pre
1769.
(SRA)

INGRAM JAMES
Son of Archibald Ingram of
Cloberhill, East Kilpatrick,
Dunbartonshire,1699-1770.
Merchant in Glasgow.
Settled in Virginia.
(SRA)

INKSON THOMAS
Morayshire. Educated in
Aberdeen - graduated M.A.
26 April 1813. M.D. in
the West Indies.
(KCA)(MCA)

INNES Dr ALEXANDER
Brother of John Innes,
deceased, Sheathyn,
Aberdeenshire. Will
27 July 1713, probate
13 August 1713. Settled
in Monmouth County, New
Jersey.
(WM)

INNES GEORGE
Born c1762, son of
Alexander Innes,
Aberdeen. Died on
9 November 1784.
Buried in Kingston
Cathedral, Jamaica.
(MIBWI)

INNES GILBERT
Aberdeen. Married
Gyles... Emigrated
from Scotland to
America. Settled in
Perth Amboy, New
Jersey. Died during
1685.
(EJD/A261)(NJA.XXI)

INNES HUGH
Born c1763, son of
Alexander Innes,
Aberdeen. Died on
6 October 1803.
Buried in Kingston
Cathedral, Jamaica.
(MIBWI)

INNES PETER
Born c1767, son of
Alexander Innes,
Aberdeen. Died on
17 June 1801.
Buried in Kingston
Cathedral, Jamaica.
(MIBWI)

INNES WILLIAM
Born c1772, son of
Alexander Innes,
Aberdeen. Died on
11 July 1791.
Buried in Kingston
Cathedral, Jamaica.
(MIBWI)

IRETON JOHN
Emigrated from Scotland
to Canada on the Commerce
in June 1820. Settled in
Upper Canada.
(PAO)

IRONS GEORGE
Old Kilpatrick,
Dunbartonshire. Applied
to settle in Canada on
3 March 1815.
(SRO/RH9)

IRONSIDE GEORGE
Born c1770. Graduated M.A.
from King's College,
Aberdeen. Emigrated from
Scotland to America.
Indian trader in Ohio c1792.
British Agent for Indian
Affairs in Canada.
Settled in Amherstburg,
Upper Canada. Died
during 1830.
(AUR)

IRVING JAMES
Born in Dumfries-shire
during 1749, son of Dr
James Irving. Emigrated
from Scotland to West
Indies. Custos of
Trelawney, Jamaica. Died
on 21 November 1798.
Buried in Kingston
Cathedral, Jamaica.
(MIBWI)

IRVING WILLIAM
Born 31 August 1731.
Shapinsay, Orkney Islands.
Emigrated from Scotland
to New York during 1763.
Married Sarah Sanders.
Father of Ebenezer and
Washington. Died in 1807.
(BAF)

ISBISTER THOMAS
Born c1791 Orkney
Islands. Hudson Bay
Company employee
from 1812 to 1836.
Postmaster. Died in
1836.
(HBRS)

ISDALE CHARLES
Emigrated from Scotland,
with wife, two sons and
three daughters, to
Canada on the Commerce
in June 1820. Received a
land grant in Lanark,
Upper Canada, on
1 October 1820.
(PAO)

IVISON HENRY
Born in Glasgow during
1808. Emigrated from
Scotland to America in
1820. Publisher in New
York. Died in New York
during 1884.
(TSA)

JACK JAMES
Emigrated from Scotland,
with wife and son, to
Canada on the Prompt.
Received a land grant
in Dalhousie, Upper
Canada, on
17 November 1821.
(PAO)

JACK WILLIAM
Emigrated from Scotland,
with wife, three sons and
two daughters, to Canada
on the Prompt. Received a
land grant in Dalhousie,
Upper Canada, on
17 November 1821.
(PAO)

JAFFRAY JOHN
Former baillie of Stirling.
Settled in Canada c1820.
(SRO/GD51.6.21131)

JAMES ROBERT
Emigrated from Scotland,
with wife, two sons and
three daughters, to Canada
on the Commerce in June
1820. Received a land
grant in Lanark, Upper
Canada, on 1 October 1820.
(PAO)

JAMES THOMAS
Minister of Cleish parish,
Fife. Died of fever on the
voyage from Scotland to
Darien on 23 October 1698.
(DP)(SHR)(NLS)

JAMIESON of BELLMOOR ALEX.
Educated at King's College,
Aberdeen, graduated M.D.
18 September 1742. Doctor.
Settled in Hampton on the
James River, Virginia.
(KCA)(SA)

JAMIESON JOHN
Emigrated from Scotland,
with wife, four sons and
three daughters, to Canada
on the Brock. Received a
land grant in Lanark,
Upper Canada, 21 October
1821. (PAO)

JAMIESON NEIL
Born in Glasgow. Partner
of John Glassford.
Settled in Norfolk,
Virginia, in 1760.
Merchant. Left with
Lord Dunmore in 1776.
Later an underwriter at
Lloyds Coffee House in
London.
(SRA/B10.15.7174)

JAMIESON ROBERT
Emigrated from Scotland
to Canada on the Greenfield
on 23 August 1816.
Received a land grant in
Drummond, Upper Canada, on
10 October 1816.
(PAO)

JAMNELL JOHN
Royalist soldier captured
at Worcester. Transported
from Gravesend, Kent, to
Boston, New England, on the
John and Sarah, master John
Greene, 13 May 1652.
(NER)

JEFFREY GEORGE
Scots merchant and
smuggler in New Hampshire.
Member of H.M.Council for
New Hampshire, 13 July
1702.
(SPAWI)

JELLER DAVID
Royalist soldier captured
at Worcester. Transported
from Gravesend, Kent, to
Boston, New England, on the
John and Sarah, master John
Greene, 13 May 1652.
(NER)

JENLER(?) ROBERT
Royalist soldier captured
at Worcester. Transported
from Gravesend, Kent, to
Boston, New England, on the
John and Sarah, master John
Greene, 13 May 1652.
(NER)

JERRIS ANDREW
Royalist soldier captured
at Worcester. Transported
from Gravesend, Kent, to
Boston, New England, on the
John and Sarah, master John
Greene, 13 May 1652.
(NER)

JOHNSTON ANDREW
Glasgow. Emigrated from
Scotland to America.
Settled in Petersburg,
Virginia, before 1785.
Merchant.
(OD)

JOHNSTON CLEMENT
Glasgow. Applied to settle
in Canada on 28 February
1815.
(SRO/RH9)

JOHNSTONE GEORGE
Indentured servant
imported from Scotland to
East New Jersey by David
Mudie in November 1684.
Headright land grant 1689.
(EJD/A196/B159)

SCOTTISH SETTLERS IN NORTH AMERICA

JOHNSTON JAMES
Indentured servant
imported from Scotland
to East New Jersey by
James Johnston during
October 1685. Land
grant 1 May 1690.
(EJD/A226/D167)

JOHNSTONE JAMES
Indentured servant
imported from Scotland
to East New Jersey,
possibly by George
Willocks, c1685.
Settled in Monmouth
County, New Jersey,c1690.
(EJD/D167)

JOHNSON JAMES
Emigrated from Scotland,
with wife, son and daughter,
to Canada on the Earl of
Buckingham in June 1821.
Received a land grant in
Ramsay, Upper Canada, on
26 July 1821.
(PAO)

JOHNSTON JOHN
Born in Annandale,
Dumfries-shire. Emigrated
from Scotland to America
before 1657. Settled on
the eastern shore of Mary-
land, before moving to
Virginia. Vestryman of
St Peter's, New Kent County,
Virginia. Married
Lucretia Massie. Father of
John.
(BAF)

JOHNSTON JOHN
Glasgow(?) Merchant and
factor for William
Cunningham and Company at
Mecklenburg, Virginia,
before 1776.
(SRA/779.1)

JOHNSTON ROBERT
Emigrated from Scotland,
with wife and two sons,
to Canada on the Brock.
Received a land grant in
Lanark, Upper Canada, on
21 October 1821.
(PAO)

JOHNSTOUN WALTER
Surgeon's mate. Died of
fever on the voyage from
Scotland to Darien on
29 September 1698.
(NLS)

JOPP ALEXANDER
Son of James Jopp, black-
smith in Cotton. Educated
at Marischal College,
Aberdeen, c1778. Settled
in Kingston, Jamaica.
(MCA)

JORIE ALEXANDER
Born c1801, son of John
Jorie, merchant in
Whithorn, Wigtownshire.
Died in Demerara on
1 August 1819.
(Whithorn GS)

130

KAY ROBERT
Emigrated from Scotland,
with wife son and daughter,
to Canada on the Commerce
in June 1821. Received a
land grant in Sherbrook,
Upper Canada, on
1 August 1821.
(PAO)

KEITH of POWBURN Sir BASIL
Governor of Jamaica.
Died on 15 June 1777.
Buried at St Catherine's,
Spanish Town, Jamaica.
(MIBWI)

KEITH GEORGE
Emigrated from Scotland,
with wife Anna and their
children Anna and
Elizabeth to East New
Jersey in February 1685.
(EJD/A236)

KEITH ISABEL
Indentured servant
imported from Scotland
to East New Jersey in
1684.
(EJD/A)

KEITH JOHN
Born in Achlossen,
Aberdeenshire during 1763.
Educated at University of
Aberdeen c1781. Emigrated
from Scotland to America
c1783. Professor at
Columbia College. Died
during 1812.
(TSA)

KELLOCK JAMES
Born in Scotland during
1794. Hudson Bay Company
employee from 1811 to
1836. Drowned on 5 June
1836 at Michiskan.
(HBRS)

KELSO JAMES
Emigrated from Scotland
to America. Settled in
New Windsor, and later,
Little Britain, New York.
Married Ludacia Goldsmith.
Father of Albert, born on
19 April 1824.
(BAF)

KELSO ROBERT HAMILTON
Born on 23 September 1779,
son of Patrick Kelso of
Hullerhurst, and Mary
Hamilton. Died in Jamaica
on 22 December 1802.
(RAF)

KEMP JAMES
Born at Keith Hall,
Aberdeenshire in 1764.
Educated at Aberdeen Grammar
School and Marischal College,
Aberdeen. Graduated 1786.
Emigrated from Scotland to
America in 1787. Tutor in
Dorchester County, Maryland.
Ordained an Episcopalian
minister during 1789. Rector
of Great Choptank, Maryland,
from 1790 to 1813. Rector
of St Paul's, Baltimore,
in 1813. Bishop 1814-1827.
Provost of the University
of Maryland. Died in
Baltimore 28 October 1827.
(HKK)(TSA)

KEMP JOHN
Born at Auchlossen,
Aberdeenshire, on
10 April 1763, son of
John Kemp in Coull.
Educated at Marischal
College, Aberdeen, -
graduated M.A. in 1781.
Awarded a D.D. from King's
College, Aberdeen,in 1787.
Emigrated from Scotland to
Virginia in 1783. Teacher
in New York during 1784.
Professor of Mathematics
and Natural Philosophy at
Columbia College, New York,
in 1786. Died in New York
on 15 November 1812.
(HKK)(KCA)

KEMP JOSEPH ALEXANDER
Born during 1777 in Perth.
Married on 20 June 1805 to
Elizabeth Jillson of Albany,
New York. Father of Joseph,
Robert, Eliza, Mary,William
and Charlotte. Died in New
York on 22 August 1832.
(HKK)

KEMPER DANIEL
Royalist soldier captured
at Worcester. Transported
from Gravesend, Kent, to
Boston,New England, on the
John and Sarah, master John
Greene, 13 May 1652.
(NER)

KENNEDY ARCHIBALD
Born in 1685, second son
of Alexander(John?)Kennedy
of Kilhenzie, Kirkoswald,
Ayrshire, and Helen
Monteith. Emigrated from
Scotland to New York 1710
or 1722. Receiver General
of Customs in New York.
Settled at Pavonia,
Second River, Hoboken,
New York. Married (1)
Miss Massam (2) Maria
Walter Schuyler in 1736.
Father of James, Robert,
Archibald, Thomas and
Catherine. Died in New
York on 14 June 1763.
(SP.II)(HCA)

KENNEDY DAVID
Born in 1773, fourth son
of Thomas Kennedy,1732-1800,
merchant in Falkland,Fife.
Merchant in Philadelphia,
Pennsylvania. Died during
1798 in Germantown,
Pennsylvania.
(Falkland GS)

KENNEDY DONALD
Born in Scotland. Received
a land grant in Beckwith,
Upper Canada, 30 May 1822.
(PAO)

KENNEDY DUNCAN
Emigrated from Scotland
to Canada. Received a
land grant in Monaghan,
Newcastle, Upper Canada,
29 November 1817.
(PAO)

KENNISS ANDREW
Emigrated from Scotland
to America. Carpenter.
Settled in Spotsylvania
County, Virginia, pre
1754.
(OD)

KENT JOHN
Pensioner. Longbride
(Lhanbryde, Morayshire?)
Applied to settle in
Canada on 5 March 1815.
(SRO/RH9)

KENT JOHN
Emigrated from Scotland,
with wife and two sons,
to Canada on the David
of London in June 1821.
Received a land grant in
Ramsay, Upper Canada, on
7 August 1821.
(PAO)

KERR ALEXANDER
Roxburghshire. Emigrated
from Scotland to America
during late seventeenth
century. Settled in
Lancaster County,
Pennsylvania. Father of
James.
(BAF)

KERR DAVID
Born in Menteith on
5 February 1749. Emigrated
from Scotland to America
in 1769. Settled in
Falmouth, Virginia, and
later during 1773 in
Annapolis, Maryland. Judge
and politician. Married (1)
Miss Hammind in Annapolis,
(2) Rachel Leeds Bozman.
Father of John Leeds Kerr.
Died on 2 November 1814.
(TSA)(BAF)

KERR MARGARET
Emigrated from Scotland
to Canada on the brig
Niagara, Hamilton, from
Greenock, Renfrewshire to
Montreal, Quebec,during
1825. Settled in McNab,
Bathurst, Upper Canada,
in 1825.
(SG)

KERR PETER
Emigrated from Scotland,
with wife, two sons and
five daughters, to Canada.
Received a land grant in
Lanark, Upper Canada, on
1 October 1821.
(PAO)

KERR THOMAS
Born during the 1790s,
son of John Kerr and Janet
Pattison. Emigrated from
Scotland to America.
Merchant in New Orleans,
Louisiana. Died in New
Orleans.
(FKK)

KERR WALTER
Born in Lanarkshire during
1656. Covenanter. Banished
to East New Jersey on the
Henry and Francis in 1685.
Married Margaret..,1661-1734.
Settled near Tennant Church,
Monmouth County, New Jersey.
Father of William, James,
Samuel, Joseph, and John.
Died on 10 June 1748.
(MNJ)

KERR Hon Justice
Born in Leith, son of a
merchant. Educated at Leith
Grammar School and University
of Glasgow. Emigrated to
Canada in 1794. Politician
and lawyer. Died in Quebec
on 5 May 1846.
(BCB)

KETCHEN WILLIAM
Parkhead. Applied to
settle in Canada on
25 February 1815.
(SRO/RH9)

KETTINS JAMES
Emigrated from Scotland,
with wife and daughter, to
Canada on the Earl of
Buckingham in June 1821.
Received a land grant in
Ramsay, Upper Canada, on
24 July 1821.
(PAO)

KIDD ALEXANDER
Blackburn. Applied to
settle in Canada on
2 March 1815.
(SRO/RH9)

KID ROBERT
Born in Scotland on
7 August 1765. Married
Sarah Ann, 1779-1811.
Died on 17 August 1850.
Buried at St Mary's,
Burlington, New Jersey.
(Burlington GS)

KIDD WILLIAM CAMPBELL
Son of James Kidd,
Marischal College,
Aberdeen. Educated in
Marischal College from
1809 to 1813, graduated
M.A. Minister in London
and America.
(MCA)

KILPATRICK EPHRAIM
Emigrated from Scotland
to Canada on the George
Canning in June 1821.
Received a land grant in
Ramsay, Upper Canada, on
10 July 1821.
(PAO)

KILPATRICK JOHN
Emigrated from Scotland,
with wife, two sons and
three daughters, to Canada
on the George Canning in
May 1821. Received a
land grant in Ramsay, Upper
Canada, on 10 July 1821.
(PAO)

KING ANDREW
Born in Scotland.
Escaped from Salem Gaol
on 6 September 1766.
(Pa. Journal.1240)

KING JAMES
Emigrated from Scotland,
with wife, two sons and a
daughter, to Canada on the
Commerce in August 1820.
Received a land grant in
Lanark, Upper Canada, on
5 September 1820.
(PAO)

KING JAMES
Emigrated from Scotland,
with wife and son, to
Canada on the Earl of
Buckingham. Received a land
grant in Ramsay, Upper
Canada, on 7 August 1821.
(PAO)

KING JOHN
Indentured servant
imported from Scotland
to East New Jersey in
1684.
(EJD/A)

KING ROBERT
Born in Scotland.
Received a land grant in
Beckwith, Upper Canada,
on 31 November 1822.
(PAO)

KINNAIRD Sir ALEXANDER
Emigrated from Scotland
to Darien. Died during
1699.
(TDD)

KINNEAR THOMAS
Born during 1803, son of
Thomas Kinnear of Kinloch,
Fife. Apprenticed to
Walter Dickson. Admitted
to the Society of Writers
to the Signet on 25 May
1826. Died in Toronto,
Canada, on 27 July 1843.
(WS)

KINNAN PATRICK
Son of Peter Kinnan.
Emigrated from Scotland
to America c1683. Settled
in Montrose, New Jersey.
Father of John, Joseph,
William, Anne, Margaret,
and Patrick. Died in 1709.
(MNJ)

KINNAN THOMAS
Son of Peter Kinnan.
Emigrated from Scotland
to America c1683.
Settled in New Jersey.
Father of Thomas.
(MNJ)

KINZIE JOHN
Born in Scotland. Indian
trader in Ohio during
the 1790s.
(AUR)

KIRBY THOMAS ALEXANDER
Born during 1692 in
Edinburgh(?) Emigrated
from Scotland to
Massachusetts in 1720.
Married in 1720 to
Elizabeth de Gast, West-
moreland County. Father
of Roger, 1746-1816.
Died in 1765.
(BAF)

KIRBY Mrs
Born c1775. Widow.
Emigrated from Scotland,
with three children, to
Canada. Settled at Little
Harbour, Pictou, Nova
Scotia, during 1815.
(PANS/RG1)

KIRKWOOD MATTHEW
Emigrated from Scotland,
with wife, son and two
daughters, to Canada on
the Commerce in June 1820.
Received a land grant in
Lanark, Upper Canada, on
1 October 1820.
(PAO)

KNIGHT JAMES
Born c1801, son of
David Knight,1759-1813,
brewer in Almerieclose,
Arbroath, Angus, and
Mary Jamieson, 1757-1829.
Died in Demerara in 1821.
(Arbroath Abbey GS)

KYLE WILLIAM
Emigrated from Scotland,
with wife, five sons and a
daughter, to Canada on the
David of London in June
1821. Received a land
grant in Ramsay, Upper
Canada, on 8 August 1821.
(PAO)

LAIDLAW Rev JOHN
Ordained in Banff during
1802. Minister in Banff
and Dunning, Perthshire.
Emigrated from Scotland
to Nova Scotia during 1814.
Minister in Nova Scotia
from 1815 to 1817. Died
in Pittsburgh,
Pennsylvania, in 1824.
(HPC)

LAING ANDREW
Prisoner in Edinburgh
Tolbooth. Stigmatised
and banished to the
Plantations on
19 February 1674.
(PC)

LAING ARTHUR
Emigrated from Scotland,
with wife, two sons and
four daughters, to Canada
on the Earl of Buckingham
in June 1821. Received a
land grant in Ramsay,
Upper Canada, on
31 July 1821.
(PAO)

LAING JOHN
Emigrated from Scotland,
with wife and son, to
Canada on the Commerce
in August 1820.
Received a land grant in
Lanark, Upper Canada, on
5 September 1820.
(PAO)

LAING ROBERT
Emigrated from Scotland
to Philadelphia,
Pennsylvania, during 1722.
Presbyterian minister
there from 1722 until 1726.
(AP)

LAING WILLIAM
Emigrated from Scotland to
America. Planter in
Freehold, Monmouth County,
New Jersey. Will dated
24 May 1709. Probate
dated 27 February 1710.
(WM)

LAIRD ALEXANDER
Emigrated from Scotland to
America before 1750.
Settled in Monmouth County,
New Jersey. Married Lydia
James. Father of William,
Robert, Richard, Amy, Lydia
and Elizabeth. Died on
8 September 1771.
(MNJ)

LAIRD WILLIAM
Emigrated from Scotland to
America before 1733. Settled
in Monmouth County, New
Jersey. Married Elizabeth
Dove. Father of Alexander,
Moses, Sarah, Jane, Elizabeth,
Mary, Bevan and William.
(MNJ)

LAMB JOHN
Born in Scotland. Former
sergeant in the 4th Royal
Veteran Battalion. Wife,
son and two daughters.
Received a land grant in
Bathurst, Upper Canada,
on 30 June 1817.
(PAO)

LAMB JOHN
Emigrated from Scotland
to Canada on the Prompt
in June 1820. Received
a land grant in
Dalhousie, Upper Canada,
on 19 November 1821.
(PAO)

LAMBIE WILLIAM
Possibly from Argyllshire.
Planter in St Thomas in
the East, Jamaica.
Testament dated 29 June
1769.
(SRA/B10.15.7303)

LAMBIE WILLIAM
Emigrated from Scotland,
with wife, four sons and
two daughters, to Canada
on the Earl of Buckingham
in June 1821. Received a
land grant in Dalhousie,
Upper Canada, on 25 July
1821.
(PAO)

LAMONT JOSEPH
Emigrated from Scotland,
with wife, son and two
daughters, to Canada on
the Brock during 1820.
Received a land grant in
Lanark, Upper Canada, on
27 October 1821.
(PAO)

LAMONT WALTER
Son of John Og Lamont,
1612-1648. Lieutenant in
Glencairn's Regiment.
Resident in Evanachan,
Strathlachlan, Argyllshire.
Married Elizabeth Hamilton
in Edinburgh during 1689.
Died in Darien during 1700.
(LC)

LANG ANDREW
Emigrated from Scotland to
Canada on the Earl of
Buckingham during 1821.
Settled in Upper Canada.
(PAO)

LANG DAVID
Inverkip, Renfrewshire.
Emigrated from Scotland
to Virginia before 1762.
Shipmaster in Virginia.
(OD)

LANG ROBERT
Forteviot, Perthshire.
Applied to settle in
Canada on 2 March 1815.
(SRO/RH9)

LAVERTY WILLIAM
Emigrated from Scotland,
with wife and three sons,
to Canada on the David of
London. Received a land
grant in Dalhousie, Upper
Canada, on 7 August 1821.
(PAO)

LAW JAMES
Belhaven,East Lothian.
Applied to settle in
Canada on 26 February 1815.
(SRO/RH9)

LAW JOSEPH
Edinburgh. Emigrated
from Scotland to
America during 1674.
Settled in Liberty
County, Georgia.
Father of Joseph, 1714-
1802.
(BAF)

LAWRIE GAVIN
Born in Scotland. To
East New Jersey in 1684.
Governor of East New
Jersey. Married Mary.
Father of James, Mary
and Rebecca. Died 1687.
(MNJ)(EJD/A)

LAURIE JOHN
Emigrated from Scotland,
with wife, four sons and
four daughters, to Canada
on the Commerce in June
1821. Received a land
grant in Dalhousie, Upper
Canada, on 15 July 1821.
(PAO)

LAWRIE THOMAS
Brother of Governor
Gavin Lawrie. Born in
Scotland. To America in
1683. Tailor. Settled in
Cheesequake Creek, and
later in Freehold, East
New Jersey. Father of
James and Anna. Died
during 1712.
(MNJ)

LAURIE THOMAS
Emigrated from Scotland
to Canada. Received a
land grant in Ramsay,
Upper Canada, on
4 April 1821.
(PAO)

LAWRIE WILLIAM
Angus. Graduated M.A.
at Aberdeen University
during March 1825.
Minister of the Scots
Episcopalian Church in
Canada.
(UKA)(KCA)

LAWRIN JOHN
Emigrated from Scotland to
Canada on the Brock during
1820. Settled in Lanark,
Upper Canada, in 1821.
(PAO)

LAWS ....
Born 1786. Housecarpenter.
Emigrated from Scotland,
with wife and two children,
to Canada. Settled in
Pictou Town, Nova Scotia,
during 1815.
(PANS/RG1)

LAWSON AGNES
Indentured servant
imported from Scotland to
East New Jersey by Lord
Neil Campbell in December
1685.
(EJD/A225)

LAWSON DAVID
Born c1720 at Muthill(?),
Perthshire. Flaxfarmer.
Married Ellen...Emigrated
from Greenock to Canada on
the Falmouth with 50 servants
8 April 1770. Landed in
June 1770 on Prince Edward
Island. Settled at Covehead,
Stanhope Cove, Prince
Edward Island. Farmer and
politician. Died after 1803.
(DCB)(TPC)

LAWSON JOHN
Emigrated from Scotland,
with wife, three sons
and four daughters, to
Canada on the Brock.
Received a land grant
in Lanark, Upper Canada,
on 25 October 1821.
(PAO)

LAWSON SICELLA
Indentured servant
imported from Scotland
to East New Jersey by
Lord Neil Campbell in
December 1685.
(EJD/A225)

LEARMONTH ALEXANDER
Indentured servant
imported from Scotland
to East New Jersey by
Lord Neil Campbell in
December 1685.
Settled in Newark,
New Jersey, by 1688.
(EJD/A225/A420)

LECKIE DAVID
Emigrated from Greenock,
Renfrewshire, to Canada
on the David of London
in May 1821. Received a
land grant in Ramsay,
Upper Canada, on
22 August 1821.
(PAO)

LECKIE JAMES
Emigrated from Scotland,
with wife, three sons and
a daughter, to Canada on
the George Canning in June
1821. Received a land
grant in Ramsay, Upper
Canada, on 10 July 1821.
(PAO)

LECKIE JOHN
Emigrated from Scotland,
with wife, four sons and
five daughters, to Canada
on the Earl of Buckingham
in June 1821. Received a
land grant in Dalhousie,
Upper Canada, on 8 August
1821.
(PAO)

LEGERWOOD JOHN
Born in Scotland. Former
private in the Royal
Artillery. Military
settler. Received a land
grant in Drummond, Upper
Canada, on 24 May 1820.
(PAO)

LEIPER JAMES
Born c1769. Chairmaker.
Emigrated from Scotland
to Canada. Settled in
Pictou Town, Nova Scotia,
during 1815.
(PANS/RG1)

LEIPER WILLIAM
Born during 1745 in Strath-
aven, Lanarkshire.
Emigrated from Scotland to
Maryland during 1763.
Settled in Philadelphia,
Pennsylvania, in 1765.
Tobacco merchant. Died in
1825.
(TSA)

LEITCH MALCOLM
North Knapdale, Argyll-
shire. Emigrated to
Canada on the Mars of
Glasgow during 1818.
(CO384/3)

LEITH JAMES
Born during 1763, son
of John Leith of Leith
Hall, Aberdeenshire.
Educated at Marischal
College, Aberdeen from
1776 to 1777, at King's
College, Aberdeen, from
1778 to 1780, and at the
University of Lille,France,
from 1780 to 1782. Army
officer and colonial
administrator. Governor
of Barbados. Died in
Barbados during 1816.
(MCA)(VI)

LEMAN JOHN
Inverness. Signed a
treaty with the Creek
Indians in Georgia on
11 August 1739. (cf the
Captain Leman who brought
43 Highlanders from
Rotherhithe to Savannah,
Georgia, on the Loyal
Judith in autumn 1737.)
(HGP)

LENNON WILLIAM
Emigrated from Scotland
to Canada. Received a
land grant in Cavan,
Newcastle, Upper Canada,
on 24 September 1817.
(PAO)

LESLIE ANTHONY
Born in Scotland. Former
lieutenant in the Glen-
garry Regiment. Military
settler. Received a
land grant in Bathurst,
Upper Canada, on
30 July 1817.
(PAO)

LESLEY DANIEL
Emigrated from Scotland
to America before 1755.
Planter in Virginia.
(OD)

LESSLIE EDWARD
Born c1764. Emigrated
from Dundee, Angus, to
Dundas, Upper Canada, in
1823. Merchant in York
and Kingston, Upper Canada.
(TO)

LESLIE GEORGE
Former Magistrate of
Edinburgh. Settled in
Schenectady, New York,
c1797.
(SRO/GD51.6.1218)

LESLIE JAMES
Son of James Leslie, Kair,
Kincardineshire. Educated
at Marischal College,
Aberdeen, from 1801 to 1803.
Merchant in Canada.
(MCA)

LESSLIE JOHN
Born in Dundee, Angus,
during 1810. Emigrated
from Scotland to Canada
during 1820. Editor and
proprietor of the
'Toronto Examiner', from
1844 to 1854. Died in 1885.
(DPL.408.2)

LESLIE ROBERT
Born c1794 in Glasgow.
Emigrated via London to
USA in 1817. Married Nancy
Gilliam Duncan, daughter of
Charles Duncan, merchant in
Roslin, Virginia. Tobacco
merchant in Petersburg.
(DU)

LESLIE THOMAS
Emigrated from Scotland
to Canada on the George
Canning in June 1821.
Received a land grant in
Dalhousie, Upper Canada,
on 15 July 1821.
(PAO)

LIDDLE ANDREW
Emigrated from Scotland,
with wife, two sons and
two daughters, to Canada
on the Commerce in June
1821. Received a land
grant in Lanark, Upper
Canada, on 1 August 1821.
(PAO)

LIGHTBODY JAMES
Emigrated from Scotland,
with wife, two sons and
four daughters, to Canada
on the Prompt in June 1820.
Received a land grant in
Dalhousie, Upper Canada,
on 25 November 1821.
(PAO)

LINDSAY ANNE
Born during 1779.
Married Patrick Glenday,
feuar in New Rattray,
Perthshire, 1777-1836.
Died at St Charles,
Mississippi on
3 November 1821.
(Rattray GS)

LINDSAY ANTHONY
Graduated M.D. at the
University of Aberdeen,
16 December 1814, and
a Fellow of the Royal
College of Physicians of
Edinburgh in 1815.
Doctor in Jamaica.
(MCA)

LINDSAY GEORGE
Son of George Lindsay of
Wormistoun and Margaret
Bethune, born on
6 February 1737.
Apprenticed to Henry
Scrymgeour, Writer to the
Signet, during 1754. Died
in Havanna, Cuba, on
9 September 1762.
(SP.V)

LINDSAY JAMES
Emigrated from Scotland,
with wife, two sons and
two daughters, to Canada
on the Commerce in June
1820. Received a land
grant in Lanark, Upper
Canada, on 1 October 1820.
(PAO)

LINDSAY JOHN
Third son of John Lindsay
of Wormiston and Margaret
Haliburton, born in Crail,
Fife, on 2 July 1694.
Merchant. Died in Albany,
New York, on 12 October 1751.
(SP.V)

LINDSAY WILLIAM
Emigrated from Scotland,
with wife and three daughters,
to Canada on the David of
London. Received a land
grant in Lanark, Upper
Canada, on 14 August 1821.
(PAO)

LISTON ANTHONY
Born in Scotland. Former
lieutenant in the Glen-
garry Fencibles. Military
settler. Received a land
grant in Lancaster, Upper
Canada, on 25 June 1818.
(PAO)

LISTON CHARLES
Royalist soldier captured
at Worcester. Transported
from Gravesend, Kent, to
Boston, New England, on
the John and Sarah, master
John Greene, 13 May 1652.
(NER)

LITTLE ANDREW
Born c1704 in Canonby,
Dumfries-shire.
Indentured servant from
London to Antigua, or any
of the Leeward Islands,
on 27 November 1724.
(LGR)

LIVINGSTONE ALEXANDER
Emigrated from Scotland,
with his wife, to Canada.
Received a land grant in
Dalhousie, Upper Canada,
on 5 November 1821.
(PAO)

LIVINGSTONE DUNCAN
Emigrated from Scotland,
with wife, three sons and
three daughters, to
Canada on the David of
London in June 1821.
Received a land grant in
Dalhousie, Upper Canada,
on 1 September 1821.
(PAO)

LIVINGSTONE JOHN ROBERT
Born on 2 July 1771, second
son of Sir Alexander Living
stone of Bedlormie, and
Anne Atkinson. Settled in
the West Indies. Died in
St Ann's, Jamaica, c1828.
(LOC)

LIVINGSTON JOHN
Emigrated from Scotland,
with wife, son and daughter,
to Canada on the Pitt on
23 September 1819.
Received a land grant in
Beckwith, Upper Canada, on
30 November 1818.
(PAO)

LIVINGSTON JOHN
Emigrated from Scotland,
with his wife, to Canada
on the David of London in
June 1821. Received a
land grant in Dalhousie,
Upper Canada, on
1 September 1821.
(PAO)

LIVINGSTON ROBERT
Born 13 December 1654,
third son of Rev John
Livingston, minister of
Ancrum, Roxburghshire,
and Janet Fleming.
Married on 9 July 1679 to
Alida Schuyler in Albany,
New York. Father of John,
Philip, Robert and Gilbert.
Politician and public
official. Died on
1 October 1728.
(BAF)

LIVINGSTON WILLIAM
Emigrated from Scotland,
with wife and son, to
Canada on the David of
London in June 1821.
Received a land grant in
Lanark, Upper Canada, on
9 September 1821, and on
24 March 1822.
(PAO)

LOCHHEAD HENRY
Son of Henry Lochhead,
merchant in Glasgow,
and Jean Park. Grand-
son of James Lochhead,
wright in Glasgow.
Merchant. Emigrated
from Scotland to
Virginia during 1769
as manager and partner
of Buchanan, Hastie and
Company. Later a factor
in Petersburg, Virginia.
(SRA/B10.12.4/B10.15.7488)

LOCHHEAD WILLIAM
Emigrated from Scotland,
with wife, son and three
daughters, to Canada on
the George Canning in June
1821. Received a land grant
in Dalhousie, Upper Canada,
on 15 July 1821.
(PAO)

LOCKARD ARCHIBALD
Emigrated from Scotland to
America before 1755.
Planter in Prince William
County, Virginia.
(OD)

LOCKHART JOHN
Emigrated from Scotland,
with wife and three
daughters, to Canada
on the Earl of Buckingham
in June 1821. Received a
land grant in Ramsay,
Upper Canada, on 31 July
1821.
(PAO)

LONGMUIR GEORGE
Born c1758 in Banffshire.
Educated at King's College,
Aberdeen. Physician.
Settled in Quebec c1781.
Died in Quebec 9 August 1811.
(DCB)

LONGMUIR ROBERT
Born in Edinburgh, son
of William Longmuir.
Hudson Bay Company
employee from 1771 to 1810.
Furtrader. Died c1813
near Montreal, Quebec.
(DCB)

LOTHIAN DUNCAN
Born in Scotland. Emigrated
from Scotland to Canada on
the Rebacco. Received a
land grant in Lancaster,
Upper Canada, on
25 December 1819.
(PAO)

LOTHIAN JOHN
Emigrated from Scotland,
with his wife, to Canada
on the Lord Middleton on
20 July 1817. Received
a land grant in Lancaster,
Upper Canada, on
25 October 1817.
(PAO)

LOTHIAN PETER
Emigrated from Scotland,
with wife and son, to
Canada on the Lord Middleton
on 20 July 1817. Received a
land grant in Lancaster,
Upper Canada, on
25 October 1817.
(PAO)

LOUFBOROW JOHN
Miller. Emigrated from
Scotland to East New Jersey
in February 1685. Head-
right land grant 1689.
(EJD/A196/B159)

LOVE ROBERT
Emigrated from Scotland,
with wife, two sons and
a daughter, to Canada on
the Commerce in June 1821.
Received a land grant in
Sherbrook, Upper Canada,
on 1 August 1821.
(PAO)

LOWE JOHN
Born during 1750 in
Kenmure, Galloway.
Emigrated from Scotland
to America in 1771.
Settled in Fredericksburg,
Virginia. Teacher - later
an Episcopalian minister.
Died in Windsor Lodge,
Virginia, during 1798.
(TSA)

LOW WILLIAM
Emigrated from Scotland to
Canada on the George Canning
in June 1821. Received a
land grant in Ramsay, Upper
Canada, on 16 July 1821.
(PAO)

LOWRIE WALTER
Born in Edinburgh in 1784.
Emigrated from Scotland to
America during 1791.
Settled in Pennsylvania.
Politician and missionary.
(TSA)

LUCKISON JOHN
Volunteer. Died of flux on
the voyage from Scotland to
Darien on 31 October 1698.
(NLS)

LUDLOW JAMES
Emigrated from Scotland
to Canada on the Phillip
during 1820. Received a
land grant in Sherbrook,
Upper Canada, on
30 March 1821.
(PAO)

LUMSDEN ALEXANDER
Son of Professor John
Lumsden and Jean Leslie,
Aberdeen. Educated at
King's College, Aberdeen,
graduated M.D. on
31 October 1770. Settled
in Jamaica.
(KCA)

LUTHMAN CHARLES
Edinburgh. Applied to
settle in Canada on
28 February 1815.
(SRO/RH9)

LYLE JAMES
Emigrated from Scotland to
America before 1756.
Carpenter in Williamsburg,
Virginia.
(OD)

LYND DAVID
Born c1745 in Scotland.
Emigrated from Scotland to
Canada before 1767. Married
Jane, daughter of Rev George
Henry in Quebec. Legal clerk
and landowner. Died in Quebec
29 June 1802.
(DCB)

LYNN WILLIAM
Scottish doctor. Settled
in Fredericksburg,
Virginia, before 1743.
(SA)

LYON HENRY
Glen Lyon, Perthshire.
Emigrated via England to
America during 1649.
Settled in Milford,
Connecticut. Married
Elizabeth Bateman, in
Fairfield, Connecticut,
during 1652. Settled in
Newark, New Jersey, in
1666. Father of Samuel,
1655-c1705. Died in 1703.
(BAF)

LYON RICHARD
Glen Lyon, Perthshire.
Emigrated via England to
America during 1649.
(BAF)

LYON THOMAS
Glen Lyon, Perthshire.
Emigrated via England to
America during 1649.
(BAF)

MacALLISTER ARCHIBALD
Son of James MacAllister.
Emigrated from Scotland
to America c1760.
Settled in Norfolk,
Virginia.
(UNC/MacA.PP.3774)

McALASTAIR DANIEL
Royalist soldier captured
at Worcester. Transported
from Gravesend, Kent, to
Boston, New England, on the
John and Sarah, master John
Greene, 13 May 1652.
(NER)

MacALLISTER HECTOR
Son of James MacAllister.
Emigrated from Scotland
to America c1760. Settled
in Norfolk, Virginia.
Merchant in a co-partnery
with a Mr Donald of
Greenock, Scotland.
(UNC/MacA.PP.3774)

McALLISTER HUGH
Argyllshire. Emigrated
from Scotland to America.
Settled in Lancaster
County, Pennsylvania, c1732.
Married Miss Harbison.
Father of Hugh. Died in
1769.
(BAF)

McALASTAIR LACHLAN
Born in 1763. Married
Mary Mackay. Father of
Donald Ban, and Marion.
Emigrated from Scotland to
Canada during 1826.
Settled in Strathlorne,
Cape Breton Island.
(CG)

McALPIN ANDREW
Emigrated from Scotland,
with wife, two sons and
two daughters, to
Canada on the Earl of
Buckingham in June 1821.
Received a land grant in
Sherbrook, Upper Canada,
on 31 July 1821.
(PAO)

McALPINE DONALD
North Knapdale, Argyll-
shire. Emigrated from
Scotland to Canada on
the Mars of Glasgow in
1818.
(CO384/3)

McALPIN HENRY
Emigrated from Scotland,
with his wife Helen
McInnes, to America in
1804. Settled in Georgia
during 1812.
(DU/WallacePP)

McANDREW GEORGE SHIRLEY
Son of James McAndrew,
merchant in Elgin,
Morayshire. Educated
at Marischal College,
Aberdeen, c1812.
Settled in Jamaica.
(MCA)

McARTHUR ALEXANDER
Emigrated from Scotland,
with his wife, son and
two daughters, to Canada
on the Trafalgar 3 July
1817. Received land grants
in Drummond, Upper Canada,
on 9 July 1818, and on
17 August 1819.
(PAO)

McARTHUR JAMES
Emigrated from Scotland,
to Canada on the Commerce
in June 1820. Received a
land grant in Dalhousie,
Upper Canada, on
1 September 1820.
(PAO)

McARTHUR JOHN
Son of Daniel McArthur
and Margaret Farquharson.
Married Margaret Campbell
in Bute during 1768.
Emigrated from Scotland
to America during 1769.
Settled in Duchess County,
New York, and later in
Washington County,
Pennsylvania, and then
in Ohio. Father of
Duncan and Eleanor.
(H)

McARTHUR JOHN
Glasgow. Applied to
settle in Canada on
27 February 1815.
(SRO/RH9)

McARTHUR PETER
Emigrated from Scotland
to Canada. Received a
land grant in Monaghan,
Newcastle, Upper Canada,
on 29 November 1817, and
in Beckwith, Upper Canada,
on 2 August 1820.
(PAO)

McARTHUR...
Emigrated from Scotland to
Canada on the Trafalgar
27 July 1817. Received a
land grant in Drummond,
Upper Canada, 15 October
1818.
(PAO)

McAULEY JAMES
Born in Scotland during
1759. Surgeon with the
British Army in Canada
1796. Settled in
Toronto. Died in 1822.
(TO)

McBAIN ARCHIBALD
Yeoman. Emigrated from
Scotland to Canada.
Received a land grant
in Thorak, Home, Upper
Canada, on 8 March 1826.
(PAO)

McBEAN ALEXANDER
Yeoman. Emigrated from
Scotland to Canada.
Received a land grant
in Eldon, Newcastle,
Upper Canada, on
8 March 1826.
(PAO)

MacBEAN ARCHIBALD
Inverness-shire(?)
Scottish settler in
Georgia sent by the
Trustees to Inverness to
recruit indentured
servants for Georgia
during 1737.
(SPAWI)

McBEAN HUGH
Born in Scotland. Former
corporal in the Canadian
Fencibles. Military
settler. Received a
land grant in Upper
Canada on 30 September
1816.
(PAO)

MacBEAN LAUGHLIN
Inverness-shire(?)
Scottish settler in
Georgia. Cousin of
Archibald MacBean(above)
(SPAWI)

McBEATH ANDREW
Emigrated from Scotland,
with wife, son and two
daughters, to Canada on
the Commerce in June 1821.
Received a land grant in
Lanark, Upper Canada, on
11 August 1821.
(PAO)

McBEATH GEORGE
Born in Scotland c1740.
Emigrated from Scotland
to Canada c1764. Married
(1) Jane Graham (2) Erie
Smith, widow of David
McRae on 9 September 1801.
Fur trader and politician.
Died in Montreal, Quebec,
3 December 1812.
(DCB)

McBRIDE ANTHONY
Emigrated from Scotland,
with wife, to Canada on the
Earl of Buckingham in June
1821. Received a land grant
in Sherbrook, Upper Canada,
on 31 July 1821.
(PAO)

McCAIN NEIL
Royalist soldier captured
at Worcester. Transported
from Gravesend, Kent, to
Boston, New England, on the
John and Sarah, master John
Greene, 13 May 1652.
(NER)

MacCAIN ROBERT
Royalist soldier captured
at Worcester. Transported
from Gravesend, Kent, to
Boston, New England, on
the John and Sarah, master
John Greene, 13 May 1652.
(NER)

MacCAIN SAMUEL
Royalist soldier captured
at Worcester. Transported
from Gravesend, Kent, to
Boston, New England, on
the John and Sarah, master
John Greene, 13 May 1652.
(NER)

McCALL ARCHIBALD
Born 28 April 1734, son
of Samuel McCall, merchant
in Glasgow, and Margaret
Adams. Merchant in Essex
County, Virginia, before
1759. Married Catherine
Flood. Died during
October 1814.
(SOF)

McCALL GEORGE
Second son of William
McCall, Kelloside,
Dumfries-shire.
Emigrated from Scotland
to America. Merchant in
Philadelphia, Pennsylvania.
Married Ann Yeates, 1697-
1746, during 1716. Settled
at Douglas Manor, Penn-
sylvania. Father of
Jasper, Samuel, George,
Archibald, Catherine, Ann,
Mary, Margaret, and
Eleanor. Died in 1740.
(SOF)

McCALL GEORGE
Son of Samuel McCall,
merchant in Glasgow.
Settled in Philadelphia,
Pennsylvania, c1701.
Merchant at Douglas
Manor, Pennsylvania.
Father of Samuel.
(SC)

McCALL JAMES
Glasgow. Storekeeper
at North Glasgow,
Essex County, Virginia,
c1765.
(SRA/T79.41)

McCALL JOHN
Born on 1 April 1771,
second son of John McCall,
merchant in Glasgow, and
Helen Cross. Died at
Castries, St Lucia, on
3 February 1821.
(SOF)

McCOLL JOHN
Emigrated from Scotland,
with wife and daughter,
to Canada on the Commerce
in June 1821. Received a
land grant in Sherbrook,
Upper Canada, on
1 August 1821.
(PAO)

McCALL ROBERT
Emigrated from Scotland
to Canada. Received a
land grant in Monaghan,
Newcastle, Upper Canada,
on 30 March 1817.
(PAO)

148

McCALL SAMUEL
Born in 1710, son of
Samuel McCall, merchant
in Glasgow, and Isobel
Blackburn. Married Anne
... 28 May 1737.
Merchant in Philadelphia,
Pennsylvania. Father of
Samuel, John, George,
Anne, Isobel, Mary,
Catherine, Margaret, and
Eleanor. Died during
April 1761 in Philadelphia.
Buried in Christ Church,
Philadelphia.
(SOF)

McCALL WILLIAM
Born in 1777, fourth son
of George McCall, merchant
in Glasgow, and Mary
Smellie. Died in Jamaica
on 14 August 1802.
(SOF)

McCALLUM ANGUS
Emigrated from Scotland,
with wife, two sons and
a daughter, to Canada on
the Brock in 1820.
Settled in Lanark, Upper
Canada, 21 October 1821.
(PAO)

McCALLUM JAMES
Emigrated from Scotland,
with wife, two sons and
two daughters, to
Canada on the David of
London in June 1821.
Received a land grant in
Lanark, Upper Canada, on
18 August 1821.
(PAO)

McCALLUM JOHN
Glasgow. Applied to
settle in Canada on
4 March 1815.
(SRO/RH9)

McCALLUM JOHN
Born c1770. Emigrated
from Scotland, with
wife and four children,
to Canada. Settled in
Pictou Town, Nova Scotia,
in 1815.
(PANS/RG1)

McALLUM JOHN
Emigrated from Scotland,
with two sons and a
daughter, to Canada on
the Fancy on 17 August
1816. Received a land
grant in Elmsley, Upper
Canada, 26 September 1816.
(PAO)

McCALLUM JOHN
Educated at King's College,
Aberdeen, - graduated M.A.
in March 1824. Church of
England minister at
Hudson Bay, Canada.
(KCA)

McCALLUM PETER
Born c1798. Emigrated from
Scotland to Canada. Clerk.
Settled at Lower Settle-
ment, Pictou, Nova Scotia,
in 1815.
(PANS/RG1)

McCALLUM WILLIAM
Emigrated from Scotland,
with three sons and two
daughters, to Canada on
the Commerce in June 1821.
Received a land grant in
Lanark, Upper Canada, on
1 August 1821.
(PAO)

McCANDLISH ROBERT
Emigrated from Scotland
to America during C18.
Tutor in Essex County,
Virginia.
(OD)

McCANN JAMES
Born in Greenock,
Renfrewshire, 4 February
1799. Merchant in Kings-
ton, Jamaica. Died on
13 March 1832. Buried in
Scots Cemetary, Jamaica.
(MIBWI)

McCARTNEY JAMES
Born in Scotland. Formerly
in the Royal Marines.
Military settler.
Received a land grant in
Upper Canada on
30 September 1816.
(PAO)

McCASKELL DANIEL
Son of Murdoch McCaskell,
born in Skye, Inverness-
shire c1760. Emigrated
from Scotland to America
before 1770. Father of
John, Alexander Bruce, and
Murdoch. Died possibly in
Georgia.
(MCF)

McCAUL COLIN
Kinnel, Perthshire(?)
Emigrated from Scotland
to Montreal, Quebec, on
the Niagara, Hamilton,
in 1825. Settled in
McNab, Bathurst, Upper
Canada, during 1825.
(SG)

McCAUL JAMES
Glasgow(?) Father of
William, John and Elizabeth.
Died in St Vincent in 1823.
(GFH)

McCAW JAMES
Son of William McCaw,
merchant in Newton
Stewart, Wigtownshire,
and Elizabeth Drew.
Emigrated from Wigtown-
shire to America in 1765.
Married Elizabeth Brough.
Father of James Drew McCaw.
Apothecary and surgeon in
Norfolk, Virginia. Died
in October 1779.
(SA)(BAF)

McCLARRIN JOHN
Emigrated from Scotland,
with wife, three sons and
a daughter, to Canada on
the Caledonia on 10 July
1816. Received a land grant
in Upper Canada on
24 September 1816.
(PAO)

McCLEMENT JOHN
Graduated University of
Edinburgh 1719. Ordained
in June 1719 for Rehoboth,
Virginia.
(AP)

McCLENNEN WILLIAM
Born in 1760. Emigrated
from Scotland to America
c1775. Settled in Boston,
Massachusetts. Father of
Joseph Jone McClennen.
(BAF)

McCLOUD WILLIAM
Born in 1730. Emigrated
from Scotland to Virginia
before 1756.
(OD)

McCLURE JOHN
Born in Edinburgh c1764.
Married Ruth Pratt on
17 September 1784 in
Middletown, Rutland County,
Vermont. Father of three
children. Revolutionary
militiaman. Died in 1790s.
(RT)

McCOLL WILLIAM jr
Emigrated from Scotland,
with wife, three sons and
four daughters, to Canada
on the Alexander 1 August
1817. Received a land grant
in Bathurst, Upper Canada,
on 23 April 1819.
(PAO)

McCOMB ANDREW
Born c1739 in Scotland(?)
Married Jane Raeburn.
Father of three children.
Revolutionary patriot.
Will dated 15 March 1788
in Augusta County,
Virginia.
(RT)

McCOMB DAVID
Royalist soldier captured
at Worcester. Transported
from Gravesend, Kent, to
Boston, New England, on the
John and Sarah, master John
Greene, 13 May 1652.
(NER)

McCOMIE ROBERT
Son of Robert McComie,
tenant farmer in Findlatrie,
Tough, Aberdeenshire, and
Isobel Ritchie. Jacobite
in 1745. Emigrated to the
West Indies via Whitehaven,
Cumberland.
(MMT)

McCOMBS JOHN
Born in 1747. Emigrated
from Scotland to America.
Married Elizabeth Marshall,
a Scot, 1748-1839, in
Lancaster County, Penn-
sylvania, c1770. Father of
William, Robert, John,
Elizabeth, Isaac, James,
and Joseph. Revolutionary
soldier. Died in Poland,
Ohio, 27 February 1822.
(ORIII)

MacCONNELL ...
Royalist soldier captured
at Worcester. Transported
from Gravesend, Kent, to
Boston, New England, on the
John and Sarah, master John
Greene, 13 May 1652.
(NER)

McCONNELL JAMES
Emigrated from Scotland,
with wife, son and daughter,
to Canada on the Commerce in
June 1821. Received a land
grant in Sherbrook, Upper
Canada, 1 August 1821.
(PAO)

McCONNELL RICHARD
Emigrated from Scotland,
with his wife, to Canada
on the Commerce in June
1821. Received a land
grant in Sherbrook,
Upper Canada, on
1 August 1821.
(PAO)

MacCORQUODALE ARCHIBALD
Kilbride, Argyllshire.
Married Laura Jones,
spinster, from
Llanbeblig, Caernarvon,
Wales, at the Anglican
Cathedral of St John
the Baptist, St Johns,
Newfoundland, on
7 November 1813.
(Gents Mag XX)

McCORKINDALE JOHN
Johnstone, Renfrewshire.
Applied to settle in
Canada on 4 March 1815.
(SRO/RH9)

McCORQUENDALE THOMAS
Born in Dumfries-shire
during 1796. Farmer.
Emigrated from Scotland,
with wife and two
children, to Canada in
1821. Received a land
grant in Caverhill,
Queensbury, New Brunswick,
during 1821.
(PANB)

McCOY ALEXANDER
Born in 1764. Emigrated
from Scotland to America
in 1772 - landed in
Philadelphia, Pennsylvania,
7 October 1772. Soldier in
the Revolution. Married
Frances Sutherland c1787.
Father of William. Died
12 August 1837. Buried at
Old Ripley Cemetery, Brown
County, Ohio.
(ORIII)(SG)

McCRACKEN JAMES
Emigrated from Scotland,
with wife, two sons and
three daughters, to Canada.
Received a land grant in
Bathurst, Upper Canada,
on 14 September 1819.
(PAO)

MacCUBBIN JOHN
Born c1630, son of Sir John
MacCubbin of Knockdolian,
Ayrshire. Settled in
Tinker Neck, Anne Arundel
County, Maryland during
1659. Married (1)Catherine
Howard, (2) Ellinor Carroll.
Father of John, c1666-1736.
Died 21 September 1685.
(BAF)

MacCULLOCH ADAM
Crofter and fisherman.
Dornoch, Sutherlandshire.
Emigrated from Scotland
to Boston, Massachusetts,
in 1765. Settled in
Kennebunkport, Maine.
Father of Hugh.
(TSA)(SO)

McCULLOCH GEORGE
Yeoman. Emigrated from
Scotland to Canada.
Received a land grant in
Eldon, Newcastle, Upper
Canada, on 8 March 1826.
(PAO)

McCULLOCH HATHORN
Born in 1772, son of
Andrew McCulloch of
Glasserton, Wigtownshire,
and Grissel Shadlin.
Emigrated from Greenock,
Renfrewshire, to America
in 1802. Settled in New
York in 1803. Married
Christina McFarlan. Father
of John Hathorn McCulloch.
(BAF)

McCULLOCH JOHN
Emigrated from Scotland
to Canada. Received a
land grant in Dalhousie,
Upper Canada, on
15 August 1821.
(PAO)

McCULLOCH PETER
Emigrated from Scotland,
with two sons and a
daughter, to Canada on
the David of London in
June 1821. Received a
land grant in Dalhousie,
Upper Canada, on
15 August 1821.
(PAO)

McCULLOCH Rev THOMAS
Born in Neilston, Renfrew-
shire during 1776.
Educated at University
of Glasgow. Ordained in
Stewarton, Ayrshire, on
13 June 1799. Emigrated
from Scotland to Nova
Scotia in 1803. Minister in
Pictou, Nova Scotia.
Founder of Pictou Academy.
Principal of Dalhousie
College, Halifax, Nova
Scotia, from 1838 to 1843.
Died during 1843.
(SF)(HPC)

McDANIEL ASA
Born on 15 September 1776.
Emigrated from Scotland to
America. Married Sarah
McCollum in Randolph County,
North Carolina, 16 December
1802. Father of William,
Harriet and Samuel. Died on
30 May 1854 in Hedricks
County, Indiana.
(SG)

McDEARMID ARCHIBALD
Emigrated from Scotland,
with wife and daughter,
to Canada on the Curlew
on 10 September 1818.
Received a land grant in
Drummond, Upper Canada, on
20 October 1818.
(PAO)

McDIARMID CATHERINE
Perthshire(?) Emigrated
from Greenock, Renfrew-
shire, to Montreal,
Quebec, on the brig
Niagara, Hamilton, 1825.
Settled in McNab, Bathurst,
Upper Canada, in 1825.
(SG)

McDIARMID DUNCAN
Son of Hugh McDiarmid,
born in Killin, Perthshire,
in 1757. Married Jane
McGregor. Soldier in the
74th(Argyllshire)Regiment
from 1775 to 1785.
Emigrated from Scotland,
with wife and children, to
Canada, in June 1801.
Died during 1847.
(TV)

McDERMID JOHN
Born in Scotland. Received
a land grant in Beckwith,
Upper Canada, on
29 September 1820.
(PAO)

McDERMID JOHN
Auchleskin, Perthshire(?)
Emigrated from Greenock,
Renfrewshire, to Montreal,
Quebec, with his mother
Margaret, his wife
Margaret, and children
Margaret and Jean, on the
brig Niagara, Hamilton, in
1825. Settled in McNab,
Bathurst, Upper Canada, in
1825.
(SG)

McDONALD ....
Emigrated from Scotland to
Canada on the Lady of the
Lake on 17 September 1816.
Received a land grant in
Beckwith, Upper Canada,
on 31 December 1816.
(PAO)

MacDONALD ALEXANDER
First son of John MacDonald
of Aberchalder. Emigrated
from Scotland to North
America before 1776. Married
Mary MacDonald. Father of
John, Hugh, Chichester,
Janet, etc. Captain in the
King's Royal Regiment of
New York. Settled in
Charlottenburg on the
River St Lawrence. Died
during 1787.
(CD)

MacDONALD ALEXANDER
Born during the 1740s,
son of Alexander MacDonald
of Keppoch and Jessie
Stewart. Married Sarah
MacDonald. Emigrated from
Scotland to Canada. Father
of Chichester, John, Mary,
Isabella and Janet. Major
in Glengarry Fencibles.
Settled in Keppoch, Prince
Edward Island. Died 1809.
(CD)(TML)

MacDONALD ALEXANDER
Son of Angus MacDonald of
Greenfield and Margaret
Grant. Emigrated from
Scotland to Canada in 1792.
Commander of the Second
Battalion of the Glengarry
Militia during the War of
1812. Married Janet
MacDonald. Father of
Hugh, Angus, Duncan, John,
Donald, Alexander, Mary,
Anne, Margery and Margaret.
Died during 1819.
(CD)

McDONALD ALEXANDER
Emigrated from Scotland
to Canada on the Green-
field on 23 August 1816.
Received a land grant in
Drummond, Upper Canada,
on 30 November 1816.
(PAO)

McDONALD ALEXANDER
Born in Scotland. Former
sergeant in the Canadian
Fencibles. Military
settler. Wife, son and
daughter. Received a land
grant in Bathurst, Upper
Canada, on 31 May 1817.
(PAO)

McDONALD ALLAN
Emigrated from Scotland to
Canada. Settled at Fort
William, Newfoundland,c1767.
(SRO/GD24.1.392)

MacDONALD ALLAN
Second son of Donald
MacDonald of Lundie, born
in 1724. Jacobite in 1745.
Emigrated from Scotland to
Canada. Settled in Chambly.
Died after 1814.
(CD)

MacDONALD ALLAN
Born in 1712, first son
of Alexander MacDonald
of Cullachie. Jacobite
in 1745. Later a captain
in the French Army. Then
returned to Scotland.
Emigrated from Scotland
to America in 1773.
Settled in Tryon Valley,
New York. Loyalist -
captain of the 84th(Royal
Highland Emigrants)
Regiment. American prisoner.
Married Helen McNab. Father
of Angus, Alexander, James,
Henrietta and Catherine.
Died in Quebec during 1792.
Buried at St Foy.
(CR)(CD)

MacDONALD ANDREW
Born in Eilean Shona,
Inverness-shire during
November 1745. Merchant in
Arisaig, Inverness-shire.
Emigrated from Scotland to
Canada during 1806. Settled
on Panmure Island, Prince
Edward Island.
(BCG)

McDONALD ANGUS
Emigrated from Scotland
to America before 1756.
Settled in King George
County, Virginia.
Seaman.
(OD)

McDONALD ANGUS
Emigrated from Scotland
to America. Settled in
Winchester, Virginia, c1750.
(DU.M.McD.PP)

McDONALD ANGUS
Emigrated from Scotland,
with family, to America
on the Frances of New
Orleans during 1812.
Settled in Highland Town,
Columbiana County, Ohio.
(SHR.LXIII)

McDONALD ANGUS
Yeoman. Emigrated from
Scotland to Canada.
Received a land grant in
Eldon, Newcastle, Upper
Canada, on 8 March 1826.
(PAO)

McDONALD ARCHIBALD
Emigrated from Scotland
to Canada on the Morning
Field on 19 September 1816.
Received a land grant in
Beckwith, Upper Canada,
on 31 December 1816.
(PAO)

McDONALD CATHARINE
Born c1755. A widow.
Emigrated from Scotland
to Canada. Settled at
Roger's Hill, Pictou,
Nova Scotia, in 1815.
(PANS/RG1)

MacDONALD DONALD
Indentured servant
imported from Scotland
to East New Jersey on the
Thomas and Benjamin, master
Thomas Pearson, on
5 November 1684.
(EJD/A)

MacDONALD DONALD
 First son of Donald
 MacDonald of Lundie.
 Jacobite in 1745.
 Emigrated from Scotland
 to Canada. Died in
 Chambly during 1805.
 (CD)(CR)

MacDONALD DONALD
 Third son of Alexander
 MacDonald of Glenaladale,
 and Margaret MacDonald.
 Emigrated from Scotland
 to Prince Edward Island
 during 1772.
 (CD)

McDONALD DONALD
 Emigrated from Scotland
 to Canada on the Fancy
 18 August 1816.
 Received a land grant in
 Drummond, Upper Canada,
 9 December 1816.
 (PAO)

McDONALD DONALD
 Emigrated from Scotland,
 with his wife, to Canada
 on the Alexander 22 July
 1817. Received a land grant
 in Beckwith, Upper Canada,
 on 6 October 1817.
 (PAO)

McDONALD DONALD
 Born in Scotland.
 Received a land grant
 in Beckwith, Upper
 Canada, 8 May 1820.
 (PAO)

McDONALD Rev DONALD
 Born on 1 January 1783,
 in Rannoch, Perthshire.
 Educated at University
 of St Andrews, Fife.
 Emigrated from Scotland
 to Cape Breton Island in
 1824. Minister in Cape
 Breton Island and Prince
 Edward Island from 1824
 to 1867. Died on
 25 February 1867. Buried
 at Uig, Prince Edward
 Island.
 (SO)(HPC)

McDONALD DONALD
 Emigrated from Scotland
 to Canada. Received a
 land grant in Ramsay,
 Upper Canada, on 23 June
 1821.
 (PAO)

McDONALD DONALD
 Yeoman. Emigrated from
 Scotland to Canada.
 Received a land grant in
 Eldon, Newcastle, Upper
 Canada, 8 March 1826.
 (PAO)

McDONALD EVEN
 Born in Scotland.
 Conductor in the Commissary
 Department. Military
 settler. Received a land
 grant in Sherbrooke, Upper
 Canada, during January 1820.
 (PAO)

McDONALD GEORGE JOHN
 Born in Scotland c1782.
 North West Company employee
 from 1801 to 1821. Hudson
 Bay Company employee from
 1821 to 1834. Died in 1834.
 (HBRS)

MacDONALD of GLENALADALE
HELEN
  Born c1750, daughter of
  Alexander MacDonald of
  Glenaladale and Margaret
  McDonnell of Scotus.
  Emigrated from Scotland
  to Prince Edward Island
  on the Alexander in 1772.
  Married Ronald McDonald
  in Grand Tracadie 1792.
  Died c1803 in Prince
  Edward Island.
  (DCB)

McDONALD HENRY
  Born in Scotland. Former
  soldier in the 8th King's
  Regiment. Military
  settler. Wife and son.
  Received a land grant in
  Drummond, Upper Canada,
  on 26 October 1816.
  (PAO)

MacDONALD HUGH
  Second son of Alexander
  MacDonald of Glenaladale
  and Margaret MacDonald.
  Educated at the Scots
  College in Rome, Italy,
  from 1757 to 1769.
  Roman Catholic priest in
  Moidart, Invernessshire.
  Emigrated from Scotland
  to Prince Edward Island.
  Buried at Scotch Fort,
  Prince Edward Island.
  (CD)

McDONALD JAMES
  Kilmahog, Perthshire(?)
  Emigrated from Greenock,
  Renfrewshire, to Montreal,
  Quebec, on the brig
  Niagara, Hamilton, in 1825
  with his wife Elizabeth
  Blair and children William
  and Archibald. Settled in
  McNab, Bathurst, Upper
  Canada, in 1825.
  (SG)

McDONALD JAMES
  Emigrated from Scotland,
  with wife, three sons and
  a daughter, to Canada on
  the Commerce in June 1820.
  Received a land grant in
  Dalhousie, Upper Canada,
  on 8 September 1820.
  (PAO)

McDONALD JOHN
  Emigrated from Scotland to
  America. Settled in Darien,
  Georgia, c1739.
  (HGP)

McDONALD JOHN
  Emigrated from Scotland to
  America before 1756.
  Planter in Carolina County,
  Virginia.
  (OD)

MacDONALD JOHN
  First son of Alexander
  MacDonald of Glenaladale
  and Margaret MacDonald.
  Educated at Ratisbon,
  Germany. Emigrated from
  Scotland to Prince Edward
  Island 1772. Married (1)
  Isabella Gordon (2)
  Catherine MacDonald. Father
  of Donald, William, Margaret,
  John and Roderick. Died 1811.
  (CD)

McDONALD JOHN
North Uist, Inverness-
shire. Educated at
King's College, Aberdeen,
graduated M.A. 2 April
1764. Minister in
Jamaica.
(KCA)

McDONALD JOHN sr
Emigrated from Scotland,
with wife, two sons and
four daughters, to Canada
on the Morning Star
19 September 1816.
Received a land grant in
Drummond, Upper Canada, on
31 December 1816.
(PAO)

McDONALD JOHN jr
Emigrated from Scotland
to Canada on the Morning
Star 19 September 1816.
Received a land grant in
Drummond, Upper Canada,
on 31 December 1816.
(PAO)

McDONALD JOHN
Born in Scotland.Wife,
five sons and three
daughters. Received
a land grant in
Drummond, Upper Canada,
on 8 October 1817.
(PAO)

McDONALD JOHN
Born in Scotland. Former
soldier in the 104th
Regiment. Military
settler. Received a
land grant in
Bathurst, Upper Canada,
on 28 June 1817.
(PAO)

McDONALD JOHN
Emigrated from Scotland,
with wife, to Canada on
the David of London in
June 1821. Received a land
grant in Dalhousie, Upper
Canada, on 1 September
1821.
(PAO)

McDONALD JOHN
Emigrated from Scotland,
with wife, son and three
daughters, to Canada.
Received a land grant in
Ramsay, Upper Canada, on
18 March 1822.
(PAO)

MacDONALD JOHN
Son of Alexander MacDonald
of Drimindarach. Surgeon
in South Uist,Inverness-
shire. Emigrated from
Scotland to America 1824.
(CD)

McDONALD JOHN
Yeoman. Emigrated from
Scotland to Canada.
Received a land grant in
Thorak, Home, Upper Canada,
on 8 March 1826.
(PAO)

McDONALD JOHN
Emigrated from Scotland to
Canada. Received a land
grant in Thorak, Home,
Upper Canada, on 14 April
1826.
(PAO)

McDONALD LACHLIN
Emigrated from Scotland
to Canada. Received a
land grant in Ramsay,
Upper Canada, on
24 June 1822.
(PAO)

McDONALD NEIL
Emigrated from Scotland
to Canada. Received a
land grant in Ramsay,
Upper Canada, on
24 June 1822.
(PAO)

McDONALD PETER
Emigrated from Scotland,
with wife and two sons,
to Canada on the David
of London in June 1821.
Received a land grant
in Dalhousie, Upper
Canada, on 1 September
1821.
(PAO)

McDONALD RANALD
Emigrated from Scotland
to America. Settled in
Georgia c1739.
(HGP)

MacDONALD RANALD
First son of Alexander
MacDonald of Geridhoil,
Uist, Inverness-shire,
and Isabella MacDonald.
Married (1) Flora
MacDonald, (2) Flora
Roy MacDonald. Father of
Donald, Catherine, Mary,
Marion, Janet, and of
Allan, Alexander.
Emigrated from Scotland
to America in 1784.
(CD)

McDONALD WILLIAM
Emigrated from Scotland,
with wife, four sons and
a daughter, to Canada on
the Commerce in June 1820.
Received a land grant in
Lanark, Upper Canada, on
8 September 1820.
(PAO)

McDONNELL ALEXANDER
Royalist soldier captured
at Worcester. Transported
from Gravesend, Kent, to
Boston, New England, on the
John and Sarah, master John
Greene, 13 May 1652.
(NER)

McDONELL ALEXANDER
Third son of Angus McDonell
of Drynachan and Leek.
Emigrated from Scotland to
North America on the Pearl
during 1773. Captain in
the King's Royal Regiment
of New York during the
American Revolution. Died
in Charlottenburg, Canada,
in 1789.
(CR)

McDONELL ALEXANDER
Son of Angus McDonell of
Greenfield. Emigrated
from Scotland to Canada in
1792. Settled in Greenfield,
Charlottenburg, Canada.
Commanding Officer of the
Glengarry Militia during
the War of 1812. Died
during 1819.
(CR)

McDONNELL ALEXANDER
Emigrated from Scotland
to Canada. Received a
land grant in
Charlottenburg,St Raphael,
Quebec, on 24 November
1787.
(PAO)

McDONELL ALEXANDER
Born in Scotland. Former
sergeant in the
Canadian Fencibles.
Military settler.
Received a land grant in
Young, Upper Canada, on
31 July 1817.
(PAO)

McDONELL ALEXANDER
Emigrated from Scotland,
with his wife Isabelle,
to Canada during the
early nineteenth century.
Settled in Glengarry,
Montreal. Father of
James, 1833-1882.
(BAF)

McDONELL ALEXANDER DHU
Yeoman. Emigrated from
Scotland to Canada.
Received a land grant in
Mora, Newcastle, Upper
Canada, 8 March 1826.
(PAO)

McDONELL ALEXANDER
Born in Inverness 1760.
Speaker of the House of
Assembly of Upper Canada.
Died in Toronto on
18 March 1842.
(BCB)

McDONELL ANGUS
Emigrated from Scotland
to Canada. Settled in
Charlottenburg, St Raphael,
Quebec, 23 November 1787.
(PAO)

McDONNELL ANGUS
From Scotland. Former
lieutenant in the 75th
Regiment. Settled in
Charlottenburg, St Raphael,
Quebec, 23 November 1787.
(PAO)

McDONELL ARCHIBALD
Emigrated from Scotland
to Canada on the Morning
Field 19 September 1816.
Received a land grant in
Drummond, Upper Canada,
on 31 December 1816.
(PAO)

McDONELL GEORGE(?)
Born in Scotland. Former
soldier in the 8th
Regiment. Military
settler. Received a land
grant in Drummond, Upper
Canada, on 23 December 1818.
(PAO)

McDONNELL HUGH
Emigrated from Scotland
to Canada. Received a land
grant in Charlottenburg,
St Raphael, Quebec, on
24 November 1787.
(PAO)

160

McDONELL JAMES
Born in Scotland. Former
sergeant in the 72nd
Regiment. Military
settler. Wife, two sons
and four daughters.
Received a land grant
in Burgess, Upper Canada,
on 27 August 1816, and on
31 July 1817 in Leeds,
Upper Canada.
(PAO)

MacDONELL JOHN
Born in 1728, son of
John MacDonell of Crowlin
and Janet McLeod. Soldier
in the Irish Brigade of
the Spanish Army.
Educated at the Scots
College, Rome, Italy.
Jacobite in 1746. Married
in 1747. Resident of
Inverguseran, Moidart,
Inverness-shire. Emigrated
from Scotland to Canada on
the Pearl during 1775.
Officer in the 84th(Royal
Highland Emigrants) Regi-
ment during the American
Revolution. Father of
Miles, John, William, Mary,
and Penelope. Died in
Cornwall, Upper Canada,
on 15 April 1810.
(CR)(CD)

McDONELL JOHN
Born in Aberchalder during
1758, son of Alexander
McDonell of Aberchalder.
Emigrated from Scotland to
New York during 1773.
Officer in the 84th(Royal
Highland Emigrants)Regiment
from 1775 to 1784. Married
Helen Yates at Fort George.
Speaker of the Parliament of
Upper Canada. Died in Quebec
on 21 November 1809.
(DCB)

McDONELL RANALD
Emigrated from Scotland
to Canada. Settled in
Charlottenburg, St Raphael,
Quebec, in 1787.
(PAO)

McDONELL RONALD
Born in Scotland. Former
lieutenant. Received a
land grant in Charlotten-
burg, St Raphael, Quebec,
on 26 November 1787.
(PAO)

McDONELL RONALD
Emigrated from Scotland
to Canada on the Morning
Field 19 September 1816.
Received a land grant in
Drummond, Upper Canada, on
9 December 1816.
(PAO)

McDOUALL EVAN
Born in Scotland. Former
sergeant in the Glengarry
Fencibles. Military
settler. Received a land
grant in Bathurst, Upper
Canada, 29 June 1817.
(PAO)

McDOUGALL ARCHIBALD
Emigrated from Scotland to
Canada on the Earl of
Buckingham in June 1821.
Received a land grant in
Sherbrook, Upper Canada,
on 24 July 1821.
(PAO)

161

McDOUGALD DONALD
Emigrated from Scotland,
with wife, two sons and
three daughters, to
Canada on the brig John
19 August 1817. Received
a land grant in Lancaster,
Upper Canada, 15 November
1817.
(PAO)

McDOUGALL JAMES
Emigrated from Scotland,
with wife and two sons,
to Canada on the Commerce
in June 1820. Received a
land grant in Lanark,
Upper Canada, on
8 September 1820.
(PAO)

McDOUGAL JOHN
Born in Dunbarton.
Emigrated from Scotland
to America. Member of
the Ohio legislature
1813-1815.
(SO)

McDOUGALL JOHN
Emigrated from Scotland
to Canada on the
Caledonian 20 July 1816.
Received a land grant in
Upper Canada 10 September
1816.
(PAO)

McDOUGALD JOHN
Born in Scotland c1800.
Hudson Bay Company
employee from 1822 to
1840.
(HBRS)

McDOUGALD MALCOLM
Emigrated from Scotland
to Canada. Received a
land grant in
Charlottenburg, St Raphael,
Quebec, 23 November 1787.
(PAO)

McDOUGALD PETER
Emigrated from Scotland,
with wife, to Canada on
the Agincourt 1 August
1817. Received a land
grant in Lancaster, Upper
Canada, on 7 October 1817.
(PAO)

McDUFFIE DUGALD
Argyllshire(?) Settled
in Kingston, Jamaica,
before 1773.
(CC)

McEACHIN ALEXANDER
Born in Scotland in 1790.
Emigrated from Scotland
to America. Died in
Richmond, Mississippi, 1881.
(Index N.C.Anc.)

McECHAN SAMUEL
Emigrated from Scotland,
with wife, son and daughter,
to Canada on the Morning
Field 19 September 1816.
Received land grants in
Beckwith, Upper Canada, on
1 November 1816, and in
Drummond, Upper Canada, on
23 July 1818.
(PAO)

McEWEN DUNCAN
  Emigrated from Scotland
  to Canada. Received a
  land grant in Beckwith,
  Upper Canada, on
  18 February 1820.
  (PAO)

McEWEN HUGH
  Emigrated from Scotland,
  with wife, three sons and
  three daughters, to
  Canada on the David of
  London. Received a land
  grant in Lanark, Upper
  Canada, 24 January 1822.
  (PAO)

McEWEN HUGH
  Cragantole, Perthshire(?)
  Emigrated from Greenock,
  Renfrewshire, to Montreal,
  Quebec, on the brig
  Niagara, Hamilton, 1825.
  Settled in McNab, Bathurst,
  Upper Canada, in 1825.
  (SG)

McEWEN JOHN
  Emigrated from Scotland
  to Canada. Received a
  land grant in Beckwith,
  Upper Canada, on
  30 November 1820.
  (PAO)

McEWAN MARGARET
  Emigrated from Scotland
  to Canada on the Commerce
  in June 1821. Received a
  land grant in Sherbrooke,
  Upper Canada, on
  7 August 1821.
  (PAO)

McEWEN ROBERT
  Dumfries. Transported
  from Scotland to America
  on the Henry and Frances
  in 1685. Settled in
  Perth Amboy, New Jersey.
  Father of Gershom.
  (BAF)

McEWAN WILLIAM
  Emigrated from Greenock,
  Renfrewshire, to Canada
  on the George Canning
  with his wife in May 1821.
  Received a land grant in
  Ramsay, Upper Canada, on
  16 July 1821.
  (PAO)

McEWING WALTER
  Emigrated from Scotland
  to Canada. Received a
  land grant in Lanark,
  Upper Canada, on
  2 April 1821.
  (PAO)

McFALIN JAMES
  Born in Scotland.
  Received a land grant in
  Beckwith, Upper Canada,
  on 23 August 1820.
  (PAO)

MacFARLANE ALEXANDER
  Glasgow. Factor in
  Chaptico, Maryland, for
  Pearls Company, shipowners
  and tobacco merchants in
  Glasgow, c1761.
  (SRA)

McFARLANE ALEXANDER
Kilburnie, Ayrshire.
Applied to settle in
Canada on
27 February 1815.
(SRO/RH9)

McFARLANE ALEXANDER
Emigrated from Scotland
to Canada. Received a
land grant in Dalhousie,
Upper Canada, on
7 November 1821.
(PAO)

MacFARLANE ALEXANDER
Perthshire(?)
Emigrated from Scotland
to Canada on the brig
Niagara, Hamilton, 1825.
Settled in McNab, Bathurst,
Upper Canada, 1825.
(SG)

MacFARLAN ANDREW
Son of .... MacFarlan and
Isabel Graeme, Loch Sloy.
Emigrated from Scotland,
via Ulster, to America
before 1772. Married Anna
Peters. Settled in
Schenectady, New York.
Father of Henry MacFarlane,
born 10 October 1772.
(CMF)

MacFARLANE DUNCAN
Emigrated from Scotland
to Canada on the brig
Niagara, Hamilton, 1825.
Settled in McNab,
Bathurst, Upper Canada.
(SG)

MacFARLANE HUGH NORMAN
Arrochar, Dunbartonshire.
Emigrated from Scotland
to America during 1784.
Settled in Chenanga County,
New York. Father of
Andrew.
(CMF)

McFARLANE JAMES
Glasgow. Applied to
settle in Canada on
27 February 1815.
(SRO/RH9)

McFARLIN JAMES
Emigrated from Scotland
to Canada. Received a
land grant in Beckwith,
Upper Canada, on
23 August 1820.
(PAO)

McFARLANE JAMES
Emigrated from Scotland
to Canada on the Earl of
Buckingham in June 1821.
Received a land grant in
Ramsay, Upper Canada, on
31 July 1821.
(PAO)

McFARLANE JAMES
Emigrated from Greenock,
Renfrewshire, to Montreal,
Quebec, with his wife Ann
Robertson and children Ann,
Janet, Christian and Janet(?)
on the brig Niagara, Hamilton
during 1825. Settled in
McNab, Bathurst, Upper
Canada, 1825.
(SG)

164

McFARLAND JAMES
Woodend, Perthshire(?)
Emigrated from Greenock,
Renfrewshire, to Montreal,
Quebec, on the brig
Niagara, Hamilton, 1825.
Settled in McNab,
Bathurst, Upper Canada,
in 1825.
(SG)

MacFARLANE JAMES
Born in Glasgow 1800,
son of James MacFarlane.
Married Jean Hunter.
Emigrated from Scotland
to America during 1829.
Settled in Wyoming Valley.
Father of James, Janet,
Margaret, Elizabeth,
Thomas and Clarinda.
(CMF)

MacFARLAN JANET
Born 13 September 1793 in
Stirlingshire(?), daughter
of Donald MacFarlan and
Mary McNee. Emigrated
from Scotland to America
during 1821. Died in
Huntingdon, Quebec, on
25 November 1869.
(CMF)

MacFARLANE JOHN
Born in Paisley, Renfrew-
shire during 1762.
Married Helen Barr, born
in Scotland during 1773.
Emigrated from Scotland
to Boston, Massachusetts,
in 1795. Settled in
Germantown, Pennsylvania.
Father of Jane, John Cameron,
Helen, Catherine, Walter,
Maria Baker, and Henry.
Died 24 December 1820.
(CMF)

MacFARLANE JOHN
Son of the Rev John
MacFarlane, Lanark.
Married ....Douglas.
Emigrated from Scotland
to Canada during 1824.
Settled in Lanark,
Upper Canada. Died 1763.
(CMF)

MacFARLANE JOHN
Perthshire(?) Emigrated
from Greenock, Renfrewshire,
to Montreal, Quebec, on the
brig Niagara, Hamilton, 1825.
Settled in McNab, Bathurst,
Upper Canada, 1825.
(SG)

McFARLANE JOHN
Emigrated from Scotland,
with wife, three sons and
two daughters, to Canada.
Settled in Lanark, Upper
Canada, 26 August 1821.
(PAO)

McFARLANE MATTHEW
Emigrated from Scotland,
with wife, son and three
daughters, to Canada on
the Earl of Buckingham in
June 1821. Received a
land grant in Ramsay, Upper
Canada, 31 July 1821.
(PAO)

McFARLANE NEIL
Emigrated from Scotland,
with wife, two sons and a
daughter, to Canada.
Received a land grant in
Dalhousie, Upper Canada,
on 3 December 1821.
(PAO)

McFARLANE PARLAN
Born 25 May 1795, son
of Donald McFarlane and
Mary McNee, Stirlingshire.
Emigrated from Scotland
to America in 1819.
Settled in Huntingdon,
Quebec. Died on
12 June 1860.
(CMF)

McFARLANE PETER
Born 25 February 1797, son
of Donald McFarlane and
Mary McNee, Stirlingshire.
Emigrated from Scotland
to America during 1819.
Settled in Huntingdon,
Quebec. Died on
9 October 1870.
(CMF)

McFARLANE P.
OldKilpatrick,
Dunbartonshire. Applied
to settle in Canada on
3 March 1815.
(SRO/RH9)

McFARLANE ROBERT
Emigrated from Scotland,
with wife and daughter,
to Canada on the Earl of
Buckingham in June 1821.
Received a land grant in
Ramsay, Upper Canada, on
31 July 1821.
(PAO)

McFARLANE WALTER
Emigrated from Scotland
on the brig Niagara,Hamilton,
to Canada in 1825.
Received a land grant in
McNab, Bathurst, Upper Canada,
1825.
(SG)

McFARQUHAR COLIN
Educated at Marischal
College, Aberdeen, from
1749 to 1753 - graduated
M.A. Minister of Apple-
cross, Pennsylvania.
(MCA)

McFEAL JOHN
Born in Scotland. Wife,
son and four daughters.
Received a land grant in
Drummond, Upper Canada,
on 13 August 1817.
(PAO)

McGIE JAMES
Carpenter. Emigrated
from Scotland to Canada.
Received a land grant in
Cavan, Newcastle, Upper
Canada, 27 May 1818.
(PAO)

McGEE JOHN
Calton. Applied to
settle in Canada on
2 March 1815.
(SRO/RH9)

McGEE JOHN
Emigrated from Scotland,
with wife, son and three
daughters, to Canada on the
Earl of Buckingham in June
1821. Received a land grant
in Lanark, Upper Canada,
20 July 1821.
(PAO)

McGEE WILLIAM
Emigrated from Scotland,
with wife and daughter,
to Canada. Received a
land grant in Lanark,
Upper Canada, on
27 July 1822.
(PAO)

McGILL JAMES
Born in Scotland c1755.
Emigrated from Scotland
to America. Married
Sarah Brashears. Soldier
in the Revolutionary army.
Died in Kentucky 1834.
(H)

McGILL PETER
Born in Dumfries or
Galloway. Emigrated from
Scotland to Canada in
1809. Merchant, banker
and politician. Died at
Beaver Hall Place,
Montreal, Quebec, on
28 September 1860.
(BCB)

McGILL PETER
Emigrated from Scotland,
with wife, son and two
daughters, to Canada on
the David of London in
May 1821. Received a
land grant in Ramsay,
Upper Canada, 18 August
1821.
(PAO)

McGILL Rev ROBERT
Born in Ayrshire.
Emigrated from Scotland
to Canada during 1829.
Minister at Niagara
from 1829 to 1845.
Minister at St Paul's,
Montreal, Quebec, from
1845 to 1856. Died on
4 February 1856.
(HPC)

McGILLIS DONALD
Yeoman. Emigrated from
Scotland to Canada.
Received a land grant in
Eldon, Newcastle, Upper
Canada, on 8 March 1826.
(PAO)

McGILLIVRAY ANGUS
Born in Inverness-shire
on 25 December 1792.
Emigrated from Scotland
to Nova Scotia in 1805.
Educated at Pictou Academy,
Nova Scotia, c1824.
Minister of Upper Settle-
ment, East River, Nova
Scotia, from 1824 to 1864.
Died on 20 July 1869.
(HPC)

McGILVRAY ARCHIBALD
Brother of Alexander
McGilvray in Inverness.
Trader to the Creek nation.
Settled in Josephtown,
Georgia, in 1735.
(HGP)

McGILLIVRAY WILLIAM
Born during 1764 in
Cloverdale, Inverness-shire.
Emigrated from Scotland to
Canada. Partner in the
North West Company. Died
during 1825.
(SO)

MacGREGOR ALEXANDER
Born in 1610. Emigrated
from Scotland to Calvert
County, Maryland, 1667.
Married (1) Margaret
Braithwaite (2) Elizabeth
Hawkins. Father of Samuel
Magruder, 1661-1734.
(BAF)

McGREGOR ALEXANDER
Emigrated from Scotland
to America. Tailor in
Isle of Wight County,
Virginia, in 1772.
(OD)

McGREGOR ALEXANDER
Fearn, Perthshire.
Emigrated, with wife, from
Greenock, Renfrewshire, to
Canada during 1817.
(CO384.1.124)

McGREGOR ALEXANDER
Emigrated from Scotland,
with wife and three sons,
to Canada on the Curlew
on 30 September 1818.
Received a land grant in
Beckwith, Upper Canada,
25 November 1818.
(PAO)

McGREGOR ARCHIBALD
Emigrated from Scotland,
with wife, two sons and
a daughter, to Canada
on the Jane 24 August 1818.
Received a land grant in
Beckwith, Upper Canada,
on 7 December 1818.
(PAO)

McGREGOR CHARLES
Son of Gregor McGregor,
1770-1854, and Ann ...,
1781-1838, Cromdale,
Morayshire. Settled in
Trinidad.
(Cromdale GS)

McGREGOR DONALD
Born in Scotland. Former
soldier in the Glengarry
Fencibles. Military
settler. Received a land
grant in Upper Canada on
27 August 1816.
(PAO)

McGREGOR DONALD
Born in Scotland. Former
soldier in the Canadian
Fencibles. Military
settler. Received a land
grant in Upper Canada on
27 September 1816.
(PAO)

McGREGOR D.
Fearn, Perthshire. Single.
Emigrated from Greenock,
Renfrewshire, to Canada in
1817.
(CO384.1.124)

McGREGOR DONALD
Fearn, Perthshire. Single.
Emigrated from Greenock,
Renfrewshire, to Canada in
1817.
(CO384.1.124)

McGREGOR DOUGALD
Emigrated from Scotland,
with his wife, to Canada
on the Trafalgar on 19 July
1817. Received a land
grant in Bathurst, Upper
Canada, on 11 February 1818.
(PAO)

MacGREGOR Rev JAMES
Born during 1759 in
Portmore, Perthshire.
Educated at the
University of Edinburgh.
Licenced as a preacher
during 1784. Appointed
a missionary to Nova
Scotia in 1786.
Emigrated from Scotland
to Halifax, Nova Scotia,
on the brig Lily 3 June
1786. Minister in Nova
Scotia from 1786 to 1830.
Died in 1830.
(HPC)

McGREGOR JOHN B.
Leith, Midlothian.
Applied to settle in
Canada on 28 February
1815.
(SRO/RH9)

McGREGOR JOHN
Emigrated from Scotland
to Canada. Received a
land grant in Monaghan,
Newcastle, Upper Canada,
23 July 1818.
(PAO)

MacGREGORIE Col PATRICK
Emigrated from Scotland
to America in 1684.
Landed in Maryland and
moved to Perth Amboy, New
Jersey. Received a land
grant in Cornwall, Orange
County, New York. Muster-
Master General of Militia
in New York in 1686. French
prisoner in Montreal, Quebec,
1687. Father of Hugh, John,
Patrick(?), Katherine, and
Jane. Killed in New York in
March 1691.
(DNY)

MacGREGOR PETER
Indentured servant.
imported from Scotland
to East New Jersey by
Captain Thomas Pearson
on the Thomas and Benjamin
5 November 1684.
(EJD/A)

McGREGOR PETER
Emigrated from Scotland
to Canada on the Sophia
6 September 1818.
Received a land grant in
Upper Canada on 31 July
1819.
(PAO)

McGRECOR PETER
Emigrated from Scotland,
with wife and two sons, to
Canada on the Earl of
Buckingham in June 1821.
Received a land grant in
Ramsay, Upper Canada, on
31 July 1821.
(PAO)

MacGREGOR Rev WILLIAM
Born in Methven, Perthshire,
during 1776. Educated at
the University of Edinburgh.
Emigrated from Scotland to
Nova Scotia during 1820.
Minister of Richmond Bay,
Prince Edward Island from
1821 to 1847. Died on
10 February 1850.
(HPC)

McGUIER PETER
Bridgeton. Applied to
settle in Canada on
2 March 1815.
(SRO/RH9)

McGURK ROBERT C.
Emigrated from Scotland
to Canada. Received a
land grant in Westminster,
London, Upper Canada, on
22 April 1818.
(PAO)

MacHATHERNE PATRICK
Royalist soldier captured
at Worcester. Transported
from Gravesend, Kent, to
Boston, New England, on the
John and Sarah, master John
Greene, 13 May 1652.
(NER)

McHATLY(?) JAMES
Emigrated from Scotland,
with wife and three sons,
to Canada on the Earl of
Buckingham in June 1821.
Received a land grant in
Lanark, Upper Canada, on
28 July 1821.
(PAO)

MacHECTOR ALEXANDER
Emigrated from Muck,
Inverness-shire, with
wife Eunice MacKinnon
and children Lachlan,
Donald, Malcolm, Christy,
and Mary, to Cape Breton
Island during 1826.
(CG)

McHELLIN(?) JOHN
Royalist soldier captured
at Worcester. Transported
from Gravesend, Kent, to
Boston, New England, on the
John and Sarah, master John
Greene, 13 May 1652.
(NER)

McILRAITH JAMES
Emigrated from Scotland
to Canada on the Earl of
Buckingham during 1821.
Settled in Upper Canada.
(PAO)

McILVAINE WILLIAM
Born during 1722. Emigrated
from Ayrshire to America
in 1745. Married Anne
Emerson. Father of Dr
William McIlvaine, 1750-
1806.
(BAF)

MacINDOE WALTER
Son of Robert MacIndoe,
Carbeth, Strathblane,
Stirlingshire. Merchant
in Virginia. Died there
unmarried - early nineteenth
century(?)
(Strathblane GS)

McINNIS ALEXANDER
Emigrated from Scotland,
with wife and five sons,
to Canada on the Commerce
in June 1820. Received a
land grant in Lanark,
Upper Canada, 1 October 1820.
(PAO)

McINNIS ALLAN
Emigrated from Scotland,
with wife, two sons and a
daughter, to Canada on the
David of London in June
1821. Received a land grant
in Dalhousie, Upper Canada,
in September 1821.
(PAO)

McINNIS DUNCAN
Emigrated from Greenock,
Renfrewshire, with wife
two sons and two
daughters, to Canada on
the George Canning in May
1821. Received a land
grant in Dalhousie,
Upper Canada, on 15 July
1821.
(PAO)

McINNIS LACHLIN
Born c1773. Emigrated
from Leith, with wife
Mary and children Penny(?),
Allan, Hector 21, Mary 19,
Donald 17, Marion 10, Flory 8,
and Jessie, to Port Hawkes-
Bury, Cape Breton Island,
on the St Lawrence of
Newcastle, master J.Cram,
in 1828.
(PANS.M6-100)

McINTOSH ALEXANDER
Inverness. Minister in
North America. Graduated
M.A. at Aberdeen on
30 March 1801.
(UKA)

McINTOSH ALEXANDER
Weaver. Emigrated from
Scotland to Canada.
Received a land grant
in Madoc township, Midland
district, Upper Canada, on
17 October 1818.
(PAO)

McINTOSH ALEXANDER
Yeoman. Emigrated from
Scotland to Canada.
Received a land grant
in Mora, Newcastle, Upper
Canada, 8 March 1826.
(PAO)

McINTOSH BENJAMIN
Emigrated from Scotland
to Canada. Received a
land grant in Charlotten-
burg, St Raphael, Quebec,
on 24 November 1787.
(PAO)

McINTOSH HUGH
Born c1745. Labourer.
Emigrated from Scotland,
with wife and child, to
Canada. Settled at
Scottshill, Pictou,
Nova Scotia, in 1815.
(PANS/RG1)

McINTOSH JAMES
Minister of the Gospel
in Dominica. Former
tutor to the children of
the late Alexander Brodie
of Lethen, husband of Ann
Simpson, daughter of James
Simpson at Mill of Brodie
1773.
(CPD)

McINTOSH JAMES
Born in Scotland. Former
sergeant. Military settler.
Wife, two sons and a
daughter. Received a land
grant in Bathurst, Upper
Canada, 13 September 1817.
(PAO)

McINTOSH JOHN
Emigrated from Scotland,
with wife, son and daughter,
to Canada on the Commerce
in June 1821. Received a
land grant in Dalhousie,
Upper Canada, 6 August 1821.
(PAO)

McINTOSH PETER
Wheelwright. Emigrated
from Scotland to Canada.
Received a land grant
in Madoc, Midland,
Upper Canada, on
17 October 1818.
(PAO)

McINTOSH WILLIAM
Emigrated from Sutherland,
with his family of twelve,
to Nova Scotia on the brig
Prince William in September
1815. Received a land grant
at Pictou, Nova Scotia.
(PANS/RG20)

McENTYRE DANIEL
Emigrated from Scotland to
America before 1756.
Planter in Fredericksburg,
Virginia.
(OD)

McINTYRE DANIEL
Emigrated from Scotland
to Canada, with wife, son
and two daughters, on the
Commerce in June 1821.
Received a land grant in
Lanark, Upper Canada, on
27 July 1821.
(PAO)

McINTYRE DONALD
Perthshire(?) Emigrated
from Greenock, Renfrew-
shire to Montreal,
Quebec, on the brig
Niagara during 1825.
Settled in McNab,
Bathurst, Upper Canada,
in 1825.
(SG)

McINTYRE DUGALD
Glasgow. Applied to
settle in Canada on
27 February 1815.
(SRO/RH9)

McINTYRE DUNCAN
Emigrated from Scotland
to Canada on the
Rothiemurcus 8 May 1817.
Received a land grant in
Bathurst, Upper Canada,
on 2 January 1818.
(PAO)

McINTYRE JANET
Emigrated from Scotland,
with a son and two daughters,
to Canada on the brig John
19 August 1817. Received
a land grant in Lancaster,
Upper Canada, 29 July 1818.
(PAO)

McINTYRE JOHN
Born 29 March 1768 in
Glenorchy, Argyllshire.
Settled in Jamaica on
4 June 1789. Died on
15 June 1842. Buried
in Kingston Cathedral,
Jamaica.
(MIBWI)

McINTYRE JOHN
Emigrated from Scotland,
with wife and daughter,
to Canada on the Earl of
Buckingham in June 1821.
Received a land grant in
Ramsay, Upper Canada, on
24 July 1821.
(PAO)

172

McINTYRE JOHN
Emigrated from Scotland,
with wife, son and daughter,
to Canada on the Prompt.
Received a land grant
in Dalhousie, Upper Canada,
on 17 November 1821.
(PAO)

McINTYRE JOHN
Leahead in Balmadrag,
Perthshire(?) Emigrated
from Scotland to Canada
with wife Catherine, and
children Donald, James,
Betty, John, Robert(?)
from Greenock, Renfrewshire,
to Montreal, Quebec, on the
brig Niagara, Hamilton, 1825.
Settled in McNab, Bathurst,
Upper Canada, in 1825.
(SG)

McINTIRE JOSEPH
Emigrated from Scotland
to Canada. Received a
land grant in Bathurst,
Upper Canada, on
21 October 1817.
(PAO)

McINTYRE PETER
Servant at Leny, Perth-
shire(?) Emigrated from
Scotland to Canada, with
wife Jean McLaren and
children Catherine and
Robert(?), on the brig
Niagara, Hamilton, from
Greenock, Renfrewshire,
to Montreal, Quebec, in
1825. Settled in McNab,
Bathurst, Upper Canada,
during 1825.
(SG)

McINTIRE WILLIAM
Born in Scotland 1760.
Revolutionary soldier.
Died during 1798.
Buried at Springfield,
Ohio.
(ORIII)

McINTYRE WILLIAM
Emigrated from Scotland,
with wife, to Canada on
the Commerce in June 1820.
Received a land grant in
Lanark, Upper Canada, on
1 October 1820.
(PAO)

McISAAC ....
Rhum, Inverness-shire.
Emigrated from Leith, Mid-
lothian, with children
Flory, Mary, Peggy, Flora,
and Donald, to Port
Hawkesbury, Cape Breton
Island, on the St Lawrence
of Newcastle, master J.Cram,
during 1828.
(PANS.M6.100)

McIVER DUNCAN
Born 1744 in Skye, Inver-
ness-shire, son of
Evander McIver. Married
Catherine Robertson pre
1780. Father of Donald,
Catherine, Margaret, Nancy,
Mary, Evander and Dorothy.
Emigrated from Liverpool,
England, to America during
August 1802 on the Duke of
Kent, Thompson.
(SG)

McIVER KENNETH
Stornaway, Isle of Lewis.
Emigrated from Scotland
to America c1772. Father
of Duncan
(BAF)

173

McKAY ALEXANDER
Emigrated from Scotland
to Canada. Received a
land grant in
Charlottenburg, St Raphael,
Quebec, 23 November 1787.
(PAO)

McKAY ALEXANDER
Born c1785. Tailor.
Emigrated from Scotland,
with wife, to Canada.
Settled at Roger's Hill,
Pictou, Nova Scotia,
during 1815.
(PANS/RG1)

McKAY ALEXANDER
Born c1775. Labourer.
Emigrated from Scotland,
with wife and five
children, to Canada.
Settled on West River,
Pictou, Nova Scotia,
during 1815.
(PANS/RG1)

McKAY ALEXANDER
Born c1785. Emigrated
from Scotland, with wife
and children Rachael 8,
William 6, John 4, Thomas
3, and Mary 4 months, to
Canada. Received a land
grant in Halifax, Nova
Scotia, during 1815.
(PANS/RG20)

McKAY ALEXANDER
Born c1788. Emigrated,
with wife, to Canada.
Received a land grant in
Halifax, Nova Scotia,
during 1815.
(PANS/RG20)

McKAY ALICE
Born c1755. Widow.
Emigrated from Scotland,
with five children, to
Canada. Settled at
Harbourmouth, Pictou,
Nova Scotia, in 1815.
(PANS/RG1)

McKAY ALLAN
Born c1816. Rhum,
Inverness-shire.
Emigrated from Leith,
Midlothian, to Port
Hawkesbury, Cape Breton
Island, on the St Lawrence
of Newcastle, master J.Cram,
during 1828.
(PANS/M6-100)

McKAY ANN
Born c1795. Servant.
Emigrated from Scotland
to Canada. Settled in
Pictou Town, Nova Scotia,
during 1815.
(PANS/RG1)

McKAY ANN
Born c1788. Rhum,
Inverness-shire.
Emigrated from Scotland,
with Duncan 20, Mary 25,
Neil 18, to Canada. From
Leith, Midlothian, to
Port Hawkesbury, Cape
Breton Island, on the
St Lawrence of Newcastle,
master J. Cram, in 1828.
(PANS/M6-100)

McKAY CATHERINE
Born c1745. Widow.
Emigrated from Scotland
to Canada. Settled at
Harbourmouth, Pictou,
Nova Scotia, in 1815.
(PANS/RG1)

McKAY CATHERINE
Born c1750. Emigrated
from Scotland to
Canada. Settled on
Fisher's Grant, Pictou,
Nova Scotia, in 1815.
(PANS/RG1)

McKAY CATHARINE
Born in 1763. Emigrated
from Scotland to Canada.
Settled on Fisher's
Grant, Pictou, Nova
Scotia, in 1815.
(PANS/RG1)

McKAY CATHERINE
Rhum, Inverness-shire.
Emigrated from Leith,
Midlothian, to Port
Hawkesbury, Cape Breton
Island, on the
St Lawrence of Newcastle,
master J. Cram, in 1828.
(PANS/RM6-100)

McKAY CHRISTIAN
Born c1791. Emigrated
from Scotland to Canada.
Settled on Fisher's Grant,
Pictou, Nova Scotia, 1815.
(PANS/RG1)

McKAY DAVID
Emigrated from Scotland
to Canada on the George
Canning in June 1821.
Received a land grant in
Dalhousie, Upper Canada,
on 2 July 1821.
(PAO)

McKAY DONALD
Born c1753. Labourer.
Emigrated from Scotland,
with wife and a child, to
Canada. Settled at
Roger's Hill, Pictou,
Nova Scotia, in 1815.
(PANS/RG1)

McKAY DONALD sr
Emigrated from Sutherland,
with family of six, to
Nova Scotia on the brig
Prince William during 1815.
Received a land grant in
Pictou, Nova Scotia.
(PANS/RG20)

McKAY DONALD jr
Emigrated from Sutherland,
with family of three, to
Nova Scotia on the brig
Prince William during
September 1815. Received
a land grant in Pictou,
Nova Scotia.
(PANS/RG20)

McKAY DONALD
Yeoman. Emigrated from
Scotland to Canada.
Received a land grant in
Thorak, Home, Upper Canada,
8 March 1826.
(PAO)

McKAY DONALD
Born c1763 Rhum,Inver-
ness-shire. Emigrated
from Leith, Midlothian, to
Port Hawkesbury, Cape Breton
Island, on the St Lawrence
of Newcastle, master J.Cram,
during 1828.
(PANS/M6-100)

McKAY FINLEY
Emigrated from Scotland
to America before 1756.
Labourer in Virginia.
(OD)

MacKAY HUGH
Emigrated from Scotland
to Georgia. Settled in
Josephstown, Georgia, in
1735. Possibly the
Adjutant Hugh MacKay who
signed a treaty with the
Creek Indians on
11 August 1739.
(HGP)

MacKAY HUGH
Glasgow. Applied to
settle in Canada on
25 February 1815.
(SRO/RH9)

McKAY HUGH
Emigrated from Sutherland,
with his family of six, to
Nova Scotia on the brig
Prince William in September
1815. Received a land grant
in Pictou, Nova Scotia.
(PANS/RG20)

McKAY HUGH
Emigrated from Sutherland,
with his family of three,
to Nova Scotia on the brig
Prince William in September
1815. Received a land
grant in Pictou, Nova
Scotia.
(PANS/RG20)

McKAY HUGH
Born c1793. Weaver.
Emigrated from Scotland
to Canada. Settled on
Fisher's Grant, Pictou,
Nova Scotia, in 1815.
(PANS/RG1)

McKAY HUGH
Emigrated from Scotland,
with his wife, to Canada
on the George Canning in
June 1821. Received a
land grant in Dalhousie,
Upper Canada, 2 July 1821.
(PAO)

MacKAY JAMES
Emigrated from Scotland
to America. Settled in
Darien, Georgia, c1739.
(HGP)

MacKAY JAMES
Educated at University
of Edinburgh. Medical
practitioner in
St Vincent. Graduated M.D.
at King's College,
Aberdeen, 8 October 1789.
(KCA)

McKAY JAMES
Emigrated from Sutherland,
with his family of three,
to Nova Scotia on the brig
Prince William in September
1815. Received a land grant
in Pictou, Nova Scotia.
(PANS/RG20)

McKAY JAMES
Born c1797. Labourer.
Emigrated from Scotland
to Canada. Settled on
Fisher's Grant, Pictou,
Nova Scotia, in 1815.
(PANS/RG1)

McKAY JAMES
Emigrated from Scotland,
with wife, son and daughter,
to Canada. Received a land
grant in Beckwith, Upper
Canada, 29 December 1819.
(PAO)

McKAY JEAN
Born c1797. Servant.
Emigrated from Scotland
to Canada. Settled in
Pictou Town, Nova Scotia,
in 1815.
(PANS/RG1)

MacKAY JOHN
Emigrated from Scotland
to Georgia. Settled in
Josephstown, Georgia,
in 1735.
(HGP)

MacKAY of STRATHY JOHN
Emigrated from Inverness
to Georgia in October
1735 on the Prince of
Wales. Landed during
January 1736.
(HGP)

McKAY JOHN
Emigrated from Scotland
to Nova Scotia. Received
a land grant on East River
Pictou, Nova Scotia, on
8 December 1813.
(PANS/RG20)

MacKAY JOHN
Glasgow. Applied to
settle in Canada on
25 February 1815.
(SRO/RH9)

McKAY JOHN
Born c1790. Emigrated
from Scotland to
Canada. Received a
land grant in Halifax,
Nova Scotia, in 1815.
(PANS/RG20)

McKAY JOHN
Son of W. McKay.
Emigrated from Scotland
to Canada. Received a
land grant on East River,
Pictou, Nova Scotia, on
10 March 1815.
(PANS/RG20)

McKAY JOHN
Born c1795. Labourer.
Emigrated from Scotland
to Canada. Settled on
Fisher's Grant, Pictou,
Nova Scotia, in 1815.
(PANS/RG1)

McKAY JOHN
Born c1755. Catechist.
Emigrated from Scotland,
with wife and eight
children, to Canada.
Settled on Fisher's Grant,
Pictou, Nova Scotia, in
1815.
(PANS/RG1)

McKAY JOHN
Born c1783. Labourer.
Emigrated from Scotland,
with wife and six children,
to Canada. Settled on
Fisher's Grant, Pictou,
Nova Scotia, in 1815.
(PANS/RG1)

MacKAY JOHN
Emigrated from Sutherland,
with family of eight, to
Nova Scotia on the brig
Prince William during
September 1815. Received
a land grant in Pictou,
Nova Scotia.
(PANS/RG20)

McKAY JOHN
Emigrated from Sutherland,
with family of nine, to
Nova Scotia on the brig
Prince William during
September 1815.
Received a land grant in
Pictou, Nova Scotia.
(PANS/RG20)

McKAY JOHN
Emigrated from Sutherland,
with family of eight, to
Nova Scotia on the brig
Prince William during
September 1815.
Received a land grant in
Pictou, Nova Scotia.
(PANS/RG20)

McKAY JOHN
Born c1790. Labourer.
Emigrated from Scotland,
with his wife, to Canada.
Settled on West River,
Pictou, Nova Scotia, in
1815.
(PANS/RG1)

McKAY JOHN
Born c1785. Labourer.
Emigrated from Scotland,
with wife and child, to
Canada. Settled on Moole
River, Pictou, Nova Scotia,
in 1815.
(PANS/RG1)

McKAY JOHN
Born c1780. Labourer.
Emigrated from Scotland,
with wife and six
children, to Canada.
Settled in Lower Settle-
ment, Pictou, Nova Scotia,
in 1815.
(PANS/RG1)

McKAY JOHN
Emigrated from Sutherland,
with family of ten, to
Nova Scotia on the brig
Prince William during
September 1815. Received
a land grant in Pictou,
Nova Scotia.
(PANS/RG20)

McKAY JOHN
Born in Scotland. Former
lieutenant in the Glen-
garry Fencibles. Military
settler. Received land
grants in Upper Canada on
7 August 1816, and in
Drummond, Upper Canada,
on 30 June 1817.
(PAO)

McKAY JOHN
Born c1809. Rhum, Inver-
ness-shire. Emigrated
from Leith, Midlothian,
to Port Hawkesbury, Cape
Breton Island, during 1828
on the St Lawrence of
Newcastle, master J.Cram.
(PANS/M6-100)

McKAY KENNETH
Born c1770. Shoemaker.
Emigrated from Scotland,
with his wife and five
children, to Canada.
Settled on Fisher's Grant,
Pictou, Nova Scotia, 1815.
(PANS/RG1)

McKAY LACHLAN
Born c1800. Rhum, Inver-
ness-shire. Emigrated
from Leith, Midlothian,
to Port Hawkesbury, Cape
Breton Island on the
St Lawrence of Newcastle,
master J.Cram, in 1828.
(PANS/M6-100)

McKAY MARGARET
Born c1785. Emigrated
from Scotland to Canada.
Settled on Moole River,
Pictou, Nova Scotia, in
1815.
(PANS/RG1)

McKAY MARGARET
Born c1795. Emigrated
from Scotland to Canada.
Settled on Fisher's Grant,
Pictou, Nova Scotia, 1815.
(PANS/RG1)

McKAY NEIL
Born c1768. Rhum, Inver-
ness-shire. Emigrated
from Leith, Midlothian,
to Port Hawkesbury, Cape
Breton Island, on the
St Lawrence of Newcastle,
master J.Cram, with
wife Mary, 57, and children
Mary, 35, Donald, 33, Flory,
30, John, 26, Christina, 21,
Jessie, 33, Ann (?) etc.,
during 1828.
(PANS/M6-100)

McKAY PETER
Born c1793. Rhum, Inver-
ness-shire. Emigrated
from Leith, Midlothian,
to Port Hawkesbury, Cape
Breton Island, on the
St Lawrence of Newcastle,
master J.Cram, with wife
Flora, 30, children
Lachlan, 5, Donald, 3,
Angus, 2, and John, an
infant, during 1828.
(PANS/M6-100)

McKAY ROBERT
Glasgow. Merchant in
Virginia c1761.
(SRA.B10.15.6729)

MacKAY ROBERT
Glasgow. Applied to
settle in Canada on
25 February 1815.
(SRO/RH9)

McKAY ROBERT
Emigrated from Sutherland,
with his family of four,
to Nova Scotia on the brig
Prince William in September
1815. Received a land
grant in Pictou, Nova Scotia.
(PANS/RG20)

McKAY ROBERT
Born c1780. Labourer.
Emigrated from Scotland,
with his wife and three
children, to Canada.
Settled in Lower Settle-
ment, Pictou, Nova Scotia,
in 1815.
(PANS/RG1)

McKAY SIMON
  Emigrated from Scotland
  to Nova Scotia.
  Received a land grant
  on East River, Pictou,
  Nova Scotia, on
  8 December 1813.
  (PANS/RG20)

McKAY WILLIAM
  Emigrated from Scotland
  to Canada. Labourer.
  Born c1787. Settled on
  West River, Pictou,
  Nova Scotia, in 1815.
  (PANS/RG1)

McKAY WILLIAM
  Emigrated from Sutherland,
  with his family of five,
  to Nova Scotia on the brig
  Prince William during
  September 1815. Received
  a land grant in Pictou,
  Nova Scotia.
  (PANS/RG20)

McKAY WILLIAM
  Born c1761. Labourer.
  Emigrated from Scotland,
  with his wife and three
  children, to Canada.
  Settled at Roger's Hill,
  Pictou, Nova Scotia, in
  1815.
  (PANS/RG1)

McKAY WILLIAM
  Born c1789. Clerk.
  Emigrated from Scotland
  to Canada. Settled in
  Pictou Town, Nova Scotia,
  during 1815.
  (PANS/RG1)

McKAY WILLIAM
  Emigrated from Scotland
  to America. Settled in
  Stirling, Ohio, in 1824.
  (SHR)

McKAY Widow
  Born c1785. Emigrated from
  Scotland, with four girls
  and a boy aged 12, to
  Canada. Received a land
  grant in Halifax, Nova
  Scotia, in 1815.
  (PANS/RG20)

McKAY Widow
  Emigrated from Sutherland,
  with her family of five,
  to Nova Scotia on the brig
  Prince William during
  September 1815. Received
  a land grant in Pictou,
  Nova Scotia.
  (PANS/RG20)

McKAY ...
  Born c1775. Labourer.
  Emigrated from Scotland,
  with his wife and seven
  children, to Canada.
  Settled on Fisher's Grant,
  Pictou, Nova Scotia, 1815.
  (PANS/RG1)

McKEAN ANDREW
  Emigrated from Scotland,
  with his wife, son and
  daughter, to Canada on the
  George Canning in June 1821.
  Received a land grant in
  Ramsay, Upper Canada, on
  16 July 1821.
  (PAO)

McKECHNIE ARCHIBALD
Emigrated from Greenock,
Renfrewshire, with his
wife, three sons and
two daughters, to Canada
on the David of London
during May 1821.
Received a land grant in
Ramsay, Upper Canada on
17 August 1821.
(PAO)

McKEE JOHN
Emigrated from Scotland,
with wife, son and three
daughters, to Canada on
the Caledonian 10 July
1816. Received a land
grant in Upper Canada on
24 September 1816.
(PAO)

McKEE THOMAS
Born in Scotland.
Received a land grant
in Beckwith, Upper Canada,
on 30 May 1821.
(PAO)

MacKELL JAMES
Royalist soldier captured
at Worcester. Transported
from Gravesend, Kent, to
Boston, New England, on
the John and Sarah, master
John Greene, 13 May 1652.
(NER)

McKELSON JOHN
Indentured servant
imported from Scotland,
with his wife Margaret
Sturrock, to East New
Jersey in October 1684
by Thomas Gordon.
(EJD/A)

McKENDRICK JAMES
Emigrated from Scotland,
with his wife, to
Canada on the Commerce.
Received a land grant in
Dalhousie, Upper Canada,
on 3 September 1821.
(PAO)

MacKENNIE ANDREW
Indentured servant
imported from Scotland
to East New Jersey by
David Mudie in November
1684.
(EJD/A196)

McKENNON JOSEPH D.
Born in Skye, Inverness-
shire, during 1734.
Emigrated from Scotland
to America. Settled in
Liverpool, Columbiana
County, Ohio. Soldier
during the American
Revolution. Died on
22 June 1809.
(ORIII)

MacKENTHOW(?) JOHN
Royalist soldier captured
at Worcester. Transported
from Gravesend, Kent, to
Boston, New England, on
the John and Sarah, master
John Greene, 13 May 1652.
(NER)

MacKENZIE Col ALEXANDER
Son of Sir Alexander
MacKenzie of Broomhill,
Kincardine. Emigrated
from Scotland to America.
Settled in Virginia c1700.
(HGM)

MacKENZIE ALEXANDER
A Scottish doctor.   Settled
in Virginia c1740.
(SA)

MacKENZIE ALEXANDER
Seventh son of Simon
MacKenzie of Allangrange,
and Isabel MacKenzie.
Physician in Jamaica.
Died during 1780.
(HGM)

McKENZIE ALEXANDER
Born in Scotland in 1769.
Forester at Tulloch Castle,
near Dingwall, Ross and
Cromarty. Emigrated from
Scotland to Nova Scotia.
Died in 1819.
(SG)

McKENZIE ALEXANDER
Emigrated from Scotland
to Canada on the
Hibernia 20 September
1816. Received a land
grant in Beckwith,
Upper Canada, on
31 March 1817.
(PAO)

McKENZIE ALEXANDER
Yeoman. Emigrated from
Scotland to Canada.
Received a land grant
in Thorak, Home, Upper
Canada, 8 March 1826.
(PAO)

McKENZIE ANDREW
Born c1780. Labourer.
Emigrated from Scotland,
with his wife and four
children, to Canada.
Settled at Scottshill,
Pictou, Nova Scotia, 1815.
(PANS/RG1)

McKENZIE ANGUS
Emigrated from Scotland
to Canada on the Green-
field on 23 August 1816.
Received a land grant in
Drummond, Upper Canada, on
30 November 1816.
(PAO)

McKENZIE CHARLES
Born in Scotland in 1774.
North West Company
employee from 1803 to 1821.
Hudson Bay Company employee
from 1821 to 1854. Died
at Red River, Canada, on
3 March 1855.
(HBRS)

MacKENZIE COLQUHOUN
Born c1786, son of Alexander
MacKenzie, 1739-1825,
tenant farmer in East Duthill
Deuthulph, Carrbridge,
Inverness-shire, and Anne
MacQueen, 1758-1845. Died
in Quebec on 30 August 1828.
(Carrbridge GS)

McKENZIE DAVID
Dundee, Angus. Actor in
New York c1810. Died in
Philadelphia, Pennsylvania,
during 1811.
(TSA)

McKENZIE DONALD
Born c1791. Labourer.
Emigrated from Scotland
to Canada. Settled at
Little Harbour, Pictou,
Nova Scotia, in 1815.
(PANS/RG1)

McKENZIE DONALD
Born in Scotland c1787.
Former army lieutenant.
Hudson Bay Company
employee from 1818 to
1850.
(HBRS)

McKENZIE DUNCAN
Born in Scotland. Former
soldier in the Royal
Artillery. Military
settler. Wife and daughter.
Received a land grant in
Burgess, Upper Canada, on
18 August 1817.
(PAO)

McKENZIE FLORY
Born c1810. Rhum, Inver-
ness-shire. Emigrated
from Leith, Midlothian,
to Port Hawkesbury, Cape
Breton Island, on the
St Lawrence of Newcastle,
master J. Cram, in 1828.
(PANS/M6-100)

MacKENZIE GEORGE
Scottish merchant in
Bridgetwon, Barbados,
c1699.
(DP)

MacKENZIE GEORGE
Apprentice physician to
Dr Donaldson. Graduated
M.D. at Marischal College,
Aberdeen, in 1767.
Physician in the West Indies.
Member of the Royal College
of Surgeons in 1801.
(MCA)

MacKENZIE HECTOR
A Scottish surgeon.
Died off Cape St Antonio
on passage from Darien
to New York during
August 1699.
(DP)

MacKENZIE HECTOR AENEAS
Son of Charles MacKenzie,
1774-1855, and Mary Mackay,
Ross-shire. North West
Company employee from
1803 to 1821. Hudson Bay
Company employee from
1821 to 1854. Possibly
died in Winnipeg after
1889.
(HBRS)

McKENZIE ISABELLA
Born c1797. Servant.
Emigrated from Scotland
to Canada. Settled in
Pictou Town, Nova Scotia,
during 1815.
(PANS/RG1)

McKENZIE JOHN
Scottish indentured
servant of John Laing,
Middlesex County, New
Jersey. Land grant on
17 January 1693.
(EJD/D)

McKENZIE JOHN
Emigrated from Scotland
to America, before 1755.
Weaver in Westmoreland,
County, Virginia.
(OD)

McKENZIE JOHN
Emigrated from Scotland
to America before 1767.
Planter in King George
County, Virginia.
(OD)

MacKENZIE JOHN
Inverness-shire.
Educated at King's
College, Aberdeen,
graduated M.A. on
26 April 1813.
Minister in Williamstown,
Canada.
(KCA)

McKENZIE JOHN
Brother(?) of Alexander
McKenzie in Edinburgh.
Former Caithness Volunteer.
Settled in St Stephens,
New Providence pre 1815.
(SRO/GD136)

McKENZIE JOHN
Born c1786. Carpenter.
Emigrated from Scotland
to Canada. Settled at
Mount Tom, Pictou, Nova
Scotia, in 1815.
(PANS/RG1)

McKENZIE JOHN
Born c1790. Labourer.
Emigrated from Scotland,
with wife and child, to
Canada. Settled at Little
Harbour, Pictou, Nova
Scotia, in 1815.
(PANS/RG1)

McKENZIE JOHN
Born c1790. Labourer.
Emigrated from Scotland,
with wife and child, to
Canada. Settled in
Lower Settlement,
Pictou, Nova Scotia, in
1815.
(PANS/RG1)

McKENZIE Rev JOHN KENNETH
Born in Stornaway, Lewis,
Inverness-shire. Emigrated
from Scotland to Nova
Scotia during 1824.
Minister in Pictou, Nova
Scotia, from 1824 to 1838.
Died in 1838.
(HPC)

McKENZIE JOHN
Born c1801 in Ross-shire.
Hudson Bay Company
employee from 1826 to
1827.
(HBRS)

McKENZIE JOHN
Born in Brahan, Ross-shire,
during 1775. Married Anne
MacDonald. Architect in
Inverness. Emigrated from
Scotland to Canada.
Settled in Glengarry County,
Upper Canada, in 1831.
(SG)

MacKENZIE KENNETH
Born in 1798, son of Alex.
MacKenzie of Hilton, Ross-
shire. Admitted to the
Society of Writers to HM
Signet in 1825. Married(1)
Ann Urquhart, 1831 (2)
Elizabeth C Jones. Died in
Canada 19 May 1874.
(WS)

McKENZIE PETER
Born c1805 in Scotland.
Hudson Bay Company
employee from 1825 to
1852. Chief trader 1844.
Died at Moose Factory
on 31 January 1852.
(HBRS)

McKENZIE ROBERT
Born c1755. Labourer.
Emigrated from Scotland,
with his wife and two
children, to Canada.
Settled on Fisher's
Grant, Pictou, Nova
Scotia, in 1815.
(PANS/RG1)

McKENZIE ROBERT
Emigrated from Sutherland,
with his family of eleven,
to Nova Scotia on the brig
Prince William in September
1815. Received a land grant
in Pictou, Nova Scotia.
(PANS/RG20)

McKENZIE RODERICK
Born in Scotland. Formerly
in the Prince of York's
Chasseurs. Military
settler. Received a land
grant in Beckwith, Upper
Canada, 22 October 1819.
(PAO)

MacKENZIE WILLIAM
Born in 1680, son of
William MacKenzie,
Commissary of Orkney,
and Margaret Stewart.
Emigrated to New England
during 1714. Episcopalian.
(HGM)

McKENZIE WILLIAM
West Linton, Peebles-
shire. Applied to
settle in Canada on
7 March 1815.
(SRO/RH9)

McKENZIE WILLIAM
Born c1793. Tailor.
Emigrated from Scotland,
with his wife, to Canada.
Settled in Lower Settle-
ment, Pictou, Nova Scotia,
in 1815.
(PANS/RG1)

MacKENZIE ...
Argyllshire. Indentured
servant for Maryland on
4 February 1724.
(LGR)

McKERCHAR JAMES
Emigrated from Scotland,
with his wife, three sons
and two daughters, to
Canada on the George
Canning in June 1821.
Received a land grant in
Ramsay, Upper Canada, on
22 October 1821.
(PAO)

McKERCHER JOHN
Emigrated from Scotland,
with his wife and son, to
Canada on the brig
Margaret 30 August 1820.
Received a land grant in
Bathurst, Upper Canada, on
28 October 1820.
(PAO)

185

McKERACHER JOHN
Emigrated from Greenock,
Renfrewshire, to Montreal,
Quebec, on the David of
London in May 1821.
Received a land grant in
Ramsay, Upper Canada, on
1 September 1821.
(PAO)

MacKETH DAVID
Royalist soldier captured
at Worcester. Transported
from Gravesend, Kent, to
Boston, New England, on
the John and Sarah, master
John Greene, 13 May 1652.
(NER)

MACKIE ALEXANDER
GLasgow. Merchant in
Virginia c1748.
(SRA/B10.5959.6653)

MACKIE JOHN
Wigtown. Emigrated from
Scotland to America pre
1750. Merchant in
Petersburg, Virginia.
(OD)

McKIE JOHN
Born c1798, son of
Peter McKie, farmer in
Morrach, and Margaret
Rodie. Died in
Antigua on
14 November 1821.
(Whithorn GS,Wigtownshire)

McKIE PETER
Son of James McKie, 1725-
1789, Dumfries. Settled
in Philadelphia, Penn-
sylvania.
(Dumfries GS)

McKIE WILLIAM
Son of James McKie, 1725-
1789. Settled in
Philadelphia, Penn-
sylvania.
(Dumfries GS)

McKILL ROBERT
Born in 1790, son of
Deacon James McKill and
Ann Ferguson, 1771-1807.
Died in Concord, Tobago,
during 1821.
(Dumfries GS)

McKILLICAN WILLIAM
Emigrated from Scotland,
with his wife, son and two
daughters, to Canada on
the Lady of the Lake 17
September 1816. Received
a land grant in Lancaster,
Upper Canada, on 11 May 1817.
(PAO)

McKILLOP NEIL
Emigrated from Scotland
to Canada. Received a
land grant in Ramsay,
Upper Canada, on
9 April 1821.
(PAO)

McKINLAY Rev JOHN
Born in Stirlingshire.
Educated at the University
of Glasgow. Emigrated
from Scotland to Nova
Scotia during 1817.
Missionary and teacher in
Pictou, Nova Scotia from
1824 to 1850. Died on
20 October 1850.
(HPC)

McKINLEY PETER
  Emigrated from Scotland,
  with his wife, son and
  daughter, to Canada on
  the Susan of Poole
  on 3 August 1817.
  Received a land grant in
  South Gower, Upper Canada,
  on 13 November 1817.
  (PAO)

McKINNELL Captain JAMES
  Born in Wigtown during
  1762, second son of John
  McKinnell. Emigrated
  from Scotland to America.
  Merchant in Baltimore,
  Maryland, New Orleans,
  Louisiana, and
  Cincinatti, Ohio. Married
  Mrs Mary Dwyer Creagh in
  Baltimore on 21 April 1801.
  Father of Henry, William,
  Charles, Elizabeth, Maria,
  and Anna. Died on 28
  January 1843.
  (BAF)

McKINNON ANN
  Born c1768. Rhum, Inverness-shire. Emigrated
  from Leith, Midlothian,
  to Port Hawkesbury, Cape
  Breton Island, on the
  St Lawrence of Newcastle,
  master J. Cram, in 1828.
  (PANS/M6-100)

McKINNON ARCHIBALD
  Born c1800. Rhum, Inverness-shire. Emigrated
  from Leith, Midlothian,
  to Port Hawkesbury, Cape
  Breton Island, on the
  St Lawrence of Newcastle,
  master J. Cram, in 1828.
  (PANS/M6-100)

MacKINNON DANIEL
  Born during 1658, son of
  Lachlan Mor McKinnon of
  McKinnon. Physician.
  Emigrated from Scotland to
  Antigua. Married Elizabeth
  Thomas before 1696.
  Father of William, Jane,
  and Samuel. Died in
  Antigua on 26 March 1720.
  (MCFI)

McKINNON DONALD
  Emigrated from Scotland,
  with his wife, two sons,
  and daughter, to Canada
  on the George Canning in
  June 1821. Received a
  land grant in Dalhousie,
  Upper Canada, on
  15 July 1821.
  (PAO)

McKINNON DONALD
  Born c1780. Rhum, Inverness-shire. Emigrated
  from Leith, Midlothian,
  to Port Hawkesbury, Cape
  Breton Island, on the
  St Lawrence of Newcastle,
  master J. Cram, in 1828.
  with wife Catharine 50.
  (PANS/M6-100)

McKINNON DONALD
  Born c1781. Rhum, Inver-
  ness-shire. Emigrated
  from Leith, Midlothian,
  to Port Hawkesbury, Cape
  Breton Island, on the
  St Lawrence of Newcastle,
  master J. Cram, in 1828
  with his wife Margaret
  46, and children Jessie 21,
  Lachlin 20, Donald 16,
  John 13, Catharine 10,
  Angus 6, and Peter 3.
  (PANS/M6-100)

McKINNON DUNCAN
Emigrated from Scotland
to Canada on the Green-
field on 17 September
1816. Received a land
grant in Beckwith,
Upper Canada, on
31 December 1816.
(PAO)

McKINNON DUNCAN
Born c1765. Rhum, Inver-
ness-shire. Emigrated
from Leith, Midlothian,
to Port Hawkesbury, Cape
Breton Island, on the
St Lawrence of Newcastle,
master J. Cram, in 1828,
with his wife Mary 58,
and children Alexander 30,
Ann 25, Lachlin 24, Ann 20,
Catharine 15, and Donald 19.
(PANS/M6-100)

McKINNON FLORY
Born c1788. Rhum, Inver-
ness-shire. Emigrated from
Leith, Midlothian, to Port
Hawkesbury, Cape Breton
Island, on the St Lawrence
of Newcastle, master J.Cram,
during 1828.
(PANS/M6-100)

MacKINNON JOHN
Eldest son of John MacKinnon
and Margaret McKenzie.
Officer in the 42nd(Black
Watch)Regiment and later
in the 77th(Montgomery
Highlanders)Regiment, from
1758 to 1763. Settled in
Yarmouth, Nova Scotia, in
1767. Father of John,
Martin, Norman and James.
Died on 7 January 1774.
Buried at Chebogue
cemetery, Nova Scotia.
(MCFI)

McKINNON JOHN jr
Emigrated from Scotland
to Canada on the Green-
field on 23 August 1816.
Received a land grant in
Drummond, Upper Canada,
on 30 November 1816.
(PAO)

McKINNON JOHN sr
Emigrated from Scotland,
with his son and two
daughters, to Canada on
the George Canning in
June 1821. Received a
land grant in Dalhousie,
Upper Canada, on
15 July 1821.
(PAO)

McKINNON JOHN jr
Emigrated from Scotland
to Canada on the George
Canning in June 1821.
Received a land grant in
Dalhousie, Upper Canada,
on 15 July 1821.
(PAO)

McKINNON JOHN
Born c1780. Rhum, Inver-
ness-shire. Emigrated
from Leith, Midlothian,
to Port Hawkesbury, Cape
Breton Island, on the
St Lawrence of Newcastle,
master J. Cram in 1828,
with his wife Ann 45,and
children Bell 20, Donald
18, Mary 15, etc.
(PANS/M6-100)

McKINNON JOHN
Born c1798. Rhum, Inver-
ness-shire. Emigrated
from Leith, Midlothian,
to Port Hawkesbury, Cape
Breton Island, on the
St Lawrence of Newcastle,
master J. Cram, in 1828.
(PANS/M6-100)

McKINNON LACHLIN
Born c1788. Rhum, Inver-
ness-shire. Emigrated
from Leith, Midlothian,
to Port Hawkesbury, Cape
Breton Island, on the
St Lawrence of Newcastle,
master J. Cram, in 1828
with his wife Marion 35,
and children Lachlin 12,
Catharine 10, Archibald
8, Donald 6, Mary - an
infant.
(PANS/M6-100)

McKINNON LACHLIN(?)
Born c1812. Rhum, Inver-
ness-shire. Emigrated
from Leith, Midlothian,
to Port Hawkesbury, Capr
Breton Island, on the
St Lawrence of Newcastle,
master J. Cram, with
Ann 12, and Allan 8.
(PANS/M6-100)

McKINNON MALCOLM(?)
Born c1740. Rhum, Inver-
ness-shire. Emigrated
from Leith, Midlothian,
to Port Hawkesbury, Cape
Breton Island, on the
St Lawrence of Newcastle,
master J. Cram, in 1828.
(PANS/M6-100)

McKINNON MALCOLM
Born c1783. Rhum, Inver-
ness-shire. Emigrated
from Leith, Midlothian,
to Port Hawkesbury, Cape
Breton Island, on the
St Lawrence of Newcastle,
master J. Cram, in 1828
with children Christina 18,
Catharine 15, John 13,
Marian 10, Peggy 6, Flory
4 and Bell 2.
(PANS/M6-100)

McKINNON MARGARET
Born c1768. Rhum, Inver-
ness-shire. Emigrated
from Leith, Midlothian,
to Port Hawkesbury, Cape
Breton Island, on the
St Lawrence of Newcastle,
master J. Cram, in 1828
with children Flory 30
and Catharine 28.
(PANS/M6-100)

McKINNON MARGARET
Born c1768. Rhum, Inver-
ness-shire. Emigrated
from Leith, Midlothian,
to Port Hawkesbury, Cape
Breton Island, on the
St Lawrence of Newcastle,
master J. Cram, in 1828
with children(?)
Alexander 28, Alyson 28,
Jessie 26, John(?) 21,
and Catharine 16.
(PANS/M6-100)

McKINNON MARGARET
Born c1790. Rhum, Inver-
ness-shire. Emigrated
from Leith, Midlothian,
to Port Hawkesbury, Cape
Breton Island, on the
St Lawrence of Newcastle,
master J. Cram, in 1828.
(PANS/M6-100)

McKINNON MARY
Born c1802. Rhum, Inver-
ness-shire. Emigrated
from Leith, Midlothian,
to Port Hawkesbury, Cape
Breton Island, on the
St Lawrence of Newcastle,
master J. Cram, in 1828
with children Ann 5,
John 3, and Flory - an
infant.
(PANS/M6-100)

McKINNON PEGGY
Born c1808. Rhum, Inver-
ness-shire. Emigrated
from Leith, Midlothian,
to Port Hawkesbury, Cape
Breton Island, on the
St Lawrence of Newcastle,
master J. Cram, in 1828
with(?) Flory 17, Mary 13,
Catharine 15, and
Archibald 10.
(PANS/M6-100)

McKINNON RANDAL
Emigrated from Scotland
to Canada on the Green-
field on 17 September
1816. Received a land
grant in Beckwith,
Upper Canada, on
31 December 1816.
(PAO)

MacKINNON RONALD
Born c1735, second son
of John MacKinnon of
Mishinish, and Margaret
McKenzie. Officer in the
77th(Montgomery Highlanders)
Regiment, from 1757 to 1763.
Married Letitia Piccott.
Settled in Nova Scotia.
Collector of Customs and
Excise. Captain in the 84th
(Royal Highland Emigrants)
Regiment at Fort Edward,
Windsor, Halifax, Nova Scotia,
from 1776 to 1783. Died
during 1805.
(MCFI)

MacINTOSH AENEAS
Brother of the laird of
MacIntosh, signed a
treaty with the Creek
Indians in Georgia on
11 August 1739.
(HGP)

MacINTOSH JOHN
Son of John MacIntosh
of Holmes. Possibly
from Inverness. Signed
a treaty with the Creek
Indians in Georgia on
11 August 1739.
(HGP)

MacINTOSH PETER
Sailor. Died of fever on
the voyage from Scotland
to Darien 23 October 1698.
(NLS)

McINTOSH WILLIAM
Yeoman. Emigrated from
Scotland to Canada.
Received a land grant in
Thorak, Home, Upper Canada,
on 8 March 1826.
(PAO)

McINTYRE JOHN
Yeoman. Emigrated from
Scotland to Canada.
Received a land grant in
Eldon, Newcastle, Upper
Canada, on 8 March 1826.
(PAO)

McLACHLAN JAMES
Eldest son of John McLachlan,
wright in Glasgow. Journey-
man tailor. Emigrated from
Scotland to America in 1756.
(SRA/B10.15.6682)

McLACHLEN JOHN
Emigrated from Scotland,
with his wife, three sons
and a daughter, to
Canada, on the Earl of
Buckingham in June 1821.
Received a land grant in
Ramsay, Upper Canada, on
28 July 1821.
(PAO)

McLACHLIN JOHN
Emigrated from Scotland
to Canada on the Brock.
Received a land grant
in Lanark, Upper Canada,
on 23 October 1821.
(PAO)

MacLAUGHLIN STEWART
Born c1802, son of John
MacLaughlan, 1758-1824,
mason in Perth, and
Margaret Kidd, 1771-1842.
Died in New York on
18 June 1855.
(Perth Greyfriars GS)

McLAUGHLAN WILLIAM
Born c1793. Married (1)
Sarah McFarlane,1788-
1837, (2) Margaret
Neilson, 1800-1882.
Father of John, James,
William and Robert.
Died in Galt, Upper
Canada, on 11 March 1882.
(Buchlyvie Stirling GS)

McLAUGHLIN ...
Emigrated from Greenock,
Renfrewshire, to New York,
with his family of eight,
on the George York in 1810.
Settled in Washington
township, Columbia County,
Ohio.
(SHR)

MacLAREN ALEXANDER
Born c1707. Cook and
butcher. Muthill, Perth-
shire. Indentured
servant for Jamaica on
7 August 1731.
(LGR)

McLAREN ARCHIBALD
Emigrated from Scotland,
to Canada on the Fancy
18 August 1816.
Received a land grant in
Drummond, Upper Canada,
on 9 December 1816.
(PAO)

MacLAREN CHRISTIAN
Perthshire(?). Emigrated
from Greenock, Renfrew-
shire, to Montreal,
Quebec, on the brig
Niagara, Hamilton, in
1825. Settled in McNab,
Bathurst, Upper Canada,
during 1825.
(SG)

McLAREN COLIN
Emigrated from Scotland
to Canada. Received a
land grant in Beckwith,
Upper Canada, on
2 August 1820.
(PAO)

McLAREN DONALD
Emigrated from Scotland,
with his wife, to Canada
on the Prompt 8 July 1817.
Received a land grant in
Lancaster, Upper Canada,
on 28 November 1817.
(PAO)

MacLAREN DONALD
Perthshire(?) Emigrated
from Greenock to Montreal
on the brig Niagara,
Hamilton, in 1825. Settled
in McNab, Bathurst, Upper
Canada, during 1825.
(SG)

191

McLAREN DUNCAN
Emigrated from Scotland
to Canada in the Prompt
8 July 1817. Received
a land grant in Beckwith,
Upper Canada, on
6 October 1817.
(PAO)

McLAREN DUNCAN
Born in Scotland.
Received a land grant in
Beckwith, Upper Canada,
on 30 November 1820.
(PAO)

McLAREN D.
Born in Scotland.
Received a land grant in
Marlborough, Upper Canada,
on 30 November 1821.
(PAO)

McLAURIN JAMES
Strathyre. Emigrated
from Scotland, with his
wife(?) Catharine, to
Canada on the brig
Niagara, Hamilton, 1825.
Settled in McNab, Upper
Canada, in 1825.
(SG)

McLAREN JANET
Perthshire(?) Emigrated
from Greenock, Renfrew-
shire to Montreal,
Quebec, on the brig
Niagara, Hamilton, in
1825. Settled in
McNab, Bathurst,
Upper Canada, in 1825.
(SG)

McLAREN JOHN
Emigrated from Scotland,
with his wife, three sons
and a daughter, to
Canada on the Caledonian
10 July 1816. Received a
land grant in Bathurst,
Upper Canada, on
24 September 1816.
(PAO)

McLAREN JOHN
Emigrated from Scotland,
with his wife, to Canada
on the Lady of the Lake
7 September 1816.
Received a land grant in
Drummond, Upper Canada,
on 9 December 1816.
(PAO)

McLAREN JOHN
Emigrated from Scotland,
with his wife and daughter,
to Canada on the Curlew
10 September 1818.
Received a land grant in
Drummond, Upper Canada,
on 20 October 1818.
(PAO)

McLAREN JOHN
Emigrated from Scotland,
with his wife, three sons
and two daughters, to
Canada on the Earl of
Buckingham in June 1821.
Received a land grant in
Lanark, Upper Canada, on
16 July 1821.
(PAO)

MacLAREN MALCOLM
Perthshire(?) Emigrated
from Scotland to Canada
via Greenock, Renfrewshire,
on the brig Niagara,
Hamilton, in 1825, with
his wife Janet Fisher, and
children Margaret, Mary,
Janet, John, Catharine,
Annie, Peter, Helen, Mary(?),
Christian, Robert and Peter.
Probably settled in McNab,
Bathurst, Upper Canada,1825.
(SG)

MacLAREN MARY
Perthshire(?) Emigrated
from Greenock, Renfrew-
shire, to Montreal, Quebec,
on the brig Niagara,
Hamilton, in 1825. Settled
in McNab, Bathurst, Upper
Canada, in 1825.
(SG)

McLAREN PETER
Emigrated from Scotland,
with his wife, to Canada
on the Prompt 8 July 1817.
Received a land grant in
Lancaster, Upper Canada,
on 28 November 1817.
(PAO)

McLAREN PETER
Emigrated from Scotland,
with his wife, three sons
and four daughters, to
Canada on the Brock in
1820. Received a land
grant in Lanark, Upper
Canada, 21 October 1821.
(PAO)

McLAREN ROBERT
Emigrated from Greenock,
Renfrewshire to Canada
with his wife, two sons
and two daughters, on the
George Canning in May 1821.
Received a land grant in
Ramsay, Upper Canada, on
3 September 1821.
(PAO)

McLAREN ROBERT
Miekyed(?), Perthshire(?)
Emigrated from Greenock,
Renfrewshire, to Montreal,
Quebec, on the brig
Niagara, Hamilton, in 1825.
Settled in McNab, Bathurst,
Upper Canada, in 1825.
(SG)

McLAREN THOMAS
Emigrated from Greenock,
Renfrewshire, to Montreal,
Quebec, with his wife and
two daughters, on the
George Canning in May 1821.
Received a land grant in
Ramsay, Upper Canada, on
4 October 1821.
(PAO)

MacLAY ARCHIBALD
Born at Killearn, Stirling-
shire, during 1778.
Emigrated from Scotland to
New York in 1805. Minister
in New York. President
of the American Bible Union.
Died in 1860.
(TSA)

McLEAN .....
A Scottish soldier. Settled
at Murray Bay or Mount
Murray, Quebec, after the
Siege of Quebec in 1762.
(PRSC/X)

McLEAN ALEXANDER
Son of Charles McLean
of Giurdal. Emigrated
from Scotland to Cape
Breton Island in 1826.
(CG)

McLEAN ALLAN
Son of Charles McLean of
Giurdal. Emigrated from
Scotland to Cape Breton
Island during 1826.
(CG)

McLEAN ALEXANDER
Born c1802. Rhum, Inver-
ness-shire. Emigrated
from Leith, Midlothian,
to Port Hawkesbury, Cape
Breton Island, in 1828
on the St Lawrence of
Newcastle, J. Cram.
(PANS/M6-100)

McLEAN ALLAN
Born c1770. Rhum, Inver-
ness-shire. Emigrated
from Leith, Midlothian,
to Port Hawkesbury, Cape
Breton Island, on the
St Lawrence of Newcastle,
master J. Cram, in 1828,
with wife Christian 42,
and children John 13,
Malcolm 11, and Flory 9.
(PANS/M6-100)

MacLEAN ALLAN
Son of Allan MacLean of
Killunaig, and Isabel
Campbell. Planter in
Jamaica. Died in 1754.
(CG)

MacLEAN ARCHIBALD
Born in 1758 son of Hector
MacLean of Torranbeg, and
Julia MacLean. Captain in
the New York Volunteers.
Wounded at the Battle of
Eutaw Spring 8 September
1781. Settled at Nashwaak
River, New Brunswick.
Politician. Married (1)
Miss French. Father of
Allan, Salome, etc. (2)
Susan Drummond. Father of
Archibald and John. Died
during 1829.
(CG)

McLEAN or McLANE ALLAN
Born in Coll, Argyllshire,
during 1719. Emigrated
from Scotland to America
in 1740. Married Jane
Erwin, Falls of Schuylkill,
Pennsylvania. Father of
Allan. Died in 1776.
(BAF)

MacLEAN ALLAN
Born at Kilbride, Coll,
Argyllshire, on 1 August
1715, fourth son of Allan
MacLean of Grishipol.
Emigrated from Scotland to
America in 1740. Merchant
in Hartford, Connecticut.
Married Mary Loomis in 1744.
Father of Mary, Alexander,
Jabez, Susanna. British
officer c1760. Farmer at
Vernon c1763. Died 1786.
(CG)

McLEAN ARCHIBALD
Old Kilpatrick, Dunbartonshire. Applied to settle
in Canada on 3 March 1815.
(SRO/RH9)

McLEAN CATHARINE
Born c1795. Rhum, Inver-
ness-shire. Emigrated
from Leith, Midlothian,
to Port Hawkesbury, Cape
Breton Island, in 1828,
on the St Lawrence of
Newcastle, master J.Cram.
(PANS/M6-100)

McLEAN CHARLES
Emigrated from Scotland
to Canada on the Brock
in 1820. Settled in
Lanark, Upper Canada, on
23 October 1821.
(PAO)

McLEAN CHARLES
Emigrated from Scotland,
with his wife and son, to
Canada on the David of
London in June 1821.
Received a land grant in
Dalhousie, Upper Canada,
on 1 September 1821.
(PAO)

McLEAN CHARLES
Born c1792. Rhum, Inver-
ness-shire. Emigrated
from Leith, Midlothian,
to Port Hawkesbury, Cape
Breton Island, in 1828,
on the St Lawrence of
Newcastle, master J.Cram.
(PANS/M6-100)

MacLANE DANIEL
Born in Scotland c1726.
Emigrated from Scotland
to America. Settled in
Winchester, Virginia.
(OD)

MacLEAN DAVID
Son of Alexander MacLean
of Loch Gorm, and ...
McBean. Soldier in the
73rd(McLeod Highlanders)
Regiment. Settled in
Pictou, Nova Scotia, in
1784. Married Isabel
Fraser. Father of
Alexander, John, Donald,
David, Catharine, William,
Simon, Hugh, Margaret, and
Marion.
(CG)

McLEAN DONALD
Eldest son of Hector McLean
of Killean and Janet McLean.
Officer in the 74th(Argyll
Highlanders)Regiment.
Stationed at Penobscot,
Nova Scotia, from 1779 to
1783. Settled in New
Brunswick, and later in
Danville, Vermont.
Resettled on the St Francis
River, Quebec, in 1812.
Married Susan Harvey.
Father of Catharine, Susan,
Janet, Hector, Archibald,
Eleanor, Betsy, Margaret,
and John. Died in 1825.
(CG)

MacLEAN DONALD
Son of John MacLean and
Margaret Patterson.
Emigrated from Scotland to
Newfoundland in 1812.
Settled at Judique, Cape
Breton Island, c1815.
Married Flora McDonald.
Father of John, Donald,
Allan, Mary, Donald and
Charles. Died in 1838.
(CG)

MacLEAN DONALD
Son of Alexander MacLean
of Loch Gorm, and ...
McBean. Soldier at the
Battle of Waterloo in
1815. Emigrated from
Scotland to Canada.
Settled in Pictou, Nova
Scotia.
(CG)

McLEAN DONALD
Old Kilpatrick, Dunbartonshire. Applied to settle
in Canada on 3 March 1815.
(SRO/RH9)

McLEAN DONALD
Emigrated from Greenock,
Renfrewshire, with his
wife and son, to Montreal,
Quebec, on the David of
London in May 1821.
Received a land grant in
Sherbrook, Upper Canada,
on 20 September 1821.
(PAO)

McLEAN DONALD
Emigrated from Scotland
to Canada with his wife,
four sons and two
daughters. Received a
land grant in Ramsay,
Upper Canada, on
27 November 1821.
(PAO)

MacLEAN HECTOR
Fifth son of Hugh MacLean
of Kingerloch, and Mary
Stewart. Emigrated from
Scotland to Canada in 1812.
Merchant in Pictou, Nova
Scotia. Married Harriet
Elizabeth Fraser. Father of
Murdoch, simon and two
daughters. Buried in Pictou.
(CG)

McLEAN HECTOR
Emigrated from Scotland,
with his wife, two sons
and three daughters, to
Canada on the David of
London in June 1821.
Received a land grant in
Dalhousie, Upper Canada,
on 1 September 1821.
(PAO)

MacLEAN HECTOR
Son of Charles MacLean of
Giurdal. Emigrated from
Scotland to Cape Breton
Island in 1826.
(CG)

McLEAN HECTOR
Born c1796. Rhum, Inver-
ness-shire. Emigrated
from Leith. Midlothian,
to Port Hawkesbury, Cape
Breton Island, in 1828
on the St Lawrence of
Newcastle, master J. Cram.
(PANS/M6-100)

McLEAN HUGH
Emigrated from Scotland,
with wife and four sons,
to Canada. Received a
land grant in Dalhousie,
Upper Canada, 1 September
1821.
(PAO)

McLEAN HUGH
Emigrated from Scotland,
with his wife, two sons
and three daughters, to
Canada. Received a land
grant in Sherbrook, Upper
Canada, on 7 September 1821.
(PAO)

McLEAN HUGH
Born c1779. Rhum, Inver-
ness-shire. Farmer.
Emigrated from Scotland,
with his wife Marion 45,
and children - sons aged
19, 13, and 10, and
daughters aged 6 and 4,
to Port Hawkesbury, Cape
Breton Island, in 1828,
on the St Lawrence of
Newcastle, master J. Cram.
(PANS/M6-100)

McLEAN JAMES
Emigrated from Scotland,
with his wife, to Canada
on the Curlew on
30 September 1818.
Received a land grant in
Drummond, Upper Canada,
on 30 November 1818.
(PAO)

McLEAN JOHN
Emigrated from Scotland
to America. Settled in
Darien, Georgia, c1739.
(HGP)

MacLEAN JOHN
Son of Neil MacLean of
Balliphetrish. Officer
in the 42nd(Black Watch)
Regiment. To America in
1757. Settled in Danbury,
Connecticut. Merchant.
Married Deborah Adams.
Revolutionary soldier.
Father of Mary, Anne,
Deborah, Alexander, Lilly,
John, Lany, Sally, Hugh or
Ewan. Died 7 April 1805.
(CG)

MacLEAN JOHN
Born during 1756 in
Mull, Argyllshire.
Revolutionary officer
under George Washington.
Artillery officer during
the War of 1812.
Commissary General of New
York. Father of George
Washington MacLean. Died
28 February 1821.
(CG)

MacLEANE JOHN
Emigrated from Scotland
to America. Settled in
Norfolk, Virginia, pre 1774.
(OD)

MacLEAN JOHN
Professor of Natural
Philosophy at the College
of New Jersey. D.D. of
King's College, Aberdeen,
26 August 1797.
(KCA)

McLEAN JOHN
Born in Scotland in 1799.
Hudson Bay Company
employee from 1821 to
1845. Died in Victoria,
Canada, 8 September 1890.
(HBRS)

McLEAN JOHN
Emigrated from Scotland,
with wife, son and daughter,
to Canada. Received a
land grant in Ramsay, Upper
Canada, 14 January 1822.
(PAO)

197

MacLEAN LACHLAN
Fifth son of Charles
MacLean of Drimmin,
and Isabel Cameron.
Planter in Jamaica.
Died there in 1764.
(CG)

MacLEAN LACHLAN
Born in Rhum, Inver-
ness-shire. Emigrated
from Scotland to Nova
Scotia during 1781.
Settled in Pictou
County, Nova Scotia.
Married Ann MacQuarrie.
Father of David, Hector,
Gormall and Catharine.
(CG)

McLEAN LAUCHLAN
Old Kilpatrick,
Dunbartonshire. Applied
to settle in Canada on
3 March 1815.
(SRO/RH9)

McLEAN LACHLAN
Emigrated from Scotland,
with his wife, three sons
and four daughters, to
Canada on the Earl of
Buckingham in June 1821.
Received a land grant in
Ramsay, Upper Canada, on
26 July 1821.
(PAO)

McLEAN LAUCHLAN
Born in Coll, Argyll-
shire during 1786.
Alderman. Died on
15 October 1829. Buried
in Kingston Cathedral,
Jamaica.
(MIBWI)

McLEAN MARION
Born c1745. Widow.
Emigrated from Scotland
to Canada. Settled in
Pictou, Nova Scotia, in
1815.
(PANS/RG1)

McLEAN MARY
Born c1768. Rhum, Inver-
ness-shire. Emigrated
from Leith, Midlothian,
to Port Hawkesbury, Cape
Breton Island, in 1828
on the St Lawrence of
Newcastle, master J.Cram.
(PANS/M6-100)

McLEAN MURDOCH
Former army sergeant.
Emigrated from Scotland
to Canada. Received a
land grant in
Charlottenburg, St Raphael,
Quebec, 24 November 1787.
(PAO)

MacLEAN Dr NEIL
Third son of Allan MacLean
of Grishipol. Emigrated
from Scotland to America
during 1736. Settled in
Wethersfield, Connecticut.
Married Hannah Stillman in
1737. Father of Lachlan,
Allan, John, Neil. Married
Hannah Knowles during 1757.
Died in 1784.
(CG)

MacLEAN NEIL
  Second son of John MacLean,
  born in Mingary, Argyll-
  shire during 1759.
  Lieutenant in the 84th
  (Royal Highland
  Emigrants) Regiment.
  Settled in St Andrews,
  Stormont County, Upper
  Canada, during 1782. Married
  .... McDonald during 1784.
  Father of John, Archibald,
  Alexander, Catharine, James,
  Jessie, Isabel and Ann.
  Politician and militia
  officer. Died in 1832.
  (CG)

McLEAN NEIL
  Born c1788. Rhum, Inverness-shire. Emigrated
  from Leith, Midlothian,
  to Port Hawkesbury, Cape
  Breton Island, in 1828
  on the St Lawrence of
  Newcastle, master J. Cram,
  with his wife Mary 30, and
  children Margaret 16 and
  John .
  (PANS/M6-100)

McLEAN NEIL
  Born c1800. Rhum, Inverness-shire. Emigrated
  from Leith, Midlothian,
  to Port Hawkesbury, Cape
  Breton Island, in 1828
  on the St Lawrence of
  Newcastle, master J.Cram.
  (PANS/M6-100)

MacLEAN RORY
  Emigrated from Rhum,
  Inverness-shire, to
  Canada during 1810 with
  his wife Ann McIsaac and
  children William, John,
  Neil, Charles, Allan and
  Donald. Settled in Prince
  Edward Island, and later
  Broad Cove, Cape Breton
  Island.
  (CG)

McLEAN WILLIAM
  Emigrated from Scotland
  to Canada. Received a
  land grant in
  Charlottenburg, St Raphael,
  Quebec, 24 November 1787.
  (PAO)

McLEAN WILLIAM
  Emigrated from Scotland
  to Canada on the Trafalgar
  31 July 1817. Received a
  land grant in Burgess,
  Upper Canada, 16 March 1818.
  (PAO)

McLEISH JOHN
  Emigrated from Scotland,
  with his wife and son,
  to Canada on the Caledonian
  10 July 1816. Received a
  land grant in Bathurst,
  Upper Canada, on
  9 September 1816.
  (PAO)

McLEISH JOHN
  Emigrated from Scotland,
  with his son, to Canada on
  the Caledonian 10 July 1816.
  Received a land grant in
  Upper Canada 24 September
  1816.
  (PAO)

McLELLAND DONALD
  Emigrated from Scotland
  to Canada on the Morning
  Field 19 September 1816.
  Received a land grant in
  Beckwith, Upper Canada, on
  30 November 1816.
  (PAO)

McLELLAN JAMES
Emigrated from Scotland,
with his wife, two sons
and a daughter, to
Canada on the Earl of
Buckingham in June 1821.
Received a land grant in
Dalhousie, Upper Canada,
on 21 July 1821.
(PAO)

McLELAND JOHN
Cambuslang,Lanarkshire.
Emigrated from Scotland,
with his wife, three sons
and a daughter, to
Canada on the Brock 1820
Received a land grant in
Dalhousie, Upper Canada,
on 27 October 1821.
(PAO)

McLELLAND JOHN
Emigrated from Scotland
to Canada on the
Morning Field.
Received a land grant in
Beckwith, Upper Canada,
on 17 February 1821.
(PAO)

McLELLAN NEIL
Born c1790. Labourer.
Emigrated from Scotland,
with wife and child, to
Canada. Settled in
Merigonish, Pictou,
Nova Scotia, in 1815.
(PANS/RG1)

McLELLAND RONALD
Born in Scotland. Former
soldier in the 37th
Regiment. Wife and two
daughter. Military
settler. Received a
land grant in Beckwith,
Upper Canada, on
28 October 1820.
(PAO)

McLELLAN THOMAS
Emigrated from Scotland
to Canada on the Earl of
Buckingham in June 1821.
Received a land grant in
Ramsay, Upper Canada, on
31 July 1821.
(PAO)

MacLELLAN WILLIAM
A boy. Died at Darien
on 11 December 1698.
(NLS)

McLELLAN WILLIAM
Emigrated from Scotland,
with his wife, four sons
and four daughters, to
Canada on the Earl of
Buckingham in June 1821.
Received a land grant in
Lanark, Upper Canada, on
31 July 1821.
(PAO)

MacLEOD ALEXANDER
Born c1769, son of Kenneth
MacLeod, tacksman of Myle
and Killiesmore. Officer
in the British Army.
Emigrated from Scotland to
Canada. Settled in Lancaster
Upper Canada. Married ...
MacDonell, died in 1794.
Father of Iain Breac, Neil,
and Alexander. Died in 1850.
Buried at Kirkhill,
Lochiel township, Upper
Canada.
(TML)

McLEOD Rev HUGH
Born in Scotland.
Emigrated from Scotland
to Nova Scotia in 1822.
Minister in Nova Scotia,
and later in Demerara.
Died in Demerara in 1832.
(HPC)

MacLEOD JAMES
Born c1750, son of
Hugh MacLeod of
Geanies, and Isabel
Fraser. Died in the
West Indies.
(TML)

MacLEOD JAMES
Born in Scotland. Former
soldier in the 90th
Regiment. Military
settler. Received a
land grant in
Montague, Upper Canada,
on 28 August 1815.
(PAO)

MacLEOD JOHN
Second son of James
MacLeod. Emigrated
from Scotland to Nova
Scotia c1760. Teacher.
(TML)

McLEOD JOHN
Born c1792 in the High-
lands of Scotland.
North West Company
employee from 1816 to
1821. Hudson Bay
Company employee from
1821 to 1842. Chief
Factor in 1834.
(NBRS)

MacLEOD MARGARET
Daughter of Roderick
MacLeod, Writer to the
Signet. Married (1) John
MacLeod of Colbecks in
Jamaica during 1773 (2)
John Grant, Chief Justice
of Jamaica.
(TML)

MacLEOD RODERICK
Second son of Norman
MacLeod, 1736-...,Pabay.
Gaelic bard and skipper
of the Marquis. Emigrated
from Scotland to New
Brunswick in 1806.
(TML)

MacLEOD RODERICK
Born in Barra, Inverness-
shire, during 1777, son
of Gilleanan MacLeod.
Emigrated from Scotland
to Prince Edward Island
during 1802. Married
Catharine MacEachern in
1811. Father of Roderick,
Lauchlan, Donald, Margaret,
Marjory, Catharine, Janet,
and Ann. Teacher, farmer
and politician. Died in
1850.
(TML)

MacLEOD WILLIAM
Born c1750, third son of
Hugh MacLeod of Geanies,
and Isabel Fraser. Died
in Maryland.
(TML)

McLURE ENOCH
Emigrated from Skye,
Inverness-shire to
America c1745.
(BAF)

McMASTERS ALEXANDER
Yeoman. Emigrated from
Scotland to Canada.
Received a land grant in
Eldon, Newcastle, Upper
Canada, 8 March 1826.
(PAO)

McMASTERS ARCHIBALD
Yeoman. Emigrated from
Scotland to Canada.
Received a land grant
in Eldon, Newcastle,
Upper Canada, on
8 March 1826.
(PAO)

McMASTERS DONALD
Yeoman. Emigrated from
Scotland to Canada.
Received a land grant
in Eldon, Newcastle,
Upper Canada, on
8 March 1826.
(PAO)

McMICHAEL JAMES
Born during 1772 in
Muirkirk, Ayrshire, the
younger son of George
McMichael. Emigrated
from Scotland to Penn-
sylvania during 1793.
Married Rosanna Demott
in Pennsylvania on 14
April 1803. Settled in
Townsend, Norfolk County,
Upper Canada, in 1820.
Father of nine sons and
one daughter. Died on
9 September 1821.
(BAF)

McMIKEN HUGH
Emigrated from Scotland
to America before 1774.
Merchant in Portsmouth,
Virginia.
(OD)

McMILLAN ALEXANDER
Emigrated from Scotland,
with his wife, son and
three daughters, to
Canada on the Commerce
in August 1820. Received
a land grant in Lanark,
Upper Canada, on
5 September 1820.
(PAO)

McMILLAN ALEXANDER
Born in Scotland. Former
captain in the Glengarry
Fencibles. Military
settler. Received a
land grant in Lanark,
Upper Canada, on
6 November 1820.
(PAO)

McMILLAN ANGUS
Born in Scotland. Former
soldier in the Canadian
Fencibles. Military
settler. Received a
land grant in Upper
Canada on 30 September
1816.
(PAO)

McMILLAN ANGUS
Yeoman. Emigrated from
Scotland to Canada.
Received a land grant in
Eldon, Newcastle, Upper
Canada, on 8 March 1826.
(PAO)

McMILLAN ANGUS
Born c1790. Rhum, Inver-
ness-shire. Emigrated
from Leith, Midlothian,
to Port Hawkesbury, Cape
Breton Island, in 1828,
on the St Lawrence of
Newcastle, master J.Cram.
(PANS/M6-100)

McMILLAN ANN
Born c1800. Rhum, Inver-
ness-shire. Emigrated
from Leith, Midlothian,
to Port Hawkesbury, Cape
Breton Island, in 1828,
on the St Lawrence of
Newcastle, master J. Cram.
(PANS/M6-100)

McMILLAN ARCHIBALD
Yeoman. Emigrated from
Scotland to Canada.
Received a land grant
in Eldon, Newcastle, Upper
Canada, on 8 March 1826.
(PAO)

McMILLAN ARCHIBALD
Born c1801. Rhum, Inver-
ness-shire. Emigrated
from Leith, Midlothian,
to Port Hawkesbury, Cape
Breton Island, in 1828,
on the St Lawrence of
Newcastle, master J. Cram,
with his wife Jessie 28,
and children Donald 2,
and Neil - an infant.
(PANS/M6-100)

McMILLAN CHRISTIANA
Born c1768. Rhum, Inver-
ness-shire. Emigrated
from Leith, Midlothian,
to Port Hawkesbury, Cape
Breton Island, in 1828,
on the St Lawrence of
Newcastle, master J.Cram.
(PANS/M6-100)

McMILLAN DONALD
Born during 1784, third
son of Donald McMillan and
Barbara McKinlay, Auchaloskin
Kintyre, Argyllshire. Married
Katharine Milloy during July
1810 in the parish of Kilberry
and Kilcalmonell. Father of
Donald, Hugh, Charles and
Archibald. Emigrated from
Campbelltown, Argyllshire,
to Canada in 1819. Settled in
Erin, Wellington, Upper
Canada, in 1822.
(CMM)

McMILLAN DONALD
Born c1771. Rhum, Inver-
ness-shire. Emigrated
from Leith, Midlothian,
to Port Hawkesbury, Cape
Breton Island, in 1828,
on the St Lawrence of
Newcastle, master J.Cram,
with his wife Marion 52.
(PANS/M6-100)

McMILLAN DOUGALD
Emigrated from Scotland
to Canada on the Morning
Field 19 September 1816.
Received a land grant in
Drummond, Upper Canada,
on 28 January 1817.
(PAO)

MacMILLAN DUNCAN BAIN
Lochaber, Inverness-shire.
Emigrated from Scotland to
Finch, Stormont County,
Quebec, c1805. Married
Mary MacMillan. Father of
Duncan, 1837-1908.
(BAF)

McMILLAN HUGH
Emigrated from Scotland,
with his wife and two
daughters, to Canada on
the George Canning in June
1821. Received a land grant
in Ramsay, Upper Canada, on
10 July 1821.
(PAOO

MacMILLAN JOHN ROY
Born c1770. Lochaber,
Inverness-shire.
Married Mary Grant.
Emigrated from Scotland
to Canada. Settled in
Glengarry County. Died
during 1896. Buried at
St Columba's, Kirkhill,
Glengarry County.
(CMM)

McMILLAN JOHN
Emigrated from Scotland,
with his wife, to Canada
on the Morning Field
19 September 1816.
Received a land grant in
Drummond, Upper Canada,
on 9 December 1816.
(PAO)

McMILLAN JOHN
Born in Scotland. Former
soldier in the Canadian
Fencibles. Military
settler. Received a
land grant in Beckwith,
Upper Canada, on
31 August 1817.
(PAO)

McMILLAN JOHN
Yeoman. Emigrated from
Scotland to Canada.
Received a land grant
in Eldon, Newcastle,
Upper Canada, on
8 March 1826.
(PAO)

McMILLAN JOHN
Born c1761. Rhum, Inver-
ness-shire. Emigrated
from Leith, Midlothian,
to Port Hawkesbury, Cape
Breton Island, in 1828
on the St Lawrence of
Newcastle, master J. Cram,
with children(?) Catharine
26, Mary 24, Ann 23, Flora
17 and Neil 13.
(PANS/M6-100)

McMILLAN MALCOLM
Second son of Donald
McMillan and Barbara
McKinley, Kintyre,
Argyllshire. Emigrated
from Scotland to America
during 1819.
(CMM)

McMILLAN MARION
Born c1788. Rhum. Inver-
ness-shire. Emigrated from
Leith, Midlothian, to Port
Hawkesbury, Cape Breton
Island, during 1828, on
the St Lawrence of
Newcastle, master J. Cram.
(PANS/M6-100)

McMILLAN MARION
Born c1811. Rhum, Inver-
ness-shire. Emigrated
from Leith, Midlothian,
to Port Hawkesbury, Cape
Breton Island, in 1828
on the St Lawrence of
Newcastle, master J. Cram.
(PANS/M6-100)

McMILLAN NEIL
  Born c1804. Rhum, Inverness-shire. Emigrated
  from Leith, Midlothian,
  to Port Hawkesbury, Cape
  Breton Island, in 1828
  on the St Lawrence of
  Newcastle, master J.Cram.
  (PANS/M6-100)

MacMILLAN P.
  Surgeon. Glasgow. Applied
  to settle in Canada on
  4 March 1815.
  (SRO/RH9)

McMILLAN PETER
  Emigrated from Greenock,
  Renfrewshire, to Montreal,
  Quebec, on the brig
  Niagara, Hamilton, 1825.
  Settled in McNab,
  Bathurst, Upper Canada,
  during 1825.
  (SG)

McMILLAN WILLIAM
  Educated at the University
  of Glasgow c1720.
  Emigrated from Scotland
  to Philadelphia, Penn-
  sylvania, during 1724.
  Presbyterian minister.
  (AP)

McMILLAN WILLIAM
  Emigrated from Scotland,
  with his wife, two sons
  and three daughters, to
  Canada on the George
  Canning in June 1821.
  Received a land grant in
  Dalhousie, Upper Canada,
  on 16 July 1821.
  (PAO)

McMONISAIL JOHN
  Emigrated from Scotland,
  with his wife, two sons
  and five daughters, to
  Canada on the Brock.
  Received a land grant in
  Dalhousie, Upper Canada,
  on 27 October 1821.
  (PAO)

McMURCHIE EWEN
  Yeoman. Emigrated from
  Scotland to Canada.
  Received a land grant in
  Eldon, Newcastle, Upper
  Canada, on 8 March 1826.
  (PAO)

McMURTRIE JAMES
  Emigrated from Scotland,
  with his wife, to Canada
  on the George Canning in
  June 1821. Received a
  land grant in Ramsay,
  Upper Canada, 16 July 1821.
  (PAO)

McNAB ALEXANDER
  Strathyre, Perthshire.
  Emigrated from Greenock,
  Renfrewshire, to Montreal,
  Quebec, on the brig
  Niagara, Hamilton, in 1825,
  with his wife Catharine
  Dewar, and children Hugh,
  Catharine, Duncan and
  Alexander. Settled in
  McNab, Bathurst, Upper
  Canada, during 1825.
  (SG)

McNAB ARCHIBALD
Perthshire(?) Emigrated
from Greenock, Renfrew-
shire, to Montreal,
Quebec, on the brig
Niagara, Hamilton, 1825,
with his wife Janet
McEwan, and children
Catharine, John, James,
Grace Buchanan, Janet,
Robert and Duncan.
Settled in McNab,
Bathurst, Upper Canada,
in 1825.
(SG)

McNAB JOHN
Glasgow. Applied to
settle in Canada on
3 March 1815.
(SRO/RH9)

McNAB JOHN
Emigrated from Scotland
with his wife, to Canada
on the brig John 18 August
1817. Received a land grant
in Bathurst, Upper Canada,
on 17 October 1817.
(PAO)

MacNAB PETER
Born during 1735 in
Breadalbane, Perthshire.
Emigrated from Scotland
to Nova Scotia in 1759.
Married Susannah Khun on
25 November 1763. Father
of Peter, John, Anne,and
Susan.   Settled on
MacNab's Island, Halifax,
Nova Scotia, during 1783.
Died there 3 November 1799.
(FC)

McNAB PETER
Born in Scotland.
Received a land grant
in Dalhousie, Upper
Canada, on 5 January 1821.
(PAO)

McNAUGHTON DONALD
Emigrated from Scotland
to Canada on the Fame
18 September 1816.
Received a land grant in
Drummond, Upper Canada,
on 1 December 1816.
(PAO)

McNAUGHTON DONALD
Cardrossmoss, Dunbarton-
shire. Emigrated from
Greenock, Renfrewshire,
to Montreal, Quebec, on
the brig Niagara, Hamilton,
in 1825 with his wife
Catharine, and children
Duncan, John, Robert,
Mary and Alexander.
Settled in McNab, Bathurst,
Upper Canada, in 1825.
(SG)

McNAUGHTON DUNCAN
Emigrated from Scotland,
with his wife, to Canada
on the Fame 18 September
1816. Received a land
grant in Drummond, Upper
Canada, on 15 November 1816.
(PAO)

McNAUGHTON DUNCAN
Emigrated from Scotland
to Canada on the Fame
18 September 1816.
Receiveda land grant in
Beckwith, Upper Canada, on
31 March 1817.
(PAO)

McNAUGHTON JACOB
Glasgow. Applied to
settle in Canada on
1 March 1815.
(SRO/RH9)

McNAUGHTON Dr JAMES
Born during 1809 in
Kenmore, Perthshire.
Emigrated from Scotland
to America during 1817.
Settled in Albany, New
York. Professor of
Medicine. Died 1874.
(TSA)

McNAUGHTON JAMES
Emigrated from Scotland
to Canada. Received a
land grant in
Monaghan, Newcastle,
Upper Canada, on
29 November 1817.
(PAO)

McNAUGHTON JOHN
Emigrated from Scotland,
with his wife, to Canada
on the Lady of the Lake
17 September 1816.
Received a land grant in
Lancaster, Upper Canada,
on 11 May 1817.
(PAO)

McNAUGHTON JOHN
Emigrated from Scotland
to Canada on the Fame
18 September 1816.
Received a land grant in
Drummond, Upper Canada,
on 15 November 1816.
(PAO)

McNAUGHTON JOHN sr
Emigrated from Scotland
to Canada. Received a
land grant in Cavan,
Newcastle, Upper Canada,
7 October 1818.
(PAO)

McNAUGHTON JOHN jr
Emigrated from Scotland
to Canada. Received a
land grant in Cavan,
Newcastle, Upper Canada,
on 7 October 1818.
(PAO)

McNAUGHTON NAUGHTON
Emigrated from Scotland
to Canada on the Neptune
5 November 1817.
Received a land grant in
Drummond, Upper Canada, on
11 January 1819.
(PAO)

McNAUGHTON THOMAS
Emigrated from Scotland,
with his wife, six sons
and two daughters, to
Canada on the David of
London. Received a land
grant in Lanark, Upper
Canada, 6 September 1821.
(PAO)

McNAUGHTON WILLIAM
Emigrated from Scotland,
with his wife and son, to
Canada on the Neptune on
5 November 1817. Received
a land grant in Bathurst,
Upper Canada, 27 March 1818.
(PAO)

McNAUGHTON WILLIAM jr
Emigrated from Scotland
to Canada on the Neptune
15 November 1817.
Received a land grant in
Drummond, Upper Canada,
11 January 1819.
(PAO)

McNEE JOHN
Emigrated from Scotland,
with his wife, son and
four daughters, to
Canada on the Caledonian
10 July 1816. Received
a land grant in Upper
Canada on 24 September
1816.
(PAO)

MacNEIL DONALD
Barra, Inverness-shire.
Soldier in the 82nd
(Fraser Highlanders)
Regiment. Settled in
Nova Scotia in 1785.
(CMN)

McNEIL DONALD
Emigrated from Scotland
to Canada. Received a
land grant in
Dalhousie, Upper Canada,
on 7 November 1821.
(PAO)

McNEIL JAMES
Royalist soldier captured
at Worcester. Transported
from Gravesend, Kent, to
Boston, New England, on the
John and Sarah, master John
Greene, 13 May 1652.
(NER)

McNEILL JOHN
Argyllshire. Emigrated
from Scotland to Prince
Edward Island. Settled
in Cavendish in 1775.
(SO)

MacNEIL JOHN
Barra, Inverness-shire.
Soldier in the 82nd
(Fraser Highlanders)
Regiment. Settled in
Nova Scotia in 1785.
(CMN)

McNEILL JOHN
Born in Scotland. Married
Nancy Martin in Richmond
County, North Carolina,
during 1801. Died c1826
in Alabama.
(Index NC Anc 27549)

McNEIL JOHN
Emigrated from Scotland,
with his wife, son and
four daughters, to
Canada on the Caledonian
10 July 1816. Received a
land grant in Bathurst,
Upper Canada, on
24 September 1816.
(PAO)

MacNEIL LACHLIN
Son of Allan MacNeil.
Emigrated from Scotland
to Prince Edward Island
during 1803.
(CMN)

MacNEIL MATHEW
Soldier in the 82nd
(Fraser Highlanders)
Regiment. Settled in Nova
Scotia during 1785.
(CMN)

MacNEIL MARY
Daughter of John MacNeil.
Emigrated from Barra,
Inverness-shire, to
Canada. Settled in Cape
Breton Island during
1817. Married ....
MacDougall.
(CMN)

McNEIL MURDOCH
Barra, Inverness-shire.
Soldier in the 82nd
(Fraser Highlanders)
Regiment. Settled in
Nova Scotia during 1785.
(CMN)

McNEIL ROBERT
Emigrated from Scotland,
with his wife and four
daughters, to Canada on
the Brock during 1820.
Received a land grant
in Lanark, Upper Canada,
on 21 October 1821.
(PAO)

MacNEIL of BREVAIG RODERICK
Emigrated from Scotland,
with his children Roderick,
Gillieonan, Catharine and
Margaret, to Canada during
1802. Settled in Vernon
Valley, Prince Edward
Island during 1803.
(CMN)

McNEIL
A Scottish soldier.
Settled at Murray Bay or
Mount Murray, Quebec,
after the Siege of
Quebec in 1762.
(PRSC/X)

MacNEISH SAMUEL
Royalist soldier captured
at Worcester. Transported
from Gravesend, Kent, to
Boston, New England, on
the John and Sarah, master
John Greene, 13 May 1652.
(NER)

MacNESTER(?) ALASTAIR
Royalist soldier captured
at Worcester. Transported
from Gravesend, Kent, to
Boston, New England, on
the John and Sarah, master
John Greene, 13 May 1652.
(NER)

McNICHOL ALEXANDER
Emigrated from Scotland,
with his wife, to Canada
on the David of London in
June 1821. Received a
land grant in Lanark,
Upper Canada, 6 August
1821.
(PAO)

McNICOLL DONALD
Glasgow. Merchant. Factor
in Pittsylvania, Virginia,
for James Murdoch and
Company, merchants in
Glasgow, c1760.
(SRA)

McNICOLL JOHN
Emigrated from Scotland,
with his wife, six sons
and a daughter, to Canada
on the Commerce in June
1820. Received a land
grant in Dalhousie, Upper
Canada, 3 September 1820.
(PAO)

McNICOL
A Scottish soldier.
Settled at Murray Bay or
Mount Murray, Quebec,
after the Siege of
Quebec in 1762.
(PRSC/X)

McNIDEN JAMES
Emigrated from Scotland,
with his wife, three sons
and two daughters, to
Canada on the Prompt in
June 1820. Received a
land grant in Dalhousie,
Upper Canada, on
19 November 1821.
(PAO)

McNISH WILLIAM
Emigrated from Scotland
to Canada. Received a
land grant in Cavan,
Newcastle, Upper Canada,
24 September 1817.
(PAO)

MacNITH DANIEL
Royalist soldier captured
at Worcester. Transported
from Gravesend, Kent, to
Boston, New England, on
the John and Sarah, master
John Greene, 13 May 1652.
(NER)

MacPETRIE JAMES
Son of James MacPetrie,
Aberdee. Educated at
Marischal College,
Aberdeen, c1815.
Surgeon in Tobago.
(MCA)

McPHADEN HECTOR
Rhum, Inverness-shire.
Emigrated from Leith,
Midlothian, to Port
Hawkesbury, Cape Breton
Island, during 1828, on
the St Lawrence of
Newcastle, master J. Cram,
with his wife Ann, and
children Donald, John
and Angus.
(PANS/M6-100)

McPHAILL ALEXANDER
Emigrated from Scotland,
with his wife, two sons
and two daughters, to
Canada. Received a land
grant in Ramsay, Upper
Canada, 16 August 1822.
(PAO)

McPHEAL JOHN
Emigrated from Scotland
to Canada. Received a
land grant in Drummond,
Upper Canada, on
5 February 1821.
(PAO)

McPHAIL PETER(?)
Emigrated from Scotland,
with his wife and daughter,
to Canada on the Prompt
8 July 1817. Received a
land grant in Drummond,
Upper Canada, 1 April 1818.
(PAO)

McPHAIL RANALD
Yeoman. Emigrated from
Scotland to Canada.
Received a land grant in
Thorak, Home, Upper Canada,
8 March 1826.
(PAO)

McPHERSON ALEXANDER
Born in Scotland.
Received a land grant
in Drummond, Upper
Canada, 15 August 1817.
(PAO)

McPHERSON ANDREW
Born during 1783 in
Scotland. North West
Company employee from
1805 to 1821. Hudson
Bay Company employee
from 1821 to 1842.
Died in 1847.
(HBRS)

MacPHERSON ANNABELLA
Perthshire(?) Emigrated
from Greenock, Renfrew-
shire, to Montreal,
Quebec, on the brig
Niagara, Hamilton, in
1825. Settled in McNab,
Bathurst, Upper Canada,
during 1825.
(SG)

MacPHERSON CATHARINE
Emigrated from Greenock,
Renfrewshire, to
Montreal, Quebec, on
the brig Niagara, Hamilton,
in 1825. Settled in McNab,
Bathurst, Upper Canada,
during 1825.
(SG)

McPHERSON DANIEL
Born in Inverness during
1752. Emigrated from Scot-
land to Canada. Settled in
Sorel, Quebec, and later
in Douglastown, Gaspe,
Quebec, 1790. Fishmonger.
Married ...Kelly. Died in
June 1840 at St Thomas,
Montmagny.
(SNF)

McPHERSON DANIEL
Emigrated from Scotland
to Canada on the George
Canning in June 1821.
Received a land grant in
Ramsay, Upper Canada, on
16 July 1821.
(PAO)

McPHERSON DONALD
Yeoman. Emigrated from
Scotland to Canada.
Received a land grant in
Thorak, Home, Upper Canada,
on 8 March 1826.
(PAO)

McPHERSON DUNCAN
Emigrated from Scotland
to Canada on the Prompt
13 July 1817. Received
a land grant in Lancaster,
Upper Canada, on
26 February 1819.
(PAO)

McPHERSON DUNCAN
Emigrated from Scotland,
with his wife, to Canada
on the Commerce in June
1820. Received a land
grant in Lanark, Upper
Canada, on 3 September 1820.
(PAO)

McPHERSON DUNCAN
Emigrated from Greenock,
Renfrewshire, to Montreal,
Quebec, on the brig
Niagara, Hamilton, in 1825.
Settled in McNab, Bathurst,
Upper Canada, during 1825.
(SG)

McPHERSON DUNCAN
Yeoman. Emigrated from
Scotland to Canada.
Received a land grant in
Eldon, Newcastle, Upper
Canada, 8 March 1826.
(PAO)

McPHERSON EVAN
Emigrated from Scotland,
with his family, to
America on the Frances
of New Orleans in 1812.
Settled in Highland Town,
Columbiana County, Ohio.
(SHR)

MacPHERSON HUGH
Aged between 2 and 8.
Emigrated from Greenock,
Renfrewshire, to Montreal,
Quebec, on the brig
Niagara, Hamilton, in
1825. Settled in McNab,
Bathurst, Upper Canada,
during 1825.
(SG)

McPHERSON JOHN
Emigrated from Greenock,
Renfrewshire, with his
wife, two sons and two
daughters, to Canada on
the George Canning in May
1821. Received a land
grant in Dalhousie,
Upper Canada, on 10 July
1821.
(PAO)

McPHERSON JOHN
Emigrated from Scotland
to Canada on the George
Canning in June 1821.
Received a land grant in
Lanark, Upper Canada, on
15 July 1821.
(PAO)

McPHERSON JOHN
Emigrated from Scotland,
with his wife, to Canada
on the George Canning in
June 1821. Received a
land grant in Ramsay,
Upper Canada, 16 July 1821.
(PAO)

McPHERSON JOHN
Emigrated from Greenock,
Renfrewshire, to Montreal,
Quebec, on the brig
Niagara, Hamilton, in 1825.
Settled in McNab, Bathurst,
Upper Canada, 1825.
(SG)

McPHERSON JOHN
Yeoman. Emigrated from
Scotland to Canada.
Received a land grant in
Mora, Newcastle, Upper
Canada, 8 March 1826.
(PAO)

McPHERSON KATHARINE
Late of Strathrushie,
Scotland. Widow of John
Campbell of Achavadi,
Lochaber, Inverness-shire.
Settled in Quebec pre 1780.
(SRO/GD214)

MacPHERSON LORN
Perthshire. Emigrated from
Greenock, Renfrewshire, to
Montreal, Quebec, on the
brig Niagara, Hamilton, 1825
Settled in McNab, Bathurst,
Upper Canada, 1825.
(SG)

McPHERSON MURDOCH
Born in Scotland 1796.
North West Company employee
1816-1821. Hudson Bay Company
employee 1821 - . Died 1863.
(HBRS)

MacPHERSON PETER
Perthshire(?) Emigrated
from Greenock, Renfrew-
shire, to Montreal,
Quebec, on the brig
Niagara, Hamilton, 1825.
Settled in McNab,
Bathurst, Upper Canada,
in 1825.
(SG)

McPHERSON ROBERT
Brother of Thomas McPherson
of Dalrada, Inverness.
Signed a treaty with the
Creek Indians in Georgia
11 August 1739.
(HGP)

McPHERSON THOMAS
Yeoman. Emigrated from
Scotland to Canada.
Received a land grant
in Thorak, Home, Upper
Canada, 8 March 1826.
(PAO)

McPHERSON SAMUEL
Born 1804, son of James
McPherson, farmer in
Kingussie, Inverness-
shire, and Elspeth ...
Died in Zaira, Upper
Canada, during October
1839.
(Kingussie GS)

McPHERSON WILLIAM
Emigrated from Scotland
to America before 1757.
Planter in Goochland,
Virginia.
(OD)

McPHIE DANIEL
Emigrated from Scotland,
with his wife, three sons
and a daughter, to Canada.
Received a land grant in
Dalhousie, Upper Canada,
on 27 October 1821.
(PAO)

McPHIE JOHN
Emigrated from Scotland,
with his wife, son and six
daughters, to Canada on
the David of London in
June 1821. Received a
land grant in Lanark, Upper
Canada, 6 September 1821.
(PAO)

McPIKE JAMES
Emigrated from Scotland
to Maryland during 1772.
Revolutionary soldier.
Married Martha Mountain.
Settled in Maysville,
Kentucky, c1795. Father
of Joseph, Richard,
Elizabeth, Nancy, Sarah,
John, Haley, George,
Martha and James.
(NYGBR)

McQUARRIE JOHN
Emigrated from Scotland,
with his wife and three
daughters, to Canada.
Received a land grant in
Ramsay, Upper Canada, on
1 March 1822.
(PAO)

McQUARRIE JOHN
Born c1763. Rhum, Inverness-shire. Emigrated
from Leith, Midlothian,
to Port Hawkesbury, Cape
Breton Island, in 1828
on the St Lawrence of
Newcastle, master J. Cram,
with his wife Marion 60,
and children Allan 30,
Donald 28, Rachael 26,
Margaret 24, and Bell 20.
(PANS/M6-100)

McQUARRIE NEIL
Emigrated from Scotland
to Canada on the George
Canning. Received a land
grant in Ramsay, Upper
Canada, on 31 July 1821.
(PAO)

MacQUEEN JAMES
Son of James MacQueen of
Corryburgh. Signed a
treaty with the Creek
Indians in Georgia on
11 August 1739.
(HGP)

McQUEEN WILLIAM
Emigrated from Scotland
to Canada. Received a
land grant in Drummond,
Upper Canada, 26 February
1817.
(PAO)

McQUEEN WILLIAM
Emigrated from Scotland,
with his wife and five
sons, to Canada on the
George Canning in June
1821. Received a land
grant in Ramsay, Upper
Canada, on 25 July 1821.
(PAO)

MacRAE ALEXANDER
Born 10 May 1756, son of
Farquhar MacRae and Mary
MacKenzie, Kintail, Ross
and Cromarty. Died in
Demerara.
(CMR)

MacRAE ALEXANDER
Born 28 August 1787, son
of Duncan MacRae and
Janet Murchison, Kintail,
Ross and Cromarty.
Educated in Aberdeen.
Planter in Demerara. Died
in Southampton 1860.
(CMR)

MacRAE ALEXANDER
Son of Duncan MacRae and
Helen Og, Kintail, Ross
and Cromarty. Emigrated
from Scotland to Canada
during 1821. Married Ann
MacKenzie. Father of
Duncan, John Alexander,
and Christopher.
(CMR)

McRAE ALEXANDER
Yeoman. Emigrated from
Scotland to Canada.
Received a land grant in
Mora, Newcastle, Upper
Canada, on 9 March 1826.
(PAO)

McRAE ALEXANDER
Yeoman. Emigrated from
Scotland to Canada.
Received a land grant in
Thorak, Home, Upper Canada,
8 March 1826.
(PAO)

MacRAE ALLEN
Scottish merchant.
Settled in Dumfries, Prince
William County, Virginia,
c1653. Married Amelia
Pearson. Father of John,
Amelia and Mary.
(FKC)

MacRAE CATHARINE
Daughter of Hugh MacRae.
Emigrated from Kintail,
Ross and Cromarty, to
Wilmington, North
Carolina, during 1770.
Married Donald MacRae.
Settled in Georgia.
(CMR)

MacRAE Rev CHRISTOPHER
Born in Urquhart, Easter
Ross, son of Christopher
MacRae, Bishop Kinkell,
Urquhart. Educated at
Aberdeen University -
graduated M.A. in 1753.
Emigrated from Scotland
to America. Settled in
Surry County, Virginia.
Returned to Virginia as
an Episcopalian minister
in 1766. Rector of
Littleton parish, Virginia,
from 1773 to 1787.
(FKC)

McRAE CHRISTOPHER
Yeoman. Emigrated from
Scotland to Canada.
Received a land grant
in Thorak, Home, Upper
Canada, on 8 March 1826.
(PAO)

MacRAE COLIN
Born 14 March 1776, son
of Farquhar MacRae and
Mary McKenzie, Kintail,
Ross and Cromarty.
Merchant and planter in
Demerara. Married Charlotte
G. Van Der Heuvel. Father
of Charlotte, Farquhar -
drowned at Cape Hateras,
U.S.A. in 1838, Maria -
married Dr James Sewell
in Quebec, John, Colin,
Justine, Alexander, Isaac,
and Margaret. Died during
1854 in Edinburgh.
(CMR)

MacRAE DONALD
Son of Farquhar MacRae,
Kintail, Ross and Cromarty.
Emigrated from Scotland to
America in 1774.
(CMR)

MacRAE DONALD
Glenelg, Inverness-shire.
Enlisted in the Canadian
Fencibles during 1804, but
discharged in Inverness as
too old. Emigrated from
Scotland, with his wife
and children, to Prince
Edward Island on the
Northern Friend in 1805.
(PAPEI.2783)

MacRAE DUNCAN
Son of Roderick MacRae
and ...MacKenzie, Kintail,
Ross and Cromarty.
Emigrated from Scotland
to Maryland. Died at Fort
Duquesne, Pennsylvania,
in 1757.
(CMR)

MacRAE DUNCAN
Son of Farquhar MacRae,
Kintail, Ross and
Cromarty. Emigrated
from Scotland to
America during 1774.
(CMR)

MacRAE DUNCAN
Son of Duncan MacRae and
Christina Bethune, Kintail,
Ross and Cromarty.
Educated at University of
Aberdeen c1820. Settled
in Demerara.
(CMR)

McRAE DUNCAN
Yeoman. Emigrated from
Scotland to Canada.
Received a land grant
in Thorak, Home, Upper
Canada, 8 March 1826.
(PAO)

McRAE FARQUHAR
Emigrated from Scotland
to Canada. Settled in
Charlottenburg, St Raphael,
Quebec, 23 November 1787.
(PAO)

MacRAE FARQUHAR
Born 30 March 1764, son of
Farquhar MacRae and Mary
MacKenzie, Kintail, Ross
and Cromarty. Doctor of
medicine. Died during 1802
in Demerara.
(CMR)

McRAE FINLAY
Yeoman. Emigrated from
Scotland to Canada.
Received a land grant in
Eldon, Newcastle, Upper
Canada, on 8 March 1826.
(PAO)

MacRAE ISABELLA
A widow. Emigrated from
Scotland to Canada.
Received a land grant in
Thorak, Home, Upper Canada,
12 November 1827.
(PAO)

MacRAE JOHN
Son of Alexander MacRae
and Anne Fraser, Kintail,
Ross and Cromarty.
Surgeon of an emigrant
ship to America in 1817.
Emigrated from Scotland
to Canada during 1817.
Settled in Glengarry,
Upper Canada, c1826.
(CMR)

MacRAE KENNETH
Born 16 July 1758, son of
Farquhar MacRae and Mary
MacKenzie, Kintail, Ross
and Cromarty. Army
officer. Paymaster General
of Jamaica. Married Miss
Mackay in Jamaica. Died
in Jamaica c1814.
(CMR)

MacRAE KENNETH
Born 19 May 1785, son of
Duncan MacRae and Janet
Murchison, Kintail, Ross
and Cromarty. Educated at
King's College, Aberdeen.
Planter in Demerara.
(CMR)

McTAVISH ALEXANDER
Emigrated from Scotland
to Canada on the Green
field 23 August 1816.
Received a land grant
in Drummond, Upper
Canada, 10 October 1816.
(PAO)

McTAVISH D.
Born in Stratherick.
Emigrated from Scotland
to Canada. Partner in
the North West Company.
Explorer and trader.
Died at Cape
Disappointment, Oregon,
on 22 May 1815.
(BCB)

McTAVISH DOUGLAS
Emigrated from Scotland
to Canada. Received a
land grant in Beckwith,
Upper Canada, on
30 August 1821.
(PAO)

McTAVISH DUNCAN
Emigrated from Scotland
to Canada on the Green-
field on 23 August 1816.
Received a land grant in
Drummond, Upper Canada, on
10 October 1816.
(PAO)

McTAVISH DUNCAN
Born in Scotland.
Emigrated from Scotland
to Canada on the Harmony
15 July 1817. Received a
land grant in Lancaster,
Upper Canada, on
25 February 1819.
(PAO)

McTAVISH HUGH
Emigrated from Scotland
to Canada on the
Agincourt 8 August 1817.
Received a land grant in
Lancaster, Upper Canada,
on 22 February 1819.
(PAO)

McTAVISH JOHN
Born in Scotland.
Received a land grant in
Beckwith, Upper Canada,
on 30 August 1820.
(PAO)

McTEAR ROBERT
Born in Scotland on
15 September 1741.
Captain in the
Revolutionary Army.
Died 8 March 1811.
Buried at Rushville, Ohio.
(ORIII)

MacTRETH(?) PATRICK
Royalist soldier captured
at Worcester. Transported
from Gravesend, Kent, to
Boston, New England, on
the John and Sarah, master
John Greene, 13 May 1652.
(NER)

McVENEE JAMES
Emigrated from Scotland
to Canada on the Success
8 September 1817. Received
a land grant in South
Gower, Upper Canada, on
13 October 1817.
(PAO)

McVICAR ALEXANDER
Emigrated from Scotland,
with his wife, son and
three daughters, to
Canada on the Earl of
Buckingham in June 1821.
Received a land grant in
Lanark, Upper Canada, on
27 July 1821.
(PAO)

McVICAR JOHN O.
Emigrated from Scotland
to Canada on the Earl of
Buckingham in June 1821.
Received a land grant in
Lanark, Upper Canada, on
27 July 1821.
(PAO)

McWALTER DUNCAN
Balvullie, Argyllshire.
Merchant in Jamaica.
Died pre 1771.
(CC)

McWHINNIE JOHN
Emigrated from Scotland,
with his wife, son and
three daughters, to
Canada on the George
Canning in June 1821.
Received a land grant
in Ramsay, Upper Canada,
16 July 1821.
(PAO)

McWILLIAM ALEXANDER
Born in Scotland. Former
captain in the Glengarry
Fencibles. Military settler.
Received a land grant in
North Gower, Upper Canada,
on 7 June 1819.
(PAO)

MABEN MATTHEW
Dumfries. Emigrated
from Scotland to
America before 1822.
Merchant in Virginia.
(OD)

MACHAR JOHN
Angus. Graduated M.A. at
the University of
Aberdeen on 25 March 1814.
Minister of St Andrews,
Kingston, Canada.
(UKA)

MACHEN JAMES
Emigrated from Scotland,
with his wife, two sons
and a daughter, to Canada
on the Earl of Buckingham
during June 1821.
Received a land grant in
Dalhousie, Upper Canada,
on 21 July 1821.
(PAO)

MAIR JOHN
Son of George Mair, Aberdeen
Educated at Marischal
College, Aberdeen, from
1811 to 1815, - graduated
M.A. Medical practitioner
and author in Canada.
(MCA)

MAIR JOHN
Emigrated from Scotland,
with his wife, to Canada
on the Commerce in June
1820. Received land
grants in Lanark, Upper
Canada, on 1 October 1820
and on 1 June 1821.
(PAO)

218

MAIR THOMAS
Blacksmith in Broxburn,
West Lothian. Applied
to settle in Canada
on 3 March 1815.
(SRO/RH9)

MAITLAND JAMES
Born in Scotland. Former
sergeant in the 90th
Regiment. Military
settler. Received a land
grant in Montague, Upper
Canada, 26 June 1817.
(PAO)

MALBON JOHN
Merchant. Died of fever
on the voyage from
Scotland to Darien on
28 October 1698.
(NLS)

MALCOLM of PELLRIVER
DUGALD
Argyllshire. Settler
in Jamaica, c1773.
(CC)

MALCOLM HUGH
Son of John Malcolm
and Catharine Campbell,
Kilmartin, Argyllshire.
Merchant in Jamaica.
Died before 1773.
(CC)

MALCOLM JAMES
Brother of Sir John
Malcolm of Lochore.
Merchant in Jamaica.
Died pre 1756.
(CPD)

MALCOLM JOHN
Emigrated from Scotland
to North Carolina after
1745. Aide to Governor
Tryon in 1771. Customs
House officer in Portland,
Maine, and in Boston,
Massachusetts.
(TSA)

MALCOLM NEIL
Argyllshire. Merchant in
Jamaica c1773.
(CC)

MANN ALEXANDER
Aberdeenshire. Educated
at the University of
Aberdeen - graduated M.A.
in March 1819. Minister
in Pakenham, Canada.
(KCA)(UKA)

MANN JAMES
Born during 1795 in Elgin,
Morayshire(?), son of John
Mann and Janet Laing.
Emigrated from Scotland to
America during 1811.
Settled in Hampstead,
Rockingham, New Hampshire.
Father of James.
(H)

MANN WILLIAM
Born during 1777 in Elgin,
Morayshire, son of John
Mann and Janet Laing. A
ship's carpenter employed
by the East India Company.
Stranded off the coast of
Africa. Rescued and landed
in Salem, Massachusetts,
during 1803. Settled in
Essex County, Massachusetts.
(H)

MANSON DAVID
Born c1783, son of
John Manson, 1745-
1823, merchant in
Perth, and Elizabeth
Key, 1754-1822. Died
in Jamaica 2 July 1821.
(Perth Greyfriars GS)

MANSON DONALD
Born during 1796 in
Scotland. Hudson Bay
Company employee from
1817 to 1857. Died in
Oregon 7 January 1880.
(HBRS)

MARSHALL AGNES
Indentured servant
imported from Scotland
to East New Jersey by
Lord Neil Campbell in
December 1685.
(EJD/A225)

MARSHALL EDMUND
Born during 1616, son of
Edmund Marshall, Aberdeen.
Emigrated from Scotland via
Chepstow, England, to
Plymouth Bay Colony in 1636.
Freeman of Massachusetts in
1637. Settled in New
London 1648, then in
Gloucester 1657, and later
in Ipswich, Massachusetts.
Married Millicent Blinman
in 1636. Father of Benjamin.
(BAF)

MARSHALL JAMES
Glasgow. Emigrated from
Scotland to America.
Settled in Frederick County,
Maryland. Father of Chloe,
William, Mary, Eleanor and
Mary Ann. Testament dated
26 October 1799.
(UNC/Williams pp)

MARSHALL MICHAEL
Indentured servant
imported from Scotland
to East New Jersey by
Lord Neil Campbell in
December 1685.
(EJD/A225)

MARSHALL WILLIAM
Born in Scotland.Former
captain in the Canadian
Fencibles. Military
settler. Received land
grants in Elmsley, Upper
Canada, 11 November 1815,
Upper Canada 30 September
1816, Beckwith, 14 June
1817, Cavan, Newcastle,
19 September 1818, and in
Drummond, Upper Canada, on
5 June 1819.
(PAO)

MARTIN ....
Third son of Donald Martin
and Isabel MacDonald, born
in Skye, Inverness-shire.
Medical practitioner. Died
during 1780 in the West
Indies.
(CD)

MARTIN DANIEL
Sailor. Died on the voyage
from Scotland to Darien,of
flux, 8 August 1698.
(NLS)

MARTIN JAMES
Emigrated from Scotland,
with his wife, four sons
and four daughters, to
Canada on the Prompt.
Received a land grant in
Dalhousie, Upper Canada,
on 25 November 1821.
(PAO)

MARTIN Rev JOHN
Born in Scotland 1790.
Ordained in Hamilton,
Lanarkshire, 31 July
1821. Emigrated from
Scotland to Halifax,
Nova Scotia, in 1821.
Minister of St Andrews
from 1821 to 1865.
Died on 22 June 1865.
(HPC)

MARTIN PETER W.
Former army sergeant.
Emigrated from Scotland
to Canada. Received a
land grant in
Charlottenburg,
St Raphael, Quebec, on
24 November 1787.
(PAO)

MASON ROBERT
Emigrated from Scotland,
with his wife, two sons
and three daughters, to
Canada on the George
Canning. Received a land
grant in Lanark, Upper
Canada, 4 August 1821.
(PAO)

MATHERS JOHN
Emigrated from Scotland,
with two daughters, to
Canada. Received a
land grant in Lanark,
Upper Canada, on
30 July 1822.
(PAO)

MATHESON ALEXANDER G.
Fourth son of Colin
Matheson of Bennetsfield,
and Grace Grant, who were
married in 1784. Merchant
in Berbice. Died 1819.
(HOM)

MATHIESON ALEXANDER
Born in Scotland. Military
settler. Received a land
grant in Bathurst, Upper
Canada, on 23 July 1816.
(PAO)

MATHESON CHARLES M.
Third son of Colin Matheson
of Bennetsfield, and Grace
Grant, who were married in
1784. Merchant in Berbice.
Married Margaret Fraser.
Father of Colin(who died
in America), Simon,
Charles, John, Donald,
Anthony and Maria.
(HOM)

MATHESON FARQUHAR
Second son of John Matheson
of Duirinish, and Mary
MacKenzie. Emigrated from
Scotland, with his family,
to America in 1774.
(HOM)

MATHESON FARQUHAR
Son of John Matheson and
Flora MacRae, Inverness.
Emigrated from Scotland to
Canada before 1812. Killed
at Fort Wellington, Upper
Canada, on 7 November 1813.
(HOM)

MATHESON FARQUHAR
Yeoman. Emigrated from
Scotland to Canada.
Received a land grant in
Eldon, Newcastle, Upper
Canada, on 8 March 1826.
(PAO)

MATHESON JOHN
Son of Murdoch Matheson,
who died 1815. Emigrated
from Scotland to Cape
Breton Island, in 1820.
(HOM)

MATHESON JOHN
Son of Donald Matheson,
1744-1845, miller at
Fernaig. Parish school
master of Lochalsh,
Inverness-shire, from
1820 to 1830.
Emigrated from Scotland
to Cape Breton Island.
(HOM)

MATTHEWSON JOHN
Born c1794. Labourer.
Emigrated from Scotland
to Canada. Settled in
Lower Settlement,
Pictou, Nova Scotia,
during 1815.
(PANS/RG1)

MATHESON MURDOCH
Son of Roderick Matheson,
farmer at Lochcarron, Ross
and Cromarty, and Margaret
McRae. Educated at King's
College, Aberdeen.
Emigrated from Scotland
to America during 1809.
Died in Lexington 1817.
(HOM)

MATHESON RODERICK
Born c1792 son of John
Matheson and Flora MacRae,
Inverness. Emigrated from
Scotland to Canada pre 1812.
Paymaster of the Glengarry
Fencibles from 1812 to 1816.
Military settler. Received
land grants in Upper Canada
in July 1816. Settled in
Perth, Lanark. Married (1)
Mary Fraser Robertson on
5 November 1823 - died 1825.
(2) Annabella Russell on
11 August 1830. Father of
John, Roderick, William,
Charles, Arthur and Allan.
Died 1873.
(HOM)(PAO)

MATHIESON RODERICK
Son of Murdoch Mathieson,
who died in 1815.
Emigrated from Scotland
to Cape Breton Island
during 1820.
(HOM)

MATHIESON WILLIAM
Born in Scotland. Former
sergeant in the Canadian
Fencibles. Military
settler. Received a land
grant in Drummond, Upper
Canada, 10 October 1816.
(PAO)

MATHEW ISABEL
Four year indentured
servant imported from
Scotland to East New
Jersey in October 1684
by John Campbell.
(EJD/A)

MATHEW SAMUEL
Four year indentured
servant imported from
Scotland to East New
Jersey in October 1684
by John Campbell.
(EJD/A)

MATHIE ALEXANDER
Emigrated from Scotland,
with his wife and three
daughters, to Canada on
the George Canning in June
1821. Received a land grant
in Dalhousie, Upper Canada,
11 July 1821.
(PAO)

MATHIE JAMES
Emigrated from Scotland,
with his wife, five sons
and a daughter, to
Canada on the David of
London in June 1821.
Received a land grant in
Lanark, Upper Canada, on
14 August 1821.
(PAO)

MAXLIE CATHARINE
Indentured servant
imported from Scotland
to East New Jersey by
David Mudie in November
1684.
(EJD/A196)

MAXTON ALEXANDER
Born c1794, son of
Rev John Maxton.
Died in Montreal,
Quebec, in 1830.
(Alloa GS
 Clackmannanshire)

MAXWELL JAMES
Emigrated from Scotland,
with his wife, four sons
and three daughters, to
Canada on the Prompt
June 1820. Received a
land grant in Lanark,
Upper Canada, on
19 November 1821.
(PAO)

MAXWELL JOHN
Scottish merchant in
New England c1699.
(DP)

MAXWELL WILLIAM
Emigrated from Paisley,
Renfrewshire, to New
York c1790.
(SO)

MAYWOOD ROBERT CAMPBELL
Born in Greenock, Renfrewshire, c1786. Actor in New
York c1819. Theatre manager
in Philadelphia, Penn-
sylvania, from 1832 to
1840. Died during 1856
in Troy, New York.
(TSA)

MELVIN JAMES
Indentured servant
imported from Scotland to
East New Jersey on
6 December 1684. Settled
in Freehold, New Jersey.
Married Alice ...Father
of James, Mary, Margaret
and John. Died in 1709.
(MNJ)(EJD/A)

MENTEITH ALEXANDER
Indentured servant
imported from Scotland
to East New Jersey by
Thomas Gordon in
October 1684.
(EJD/A)

MEICKLE ALEXANDER
Four year indentured
servant imported from
Scotland to East New Jersey
in October 1684 by John
Campbell. Carpenter in
Topanemus, New Jersey, 1689.
(EJD/A/B)

223

MEIN PATRICK
Scottish merchant in
Barbados c1701. Member
of the Council of
Barbados.
(SPAWI)

MENZIES GEORGE
Planter. Died of flux
on the voyage from
Scotland to Darien
30 August 1698.
(NLS)

MENZIES ROBERT
Emigrated from Scotland
to Canada on the Earl of
Buckingham in June 1821.
Received a land grant in
Dalhousie, Upper Canada,
on 31 July 1821.
(PAO)

MIDDLETON ALEXANDER
Third son of Alexander
Middleton, 1676-1751,
Customs Collector in
Aberdeen, and Elspet
Burnet, 1683-1767.
Baptised 3 September
1709. Emigrated from
Scotland to America.
Married Ann Todd in
Boston, Massachusetts.
Died 21 August 1750.
(SP.VI)

MIDDLETON JOHN
Second son of Alexander
Middleton, 1676-1751,
Customs Collector in
Aberdeen, and Elspet
Burnet, 1683-1767.
Baptised 21 March 1708.
Married Mary Allister
31 July 1731. Settled in
Barbados. Father of John
and Alex. Died in 1792.
(SP.VI)

MILL ANNA
Daughter of Robert Mill,
master mason in Edinburgh.
Indentured servant
imported from Scotland to
East New Jersey. Headright
land grant 3 May 1687.
(EJD/B139)

MILLER ALEXANDER
Arnprior, Perthshire.
Emigrated from Greenock,
Renfrewshire, to Montreal,
Quebec, with his wife Agnes
Moir and children Janet
and Peter, on the brig
Niagara, Hamilton, 1825.
Settled in McNab, Bathurst,
Upper Canada, 1825.
(SG)

MILLER ANDREW
Emigrated from Scotland
to Canada on the George
Canning in June 1821.
Received a land grant in
Dalhousie, Upper Canada,
on 16 July 1821.
(PAO)

MILLER DAVID
Planter. Died in Darien
on 6 December 1698.
(NLS)

MILLER HUGH
Emigrated from Scotland,
with his wife, son and
daughter, to Canada on
the Earl of Buckingham in
June 1821. Received a land
grant in Ramsay, Upper
Canada, 31 July 1821.
(PAO)

MILLER JAMES
Scotland. Merchant.
Settled in Perth
Amboy, New Jersey.
Received a land grant
on 30 June 1685.
(EJD/A282)

MILLER JAMES
Emigrated from Scotland
to America. Planter in
Norfolk, Virginia, 1764.
(OD)

MILLAR JAMES
Emigrated from Scotland,
with his wife, son and
two daughters, to Canada
on the George Canning in
June 1821. Received a
land grant in Dalhousie,
Upper Canada, 16 July 1821.
(PAO)

MILLER JAMES
Emigrated from Scotland,
with his wife, two sons
and two daughters, to
Canada on the Commerce in
June 1821. Received a
land grant in Lanark,
Upper Canada, on
22 August 1821.
(PAO)

MILLER JOHN
Emigrated from Scotland,
with his wife, three sons
and three daughters, to
Canada on the Commerce
in June 1821. Received a
land grant in Lanark,
Upper Canada, 21 July 1821.
(PAO)

MILLER JOHN
Emigrated from Scotland,
with his wife, two sons
and a daughter, to Canada
on the George Canning in
June 1821. Received a land
grant in Dalhousie, Upper
Canada, 25 July 1821.
(PAO)

MILLER ROBERT
Born in Aberdeen c1690.
Married Elizabeth
Gordon c1730. Emigrated
from Scotland to America
c1732. Settled in Penn-
sylvania. Father of William.
(BAF)

MILLER WILLIAM
Volunteer. Died of fever
on the voyage from Scot-
land to Darien on
26 October 1698.
(NLS)

MILLER Rev WILLIAM
Born in Ayrshire during
1786. Emigrated from
Scotland to Nova Scotia
c1821. Ordained at West
River, Pictou, Nova Scotia,
during 1821. Minister in
Mabou and Port Hood, Cape
Breton Island from 1821
to 1861. Died 16 November
1861.
(HPC)

MILLER WILLIAM
Emigrated from Scotland,
with his wife, son and
three daughters, to
Canada on the Prompt in
June 1820. Received a
land grant in Dalhousie,
Upper Canada, on
19 November 1821.
(PAO)

MILLER WILLIAM
Emigrated from Scotland
to Canada on the Commerce
in June 1820. Received a
land grant in Lanark,
Upper Canada, 18 March 1821.
(PAO)

MILLER WILLIAM
Emigrated from Scotland,
with his wife, four sons
and a daughter, to
Canada on the George
Canning in June 1821.
Received a land grant in
Lanark, Upper Canada, on
16 July 1821.
(PAO)

MILLER WILLIAM
Emigrated from Scotland
to Canada on the Earl of
Buckingham in June 1821.
Received a land grant in
Ramsay, Upper Canada, on
20 July 1821.
(PAO)

MILLS JAMES
Emigrated from Scotland
to America before 1755.
Hatter in Leedstown,
Virginia.
(OD)

MILNE WILLIAM
Born in Falkirk,
Stirlingshire, son of
Alexander Milne, Writer
to the Signet, and Sarah
Swan. Lieutenant in the
Royal Navy. Married Johanna
Gallwey in London. Settled
in Canada. Died in
Ancaster, Upper Canada, on
27 February 1825.
(DF)

MILNER JOSEPH
Born in Scotland.
Received a land grant in
Lanark, Upper Canada, on
26 January 1821.
(PAO)

MILROY WILLIAM
Born c1784, son of John
Milroy, town clerk of
Whithorn, Wigtownshire,
and Janet McMillan. Died
in Dominica on 3 June 1804.
(Whithorn GS)

MINGEESE (MENZIES?) PETER
Emigrated from Scotland
to America. Tailor in
Chesterfield County,
Virginia, by 1756.
(OD)

MINTO ROBERT
Born 1743 in Scotland(?)
Father of Walter Minto,
1779-1830. Grandfather
of Robert Minto, 1809-1840.
Died on 3 May 1803.
Buried in Roslyn Castle
Estate, Jamaica.
(MIBWI)

MITCHELL DAVID BRYDIE
Born in Scotland on
22 October 1766.
Emigrated from Scotland
to America during 1783.
Inherited property of
his uncle David Brydie
in Savannah, Georgia.
Politician, militiaman,
Solicitor General of
Georgia, Governor of
Georgia. Died in
Milledgeville, Georgia,
on 22 April 1837.
(DU/DBM pp)

MITCHELL FRANCIS
Emigrated from Scotland
to Canada on the Prompt
26 September 1817.
Received a land grant in
Leeds, Upper Canada, on
15 October 1817.
(PAO)

MITCHELL HENRY
Glasgow. Merchant in
Fredericksburg, Virginia.
Partner in McCall, Smellie
and Company, merchants in
Glasgow c1770.
(SRA)

MITCHELL JAMES
Merchant in Virginia.
Legatee in settlement of
John Wilson of Shieldhall,
29 October 1761.
(SRA/B10.15.7118)

MITCHELL JAMES
Emigrated from Scotland,
with his wife and three
daughters, to Canada on
the Earl of Buckingham
in June 1821. Received
a land grant in Lanark,
Upper Canada, 1 August 1821.
(PAO)

MITCHELL JOHN
Glasgow. Tobacco factor
in Culpepper County and
in Fredericksburg,
Virginia, for Anderson
and Dalziel, and also for
Anderscn and Horsburgh,
pre 1776.
(SRA/T79.32)

MITCHELL JOHN
Born 1770, son of David
Mitchell of Kirkmoatland,
Dumfries-shire, 1729-1780,
and Jean Richardson.
Died 8 September 1794 at
Montego Bay, Jamaica.
(Dumfries GS)

MITCHELL JOHN sr
Emigrated from Scotland,
with his wife, four sons
and three daughters, to
Canada on the Earl of
Buckingham in June 1821.
Received a land grant in
Ramsay, Upper Canada, on
8 August 1821.
(PAO)

MITCHELL JOHN jr
Emigrated from Scotland
to Canada on the Earl of
Buckingham in June 1821.
Received a land grant in
Ramsay, Upper Canada, on
8 August 1821.
(PAO)

MITCHELL MARY
Widow. Transported from
Scotland, with her late
husband and four sons, to
East New Jersey by Arent
Sonmans. Petitioned the
Governor and Council on
29 February 1683.
(EJD)

MITCHELL MARY
Four year indentured
servant. Imported
from Scotland to
East New Jersey in
October 1684 by John
Campbell.
(EJD/A)

MITCHELL WILLIAM
Born c1766, son of
William Mitchell, 1725-
1794, tenant farmer in
West Seatoun, Maryton,
by Arbroath, Angus, and
Jean Deas, 1733-1802.
Died in Grenada on
19 February 1823.
(Maryton GS)

MOFFAT GEORGE
Agent in New York c1699
for Messrs Joseph
Ormston, Alexander
Hamilton and Company.
(DP)

MOFFAT JAMES
Son of David Moffat,
tanner in Musselburgh,
East Lothian. A tanner.
Married Jean Hogg.
Settled in Quebec pre
1816.
(SRO/GD81.310.1)

MOFFAT SAMUEL
Covenanter - fought at
Battle of Bothwell Bridge
1679. Emigrated from Scotland, via Ireland, to
America in 1708. Settled
in Woodbridge, New Jersey,
in 1710. Father of William
and Samuel.
(BAF)

MOGG DAVID
Born in Scotland. Former
bombardier in the Royal
Artillery. Wife and a
daughter. Received a land
grant in Drummond, Upper
Canada, 21 November 1815.
(PAO)

MOIR ALEXANDER
Educated at King's College,
Aberdeen, - graduated M.A.
during 1730s. Settled in
St Croix. Graduated M.D.
of Aberdeen 27 September
1763.
(KCA)

MOIR WILLIAM
Son of George Moir, minister
in Peterhead, Aberdeenshire.
Educated at Marischal
College, Aberdeen, c1792.
Writer in Edinburgh and in
Trinidad.
(MCA)

MOIR WILLIAM
Emigrated from Scotland,
with his wife, three sons
and a daughter, to Canada
on the Earl of Buckingham
in June 1821. Received a
land grant in Ramsay,
Upper Canada, 31 July 1821.
(PAO)

MOLISON JOHN
Indentured servant
imported from Scotland to
East New Jersey c1684.
Headright land grant 1688.
(EJD/A403)

MONDAY ROBERT
Emigrated from Scotland
to Canada on the Commerce
in June 1820. Settled in
Upper Canada.
(PAO)

MONKE WILLIAM
A Scottish soldier taken
to Jamaica on the
Grantham by General
Brayne during 1659.
Discharged in Jamaica
in April 1659.
(SPAWI)

MONROE ANDREW
Third son of David Monroe
and Agnes Monroe.
Emigrated from Scotland
to St Mary's County, Mary-
land c1641. Royalist
officer captured and
banished from England to
Virginia in 1648.
Settled in Northumberland
County, Virginia. Married
Elizabeth Alexander.
Father of William, 1666-
1737. Died in 1668.
(BAF)

MONRO JAMES
Born in 1771, son of
Rev James Monro, minister
of Cromarty, and Mary
Stark. Cabinet-maker in
Inverness. Married Helen
Gordon, 1769-1841, on
20 October 1799. Settled
in Pictou, Nova Scotia.
Father of George and James.
Died in September 1843.
(DF)

MONTEITH ALEXANDER
Settled in Kingston,
Jamaica, pre 1749.
(SRO/GD30)

MONTGOMERY CHARLES
Son of Hugh Montgomery of
Broomlands, 1686-1766,and
Margaret McLaren.
Emigrated from Scotland,
via Portsmouth, England,
to Jamaica. Settled at
Montego Bay, and later in
Rozelle Plantation,
Kingston, Jamaica.
Merchant. Died 1766.
(RAF)

MONTGOMERIE HUGH
Son of Hugh Montgomerie
of Blackhouse, Ayrshire.
Died in Trinidad 1822.
(RAF)

MONTGOMERY JAMES
Died of flux on the voyage
from Scotland to Darien
28 October 1698.
(NLS)

MONTGOMERY JAMES
Planter. Died at Darien
on 29 November 1698.
(NLS)

MONTGOMERIE JOHN
Ayrshire. Settled in
Trinidad. Father of Hugh
born during 1822 in
Trinidad.
(RAF)

MONTGOMERIE ROBERT
Son of Patrick Montgomerie
of Blackhouse, Ayrshire.
Settled in Sevilla,
Trinidad, c1800. Merchant.
(RAF)

MONTGOMERIE THOMAS
Third son of Alexander
Montgomerie of Coilsfield,
and Lilias Montgomerie.
Died in Dumfries, Virginia,
13 August 1793.
(HCA)

MONTGOMERIE WILLIAM
Born c1655, eldest son of
Hew Montgomerie of Brigend,
and Catharine Scott.
Married in 1684 to Isobel
Burnet, daughter of Robert
Burnet of Lethendie, in
Maybole, Ayrshire. Father
of Robert, Anna, William,
James and Alexander.
Emigrated from Scotland to
America during 1701.
Settled at Doctor's Creek,
East New Jersey.
(HCA)

MOODIE JEAN
Daughter of James Moodie,
Jamaica, married William,
eldest son of Dr William
Keith, South Carolina.
Both in New Kirk parish,
Edinburgh. Married in
Edinburgh 12 March 1769.
(EMR)

MOORE JOHN
Indentured servant
imported from Scotland
to East New Jersey in
October 1684 by John Dobie.
(EJD/A)

MOORE JOHN
Forres, Morayshire,
married Betty Taylor,
Elgin, Morayshire.
Emigrated from Scotland
to America during 1772.
Settled in Moresville,
Delaware County, New York.
(NYGBR.XXV)

MOORE ROBERT
Indentured servant
imported from Scotland
to East New Jersey in
October 1684.
(EJD/A)

MOOR SAMUEL
Glasgow. Student.
Applied to settle in
Canada on 6 March 1815.
(SRO/RH9)

MOORE SAMUEL
Glasgow. Applied to
settle in Canada on
3 March 1815.
(SRO/RH9)

MOORE WILLIAM
Minister of Halifax, Nova
Scotia. Graduated D.D. at
University of Aberdeen on
2 March 1770.
(KCA)

MORE JOHN
Emigrated from Scotland to
Canada, with his wife, two
sons and two daughters, on
the George Canning in June
1821. Received a land
grant in Ramsay, Upper
Canada, on 16 July 1821.
(PAO)

MORGAN THOMAS
Emigrated from Scotland
to Canada. Received a
land grant in Brock,
Home, Upper Canada, on
14 July 1817.
(PAO)

MORGAN WILLIAM
Indentured servant
imported from Scotland
to East New Jersey in
October 1684 by John
Campbell for Captain
Andrew Hamilton.
(EJD/A)

MORGAN WILLIAM
Son of George Morgan.
Educated at University of
Aberdeen. Rector of
Kingston, Jamaica. Married
Martha Jopping. Father of
James..D.D. of King's
College, Aberdeen, on
20 November 1780. Died
2 September 1788.
(KCA)(MCA)

MORRIS JAMES
Son of Alexander Morris.
Born in Paisley, Renfrew-
shire, during 1798.
Emigrated from Scotland
to Canada in 1801.
Politician.
(BCB)

MORRIS WILLIAM
Born on 31 October 1786
in Paisley, Renfrewshire.
Emigrated from Scotland,
with his parents, to
Upper Canada in 1801.
Merchant and public
official. Died in Montreal,
Quebec, 29 June 1858.
(BCB)

MORRIS WILLIAM
Emigrated from Scotland
to Canada on the Brock
in 1820. Received a land
grant in Lanark, Upper
Canada, 1 November 1821.
(PAO)

MORRIS WILLIAM
Married Elizabeth,
daughter of John Cochran,
in Kirktonfield. Settled
in Perth, Upper Canada,
before 1826.
(SRO/RH4)

MORISON Rev
Minister in Nevis c1700.
Brother-in-law of James
Gentleman in Montrose,
Angus.
(DP)

MORRISON ALEXANDER
Emigrated from Scotland
to Canada. Received a
land grant in Cavan,
Newcastle, Upper Canada,
on 10 October 1818.
(PAO)

MORRISON ALEXANDER
Emigrated from Scotland,
with his wife and daughter,
to Canada on George Canning
in June 1821. Received a
land grant in Ramsay,
Upper Canada, 16 July 1821.
(PAO)

MORRISON HUGH
Emigrated from Scotland to
America. Settled in
Darien, Georgia, c1739.
(HGP)

MORRISON HUGH
Emigrated from Scotland
to Canada. Received a
land grant in Smith,
Newcastle, Upper Canada,
on 7 October 1818.
(PAO)

MORRISON JAMES
Son of Marion Young in
Glasgow. A 'slave' in
Barbados c1654.
(GR)

MORRISON JAMES
Emigrated from Scotland
to Canada. Received a
land grant in Cavan,
Newcastle, Upper Canada,
on 10 October 1818.
(PAO)

MORRISON JOHN
Shoemaker. Emigrated
from Scotland to Canada.
Received a land grant in
Smith, Newcastle, Upper
Canada, on 7 October 1818.
(PAO)

MORRISON JOHN
Emigrated from Scotland
to Canada. Received a
land grant in Cavan,
Newcastle, Upper Canada,
on 10 October 1818.
(PAO)

MORRISON JOHN
Emigrated from Scotland
to Canada on the Martha
11 June 1819. Received
a land grant in
Drummond, Upper Canada,
on 18 June 1819.
(PAO)

MORRISON JOHN
Emigrated from Scotland
to Canada on the Earl of
Buckingham in June 1821.
Received a land grant in
Dalhousie, Upper Canada,
on 31 July 1821.
(PAO)

MORRISON JOHN
Emigrated from Scotland,
with his wife, three sons
and a daughter, to Canada
on the Prompt. Received a
land grant in Dalhousie,
Upper Canada, on
25 November 1821.
(PAO)

MORRISON ROBERT
Emigrated from Scotland,
with his wife and two
daughters, to Canada on
the Prompt. Received a
land grant in Dalhousie,
Upper Canada, on
25 November 1821.
(PAO)

MORISON RODERICK
Second son of John Morison
and Elizabeth Tolmie.
Emigrated from Scotland to
New Orleans during
November 1828. Settled in
Lexington City, Kentucky.
Educated at the University
of Pennsylvania, and at
Georgia Medical College.
Graduated M.D. in Georgia
on 15 April 1835.
(MB)

MORRISON WILLIAM
Emigrated from Scotland to
Canada on the Commerce 1820.
Received a land grant in
Lanark, Upper Canada, on
1 September 1820.
(PAO)

MORROT(?) ALEXANDER
Royalist soldier
captured at Worcester.
Transported from
Gravesend, Kent, to
Boston, New England, on
the John and Sarah, master
John Greene, 13 May 1652.
(NER)

MORSON ARTHUR
Glasgow. Merchant in
Falmouth, Rappahannock
River, Virginia, 1768.
Storekeeper for Glass-
ford and Company. Father
of Alexander, born 1759.
(SRA/B10.15.7174)

MORSON JAMES
Brother of Alexander
Morson, merchant in
Greenock, Renfrewshire.
Merchant in St Kitts
c1755.
(SRA)

MORTIMER EDWARD
Born in 1768 son of
Alexander Mortimer,
burgess of Forres, Moray-
shire, and Mary Smith,
1740-1802. Merchant in
Pictou, Nova Scotia.
Assemblyman for Halifax,
Nova Scotia. Judge in the
Court of Common Pleas.
Died in Pictou on
10 October 1819.
(CK)

MORTIMER WILLIAM
Son of John Mortimer,
fisher in Aberdeen.
Educated at Marischal
College, Aberdeen, 1812-
1816. Graduated M.A.
Merchant in Pictou, Nova
Scotia.
(MCA)

MORTON DAVID
Prisoner in Edinburgh
Tolbooth. Banished to
Virginia for conducting
an irregular marriage,
5 May 1669. Transported
from Leith to America
22 June 1671.
(PC)

MOSSMAN ARCHIBALD
Volunteer. Died in
Darien on 15 November
1698.
(NLS)

MOULTON JOHN
Emigrated from Scotland
to Canada on the Brock
in 1820. Received a land
grant in Lanark, Upper
Canada, in 1821.
(PAO)

MOUNT GEORGE
Prisoner in Edinburgh
Tolbooth. Stigmatised
and banished to the
Plantations on
19 February 1674.
(PC)

MOUNTT WILLIAM
Indentured servant
imported from Scotland
to East New Jersey in
October 1685 by James
Johnston.
(EJD/A226)

MOWAT JOHN
Canisby, Caithness.
Emigrated from Scotland
to Canada in 1816.
Settled in Kingston, Upper
Canada.
(BCG)

MOWBRAY ROBERT
Emigrated from Scotland,
with his wife, to Canada
on the Commerce in August
1820. Received a land grant
in Lanark, Upper Canada, on
1 September 1820.
(PAO)

MUCKART JOHN
Lanark. Applied to settle
in Canada on 27 February
1815.
(SRO/RH9)

MUDIE DAVID
Emigrated from Scotland,
with his children David,
James, Isabella, and
Margaret, to East New
Jersey during November
1684. Settled in Perth-
Amboy, New Jersey.
Merchant in New York 1690.
(EJD/A197/D330)

MUDIE MARGARET
Indentured servant
imported from Scotland
to East New Jersey by
David Mudie during
November 1684.
(EJD/A196)

MUIR ALEXANDER
Strathaven, Lanarkshire.
Applied to settle in
Canada on 27 February
1815.
(SRO/RH9)

MUIR ARCHIBALD
Emigrated from Scotland,
with his wife, two sons
and a daughter, to Canada.
Received a land grant in
Ramsay, Upper Canada, on
25 January 1822.
(PAO)

MUIR JAMES
Emigrated from Scotland,
with his wife, three sons
and five daughters, to
Canada on the Prompt in
June 1820. Received a
land grant in Dalhousie,
Upper Canada, on
25 November 1821.
(PAO)

MUIR JOHN
Emigrated from Scotland,
with his wife, four sons
and two daughters, to
Canada on the George Canning
June 1821. Received a
land grant in Dalhousie,
Upper Canada, 18 July 1821.
(PAO)

MUIR JOHN
Emigrated from Scotland,
with his wife, son and
three daughters, to Canada
on the Earl of Buckingham
in June 1821. Received a
land grant in Ramsay,
Upper Canada, on
25 July 1821.
(PAO)

MUIR ROBERT
Indentured servant
imported from Scotland to
East New Jersey by James
Johnston in October 1685.
(EJD/A226)

234

MUIR THOMAS
Emigrated from Scotland,
with his wife, two sons
and three daughters, to
Canada on the Commerce
in August 1820.
Received a land grant in
Lanark, Upper Canada, on
5 September 1820.
(PAO)

MUIR WILLIAM
Born in Kirkcudbright
during 1754. Emigrated
from Scotland to New York
in 1774. Married Mary
Ritchie. Father of John,
1793-1870. Died on
9 February 1809.
(BAF)

MUIR WILLIAM
Glasgow. Applied to
settle in Canada on
2 March 1815.
(SRO/RH9)

MUIR WILLIAM
Emigrated from Scotland,
with his wife, son and
two daughters, to Canada
on the Prompt in June
1820. Received a land
grant in Dalhousie, Upper
Canada, 19 November 1821.
(PAO)

MUIRHEAD JOHN
Scottish merchant in
Philadelphia, Penn-
sylvania, c1699.
(SPAWI)

MUIRHEAD JOHN
Emigrated from Scotland
to America before 1776.
Shoemaker in Norfolk,
Virginia.
(OD)

MUIRHEAD ROBERT
Born in Scotland. Former
sergeant in the 137th
Regiment. Wife and three
sons. Military settler.
Received a land grant in
Lanark, Upper Canada, on
1 August 1821.
(PAO)

MULLOCK GEORGE
Emigrated from Scotland
to Canada on the Grace
in June 1818. Received
a land grant in Drummond,
Upper Canada, 28 May 1819.
(PAO)

MUNCKLAND ROGER
Volunteer. Died in Darien
on 22 November 1698.
(NLS)

MUNGALL HENRY
Emigrated from Scotland
to Canada. Received a
land grant in Ramsay, Upper
Canada, on 26 August 1821.
(PAO)

MUNGALL WILLIAM
Royalist soldier captured
at Worcester. Transported
from Gravesend, Kent, to
Boston, New England, on the
John and Sarah, 13 May 1652.
(NER)

MUNRO ALEXANDER
Emigrated from Scotland
to America. Settled in
Darien, Georgia, c1739.
(HGP)

MUNRO ALEXANDER
Born c1785. Labourer.
Emigrated from Scotland,
with his wife and child,
to Canada. Settled at
Scottshill, Pictou, Nova
Scotia, in 1815.
(PANS/RG1)

MUNRO ALEXANDER
Born c1793. Carpenter.
Emigrated from Scotland
to Canada. Settled in
Lower Settlement, Pictou,
Nova Scotia, in 1815.
(PANS/RG1)

MUNRO ALEXANDER
Emigrated from Sutherland,
with his family of five,
to Nova Scotia on the brig
Prince William in September
1815. Received a land grant
in Pictou, Nova Scotia.
(PANS/RG20)

MUNRO ANDREW
Born during 1794 in Dumfries.
Emigrated from Scotland to
Jamaica during 1818. Died
on 18 December 1841. Buried
in the Scots cemetery,
Kingston, Jamaica.
(MIBWI)

MUNRO DAVID
Scottish settler in Darien.
Moved from Darien to New
York on the Unicorn in
August 1699.
(SPAWI)

MUNRO Rev JAMES
Born at Orbiston, Moray-
shire, during 1747.
Ordained on 18 June 1781.
Emigrated from Scotland
to America during 1785.
Pastor in Nottingham,
Maryland. Later settled
in Nova Scotia c1792. Died
in Antigonish, Nova Scotia,
on 17 May 1819.
(HPC)

MUNRO JAMES
Joiner. Emigrated from
Scotland, with his wife
and child, to Canada.
Settled in Pictou Town,
Nova Scotia, in 1815.
(PANS/RG1)

MUNROE JOHN
Born in Ross-shire 1796.
Emigrated from Scotland,
with his parents, to
America. Graduated from
West Point in 1814. U.S.
Army officer, and later
Governor of New Mexico.
Died in New Brunswick 1861.
(TSA)

MUNRO JOHN
Emigrated from Scotland
to Canada on the George
Canning in June 1821.
Received a land grant in
Ramsay, Upper Canada, on
16 July 1821.
(PAO)

MUNRO KENNETH
Emigrated from Sutherland,
with his family of six, to
Nova Scotia on the brig
Prince William in September
1815. Received a land grant
in Pictou, Nova Scotia.
(PANS/RG20)

MUNRO PETER
Emigrated from Scotland,
with his wife, two sons
and five daughters, to
Canada on the Commerce
in June 1820. Received
a land grant in
Dalhousie, Upper Canada,
on 1 October 1820.
(PAO)

MUNRO WILLIAM
Emigrated from Scotland
to America. Settled in
Darien, Georgia, c1739.
(HGP)

MUNRO WILLIAM
Emigrated from Scotland,
with his wife, two sons
and four daughters, to
Canada on the Hibernia
on 20 September 1816.
Received a land grant
in Drummond, Upper Canada,
on 31 March 1817.
(PAO)

MURCHISON ALEXANDER
Educated at Marischal College,
Aberdeen, - graduated M.D. on
7 July 1813. Medical
practitioner in Jamaica.
(MCA)

MURDOCK EDWARD C.
Emigrated from Scotland,
with his wife and three
sons, via the United
States to Canada.
Received a land grant in
Drummond, Upper Canada,
on 8 April 1817.
(PAO)

MURDOCH Rev GEORGE
Glasgow(?) Emigrated
from Scotland to America
after 1720. Rector of
Prince George County,
Maryland. Father of
William, born during 1720
in Glasgow. Died 1775.
(TSA)

MURDOCH JOHN
Emigrated from Scotland,
to Canada on the Peace of
Hull on 16 July 1817.
Received a land grant in
Drummond, Upper Canada,
on 25 July 1818.
(PAO)

MURDOCH WILLIAM
Born in Glasgow during 1720
son of Rev George Murdoch.
Emigrated from Scotland,
with his father, to
America. Member of the
General Assembly of Maryland
from 1745 to 1770. Died 1775.
(TSA)

MURE JOHN
Son of Robert Mure of Blair-
stoun, and Mary Mitchell.
Trained as a surgeon in
Edinburgh. Died in Jamaica
during 1744.
(HCA)

237

MURRAY ALEXANDER
Educated at King's College,
Aberdeen, - graduated M.A.
in 1746. Episcopalian
missionary in Reading,
Pennsylvania. Awarded a
Doctor of Divinity at
Aberdeen, 17 February 1784.
(KCA)

MURRAY ALEXANDER
Emigrated from Scotland
to America in 17..
Planter in Pittsylvania
County, Virginia.
(OD)

MURRAY ALEXANDER
Emigrated from Scotland,
with his wife and daughter,
to Canada on the George
Canning in June 1821.
Received a land grant in
Ramsay, Upper Canada, on
10 July 1821.
(PAO)

MURRAY ANGUS
Born c1743. Labourer.
Emigrated from Scotland,
with his wife, to Canada.
Settled at Roger Hill,
Pictou, Nova Scotia, 1815.
(PANS/RG1)

MURRAY ARCHIBALD
Alloa, Clackmannanshire.
Applied to settle in
Canada on 29 February
1815.
(SRO/RH9)

MURRAY DONALD
Born c1775. Labourer.
Emigrated from Scotland,
with his wife and five
children, to Canada.
Settled at Roger Hill,
Pictou, Nova Scotia, 1815.
(PANS/RG1)

MURRAY DONALD
Born c1790. Labourer.
Emigrated from Scotland,
with his wife and two
children, to Canada.
Settled at West River,
Pictou, Nova Scotia, 1815.
(PANS/RG1)

MURRAY DONALD
Born c1793. Emigrated
from Scotland, with his
wife and children,
Christina 4, and Margaret
2, to Canada. Received a
land grant in Halifax,
Nova Scotia, in 1815.
(PANS/RG20)

MURRAY DUNCAN
Emigrated from Scotland to
America before 1755.
Seaman. Settled in Fairfax
County, Virginia.
(OD)

MURRAY JAMES
Born in Scotland. Married
Ann ... in 1742(?) Father
of James, John, Anne,
Margaret, William, Mary
and Thomas. Churchwarden
and vestryman of Bristol
County, Virginia, 1746.
Settled in Athol, Peters-
burg, Virginia.
(HBV)

238

MURRAY JAMES
Born in Perthshire.
Emigrated from Scotland
to America during 1766.
Settled in Dauphin,
Pennsylvania. Soldier in
the Revolution.
(TSA)

MURRAY JAMES
Emigrated from Scotland,
with his wife, five sons
and three daughters, to
Canada on the Commerce
in June 1820. Received
a land grant in Lanark,
Upper Canada, on
18 March 1821.
(PAO)

MURRAY JOHN
Born in Perthshire 1731.
Emigrated from Scotland
to America during 1766.
Settled in Dauphin,
Pennsylvania. Soldier in
the Revolution.Died 1798.
(TSA)

MURRAY JOHN
Glasgow. Factor at Aquia,
Virginia, for Oswald
Dennistoun and Company,
tobacco merchants in
Glasgow, c1770.
(SRA/779.21)

MURRAY JOHN
Born c1799. Emigrated
from Scotland, with two
sisters, to Nova Scotia c1815.
(PANS/RG20)

MURRAY Lord MUNGO
Emigrated from Scotland
to Darien. Died in
Darien during 1699.
(TDD)

MURRAY WILLIAM
Merchant traveller in
Virginia, married Margaret,
daughter of Robert
Robertson, merchant in
Edinburgh, on 8 July 1662
in Edinburgh.
(EMR)(Register of Deeds)

MURRAY WILLIAM
Scottish settler in Darien.
Moved from Darien to New
York on the Unicorn during
August 1699.
(SPAWI)

MURRAY WILLIAM
Born c1784, son of
Alexander Murray and
Catharine McGuffie.
Died in Jamaica on
22 August 1800.
(Wigtown GS)

MURRAY WILLIAM
Born c1790. Farmer.
Emigrated from Scotland
to Canada. Settled in
Merigonish, Pictou, Nova
Scotia, in 1815.
(PANS/RG1)

MURT ALEXANDER
Indentured servant
imported from Scotland to
East New Jersey in 1684.
(EJD/A)

MUSHET JOHN
Brother of Dr Mushet, and
nephew of 'Old Lendricks',
Stirlingshire. Settled in
Portobacco, Maryland,
before 1747.
(LM)

MUSHET Dr
Brother of John Mushet, and
nephew of 'Old Lendricks',
Stirlingshire. Settled in
Portobacco, Maryland,
before 1747.
(LM)

NAIRN ARCHIBALD
Emigrated from Scotland,
with his wife, three sons
and a daughter, to Canada
on the Earl of Buckingham
in June 1821. Received a
land grant in Lanark,
Upper Canada, on
1 August 1821.
(PAO)

NAIRN Captain JOHN
Born in Scotland on
1 March 1731. Officer in
a Highland Regiment from
1745 to 1762. To Canada
during 1759. Settled at
Murray Bay c1764, after
the Siege of Quebec.
Married Christiana Emery
in Quebec 20 July 1789.
Landowner. Died on
14 July 1802.
(DCB)(PRSC.X)(CP)

NAPIER ALEXANDER
Indentured servant
imported from Scotland
to East New Jersey 1684.
(EJD/A)

NAPIER DAVID
Linen manufacturer.
Emigrated from Scotland
to Philadelphia, Penn-
sylvania, in August 1783.
(SO)

NAPIER Dr PATRICK
Son of Robert Napier,
Edinburgh, born in 1610.
Emigrated to America in
1655. Settled in
Virginia. Married Elizabeth
Booth. Father of Robert,
1660-c1715. Died in 1669.
(BAF)

NAPIER Lieutenant
Born in Scotland. Military
settler. Received a land
grant in Bathurst, Ketley
and Elmsley, Upper Canada,
on 21 June 1817.
(PAO)

NAUGHTY WILLIAM
Born in Scotland. Formerly
in the Military Field Train.
Military settler. Received
a land grant in Ketley,
Upper Canada, 18 June 1817.
(PAO)

NEILSON JOHN
Sixth child of William
Neilson and Isabel Brown,
born at Dornald, Balmaghie,
Kirkcudbrightshire.
Emigrated from Scotland to
Canada c1790. Editor of the
Quebec Gazette. Politician.
Died at Cap Rouge, Quebec,
on 1 February 1843.
(SNF)(BCB)

NEILSON JOHN
Emigrated from Scotland
to Canada. Received a
land grant in Cavan,
Newcastle, Upper Canada,
on 27 May 1818.
(PAO)

NEILSON SAMUEL
Born in Scotland pre1776.
Emigrated from Scotland
to Canada. Editor of the
Quebec Gazette. Died 1793.
(SNF)

NEISMITH JOHN
Indentured servant
imported from Scotland
to East New Jersey 1684.
(EJD/A)

NEWLANDS Captain JOHN
Born in Glasgow during 1781.
Shipmaster. Died on 31 July
1836. Buried in the Scots
cemetery, Jamaica.
(MIBWI)

NICOL Rev ANDREW
Ordained in Glasgow 1818.
Emigrated from Scotland
to Nova Scotia during 1818.
Minister in Prince Edward
Island. Died in 1819.
(HPC)

NICOL JOHN
Aberdeen. Educated at
King's College, Aberdeen,
graduated M.A. 28 March 1812.
Planter in Jamaica.
(KCA)

NICOLL JOHN
Born in Scotland. Former
soldier in the 4th Royal
Veteran Battalion. Military
settler. Received a land
grant in Drummond, Upper
Canada, on 4 June 1817.
(PAO)

NICHOL JOHN
Emigrated from Scotland,
with his wife, four sons
and a daughter, to Canada
on the David of London in
June 1821. Received a land
grant in Ramsay, Upper
Canada, on 7 August 1821.
(PAO)

NICOL WALTER
Born in Scotland.
Emigrated from Scotland to
Louisiana. Settled in
St Helen's parish. Married
Jane Harvey, Springfield,
Livingston parish, 1821.
Resettled in New Orleans.
Timber executive. Died in
1861.
(UNC/WN's diary)

NICOL WILLIAM
Born c1775. Labourer.
Emigrated from Scotland,
with his wife and four
children, to Canada.
Settled at Mount Tom,
Pictou, Nova Scotia, 1815.
(PANS/RG1)

NICOLL WILLIAM
Emigrated from Sutherland,
with his family of eight,
to Nova Scotia on the brig
Prince William September
1815. Land grant in Pictou.
(PANS/RG20)

NICHOLSON ALEXANDER
Emigrated from Scotland,
with his wife and son,
to Canada on the George
Canning in June 1821.
Received a land grant
in Ramsay, Upper Canada,
on 16 July 1821.
(PAO)

NICHOLSON DUNCAN
Born in Scotland c1777.
Emigrated from Scotland
to America. Married Mary
Blackman in Moore County,
North Carolina, c1808.
Died in Alabama in 1861.
(Index NC Anc.60040)

NICHOLSON MARGARET
Indentured servant
imported from Scotland
to East New Jersey by
Thomas Gordon during
1684.
(EJD/A)

NIMMO JAMES
Linlithgow, West Lothian.
Emigrated from Scotland
to America c1723. Merchant
in Virginia.
(OD)

NIMMO ROBERT
Born in Edinburgh on
22 March 1741. Died in
Jamaica. Buried in
St Andrews parish.
(MIBWI)

NISBET ALEXANDER
Born in Montrose, Angus,
on 26 June 1777.
Emigrated from Scotland
to America during 1784.
Married Mary C. Owings.
Father of Charles, Thomas
Deye, John Owings. Judge
in Baltimore, Maryland.
President of the St Andrews
Society. Died 22 November
1857. Buried in Baltimore
County, Maryland.
(HGM)

NISBET JAMES
Emigrated from Scotland,
with his wife, two sons
and a daughter, to
Canada on the Earl of
Buckingham in June 1821.
Received a land grant in
Sherbrook, Upper Canada,
on 24 July 1821.
(PAO)

NOBLE ANGUS
Emigrated from Scotland,
with his family, to
America on the Frances
of New Orleans in 1812.
Settled in Highland Town,
Columbiana County, Ohio.
(SHR.LXIII)

NOURSE WILLIAM
Born in Scotland c1792.
Hudson Bay Company
employee from 1817 to
1851. Chief factor in
1838. Died in Cobourg,
Canada, on 4 May 1855.
(HBRS)

O'CONNOR C.
Gorbals, Glasgow.
Applied to settled in
Canada on 3 March 1815.
(SRO/RH9)

OGILVIE GEORGE
Born c1731. Langley Park
and Tayock, Montrose,
Angus, and of Langley
Estate, Jamaica. Died
at Langley Park in 1791.
(Montrose GS)

OGILVIE JOHN
Born in 1728, son of
James Ogilvie of Auchiries.
Jacobite in 1745. Doctor.
Settled in St Eustatia.
(JAB)

OGILVY JOHN
Born c1769 in Leith(?)
Midlothian, son of Jane
Dunlop or Ogilvie.
Emigrated from Scotland
to Canada c1790. Merchant
and farmer. Died on
28 September 1819 in
Amherstburg, Upper Canada.
(DCB)

OGILVIE PATRICK
Son of John Ogilvie,
minister of Midmar,
Aberdeenshire. Educated
at Marischal College,
Aberdeen, from 1787 to
1791 - graduated M.A.
Surgeon in St Domingo.
(MCA)

OGILVIE WILLIAM
Emigrated from Scotland
to Canada in 1802.
Settled in Georgetown,
Quebec.
(CP)

OGILVIE WILLIAM
Born in 1728, son of
James Ogilvie of Auchiries.
Jacobite in 1745.
Emigrated from Scotland
to America. Died in
Virginia during 1750.
(JAB)

OLIPHANT JOHN
With his wife Janet
Gilchrist, and daughters
Margaret and Janet, in
Pencaitland, East Lothian,
indentured as servants for
four years in East New
Jersey, the daughters until
they were 21, to John
Hancock in Edinburgh on
19 August 1685.
(EJD/A252)

OLIVER GEORGE
Born in Scotland. Military
settler. Received a land
grant in Bathurst, Upper
Canada, in April 1816.
(PAO)

OLIVER GEORGE
Born during 1781 at
Blinkbonny, Castleton,
Roxburghshire, son of
William Oliver and Jean
Nicol. Married Elizabeth
Irving. Settled in Indiana.
Died in 1837.
(OS)

OLIVER ROBERT
Baptised in 1777, son
of John Oliver and
Margaret Douglas,
Wilton, Roxburghshire.
Emigrated from Scotland
to Nova Scotia in 1814.
Married Elizabeth ...
Father of John, William
and James. Died in 1870s.
(OS)

OLIVER WILLIAM
Born 31 January 1795 in
Hawick, Roxburghshire,
son of Robert Oliver,
shoemaker, and Helen Scott.
Emigrated from Scotland to
America. Father of Henry,
William, Andrew and
Margaret.
(OS)

ORR JOHN
Second son of Rev Alexander
Orr and Agnes Dalrymple,
born in Muirkirk, Ayrshire,
on 25 July 1726.
Emigrated from Scotland
to America. Merchant in
Virginia. Father of John,
Alexander, Benjamin, William,
Ann, Elizabeth and Susanna.
(SOF)

ORR THOMAS
Emigrated from Scotland to
Canada on the Brock 1820.
Received a land grant in
Lanark, Upper Canada, on
21 October 1821.
(PAO)

ORR WILLIAM
Edinburgh. Applied to
settle in Canada on
28 February 1815.
(SRO/RH9)

OUCHTERLONY ROBERT
Born c1776, son of
Robert Ouchterlony, 1737-
1816, and Anne Renny, 1734-
1787, Montrose, Angus.
Died in Kingston, Jamaica,
on 14 April 1827.
(Montrose GS)

PAGAN WILLIAM
Born in Glasgow during
1744, eldest son of
William Pagan and Margaret
Maxwell. Emigrated from
Scotland to America.
Settled in New York pre
1769. Moved to St John,
New Brunswick in 1783.
Merchant. Died in St John
on 12 March 1819.
(DCB)

PANTON JOHN
Son of Patrick Panton,
Turiff, Aberdeenshire.
Educated at Marischal
College, Aberdeen, c1796.
Hudson Bay Company
employee.
(MCA)

PARK ALEXANDER
Emigrated from Scotland,
with his wife, to Canada
on the Prompt. Received a
land grant in Dalhousie,
Upper Canada, 17 November
1821.
(PAO)

PARK ANDREW
Emigrated from Scotland
to Canada on the Prompt.
Received a land grant in
Dalhousie, Upper Canada,
on 17 November 1821.
(PAO)

PARK BREDDIE
Born in Greenock,
Renfrewshire, c1784.
Died on 20 June 1811.
Buried in Kingston
Cathedral, Jamaica.
(MIBWI)

PARK HUGH
Emigrated from Scotland,
with his wife, two sons
and two daughters, to
Canada on George Canning
in June 1821. Received a
land grant in Dalhousie,
Upper Canada, 10 July 1821.
(PAO)

PARK JAMES
Emigrated from Scotland,
with his wife, three sons
and a daughter, to Canada
on the George Canning in
June 1821. Received a
land grant in Dalhousie,
Upper Canada, on
10 July 1821.
(PAO)

PARK JAMES
Emigrated from Scotland,
with his wife, son and two
daughters, to Canada on
the Prompt. Received a
land grant in Dalhousie,
Upper Canada, on
17 November 1821.
(PAO)

PARKER JAMES
Born during 1729 in Port
Glasgow. Indentured
servant of Alexander
Speirs. Merchant in
Norfolk, Virginia.
Married Margaret Elligood.
Loyalist.
(Colonial Williamsburg
(M-77-1/3)

PARKER JOHN
Emigrated from Scotland
to Canada on the Commerce
in June 1821. Received a
land grant in Dalhousie,
Upper Canada, 27 July 1821.
(PAO)

PATERSON ANDREW
Emigrated from Scotland
to Canada on the Commerce
Received a land grant in
Lanark, Upper Canada, on
13 October 1821.
(PAO)

PATERSON ARCHIBALD
Emigrated from Greenock,
Renfrewshire, with his
wife and three daughters,
to Canada on the David of
London in May 1821.
Received a land grant in
Dalhousie, Upper Canada,
on 26 July 1821.
(PAO)

PATERSON GEORGE
Born in Perth, Scotland.
Former soldier in the 37th
Regiment. Wife and two
sons. Military settler.
Received a land grant in
Upper Canada 18 July 1816.
(PAO)

PATERSON JAMES
 Volunteer. Died of flux
 on the voyage from
 Scotland to Darien on
 7 October 1698.
 (NLS)

PATTERSON JAMES
 Mason in Lockerbie,
 Dumfries-shire.
 Emigrated from Scotland
 to Halifax, Nova Scotia,
 during 1815. Father of
 James, born 4 March 1816
 in Torthorwald, Dumfries-
 shire.
 (Torthorwald OPR)

PATTERSON JAMES
 Emigrated from Scotland,
 with his wife, three sons
 and two daughters, to
 Canada on the George
 Canning in May 1821.
 Received a land grant in
 Ramsay, Upper Canada, on
 16 July 1821.
 (PAO)

PATTERSON JAMES
 Emigrated from Scotland,
 with his wife, to Canada
 on the George Canning .
 Received a land grant in
 Ramsay, Upper Canada, on
 31 July 1821.
 (PAO)

PATERSON JOHN
 Brother in law of James
 Maxwell, merchant in
 Glasgow. Merchant(?) in
 Boston, Massachusetts,
 c1690, and owner of the
 Two Brothers of Boston.
 (PC)

PATTERSON MATTHEW
 Emigrated from Scotland
 to New York before 1776.
 Mason, soldier and
 politician. Settled in
 Putnam County, New York.
 (TSA)

PATERSON PETER
 Sailor. Died of flux on
 the voyage from Scotland
 to Darien on
 28 October 1698.
 (NLS)

PATTERSON PETER
 Emigrated from Scotland
 to Canada. Merchant in
 York, Upper Canada, 1819.
 Died in 1846.
 (TO)

PATTERSON ROBERT
 Born in Renfrew in 1732.
 Emigrated from Scotland
 to America during 1763.
 Settled in Churchville,
 Maryland, in 1767. Surveyor.
 Moved with his wife and five
 children, via Philadelphia,
 Pennsylvania, to Pictou,
 Nova Scotia, on the Betsey,
 John Hull, during 1768.
 Died in Pictou on
 30 September 1808.
 (DCB)(SF)

PATTERSON THOMAS
 Emigrated from Scotland
 to Canada on the George
 Canning in June 1821.
 Received a land grant in
 Ramsay, Upper Canada, on
 16 July 1821.
 (PAO)

PATERSON Mrs WILLIAM
Emigrated from Scotland
to Darien. Died in Darien
on 14 November 1698.
(NLS)

PATERSON ....
Born c1779. Housecarpenter.
Emigrated from Scotland,
with his wife and four
children, to Canada.
Settled in Pictou Town,
Nova Scotia, 1815.
(PANS/RG1)

PATOUN ROBERT
Covenanter and rebel in
1666. Prisoner in Edin-
burgh Tolbooth.
Banished to Virginia on
10 June 1669. Paroled
in Edinburgh, awaiting
transport, September
1669.
(PC)

PATTON ROBERT
Glasgow. Merchant and
factor in Culpepper,
Virginia, for William
Cunningham and Company
before 1776.
(SRA)

PATON ROBERT
Gorbals, Glasgow.
Applied to settle in
Canada on 2 March 1815.
(SRO/RH9)

PATRICK JOHN
Son of John Patrick of
Treearne, Ayrshire, and
Marion Shedden, who
were married in 1762.
Emigrated from Scotland
to America. Merchant in
New York.
(RAF)

PATRICK ROBERT
Son of James Patrick of
Drumbuie, Ayrshire, and
Anne Shedden. Merchant
in Bermuda. Died 1809.
(RAF)

PATRICK WILLIAM
Son of James Patrick of
Drumbuie, Ayrshire, and
Anne Shedden. Merchant
in Virginia c1800.
Father of Margaret.
(RAF)

PATRICK Rev WILLIAM
Born in Kilsyth,
Stirlingshire. Minister
of Lockerbie, Dumfries-
shire. Emigrated from
Scotland to Miramachi,
New Brunswick, during 1815.
Minister of Merigomish,
Nova Scotia, from 1815
to 1844. Died on
25 November 1844.
(HPC)

PAUL JAMES
Indentured servant
imported from Scotland
to East New Jersey 1684.
(EJD/A)

PAUL JAMES
Emigrated from Greenock,
Renfrewshire, to Canada
on the George Canning
in May 1821. Received a
land grant in Dalhousie,
Upper Canada, 2 July 1821.
(PAO)

PAUL JOHN
Emigrated from Scotland,
with his wife, two sons
and four daughters, to
Canada on the Commerce
Received a land grant
in Dalhousie, Upper Canada,
on 9 September 1821.
(PAO)

PAUL JOHN
Son of John Paul, farmer,
Dyce, Aberdeenshire.
Educated at Marischal
College, Aberdeen, from
1816 to 1820. Army officer.
Served in the Canadian
Rebellion, 1836/1837.
Clerk of Court in Weston,
Canada.
(MCA)

PAUL MONTGOMERY
Emigrated from Scotland
to Canada on the George
Canning in June 1821.
Received a land grant in
Dalhousie, Upper Canada,
on 2 July 1821.
(PAO)

PAUL WILLIAM
Emigrated from Scotland,
with his wife and two
daughters, to Canada on
the Earl of Buckingham
in June 1821. Received
a land grant in Ramsay,
Upper Canada, 24 July 1821.
(PAO)

PEACOCK WILLIAM
Emigrated from Scotland,
with his wife, three sons
and two daughters, to
Canada on the Commerce
in August 1820. Received
a land grant in Lanark,
Upper Canada, 5 September
1821.
(PAO)

PEARSON MICHAEL
Emigrated from Scotland
to Darien. Self-marooned
on Crab Island in the
West Indies, on
7 October 1698.
(DSP)

PEARSON THOMAS
Mariner. Scotland.
Received a land grant
in East New Jersey on
24 April 1684.
(EJD/A)

PEDDIE WILLIAM
Indentured servant
imported from Scotland
to East New Jersey during
1685 by Dr John Gordon.
(EJD/A302)

PEDEN HUGH
Emigrated from Scotland
to Canada on the Caledonian
10 July 1816. Received a
land grant in Bathurst,
Upper Canada, on
10 October 1816.
(PAO)

PENDREICK ROBERT
Emigrated from Scotland
to Darien. Died in Darien
on 11 December 1698.
(NLS)

PENMAN ROBERT sr
Emigrated from Scotland
to Canada. Received a
land grant in Lanark,
Upper Canada, on
4 April 1821.
(PAO)

PENMAN ROBERT
Emigrated from Scotland,
with his wife, four sons
and two daughters, to
Canada on the Prompt in
June 1820. Received a
land grant in Lanark,
Upper Canada, on
25 November 1821.
(PAO)

PENMAN WILLIAM
Emigrated from Scotland
to Canada on the Commerce.
Received a land grant in
Lanark, Upper Canada, on
13 October 1821.
(PAO)

PENNY WILLIAM
Indentured servant
imported from Scotland
to East New Jersey in
October 1684 by John
Campbell for Captain
Andrew Hamilton.
(EJD/A)

PETER ROBERT
Born during 1726, son of
Thomas Peter, Corsbasket
Castle, Glasgow, and Jean
Dunlop. Emigrated from
Scotland to America c1745.
Married Elizabeth Scott.
Father of Thomas, 1769-
1834, and George. Died on
15 November 1806.
(BAF)

PETRIE WILLIAM
Born in Scotland. Former
sergeant in the Royal
Artillery. Military
settler. Received a
land grant in Edwardsburgh,
Upper Canada, on 21 July
1817.
(PAO)

PHILIPS ARCHIBALD
Emigrated from Oban,
Argyllshire, to Quebec
during 1819. Settled in
Argyle, Upper Canada,
on 24 December 1819.
(NRP)

PHYFE DUNCAN
Born in Glasgow during
1770. Emigrated from
Scotland to America in
1783. Furniture maker in
New York from 1796 to
1850. Died in 1850.
(TSA)

PHYFE GABEL
Born near Loch Fannich,
Ross and Cromarty.
Emigrated from Scotland,
with his wife and children,
to America. Settled in
Albany, New York.
(BAF)

PIERY ALEXANDER
Planter. Died of fever on
the voyage from Scotland
to Darien on 23 July 1698.
(NLS)

PICKEN ANDREW
Born in Paisley, Renfrew-
shire, during 1802 son of
Ebenezer Picken. Teacher.
Settled in the West Indies
from 1822 to 1828.
Emigrated from Scotland
to America during 1830.
Died in Montreal, Quebec,
in 1849.
(TSA)

PINKERTON ROBERT
Emigrated from Scotland
to Canada on the Commerce
in June 1821. Received a
land grant in Sherbrook,
Upper Canada, 1 August 1821.
(PAO)

PIRIE GEORGE
Born in Aberdeen on
28 February 1798. Educated
in Aberdeen and in London.
Mercantile agent in Montreal,
Quebec, from 1818 to 1821.
Returned to Scotland. Farmer
in Bon Accord, Canada, from
1838 to 1848. Editor and
proprietor of the Guelph
Herald. Died in Guelph,
Upper Canada, c1869.
(AG)

PIRIE GEORGE
Educated at Marischal
College, Aberdeen, c1820.
Surgeon in U.S.A.
(MCA)

PLAYFAIR ANDREW
Born in Scotland. Former
lieutenant in the 104th
Regiment. Military settler.
Wife and four daughters.
Received land grants in
Younge 31 July 1817,
Bathurst 24 November 1819,
and Dalhousie 6 November
1820, - all Upper Canada.
(PAO)

POLLOCK BESSIE
Indentured servant
imported from Scotland
to East New Jersey by
Lord Neil Campbell in
December 1685.
(EJD/A225)

POLLOCK GEORGE
Eldest son of George
Pollock and Helen Orr,
Glasgow. Educated at the
University of Glasgow c1664.
Married Elizabeth Douglas.
"left issue in Virginia".
(HHG)

POLLOCK JAMES
Emigrated from Scotland,
with his wife, two sons
and two daughters, to
Canada on the David of
London in May 1821.
Received a land grant in
Ramsay, Upper Canada, on
3 September 1821.
(PAO)

POLLOCK JOHN
Indentured servant
imported from Scotland
to East New Jersey by
Lord Neil Campbell in
December 1685.
(EJD/A225)

POLLOCK of LOGIEGREEN
JOHN
Fifth son of Allan Pollock,
merchant in Glasgow.
Apprenticed to John
Campbell. Admitted to the
Society of Writers to the
Signet on 16 June 1807.
Died in Yancieville,
Virginia, on 28 April 1817.
(WS)

POLLOCK ROBERT
Glasgow. Emigrated from
Scotland to America pre 1811.
Merchant in Petersburg,
Virginia.
(OD)

POLLOCK THOMAS
Emigrated from Greenock,
Renfrewshire, to Canada,
with his wife, son and
three daughters, on the
David of London in May 1821.
Received a land grant in
Ramsay, Upper Canada, on
3 September 1821.
(PAO)

POLLOCK WILLIAM
Emigrated from Scotland,
with his wife, three sons
and a daughter, to Canada
on the George Canning in
June 1821. Received a land
grant in Ramsay, Upper
Canada on 25 July 1821.
(PAO)

PORTER JOHN
Emigrated from Scotland,
with his wife, three sons
and a daughter, to Canada
on the Earl of Buckingham
in June 1821. Received a
land grant in Sherbrook,
Upper Canada, on
31 July 1821.
(PAO)

PORTERSFIELD JOHN
Scottish merchant in
Bristol(?), New England.
Part owner of the
Society c1699.
(SPAWI)

POTTY ROBERT
Emigrated from Scotland
to Canada on the Fame on
17 September 1816.
Received a land grant in
Drummond, Upper Canada, on
9 December 1816.
(PAO)

PRENTICE THOMAS
Born during 1798 son of
Archibald Prentice, 1734-
1813, and his second wife
Helen, 1757-1836,
Covington Mains, Lanarkshire,
former tenant farmer in
Cleghorn Mill, Lanark.
Died in Philadelphia,
Pennsylvania, on 28 June
1823.
(Covington GS)

PRESTON JAMES
Stirling. Applied to
settle in Canada on
1 March 1815.
(SRO/RH9)

PRINGLE ROBERT
Emigrated from Scotland
to Canada. Received a
land grant in Ramsay,
Upper Canada, on
16 August 1822.
(PAO)

PRINGLE WILLIAM
Born c1791. Died in
Demerara during
December 1815.
(Perth Greyfriars GS)

PROCTOR WILLIAM
Emigrated from Scotland
to Virginia before 1739.
Tutor librarian to Col.
William Byrd, Westover
upon the James River,
Virginia. Presbyterian
converted to Anglicanism.
Episcopalian minister in
Virginia.
(VMHB/1902)

PROUDFIT JAMES
Son of Andrew Proudfit,
farmer in Perthshire,
born during 1732.
Theological student.
Licenced to preach 1753
and ordained 1754.
Emigrated from Scotland
to America. Landed in
Boston, Massachusetts, in
September 1754. Missionary
and later a minister in -
Lancaster County, Penn-
sylvania, and Salem, New
York. Married (2) Miss
Houston, Philadelphia,
Pennsylvania. Father of
Andrew, John, James, Daniel,
Alexander, Ebenezer, William
and Mary. Died in 1802.
(NYGBR.XXIX)

PROUDFOOT WILLIAM
Emigrated from Scotland
to Canada c1816. Merchant.
President of the Bank of
Upper Canada from 1835
to 1860.
(TO)

PROVAND ARCHIBALD
Emigrated from Scotland,
with his wife and son,
to Canada on the George
Canning in June 1821.
Received a land grant in
Dalhousie, Upper Canada,
on 2 July 1821.
(PAO)

PUNN(?) EDWARD
Royalist soldier captured
at Worcester. Transported
from Gravesend, Kent, to
Boston, New England, on the
John and Sarah, master John
Greene on 13 May 1652.
(NER)

PURCEL JAMES
Emigrated from Scotland to
Canada on the Commerce.
Received a land grant in
Lanark, Upper Canada, on
13 October 1821.
(PAO)

PURDIE ALEXANDER
Born in 1767 son of
Alexander Purdie, 1716-
1772, and Janet Scott,
1728-1804. Married
Janet Lawrie, 1764-1808.
Father of Thomas, William,
Mary, Janet, William.
Died in Syracuse, North
America, on 9 October 1834.
(Thankerton, Lanark, GS)

PURDIE W.
Widow. Emigrated from
Scotland to Canada on
the David of London.
Received a land grant
in Lanark, Upper Canada,
on 4 October 1821.
(PAO)

PURDON ROBERT
Emigrated from Scotland,
with his wife, two sons
and two daughters, to
Canada on the George
Canning in June 1821.
Received a land grant in
Dalhousie, Upper Canada,
on 18 July 1821.
(PAO)

PURSS JOHN
Born 12 December 1732 in
Elgin, Morayshire, son of
Alexander Purss, tailor,
and Isabel Blenshel.
Emigrated from Scotland
to Canada before 1762.
Merchant and public
official. Died in Quebec
on 8 April 1803.
(DCB)

RAE JAMES
Emigrated from Scotland,
with his wife, son and
three daughters, to Canada
on the David of London in
May 1821. Received a land
grant in Ramsay, Upper
Canada, 22 August 1821.
(PAO)

RAE JAMES
Emigrated from Scotland,
with his wife, to Canada
on the Commerce. Received
a land grant in Lanark,
Upper Canada, 11 October
1821.
(PAO)

RAE WILLIAM
Born in Dumfries during
1762. Settled in Jamaica
during 1782. Died in
Kingston, Jamaica, on
7 May 1837. Buried in the
Scots cemetery.
(MIBWI)

RAIT JOHN
Born c1653, son of Rev
John Rait, minister of
Inverkeilor, Angus.
Died in Nevis in 1675.
(Inverkeilor GS)

RALSTON DAVID
Glasgow. Merchant in
Cabin Point, on the
James River, Virginia,
c1762.
(SRA)

RALSTON JOSEPH
Emigrated from Scotland
to Canada. Received a
land grant in Cavan,
Newcastle, Upper Canada,
on 22 October 1817.
(PAO)

RAMAGE HENRY
Born in Scotland. Former
soldier in the Royal
Artillery. Military settler.
Wife, two sons and three
daughters. Received a land
grant in Upper Canada on
30 September 1816.
(PAO)

RAMSAY DAVID
Emigrated from Scotland
to America during the
eighteenth century.
Settled in Norfolk,
Virginia.
(OD)

RAMSAY DAVID
Born c1740 in Leven,
Fife. Served in the
Royal Navy from c1756
to 1765. Emigrated to
Canada during 1765.
Fur trader. Died c1810
probably in Quebec.
(DCB)

RAMSAY GILBERT jr
Educated at Marischal
College, Aberdeen, c1674.
Rector of Christchurch
in Barbados.
(MCA)

RAMSAY JAMES
Born in Scotland. Former
sergeant in the Prince
of York's Chasseurs.
Military settler.
Received a land grant
in Bathurst, Upper Canada,
on 7 October 1819.
(PAO)

RAMSAY JOHN
Emigrated from Scotland
to Canada on the George
Canning in June 1821
Received a land grant in
Lanark, Upper Canada, on
12 July 1821.
(PAO)

RAMSAY PATRICK
Son of Andrew Ramsay, Provost
of Glasgow. Married Elizabeth
Poythress on 26 November 1760.
Father of Andrew, Eliza, etc.
Died in Scotland c1790. His
widow and children settled in
Alexandria, Virginia, in 1791.
(HBV)

RAMSEY WILLIAM
Born 1747. Emigrated from
Scotland, via Londonderry
Ireland, to America.
Settled in Lancaster County,
Pennsylvania, in 1768.
Married (1) Elizabeth Lackey
in 1771 (2) Martha
Ochiltree in 1796. Father
of George. Died in 1838.
(BAF)

RANKINE ARCHIBALD
Emigrated from Scotland,
with his wife, to Canada
on the David of London in
June 1821. Received a land
grant in Lanark, Upper
Canada, on 31 July 1821.
(PAO)

RANKINE DONALD jr
Yeoman. Emigrated from
Scotland to Canada.
Received a land grant in
Mora, Newcastle, Upper
Canada, on 8 March 1826.
(PAO)

RANKINE DONALD sr
Emigrated from Scotland
to Canada. Received a
land grant in Thorak, Home,
Upper Canada, on 14 April
1826.
(PAO)

RANKIN HUGH
Yeoman. Emigrated from
Scotland to Canada.
Received a land grant in
Eldon, Newcastle, Upper
Canada, on 8 March 1826.
(PAO)

RANTOUL ROBERT
Emigrated from Scotland
to America during the
early eighteenth century.
(BAF)

RATTRAY JOHN
Eldest son of Thomas
Rattray, merchant in
Glasgow, and Janet
Marshall. Emigrated
from Scotland to Jamaica
on 15 November 1763.
(SRA)

REDFORD THOMAS
Indentured servant
imported from Scotland
to East New Jersey 1684.
(EJD/A)

REDFORD WILLIAM
Born in Scotland 1642 at
Friershaw, Teviotdale.
Married Margaret ....
1645-17 April 1729.
Father of seven children.
Indentured as a servant
to Arens Sonmans, Wallyford,
East Lothian, on 18 July
1681. Emigrated from Scot-
land to East New Jersey in
1682. Land grant in Essex
County, New Jersey, 1692.
Died 1 March 1725. Buried at
Old Scots cemetery, Freehold,
New Jersey.
(EJD/A/D)

REID ANDREW
Son of John Reid. Emigrated
from Leith to Staten Island
on the Exchange, James Peacock,
December 1683. Settled in East
New Jersey. Father(?) of
Andrew and Sarah. Died 1769.
(MNJ)

REID ANDREW
Emigrated from Scotland
to Canada. Received a
land grant in Ramsay,
Upper Canada, 12 July 1821.
(PAO)

REID EBENEZER sr
Born in Scotland in 1777.
Teacher. Emigrated from
Scotland to Jamaica in
1800. Died 25 May 1843.
Buried in Kingston
Cathedral, Jamaica.
(MIBWI)

REID GEORGE
Indentured servant
imported from Scotland
to East New Jersey 1684.
(EJD/A)

REID GEORGE
Emigrated from Scotland
to Canada. Received a
land grant in Cavan,
Newcastle, Upper Canada,
7 April 1818.
(PAO)

REID JAMES
Son of John Reid. Emigrated
from Leith to Staten Island
on the Exchange, James
Peacock, in December 1683.
Settled in Perth Amboy, New
Jersey, and later inFree-
hold, Monmouth County, New
Jersey. Father of Samuel,
John, Anna, Helena and
Andrew. Surveyor General.
Died c1711.
(MNJ)(HOT)

REID JAMES
Born c1787. Labourer.
Emigrated from Scotland,
with his wife and four
children, to Canada.
Settled on Mount Tom,
Pictou, Nova Scotia,
in 1815.
(PANS/RG1)

REID JAMES
Emigrated from Scotland,
with his wife and two
daughters, to Canada on
the Commerce in June 1820.
Received a land grant in
Lanark, Upper Canada, on
3 September 1820.
(PAO)

REID JOHN
Born at Mildrew Castle,
Kirkliston, West Lothian,
on 16 February 1656 son
of John Reid, gardener.
Author of "The Scotch
Gardener". Bookseller.
Quaker. Married Margaret
Miller, 1644-1728.
Emigrated from Leith to
Staten Island on the
Exchange, James Peacock,
in December 1683. Settled
in Perth Amboy, New Jersey,
and later in Hortencie,
Monmouth County, New Jersey.
Surveyor General of New
Jersey. Father of Anna,
Helena, Margaret and John.
Died on 16 November 1723.
Buried at Topanemus,
Monmouth County, New Jersey.
(MNJ)

REID JOHN
Emigrated from Scotland,
with his wife, to Canada
on the George Canning in
June 1821. Received a
land grant in Lanark,
Upper Canada, 12 July 1821.
(PAO)

REID PETER
Emigrated from Scotland,
with his wife, two sons
and three daughters, to
Canada on the Commerce.
Received a land grant in
Lanark, Upper Canada, on
11 October 1821.
(PAO)

REID THOMAS
Emigrated from Scotland,
with his wife, to Canada
on the Commerce in June
1821. Received a land
grant in Dalhousie, Upper
Canada, 19 July 1821.
(PAO)

REID THOMAS
Born in Scotland. Former
cornet in the 22nd Light
Dragoons. Military settler.
Wife, two sons and a daughter.
Received a land grant in
Lanark, Upper Canada, on
4 October 1821.
(PAO)

REID WILLIAM
Glasgow. Merchant and
tobacco factor in
Fredericksburg, Virginia,
for William Cunningham and
Company c1775.
(SRA/T79.1)

REID WILLIAM
Johnstone, Renfrewshire.
Applied to settle in
Canada on 28 February
1815.
(SRO/RH9)

RENWICK JOHN
Born in Dumfries in 1771.
Emigrated from Scotland
to Jamaica before 1797.
Died there 24 April 1847.
Buried in the Scots
cemetery.
(MIBWI)

RHEA ROBERT
Quaker. Carpenter.
Emigrated from Scotland
to America during 1685.
Settled in Monmouth County,
New Jersey, in 1688.
Married Janet, c1668-1761,
daughter of John Hampton,
in Shrewsbury 10 February
1690. Father of David,
Elizabeth, Catharine,
Margaret, Isabel and Mary.
Died on 18 January 1720.
(MNJ)

RICHARDSON BESSIE
Indentured servant
imported from Scotland
to East New Jersey by
Lord Neil Campbell in
December 1685.
(EJD/A225)

RICHARDSON GEORGE
Emigrated from Scotland
to America. Settled in
Stirling, Ohio, in 1824.
(SHR)

RICHMOND GEORGE
Emigrated from Scotland,
with his wife, six sons
and four daughters, to
Canada on the Prompt.
Received a land grant in
Dalhousie, Upper Canada,
on 27 November 1821.
(PAO)

RICHMOND ROBERT
Emigrated from Scotland,
with his daughter, to
Canada on the Prompt.
Received a land grant in
Dalhousie, Upper Canada,
on 27 November 1821.
(PAO)

RIDDELL HENRY
Glasgow. Merchant and
partner of John Glassford
and Company at Pitscataway,
Maryland, pre 1776.To
Britain in 1778.
(SRA/AO.12.9)

RIDDELL HENRY
Eldest son of John Riddell,
Roxburghshire. Married
Elizabeth Dixon. Farmer.
Emigrated from Scotland
to Canada during 1827.
Settled at Kirkwall
Beverley. Father of
Margaret, Christiana,
Elizabeth, Janet, John,
Robert, Isabella, William
and Jane.
(HAR)

RIDDELL JAMES
Born in Scotland c1700.
Emigrated from Scotland
to America. Married Mary.
Settled in Orange County,
Virginia. Planter. Father
of William.
(HAR)

RIDDELL JOHN
Born in Scotland c1694.
Emigrated from Scotland
to America during 1730.
Settled in Derryfield,
New Hampshire. Married
Janet ... ,1696-1746.
Father of James.
(HAR)

RIDDELL JOHN
Glasgow. Merchant in
Dumfries, Prince William
County, Virginia, with
stores at Aquia, Dumfries
and Fredericksburg,
Virginia. Attorney for
Henderson and Glassford
in Virginia 1769.
(SRA)

RIDDAL JOHN
Emigrated from Scotland
to Canada on the George
Canning in June 1821.
Received a land grant in
Ramsay, Upper Canada, on
16 July 1821.
(PAO)

RIDDELL THOMAS
Born during 1815 at
Lilliesleaf, Roxburghshire.
Emigrated from Scotland to
America in 1820. Settled
in Lawrence, Massachusetts.
Married Sarah S. Henderson.
Father of James, Walter
and David. Died on
27 December 1862.
(HAR)

RIGG WILLIAM
Son of Thomas Rigg of
Athorny. Brother of
Walter and James Rigg in
Scotland. Died 27 November
1685 aboard the Henry and
Francis on route from
Scotland to East New Jersey.
(EJD/A238)

RITCHIE ALEXANDER
Indentured as a servant for
four years in East New
Jersey in Edinburgh to
John Hancock on the
12 August 1685.
(EJD/A252)

RITCHIE ARCHIBALD
Scottish merchant at
Tappahannock, Virginia,
before 1766. Married
Mary, daughter of William
Roane, Essex County,
Virginia, during 1753.
Father of Thomas (later
editor of the Richmond
Enquiror) and John (later
captain in the American
army - killed at the
Battle of Lundy's Lane)
Died in 1784.
(VMHB.1917)

RITCHIE DAVID
Emigrated from Scotland,
with his wife, four sons
and three daughters, to
Canada on the Earl of
Buckingham in June 1821.
Received a land grant in
Sherbrook, Upper Canada,
on 24 July 1821.
(PAO)

RITCHIE THOMAS
Son of David Ritchie,
Brechin, Angus.
Educated at Marischal
College, Aberdeen,
from 1784 to 1787.
Judge in Nova Scotia.
(MCA)

ROBB JAMES
Son of William Robb,
merchant in Glasgow.
Factor at Port Royal,
Virginia, for Patrick
Mitchell, from 1753
to 1756.
(SRA/t-MJ)

ROBERTSON ALEXANDER
Son of William Robertson
in Aberdeen. Educated at
Marischal College,
Aberdeen, from 1786 to
1787. Painter in New
York.
(MCA)

ROBERTSON ALEXANDER
Born in Edinburgh during
1775. Emigrated from
Scotland to New Brunswick
c1798. Married Margaret
Stuart in 1804. Father
of Albert James, 1806 -
1851. Died in 1842.
(BAF)

ROBERTSON ALEXANDER
Born in Glasgow during 1791.
Hudson Bay Company employee
from 1811 to 1845.
(HBRS)

ROBERTSON ARCHIBALD
Edinburgh. Emigrated from
Scotland to America.
Settled in Prince George
County, Virginia, in 1746.
(OD)

ROBERTSON ARCHIBALD
Son of William Robertson
in Aberdeen. Educated at
Marischal College, Aber-
deen, c1785. Painter and
author in New York.
(MCA)

ROBERTSON COLIN
Born the son of a weaver
in Perth on 27 July 1783.
Emigrated from Scotland
to New York c1805. Moved
to Canada. North West
Company employee from
1805 to 1809. Hudson Bay
Company employee from
1814 to 1840. Died on
4 February 1842.
(HBRS)

ROBERTSON DANIEL
Born c1733 in Dunkeld,
Perthshire. Surgeon in
America with the 42nd
(Black Watch) Regiment
from 1754. Married Marie
Louise Reaume in Montreal,
Quebec, during 1761.
Settled in Montreal c1763.
Died there 5 April 1810.
(DCB)

ROBERTSON DAVID
Emigrated from Scotland to
Canada. Received a land
grant in Monaghan, Newcastle,
Upper Canada, 20 August 1818.
(PAO)

ROBERTSON DONALD
Emigrated from Scotland
to Canada on the Curlew
1 September 1818.
Received a land grant in
Drummond, Upper Canada,
on 5 September 1820.
(PAO)

ROBERTSON FARQUHAR
Tacksman of Scalasaig,
Glen Elg, Inverness-
shire. Married Katharine
McLeod. Emigrated from
Scotland to Canada 1823.
(TML)

ROBERTSON HUGH
Slateville, Denoon,
Perthshire. Emigrated
from Scotland to America
in 1790. Married
Elizabeth Fraser 1 June
1820. Father of John.
(BAF)

ROBERTSON HUGH
Emigrated from Scotland
to Canada on the Lady of
the Lake 7 September 1816.
Received a land grant in
Drummond, Upper Canada,
on 9 December 1816.
(PAO)

ROBERTSON JAMES
Eldest son of Patrick
Robertson, writer in
Glasgow. Apprenticed
to David Erskine.
Admitted to the Society
of Writers to the Signet
on 26 June 1789. Died in
Jamaica in April 1794.
(WS)

ROBERTSON JAMES
Born in the Orkney
Islands c1785. Hudson
Bay Company employee
from 1799 to 1857.
(HBRS)

ROBERTSON JAMES
Emigrated from Scotland,
with his wife and son,
to Canada on the George
Canning in June 1821.
Received a land grant in
Lanark, Upper Canada, on
10 July 1821.
(PAO)

ROBERTSON JAMES
Emigrated from Scotland,
with his wife, son and
two daughters, to Canada
on the Prompt. Received
a land grant in Dalhousie,
Upper Canada, 17 November
1821.
(PAO)

ROBERTSON JAMES
Edinburgh. Emigrated from
Greenock, Renfrewshire,
with his wife Margaret
MacGregor, and her mother,
and his children John,
Peter, Elizabeth, Donald,
Christian and Duncan, to
Montreal, Quebec, on the
brig Niagara, Hamilton, in
1825. Settled in McNab,
Bathurst, Upper Canada,
during 1825.
(SG)

ROBERTSON JOHN
Emigrated from Scotland,
with his wife and son,
to Canada on the Curlew
10 September 1818.
Received a land grant
in Drummond, Upper Canada,
20 October 1818.
(PAO)

ROBERTSON JOHN
Emigrated from Scotland,
with his wife, three sons
and two daughters, to
Canada on the Commerce
in June 1820. Received a
land grant in Lanark,
Upper Canada, on
1 October 1820.
(PAO)

ROBERTSON JOHN
Emigrated from Greenock,
Renfrewshire, with his
wife, son and daughter,
to Canada on the David
of London in May 1821.
Received a land grant in
Ramsay, Upper Canada, on
17 August 1821.
(PAO)

ROBERTSON JOHN
Yeoman. Emigrated from
Scotland to Canada.
Received a land grant
in Eldon, Newcastle,
Upper Canada, on
8 March 1826.
(PAO)

ROBERTSON MARGARET
Indentured servant
imported from Scotland
to East New Jersey by
Lord Neil Campbell in
December 1685.
(EJD/A225)

ROBERTSON WILLIAM
Son of Archibald Robertson,
baillie in Edinburgh.
Emigrated from Scotland
to Virginia during 1745.
Clerk of the Council of
Virginia. Married Elizabeth
Fitzgerald in 1748.
Father of Archibald,
William, John, Christian
and Susan.
(VMHB.1926)(HBV)

ROBERTSON WILLIAM
Emigrated from Scotland,
with his wife, three sons
and two daughters, to
Canada on the Commerce
in June 1821. Received a
land grant in Lanark,
Upper Canada, 27 July 1821.
(PAO)

ROBERTSON WILLIAM
Born in Scotland. Former
soldier in the Inverness
Local Militia. Military
settler. Wife and daughter.
Received a land grant in
Bathurst, Upper Canada,
on 7 July 1822.
(PAO)

ROBESON JOHN
Emigrated from Scotland,
with his wife, son and
four daughters, to Canada
on the George Canning in
June 1821. Received a land
grant in Ramsay, Upper
Canada, 25 July 1821.
(PAO)

ROBINSON DUNCAN
Emigrated from Scotland,
with his wife, son and
daughter, to Canada on the
brig Fame 18 September 1816.
Received a land grant in
Drummond, Upper Canada, on
15 November 1816.
(PAO)

ROBINSON JAMES
Glasgow. Merchant and
partner in Falmouth,
Virginia, of William
Cunningham and Company,
from 1767 to 1774.
(SRA)

ROBINSON JAMES
Emigrated from Scotland,
with his wife, to Canada
on the Fame 18 September
1816. Received a land
grant in Drummond, Upper
Canada, 15 November 1816.
(PAO)

ROBINSON JOHN
Emigrated from Scotland
to America before 1754.
Planter in Fredericksburg,
Virginia.
(OD)

ROBINSON MARGARET
Indentured servant
imported from Scotland
to East New Jersey by
Governor Gavin Lawrie
during 1684.
(EJD/A)

ROBINSON PATRICK
Four year indentured
servant imported from
Scotland to East New
Jersey by John Campbell
in October 1684.
(EJD/A)

ROBINSON ROBERT
Born in southern Scotland
c1747. Joiner and
carpenter. Indentured
servant. Emigrated from
Scotland to Virginia on
the Friendship from
Glasgow in 1775. Runaway
servant in June 1775.
(Va. Gaz.)

ROBINSON WILLIAM
Doctor of Physics.
Emigrated from Scotland
to East New Jersey.
Settled in Monmouth
County, New Jersey, on
19 July 1690.
(EJD/D209)

ROBINSON WILLIAM
Born in Scotland. Former
sergeant in the 70th
Regiment. Military settler.
Received a land grant in
Bathurst, Upper Canada,
on 17 March 1820.
(PAO)

ROBINSON WILLIAM
Emigrated from Scotland,
with his wife and son, to
Canada on the Commerce in
June 1821. Received a land
grant in Dalhousie, Upper
Canada, on 1 August 1821.
(PAO)

ROBSON ADAM
Born in Scotland. Wife,
two sons and four daughters.
Received a land grant in
Drummond, Upper Canada, on
13 August 1817.
(PAO)

ROBSON ADAM
Emigrated from Scotland,
with his wife, son and
daughter, to Canada on
the Lord Middleton on
27 July 1818. Received
a land grant in
Drummond, Upper Canada,
13 January 1819.
(PAO)

ROBSON Rev JAMES
Born in Kelso, Roxburgh-
shire during 1775.
Minister of Lochwinnoch,
Renfrewshire. Emigrated
from Scotland to Nova
Scotia in 1811. Minister
in Halifax from 1812 to
1820. Clerk of the Synod
of Nova Scotia from 1817
to 1838. Died in Pictou,
Nova Scotia, on
8 December 1838.
(HPC)

ROBSON JOHN
Emigrated from Scotland
to Canada on the brig
Ann on 1 September 1816.
Received a land grant in
Drummond, Upper Canada,
on 8 October 1816.
(PAO)

ROCKHED JOHN
Second son of Thomas
Rockhed of Whitsomhill,
Berwickshire, born 1681.
Emigrated from Scotland
to East New Jersey. Died
12 September 1737. Buried
in Topanemus cemetery,
Monmouth County, New
Jersey.
(HOT)

ROGERS JAMES
Emigrated from Scotland,
with his wife and daughter,
to Canada on the Prompt
during June 1820. Received
a land grant in Dalhousie,
Upper Canada, on
25 November 1821.
(PAO)

ROGERS JOHN
Born in Glasgow. Emigrated
from Scotland to Maryland.
Moved, with his wife and
four children, via
Philadelphia, Pennsylvania,
to Pictou, Nova Scotia, on
the Betsey, John Hill, in
1767.
(SF)

ROGERS ROBERT
Emigrated from Scotland
to Canada on the Prompt
during June 1820.
Received a land grant in
Dalhousie, Upper Canada,
on 27 November 1821.
(PAO)

ROGERSON RICHARD
Born in Scotland. Former
sergeant in the 5th Royal
Veteran Battallion. Wife.
Military settler. Received
a land grant in Bathurst,
Upper Canada, 9 August 1817.
(PAO)

ROLLO JAMES
 Born c1788 in Scotland(?)
 Cabinet-maker and
 merchant in Montreal,
 Quebec. Settled there pre
 1816. Died in Montreal on
 30 June 1820.
 (DCB)

ROLLO JAMES
 Emigrated from Scotland,
 with his wife and two sons,
 to Canada on the David of
 London in June 1821.
 Received a land grant in
 Lanark, Upper Canada, on
 22 August 1821.
 (PAO)

RONALD WILLIAM
 Indentured servant
 imported from Scotland
 to East New Jersey 1684.
 (EJD/A)

ROSE ALEXANDER
 Emigrated from Scotland,
 with his wife and daughter,
 to Canada on the Brock.
 Received a land grant in
 Dalhousie, Upper Canada,
 on 27 October 1821.
 (PAO)

ROSE DUNCAN
 Brother of John Rose,
 merchant in Glasgow.
 Merchant in Virginia
 c1764.
 (SRA/B10.15.6969)

ROSE JOHN
 Son of John Rose and
 Margaret Grant. Married
 Anne Cumming in 1735.
 Merchant in Forres, Moray-
 shire. Father of Jean,
 Margaret, William, Patrick,
 Rachel, Alexander. A
 Jacobite in 1745. Fled
 to America after 1746.
 Died in Virginia 1762.
 (DRF)

ROSS ALEXANDER
 Born c1756 son of Alexander
 Ross, 1712-1785, and
 Catharine Rutherford, 1713-
 1785. Died in New York on
 26 December 1805.
 (Kinnoull, Perth, GS)

ROSS ALEXANDER
 Born c1755. Millwright.
 Emigrated from Scotland,
 with his wife and five
 children, to Canada. Settled
 at West River, Pictou,
 Nova Scotia, in 1815.
 (PANS/RG1)

ROSS ALEXANDER
 Born c1780. Blacksmith.
 Emigrated from Scotland,
 with his wife and five
 children, to Canada.
 Settled in Pictou Town,
 Nova Scotia, in 1815.
 (PANS/RG1)

ROSS DONALD
 Born c1793. Labourer.
 Emigrated from Scotland
 to Canada. Settled on
 Fisher's Grant, Pictou,
 Nova Scotia, in 1815.
 (PANS/RG1)

ROSS DONALD
Born c1755. Labourer.
Emigrated from Scotland,
with his wife and child,
to Canada. Settled in
Pictou Town, Nova Scotia,
1815.
(PANS/RG1)

ROSS Rev DUNCAN
Born in Tarbet, Ross-shire,
during 1769. Educated at
University of Edinburgh.
Ordained in 1795.
Emigrated from Scotland
to Nova Scotia via New
York in 1795. Minister in
Pictou, Nova Scotia, from
1795 to 1834. Father of
James and Ebenezer. Died
25 October 1834.
(HPC)

ROSS FINLAY
Born c1765. Shoemaker.
Emigrated from Scotland,
with his wife and seven
children, to Canada.
Settled in Pictou Town,
Nova Scotia, 1815.
(PANS/RG1)

ROSS GEORGE
Born c1806 in Scotland.
Hudson Bay Company
employee from 1825 to
1846. Clerk at Mincan,
Canada. Died on
14 May 1846.
(HBRS)

ROSS HUGH
Born in Inverness-shire
during 1797. Emigrated
from Scotland to Nova
Scotia in 1813.
Minister in Nova Scotia
from 1827 to 1858. Died
1 December 1858.
(HPC)

ROSS HUGH
Emigrated from Scotland
to Canada on the Garland
during 1819. Received a
land grant in Bathurst,
Nova Scotia, on
9 September 1820.
(PAO)

ROSS JOHN
Born c1745. Farmer.
Emigrated from Scotland,
with his wife and three
children, to Canada.
Settled at Roger's Hill,
Pictou, Nova Scotia, in
1815.
(PANS/RG1)

ROSS JAMES
Born c1764. Labourer.
Emigrated from Scotland,
with his wife and nine
children, to Canada.
Settled on Fisher's Grant,
Pictou, Nova Scotia, 1815.
(PANS/RG1)

ROSS JOHN
Emigrated from Scotland,
with his wife and daughter,
to Canada on the Commerce,
in August 1820. Received
a land grant in Lanark,
Upper Canada, on
5 September 1820.
(PAO)

ROSS WILLIAM
Emigrated from Scotland
to America before 1757.
Planter in Caroline County,
Virginia.
(OD)

ROSS WILLIAM
Born in Scotland on
28 April 1753. Died
on 10 July 1815.
Buried in Kingston
Cathedral, Jamaica.
(MIBWI)

ROSS WILLIAM
Emigrated from Sutherland,
with his family of five,
to Nova Scotia on the brig
Prince William in September
1815. Received a land grant
in Pictou, Nova Scotia.
(PANS/RG20)

ROSS WILLIAM
Born c1785. Labourer.
Emigrated from Scotland,
with his wife and three
children, to Canada.
Settled on Fisher's Grant,
Pictou, Nova Scotia, 1815.
(PANS/RG1)

ROWE JAMES
Royalist soldier captured
at Worcester. Transported
from Gravesend, Kent, to
Boston, New England, on
the John and Sarah, master
John Greene, 13 May 1652.
(NER)

ROY Rev Dr DANIEL
Born in 1791 at Kinkell,
Perthshire. Emigrated
from Scotland to Nova
Scotia in 1830. Minister
of East River from 1831
to 1873. Died 5 August
1873.
(HPC)

RUMMAGE WILLIAM sr
Emigrated from Scotland
to Canada on the Prompt
8 July 1817. Received
land grants in Edwards-
burgh, Upper Canada, on
18 August 1817, and on
29 December 1819.
(PAO)

RUSSELL ROBERT
Born in Scotland(?) 1630.
Emigrated to America in
c1640. Settled in Andover,
Massachusetts. Married Mary,
daughter of Captain Thomas
Marshall, Lynn, Massachusetts
6 July 1659. Died in 1710.
Buried at Andover,
Massachusetts.
(BAF)

RUSSELL THOMAS
Emigrated from Scotland
to Canada on the Prompt.
Received a land grant in
Dalhousie, Upper Canada,
on 17 November 1821.
(PAO)

RUTHERFORD JOSEPH
Emigrated from Scotland to
Canada. Received a land
grant in Cavan, Newcastle,
Upper Canada, 11 June 1818.
(PAO)

RUTHERFORD THOMAS
Born in Kirkcaldy, Fife,
during 1766 son of Thomas
Rutherford, excise officer
in Glasgow, and Janet Mel-
drum. Educated at Glasgow
University. Emigrated from
Scotland to Virginia 1784.
Settled in Richmond. Married
Sallie Winston in 1790.
Died in 1852.
(BAF)(TSA)

RUTHERFORD WALTER
Born 29 December 1723,
sixth son of Sir John
Rutherford and
Elizabeth Cairncross.
Emigrated via England
to America in 1759.
British Army officer.
Married Catharine
Alexander during 1758.
Father of John. Died
during 1804.
(BAF)

RUTHERFORD WILLIAM
Emigrated from Scotland,
with his son and daughter,
to Canada on the Commerce
in June 1821. Received a
land grant in Sherbrook,
Upper Canada, 1 August
1821.
(PAO)

RUTHVEN ROBERT
Emigrated from Scotland,
with his wife and four
sons, to Canada on the
David of London in June
1821. Received a land
grant in Lanark, Upper
Canada, 1 August 1821.
(PAO)

RUXTON ROBERT
Born in 1747, son of
Robert Ruxton of Cairnhill,
Esslemont, Aberdeenshire.
Married Margaret Brown,
Conansyth, Angus.
Emigrated from Scotland
to America during 1788.
Father of William, 1797-
1842. Died in 1828.
(BAF)

RYNAN WILLIAM
Born in Scotland. Weaver.
Emigrated via Ireland to
America in 1766. Indent-
ured servant. Absconded
during April 1768.
(Penn. Chron.67)

SANDEMAN ROBERT
Born in Perth during 1718.
Educated at the University
of Edinburgh. Minister.
Married a daughter of Rev
John Glass, Tealing, Angus.
Emigrated from Scotland to
Boston, Massachusetts, 1764.
Settled in Danbury, Massa-
chusetts. Died in 1771.
(TSA)

SANDILANDS ROBERT
Born in 1790, fourth son
of George Sandilands of
Nuthill, Fife. Apprenticed
to John Tod. Admitted to
the Society of Writers to
the Signet on 26 May 1818.
Married Mary Style, Kent,
on 14 July 1829. Assistant
Judge at Nassau, New
Providence. Died on
20 May 1872.
(WS)

SCAMBLE JOHN
Born c1809, son of
George Scamble. Died in
Trinidad on 27 July 1828.
(Wigtown GS)

SCOON JOHN
Born on 27 April 1771 in
Hawick, Roxburghshire.
Married Margaret Renwick.
Settled in Geneva, New York,
c1820. Father of William.
Died 26 January 1861.
(BAF)

SCOTT Rev ADAM
Minister. Jedburgh,
Roxburghshire.
Emigrated from Scotland
to Darien. Died there
on 20 November 1698.
(SHR)(NLS)

SCOTT ALEXANDER
Four year indentured
servant imported from
Scotland to East New
Jersey in October
1684 by John Campbell.
(EJD/A)

SCOTT ALEXANDER
Born in 1716, son of
Rev John Scott of Loch,
1651-1726, and Marjory
Stuart. Grandson of
John Scott, burgess of
Forres, Morayshire.
Episcopalian minister
in Virginia. Died 1737.
(Dipple Speymouth GS)

SCOTT ALEXANDER
Glasgow. Merchant in
Gosport, Norfolk, Virginia,
from c1755. Partner of
Andrew Sproule.
(SRA)

SCOTT ANDREW
Emigrated from Scotland
to Canada on the David
of London in June 1821.
Received a land grant in
Lanark, Upper Canada, on
3 September 1821.
(PAO)

SCOTT HUGH
Emigrated from Scotland
to Canada on the Success
in August 1819. Received
a land grant in Sherbrook,
Upper Canada, on
8 December 1820.
(PAO)

SCOTT JAMES
Born in 1715, son of Rev
John Scott of Loch, 1651-
1726, and Marjory Stuart.
Grandson of John Scott,
burgess of Forres, Moray-
shire. Episcopalian
minister in Virginia.
(Dipple Speymouth GS)

SCOTT JAMES
Emigrated from Scotland,
with his wife and daughter,
to Canada on the Lord
Middleton 2 July 1817.
Received a land grant in
Elmsley, Upper Canada,
23 March 1818.
(PAO)

SCOTT JAMES
Emigrated from Scotland
to Canada on the Brothers
14 August 1817. Received
a land grant in Burgess,
Upper Canada, 3 December
1817.
(PAO)

SCOTT JANET
Born in 1787, fourth
daughter of Allan Scott,
Glasgow. Died 4 January
1819. Buried in Kingston
Cathedral, Jamaica.
(MIBWI)

SCOTT JOHN
Emigrated from Scotland
to America before 1757.
Planter in Prince
William County, Virginia.
(OD)

SCOTT JOHN
Born in 1775, son of
Robert Scott, banker in
Glasgow. Died on
26 October 1815. Buried
in Kingston Cathedral,
Jamaica.
(MIBWI)

SCOTT JOHN
Born c1771. Labourer.
Emigrated from Scotland,
with his wife, to Canada.
Settled at Mount Tom,
Pictou, Nova Scotia, in
1815.
(PANS/RG1)

SCOTT JOHN
Emigrated from Scotland,
with his wife, son and
daughter, to Canada on
the Success in August 1819.
Received a land grant in
Sherbrook, Upper Canada,
on 8 December 1820.
(PAO)

SCOTT Rev JOHN
Ordained in Jedburgh,
Roxburghshire.
Emigrated from Scotland
to Nova Scotia in 1826.
Minister of St Matthew's,
Halifax, from 1827 to 1863.
Died in February 1864.
(HPC)

SCOTT ROBERT
Born c1708. Berwick.
Husbandman. Indentured
servant for Maryland,
7 January 1736.
(LGR)

SCOTT ROBERT
Born c1773, Biggar,
Lanarkshire. Saddler in
Edinburgh. Emigrated from
Scotland, with his wife
Marion Young 33, and
children James 8, Robert 6,
John 5, Margaret 2, and
Alice 15, to Canada in 1818.
(CO.384.3)

SCOTT ROBERT
Emigrated from Scotland,
with his wife, son and
four daughters, to Canada
on the George Canning in
June 1821. Received a land
grant in Dalhousie, Upper
Canada, on 10 July 1821.
(PAO)

SCOTT JOHN
Third son of Sir John Scott
of Ancrum, died 1712, and
Margaret Rutherford.
Merchant in New York.
(NHP)

SCOTT THOMAS
Born in 1774, eighth son
of Walter Scott, W.S.
Apprenticed to George
Johnston. Admitted to the
Society of Writers to the
Signet 19 November 1797.
Married Elizabeth, daughter
of David McCulloch of Ard-
well, Kirkcudbright, on 16
December 1799. Extractor
of the Court of Session in
1810. Officer of the Manx
Fencibles. Paymaster of the
70th Regiment. Died in Canada
14 February 1823.
(WS)

SCOTT THOMAS
 Emigrated from Scotland,
 with his wife, three sons
 and a daughter, to Canada
 on the Success in August
 1819. Received a land
 grant in Sherbrook,
 Upper Canada, on
 8 December 1820.
 (PAO)

SCOTT THOMAS
 Emigrated from Scotland,
 with his wife, three sons
 and five daughters, to
 Canada on the Prompt in
 June 1820. Received a
 land grant in
 Dalhousie, Upper Canada,
 on 27 November 1821.
 (PAO)

SCOTT THOMAS jr
 Emigrated from Scotland
 to Canada on the
 Manhattan during 1820.
 Received a land grant in
 Sherbrook, Upper Canada,
 on 17 February 1821.
 (PAO)

SCOTT WALTER
 Scotland. Emigrated via
 Sligo, Ireland, to New
 York on the Foundling.
 Landed on 30 June 1816.
 (NWI)

SCOTT WILLIAM
 Born c1780, son of
 Patrick Scott of Rossie,
 1728-1814, and Margaret
 Forbes of Craigievar,
 1752-1839. Died in the
 West Indies during 1798.
 (Craig, Angus, GS)

SCOTT WILLIAM
 Emigrated from Scotland
 to Canada on the Lord
 Middleton 20 June 1818.
 Received a land grant in
 Drummond, Upper Canada,
 on 15 October 1818.
 (PAO)

SCOTT WILLIAM
 Born c1807 Bellshill,
 Lanarkshire. Saddler.
 Died in Jamaica on
 30 November 1838. Buried
 in the Scots cemetery,
 Kingston, Jamaica.
 (MIBWI)

SCOULAR JOHN
 Indentured servant
 imported from Scotland
 to East New Jersey by
 Lord Neil Campbell in
 December 1685.
 (EJD/A225)

SCOULER ROBERT
 Emigrated from Scotland,
 with his wife, four sons
 and six daughters, to
 Canada on the Prompt in
 June 1820. Received a land
 grant in Lanark, Upper
 Canada, 27 November 1821.
 (PAO)

SCRIMGEOUR JAMES
 Indentured servant
 imported from Scotland to
 East New Jersey by Lord
 Neil Campbell in
 December 1685.
 (EJD/A225)

SCRIMGEOUR SICELLA
Indentured servant
imported from Scotland
to East New Jersey by
Lord Neil Campbell in
December 1685.
(EJD/A225)

SEATON DAVID
Emigrated from Scotland,
with his wife, son and
daughter, to Canada on
the Prompt. Received a
land grant in Dalhousie,
Upper Canada, on
17 November 1821.
(PAO)

SEATON JAMES
Indentured servant
imported from Scotland
to East New Jersey 1684.
(EJD/A)

SETON JAMES
Son of Robert Seton of
Parbroath, Fife. Married
Margaret Newton. Moved to
London. Father of John,
Mary and Margaret. Died
at Cape Francais, San
Domingo.
(SOP)

SEATON JAMES
Emigrated from Scotland,
with wife and daughter,
to Canada on the Prompt.
Received a land grant in
Dalhousie, Upper Canada,
on 17 November 1821.
(PAO)

SETON JOHN
Second son of Sir David
Seton of Parbroath, Fife,
and Mary Gray. Emigrated
to Virginia in 1635.
(SOP)

SETON JOHN
Son of John and Elisabeth
Seton. Emigrated to the
West Indies. Buried in
St James parish, Barbados,
22 December 1768.
(SOP)

SETON WILLIAM
Born 24 April 1746, son
of John and Elisabeth
Seton. Emigrated from
Scotland to America 1758.
Married Rebecca Curzon,
Baltimore, Maryland, 1767.
Merchant and banker.
Loyalist. Father of William,
James, John and Anna Maria.
Died on 9 June 1798.
(SOP)

SEGGIE SAMUEL
Tullibody, Clackmannan-
shire. Applied to settle
in Canada on 27 February
1815.
(SRO/RH9)

SELLAR ROBERT
Born in 1800, second son
of Robert Sellar, 1758-1815,
blacksmith in Tenantown,
and Isabella Hay, 1771-1851.
Died in Pitsfield,
Massachusetts, 4 March 1821.
(CK)

SEMPLE JOHN
Merchant and tobacco
imported in Glasgow.
Emigrated from Scotland
to America. Iron merchant
in Virginia and Maryland
c1765.
(SRA/B10.15.7082)

SETTER GEORGE
Born c1782 in the Orkney
Islands. Hudson Bay
Company employee from
1805 to 1853. Postmaster.
(HBRS)

SHAND FRANCIS
Son of John Shand,
minister of Kintore,
Aberdeenshire. Educated
at Marischal College,
Aberdeen, from 1799 to
1803. Advocate in
Aberdeen c1811.
Settled in Jamaica.
(MCA)

SHAND JOHN
Born 6 January 1801,
son of Rev James Shand,
minister of Marykirk,
Kincardineshire, and
Margaret Farquhar.
Married Isabella Lister.
Settled at Mornefendue,
Grenada. Father of John,
George, David, Janet and
Isabella. Died on
25 October 1876.
(DF)

SHARP GEORGE
Indentured servant
imported from Scotland
to East New Jersey by
Gilbert Innes in 1684.
Land grant 4 January 1695.
(EJD/E330)

SHARP GIDEON
Brother of Thomas Sharp
of Houston. Settled in
Shelbourne, Nova Scotia,
c1784.
(SRO/GD24.1598)

SHARP JOHN
Indentured servant
imported from Scotland
to East New Jersey by
Gilbert Innes in 1684.
Land grant on 4 January
1695. Carpenter in New
York.
(EJD/E330)

SHARP JOHN
Educated at King's College,
Aberdeen. Army chaplain
in New York from 1702.
Granted a D.D. in Aberdeen
on 2 January 1714.
(KCA)

SHARPE WILLIAM
Indentured servant
imported from Scotland
to East New Jersey by
Lord Neil Campbell in
December 1685.
(EJD/A225)

SHAW AENEAS
Son of Angus Shaw of
Tordarroch. Emigrated
from Scotland to America
in 1770. Settled on Staten
Island. Loyalist - captured
at Yorktown 1781. Married
Ann Goslin in New York.
Settled on River Nashwauk,
New Brunswick, and later
in York, Upper Canada, 1796.
Father of John. Alexander,
Charles, Isabella, Aeneas,
Richard, Sophia, Ann, George,
Anne, David, Charlotte, and
Mary.
(HCS)

SHAW AENEAS
Born at Tordarroch House,
second son of Angus Shaw
and Anne Dallas. Married
(1) Ann Gosline (2)
Margaret Hickman.
Emigrated from Scotland
to Staten Island, New York,
in 1770. Officer in the
Queen's Rangers. Farmer
in New Brunswick c1791.
Public administrator in
Upper Canada. Died in
Toronto 6 February 1814.
(DCB)(TO)

SHAW JAMES
Born 20 October 1760,
seventh son of Rev David
Shaw and Marion Dalrymple.
Emigrated from Scotland
to Jamaica on 1 March 1777.
Died in Jamaica on
12 July 1779.
(CFG)

SHAW JANE
Indentured servant
imported from Scotland
to East New Jersey 1684.
Sold to Robert Hamilton
in Middletown.
(EJD/A)

SHAW JOHN
Cabinet maker in
Glasgow. Emigrated from
Scotland to America 1775.
Settled in Annapolis,
Maryland. Partner of
Andrew Chisholm,
blacksmith and armourer.
(SRA)

SHAW JOHN
Emigrated from Scotland,
with his wife, two sons
and two daughters, to
Canada. Received a land
grant in Ramsay, Upper
Canada, on 31 July 1821.
(PAO)

SHAW THOMAS
Born in Scotland 1771.
Married Elizabeth Booth.
Died 12 February 1821.
Buried in St Michael's,
Barbados.
(MIBWI)

SHEARER THOMAS
Indentured servant
imported from Scotland
to East New Jersey by
Lord Neil Campbell in
December 1685.
(EJD/A225)

SHEDDEN ANNABELLA
Born during 1742 in
Beith, Ayrshire, third
daughter of John Shedden
of Roughwood, and Jean
Ralston. Emigrated from
Scotland to Bermuda during
the 1770s. Died in
Bermuda during 1783.
(HCA)(RAF)

SHEDDEN JAMES
Second son of John Shedden
of Muirston, Ayrshire, and
Beatrix Shedden. Settled
in Jamaica during late
eighteenth century.
(RAF)

SHEDDEN WILLIAM RALSTON
Born on 23 April 1747,
fifth son of John Shedden
of Roughwood, and Jean
Ralston, Beith, Ayrshire.
Emigrated from Scotland
to America. Merchant in
Virginia from 1770 to
1775, Bermuda from 1775
to 1783, and in New York
from 1783. Father of Jane
and a son. Died in New
York during 1798.
(RAF)(HCA)

SHEED Rev GEORGE
Born in Scotland.
Educated in Aberdeen.
Emigrated from Scotland
to Canada in 1825 as a
tutor to the family of
Hon. James Crooks.
Ordained in Scotland in
1827. Minister in
Ancaster and Flamboro,
Canada, from 1827 to
1832. Died in 1832.
(HPC)

SHEPHERD ANDREW
Son of George Shepherd,
Aberdeen. Educated at
Marischal College,
Aberdeen, from 1772 to
1774. Merchant in
Virginia.
(MCA)

SHEWAN ANSELL
Royalist soldier captured
at Worcester. Transported
from Gravesend, Kent, to
Boston, New England, on
the John and Sarah, master
John Green, 13 May 1652.
(NER)

SHEWAN DANIEL
Royalist soldier captured
at Worcester. Transported
from Gravesend, Kent, to
Boston, New England, on the
John and Sarah, master John
Greene, 13 May 1652.
(NER)

SHIELDS Rev ALEXANDER
Minister of the Second
Charge in St Andrews, Fife.
Emigrated from Scotland to
Darien on 24 September 1699.
Landed in Darien 30 November
1699. Died at Port Royal,
Jamaica, on 14 June 1700.
(SHR)

SHIELDS JAMES
Ayr. Applied to settle in
Canada on 4 March 1815.
(SRO/RH9)

SHIELDS PETER
Emigrated from Scotland,
with his wife, two sons
and a daughter, to Canada
on the Prompt. Received a
land grant in Dalhousie,
Upper Canada, on
27 November 1821.
(PAO)

SHONE JAMES
Royalist soldier captured
at Worcester. Transported
from Gravesend, Kent, to
Boston, New England, on the
John and Sarah, master John
Greene, 13 May 1652.
(NER)

SHUNGER JOHN
Ploughman. Glen Ogilvy,
Angus. Jacobite in the
Forfarshire Regiment in
1745. Transported to the
Plantations.
(MR)

SHUTTLETON ARCHIBALD
Emigrated from Scotland
to Canada on the Commerce
in August 1820. Received
a land grant in Lanark,
Upper Canada, on
3 September 1820.
(PAO)

SIM HUGH
Born in Scotland.
Graduated B.A. at
Princeton University,
New Jersey, in 1768.

SIM JOHN
Sailor. Died at Darien
on 16 November 1698.
(NLS)

SIMSON ADAM
Indentured servant
imported from Scotland
to East New Jersey by
Lord Neil Campbell in
December 1685.
(EJD/A225)

SIMPSON ALEXANDER
Son of Alexander Simpson,
minister of New Machar,
Aberdeenshire. Educated
at Marischal College,
Aberdeen, from 1816 to
1820. Settled in Jamaica.
(MCA)

SIMPSON ALEXANDER
Brother of Aemilius Simpson.
Born in Scotland during 1811.
Hudson Bay Company employee
from 1827 to 1843. Temporary
Consul to the Hawaiian Is
Islands.
(HBRS)

SIMPSON ARTHUR
Indentured servant
imported from Scotland
to East New Jersey by
George Willocks in
October 1684. Later
employed by John Laing
in Middlesex County, New
Jersey. Received a land
grant on 17 January 1693.
(EJD/A267/D)

SIMSON DAVID
Indentured servant
imported from Scotland
to East New Jersey by
Lord Neil Campbell in
December 1685.
(EJD/A225)

SIMSON DOUGALD
Indentured servant
imported from Scotland
to east New Jersey by
Lord Neil Campbell in
December 1685.
(EJD/A225)

SIMSON JAMES
Indentured servant
imported from Scotland
to East New Jersey 1684.
(EJD/A)

SIMPSON JOHN
Born c1753. Farmer.
Emigrated from Scotland,
with his wife and seven
children, to Canada.
Settled at Mount Tom,
Pictou, Nova Scotia, 1815.
(PANS/RG1)

SIMPSON MARGARET
Indentured servant
imported from Scotland
to East New Jersey by
David Mudie during
November 1684.
(EJD/A196)

SIMSON PATRICK
Indentured servant
imported from Scotland
to East New Jersey by
Lord Neil Campbell in
December 1685.
(EJD/A225)

SIMPSON THOMAS
Born in Scotland 1808.
Educated at King's College,
Aberdeen. Brother of
Aemilius and Alexander
Simpson. Hudson Bay
Company employee from
1828 to 1840. Died at
Turtle River, North Dakota
on 14 June 1840.
(HBRS)

SINCLAIR ALEXANDER
Emigrated from Scotland
to Canada on the Harmony
16 July 1817. Received a
land grant in Lancaster,
Upper Canada, on
24 November 1817.
(PAO)

SINCLAIR ALEXANDER
Born at Murr, Ayrshire, in
1806. Died 20 January 1825.
Buried in Kingston
Cathedral, Jamaica.
(MIBWI)

SINCLAIR ARTHUR
Scalloway, Shetland Islands.
Emigrated from Scotland to
Virginia c1745. Sea-captain
based in Virginia trading
to Glasgow.
(VMHB.1923)

SINCLAIR DONALD
Emigrated from Scotland,
with his wife and five
daughters, to Canada on
the Sophia 6 September 1818.
Received a land grant in
Drummond, Upper Canada, on
21 December 1818.
(PAO)

SINCLAIR FRANCIS
Emigrated from Scotland
to Canada on the Lady of
the Lake on 19 September
1816. Received a land
grant in Drummond, Upper
Canada, 27 January 1817.
(PAO)

SINCLAIR HUGH
Emigrated from Scotland,
with his wife, son and two
daughters, to Canada on
the George Canning in June
1821. Received a land grant
in Lanark, Upper Canada,
on 16 July 1821.
(PAO)

SINCLAIR WILLIAM
Pulteneytown, Wick,
Caithness. Emigrated
from Scotland to
Hudson Bay in 1812.
(SRO/GD.136.468.321)

SINCLAIR WILLIAM
Emigrated from Scotland
to Canada. Received a
land grant in Cavan,
Newcastle, Upper Canada,
on 7 April 1818.
(PAO)

SIVEWRIGHT JOHN
Born in Scotland c1779.
Emigrated from Scotland
to Canada. Employed by
the XY Company, then the
North West Company, and
after 1821 the Hudson Bay
Company. Chief trader in
1828. In charge of Fort
Coulonge district from
1823 to 1843. Chief factor
1846. Died 4 September 1856.
(HBRS)

SKAKEL ALEXANDER
Aberdeen. Educated at
King's College, Aberdeen,
- graduated M.A. 28 March
1794. Master of the Royal
Grammar School in Montreal.
(KCA)

SKENE ALEXANDER
Born 9 July 1706, sixth
son of Alexander Skene of
Skene, and Giles Adie.
Died in Jamaica in 1732.
(NHP)

SKENE JOHN
Educated at Marischal
College, Aberdeen, from
1662 to 1663. Governor of
New Jersey.
(MCA)

SKIMMINGS WILLIAM
Born in Scotland. Former
soldier in the Glengarry
Fencibles. Military settler.
Received land grants in
Upper Canada 16 July 1816,
and in Bathurst, Upper
Canada, 24 November 1819.
(PAO)

SESSOR DANIEL
Royalist soldier captured
at Worcester. Transported
from Gravesend, Kent, to
Boston, New England, on the
John and Sarah, master John
Greene, 13 May 1652.
(NER)

SLOANE JOHN
Born in Dumfries-shire 1791.
Farmer. Emigrated from Scot-
land, with his wife and four
children, to Canada 1821.
Received a land grant in
Caverhill, Queensbury,
York County, New Brunswick,
in 1821.
(PANB)

SMEWREY CORNELIUS
Born c1662. Weaver.
Berwick. Indentured servant
for Barbados 15 May 1686.
(LGR)

SMILIE GAVIN
Emigrated from Scotland
to Canada on the Earl of
Buckingham in June 1821.
Received a land grant in
Dalhousie, Upper Canada,
on 1 August 1821.
(PAO)

SMILEY JAMES
Emigrated from Edinburgh
to America in 1747.
Married Sarah McFarland
in Haverhill, Massachusetts
29 April 1781. Father of
Francis, Poley, Nathan,
James, Nancy and Louisa.
Died 15 April 1824.
(CMF)

SMILLIE JAMES
Emigrated from Scotland
to Quebec during 1821.
Engraver. Settled in
New York during 1829.
Died in 1884 at
Poughkeepsie, New York.
(TSA)

SMITH ANDREW
Emigrated from Scotland,
with his wife, two sons
and two daughters, to
Canada on the George
Canning in June 1821.
Received a land grant
in Ramsay, Upper Canada,
16 July 1821.
(PAO)

SMITH ANGUS
Yeoman. Emigrated from
Scotland to Canada.
Received a land grant
in Eldon, Newcastle,
Upper Canada, 8 March 1826.
(PAO)

SMITH Rev DAVID
Born in 1732. Minister in
St Andrews, Fife, 1764.
Emigrated from Scotland
to Nova Scotia during 1771.
Settled in Londonderry,
Nova Scotia. Presbyterian
minister there from 1771
to 1795. Died 1795.
(HPC)

SMITH DAVID
Emigrated from Scotland,
with his wife, four sons
and two daughters, to
Canada on the Earl of
Buckingham in June 1821.
Received a land grant in
Dalhousie, Upper Canada,
on 21 July 1821.
(PAO)

SMITH GEORGE
Emigrated from Scotland
to America c1785. Took the
Oath of Allegience in
Philadelphia, Pennsylvania,
10 October 1786.
('Names of Persons taking
   Oaths of Allegiance
   1779-1789')

SMITH GEORGE
Son of James Smith, farmer,
Old Deer, Aberdeenshire.
Educated at Marischal
College, Aberdeen,c1823.
Land speculator in Chicago.
(MCA)

SMITH JAMES
Indentured servant
imported from Scotland
to East New Jersey by
John Forbes during
October 1684.
(EJD/A266)

SMITH JAMES
Emigrated from Scotland
to Canada on the George
Canning in June 1821.
Received a land grant in
Ramsay, Upper Canada, on
16 July 1821.
(PAO)

SMITH JAMES
Emigrated from Scotland,
with his wife, three sons
and a daughter, to Canada
on the Commerce. Received
a land grant in Lanark,
Upper Canada, 31 July 1821.
(PAO)

SMITH JAMES
Emigrated from Scotland,
with his wife, to Canada
on the Earl of Buckingham
in June 1821. Received a
land grant in Sherbrook,
Upper Canada, 31 July 1821.
(PAO)

SMITH Rev JAMES
Born in Methven, Perthshire.
Educated at the University
of Glasgow. Emigrated from
Scotland to Nova Scotia in
1829. Minister in Nova
Scotia. Professor at
Divinity Hall, Halifax,
Nova Scotia, 1860. Died on
17 May 1871.
(HPC)

SMITH JOHN
Sailor. Died of fever on
the voyage from Scotland
to Darien 23 September
1698.
(NLS)

SMITH JOHN
Emigrated from Scotland,
with his wife, two sons
and two daughters, to
Canada on the Earl of
Buckingham in June 1821.
Received a land grant in
Ramsay, Upper Canada, on
4 August 1821.
(PAO)

SMITH JOHN
Emigrated from Scotland,
with his wife and three
sons, to Canada on the
Prompt. Received a land
grant in Dalhousie, Upper
Canada, 27 November 1821.
(PAO)

SMITH MARY
Indentured servant
imported from Scotland
to East New Jersey by
George Keith during
February 1685.
(EJD/A226)

SMITH PATRICK
Son of Patrick Smith,
merchant in Glasgow, and
Janet Maxwell. Merchant.
Emigrated from Scotland
to Jamaica in 1763.
(SRA/B10.15.7085)

SMITH ROBERT THOMSON
Aberlady, East Lothian.
Convicted of the murder
of George Forester,
land labourer, to be
transported in 1739.
(SM.I)

SMITH ROBERT
Emigrated from Greenock,
Renfrewshire, to Montreal,
Quebec, on the David of
London in May 1821.
Received a land grant in
Ramsay, Upper Canada, on
10 September 1821.
(PAO)

SMITH ROBERT sr
Emigrated from Scotland,
with his wife, son and
two daughters, to Canada
on the Earl of Buckingham
in June 1821. Received a
land grant in Sherbrook,
Upper Canada, 24 July 1821.
(PAO)

SMITH ROBERT jr
Emigrated from Scotland
to Canada on the Earl of
Buckingham in June 1821.
Received a land grant in
Sherbrook, Upper Canada,
24 July 1821.
(PAO)

SMITH WILLIAM
Emigrated from Scotland
to Canada on the David of
London in June 1821.
Received a land grant in
Lanark, Upper Canada, on
16 August 1821.
(PAO)

SNEDDON JAMES
Emigrated from Scotland,
with his wife, son and
daughter, to Canada on
the Commerce. Received a
land grant in Ramsay,
Upper Canada, 9 September
1821.
(PAO)

SNODGRASS JOHN
Glasgow. Factor in Gooch-
land, Virginia, for
Thompson and Snodgrass,
tobacco importers in
Glasgow, c1776.
(SRA/B10.12.4)

SOLOMANS GEORGE
Born in Scotland c1723.
Emigrated from Scotland
to America before 1760.
Planter in Stafford County,
Virginia.
(OD)

SOMERVILLE B. ANDREW
Emigrated from Scotland,
with his two sons, to
Canada on the Commerce.
Received a land grant in
Lanark, Upper Canada, on
28 July 1821.
(PAO)

SOMERVILLE JAMES
Eldest son of John
Somerville of Jenlaw.
Tenant in Hillhouse.
Planter in Forest Estate,
Westmoreland, Jamaica,
c1794.
(CPD)

SOMERVILLE JOHN
Glasgow. Applied to
settle in Canada on
26 February 1815.
(SRO/RH9)

SOMERVILLE JOHN
Emigrated from Scotland,
with his wife, son and
daughter, to Canada on
the Commerce in August
1820. Received a land
grant in Lanark, Upper
Canada, 5 September 1820.
(PAO)

SPALDING WILLIAM
Emigrated from Scotland
to Canada on the Dorothy
during 1815. Received a
land grant in Elmsley,
Upper Canada, on
8 December 1818.
(PAO)

SPARK ALEXANDER
Born 7 January 1762(?),
in Marykirk, Kincardine-
shire, son of John Spark
and Mary Low. Educated at
King's College, Aberdeen,
c1776. Emigrated from
Scotland to Quebec in
1780. Teacher and minister.
Granted a D.D. by King's
College, Aberdeen, on
31 January 1804. Married
Mary Ross in Quebec on
13 July 1805. Died there
7 March 1819.
(DCB)((KCA)

SPEIRS ALEXANDER
Born 1714 in Edinburgh, son
of John Speirs. Emigrated
from Scotland to Virginia
c1740. Married (1) Sarah
Carey in Virginia in 1741.
Plantation owner at Elderslie,
Virginia, (managed by his
sister Mrs Judith Bell)
Returned to Glasgow in 1749.
Merchant and tobacco
importer. Married (2) Mary
Buchanan during 1755. Died
in 1782.
(SRA/B10.15.5943)

SPEIRS JAMES
Glasgow. Tobacco merchant
and planter in Virginia
c1754.
(SRA/B10.15.6653)

SPENCE JEREMY
Sailor. Died of fever on the
voyage from Scotland to Darien
27 September 1698.
(NLS)

SPENCE MARGARET
Daughter of James Spence,
Queensferry, and widow of
John Vernor of Dattvick.
Died on the Henry and Francis
on the voyage from Scotland
to East New Jersey during
November 1685.
(EJD)

SPENCER MARY ELISABETH
Daughter of William
Spencer, H.M. Customs
Collector of Savannah,
Georgia, married
Alexander Thomson, son
of James Thomson,
accountant in the
Excise Office in Savannah,
Georgia. Married by Rev
Samuel Frink, minister of
Christ Church, Savannah,
Georgia, on
24 November 1770.
(EMR)

SPROTT Rev JOHN
Born at Stoneykirk,
Wigtownshire, in March
1790. Educated at the
University of Edinburgh
from 1808 to 1812.
Emigrated from Scotland
to Nova Scotia in 1818.
Minister in Musquodoboit,
Nova Scotia, from 1825 to
1845. Died September 1869.
(HPC)

SPROWLE ANDREW
Glasgow. Merchant in
Gosport and in Norfolk,
Virginia, from 1755.
Partner of Alexander
Scott. Died in 1776.
(SRA)

STANDBURGH RECOMPENCE
Mate of the St Andrew.
Died in Darien on
10 December 1698.
(NLS)

STARKE JAMES
Emigrated from Scotland
to America before 1754.
Planter in Stafford
County, Virginia.
(OD)

STARKE JOHN
Emigrated from Scotland
to Canada on the Commerce
in June 1821. Received a
land grant in Dalhousie,
Upper Canada, 16 July 1821.
(PAO)

STARKE THOMAS
Emigrated from Scotland,
with his wife and two sons,
to Canada on the Commerce
in August 1820. Received
a land grant in Lanark,
Upper Canada, on
5 September 1820.
(PAO)

STEEL ALEXANDER
Emigrated from Scotland,
with his wife and four
sons, to Canada on the
Commerce in June 1821.
Received a land grant in
Ramsay, Upper Canada, on
14 August 1821.
(PAO)

STEEL GEORGE
Emigrated from Scotland,
with his wife and four
daughters, to Canada on the
George Canning in June 1821.
Received a land grant in
Lanark, Upper Canada, on
12 July 1821.
(PAO)

STEEL MARY
Four year indentured servant
imported from Scotland to
East New Jersey by John
Campbell in October 1684.
(EJD/A)

STEVEN Rev JAMES
  Born in 1801. Ordained
  in Stranraer, Wigtown-
  shire. Emigrated from
  Scotland to Chaleur, New
  Brunswick in October
  1831. Minister in New
  Brunswick from 1831 to
  1864. Died on
  22 January 1864.
  (HPC)

STEPHEN JOHN
  Educated at Marischal
  College, Aberdeen, -
  graduated M.A. in 1780.
  Episcopalian minister
  in Cruden, Aberdeenshire.
  Master of the Academy of
  Nassau, New Providence.
  (MCA)

STEPHEN WILLIAM
  Born on 25 March 1801 in
  Dufftown, Banffshire, son
  of William Stephen of
  Hillside, and Elizabeth
  Cameron. Married Elspet
  Smith, Knockando, Moray-
  shire, in 1828. Settled
  in Montreal, Quebec.
  (BCG)

STEVENSON ALLAN
  Born in June 1750,
  fourth son of Robert
  Stevenson and Margaret
  Fulton. Died in St Kitts
  on 26 May 1774.
  (S)

STEVENSON HUGH
  Born 26 February 1749,
  second son of Robert
  Stevenson and Margaret
  Fulton. Died in Tobago.
  (S)

STEVENSON JAMES
  Emigrated from Scotland
  to America after 1715.
  Settled in Albany, New
  York. Father of John
  born 13 March 1735.
  Died 2 February 1769.
  (TSA)

STEPHENSON NATHANIEL
  Emigrated from Scotland
  to America before 1756.
  Barber in Northampton
  County, Virginia.
  (OD)

STEVENSON SAMUEL
  Emigrated from Greenock,
  Renfrewshire, with his
  wife and daughter, to
  Canada on the David of
  London in May 1821.
  Received a land grant in
  Lanark, Upper Canada, on
  10 September 1821.
  (PAO)

STEWART AGNES
  Indentured servant
  imported from Scotland
  to East New Jersey by
  Charles Gordon in October
  1684.
  (EJD/A255)

STEWART ALEXANDER
  Born in Scotland in 1680.
  Possibly imported into
  East New Jersey by Thomas
  Yallerton in 1684.
  Apprenticed to Francis
  Chadsey, Chester County,
  Pennsylvania, 1697, and to
  Henry Nayle, shoemaker,
  also there, in 1701.
  Married Mary Bailey 1707.
  Father of Jane, Robert,
  Mary and Ann. Died 1724.
  (EJD/A)(NCGenJ.XII)

STEWART ALEXANDER
Born c1735. Emigrated
from Scotland to America
before 1755. Planter in
Virginia.
(OD)

STEWART ALEXANDER
Born in Scotland. Educated
at the University of Edin-
burgh. Emigrated from
Scotland to Canada in 1818.
Teacher in York, Upper
Canada c1819. Land agent.
Baptist minister in York
from 1829 to 1836.
(TO)

STEWART CHARLES
Son of Charles Stewart of
Ardsheal, and Isobel
Haldane. Died in Jamaica
during 1767.
(SAE)

STEWART CHARLES
Born c1759 in Campbelltown,
Argyllshire, son of Peter
Stewart. Emigrated from
Scotland to Prince Edward
Island in 1775. Lawyer
and administrator. Died
in Charlottetown, Prince
Edward Island, on
6 January 1813.
(DCB)

STEWART CHARLES JAMES
Born 15 April 1775, fifth
son of John, Earl of
Galloway, Galloway House,
Wigtownshire. Educated at
Oxford University. Ordained
as an Anglican minister in
1800. Emigrated to Quebec
c1808. Bishop of Quebec
1825 to 1837. Died 1837.
(TSA)(SP.IV)

STEWART DANIEL
Emigrated from Scotland
to Canada. Received a
land grant in Cavan,
Newcastle, Upper Canada.
10 June 1818.
(PAO)

STEWART JAMES
Indentured servant
imported from Scotland
to East New Jersey by
Thomas Yallerton 1684.
(EJD/A)

STEWART JAMES
Born in 1778, son of
Andrew Stewart, Inver-
nahyle. Married
Isabella Tod. Father of
David. Died in New York
during 1813.
(SAE)

STEWART JOHN
Indentured servant
imported from Scotland
to East New Jersey by
Thomas Yallerton 1684.
(EJD/A)

STEWART JOHN
Volunteer. Died of fever
on the voyage from Scotland
to Darien 21 September 1698.
(NLS)

STEWART JOHN
Born in Edinburgh during
1682, son of Robert Stewart,
and grandson of Walter
Stewart in Perthshire.
Emigrated from Scotland via
Ulster to America in 1718.
Settled in Londonderry,
New Hampshire.
(SG)

STEWART JOHN
Emigrated from Scotland,
with his wife and two
daughters, to Canada on
the Prompt. Received a
land grant in Dalhousie,
Upper Canada, 21 November
1821.
(PAO)

STEWART NEIL
Born c1802. Rhum, Inver-
ness-shire. Emigrated
from Leith, Midlothian,
with his wife Marion 28,
to Port Hawkesbury, Cape
Breton Island, in 1828
on the St Lawrence of
Newcastle, J. Cram.
(PANS.M6-100)

STEWART PETER
Born in 1725 son of Rev
Charles Stewart and Anna-
bella Campbell, Campbell-
town, Argyllshire. Married
(1) Helen MacKinnon in 1758
(2) Sarah Hamilton.
Emigrated from Scotland,
via Cork, Ireland, to
Canada on the Elizabeth on
10 September 1775. Public
official in Prince Edward
Island. Died 10 October 1805
in Charlottetown, Prince
Edward Island.
(DCB)

STEWART ROBERT
Born in Scotland c1732.
Emigrated from Scotland
to America. Planter in
Stafford County, Virginia.
(OD)

STEWART WILLIAM
Educated at the University
of Glasgow. Emigrated from
Scotland via London to
America in 1718. Ordained
in June 1719 for Monokin
and Wicomico, Virginia.
Presbyterian minister.
(AP)

STEWART WILLIAM
Brother of Dr Stewart,
Annapolis, Maryland, and
of David Stewart of
Ballachulin, Stirlingshire.
Settled in Annapolis pre
1747.
(LM)

STEWART WILLIAM
Yeoman. Emigrated from
Scotland to Canada.
Received a land grant
in Thorak, Home, Upper
Canada, 8 March 1826.
(PAO)

STEWART Dr
Born in Scotland. Settled
in Port Morant, Jamaica,
c1699.
(DP)

STEWART Dr
Brother of William Stewart,
Annapolis, Maryland, and
of David Stewart of Balla-
chulin, Stirlingshire.
Settled in Annapolis pre
1747.
(LM)

STIRLING CHARLES
Planter in Jamaica
from c1765 to 1797.
(SRO/GD24)

STIRLING JAMES
Stirling. Born in 1752.
Emigrated from Scotland
to America during 1774.
Settled in Baltimore,
Maryland. Married
Elizabeth Gibson, Carlisle,
Pennsylvania, on 19 May
1782. Father of Archibald,
1798-1892. Died 25 June 1820.
(BAF)

STIRLING ROBERT
Born in 1772, fifth son of
William Stirling of Keir,
Perthshire. Died in Hampton,
St James parish, Jamaica, on
28 September 1808. Buried in
Kingston Cathedral, Jamaica.
(MIBWI)

STIRLING ROBERT
Born in Scotland. Received
a land grant in Burgess,
Upper Canada, 12 August 1817.
(PAO)

STIRLING WALTER
Emigrated from Scotland,
with his wife and three sons,
to Canada on the George Canning
in June 1821. Received a land
grant in Ramsay, Upper Canada,
16 July 1821.
(PAO)

STIRLING WILLIAM
Emigrated from Scotland,
with his wife, two sons
and three daughters, to
Canada on the George
Canning in June 1821.
Received a land grant in
Lanark, Upper Canada, on
10 July 1821.
(PAO)

STOBO ROBERT
Born in Glasgow in 1727,
son of William Stobo,
merchant. Educated at the
University of Glasgow from
1740 to 1742. Merchant in
Virginia. Militiaman.
(VMHB.1941)

STOCKS ARTHUR sr
Emigrated from Scotland,
with his wife, three sons
and a daughter, to Canada
on the Earl of Buckingham
in June 1821. Received a
land grant in Sherbrook,
Upper Canada, 24 July 1821.
(PAO)

STOCKS ARTHUR jr
Emigrated from Scotland
to Canada on the Earl of
Buckingham in June 1821.
Received a land grant in
Sherbrook, Upper Canada,
24 July 1821.
(PAO)

STODART JOHN
Born c1782, son of James
Stodart, 1757-1829, and
Agnes Thomson, 1757-1839,
Hillhead, Covington, Lanark-
shire. Died in Uttica, USA
on 15 December 1834.
(Covington GS)

STORIE JAMES
Emigrated from Greenock,
Renfrewshire, to Montreal,
Quebec, on the brig
Niagara, Hamilton, 1825.
Settled in McNab, Bathurst,
Upper Canada, 1825.
(SG)

STORIE ROBERT
Emigrated from Greenock,
Renfrewshire, to Montreal,
Quebec, on the brig
Niagara, Hamilton, 1825.
Settled in McNab, Bathurst,
Upper Canada, 1825.
(SG)

STRACHAN JOHN
Educated at King's College,
Aberdeen. Rector of Corn-
wall, Upper Canada. D.D.
of Aberdeen 22 January 1811.
(KCA)

STRACHAN THOMAS
Emigrated from Scotland,
with his wife, two sons
and three daughters, to
Canada on the Commerce
in June 1821. Received
a land grant in Lanark,
Upper Canada, on
1 August 1821.
(PAO)

STRATTON EFFIE
Indentured servant
imported from Scotland
to East New Jersey by
David Mudie during
November 1684.
(EJD/A196)

STRONTIAN SANDY
Scottish settler at
La Chine, Montreal,
Quebec, c1805.
(GD.202.70.12)

STRUTHER JOHN
Brewer in Glasgow. Died
in Savannah, Georgia,
during February 1790.
Buried in the Colonial
Cemetery, Savannah.
(HGP)

STRUTHERS ROBERT
Emigrated from Scotland
to Canada on the George
Canning in June 1821.
Received a land grant in
Ramsay, Upper Canada, on
10 July 1821.
(PAO)

STUART ANDREW
Brother of the Earl of
Galloway. Emigrated from
Scotland to Darien. Died
in Darien during 1699.
(TDD)

STUART ARCHIBALD
Emigrated from Scotland,
with his wife and son, to
Canada on the George Canning
in June 1821. Received a
land grant in Lanark,
Upper Canada, 24 July 1821.
(PAO)

STUART CALLUM
Servant of James Calder,
Miltoun of Redcastle.
Jacobite in the Earl of
Cromarty's Regiment 1745.
Transported to the Plant-
ations.
(LP)

STUART CHARLES
Son of John Stuart.
Educated at Marischal
College, Aberdeen, from
1811 to 1813. Merchant
in Quebec.
(MCA)

STUART DUNCAN
Emigrated from Scotland,
with his wife and three
sons, to Canada on the
David of London in June
1821. Received a land
grant in Dalhousie,
Upper Canada, on
1 September 1821.
(PAO)

STUART JAMES
Emigrated from Scotland
to Canada on the George
Canning in June 1821.
Received a land grant in
Ramsay, Upper Canada, on
25 July 1821.
(PAO)

STUART JOHN
Born in Scotland in 1779.
North West Company
employee from 1799 to
1821. Hudson Bay Company
employee from 1821 to
1824. Trader in the New
Caledonia region.
(HBRS)

STUART JOHN
Glasgow. Emigrated from
Scotland to Virginia
before 1814.
(OD)

STUART JOHN
Emigrated from Scotland,
with his wife, two sons
and three daughters, to
Canada on the George Canning
in June 1821. Received a
land grant in Lanark,
Upper Canada, on
24 July 1821.
(PAO)

STUART(?) MARGARET
Four year indentured
servant imported from
Scotland to East New
Jersey in October 1684
by John Campbell. Land
grant 1 May 1690.
Servant to Colin
Campbell in 1690.
(EJD/A/D325)

STUART PETER
Son of Rev Charles Stuart
and Annabella Campbell,
Campbelltown, Argyllshire.
Married Helen MacLeod.
Father of ten children.
Emigrated from Scotland to
Prince Edward Island in
November 1775. Later the
Chief Justice of Prince
Edward Island.
(TML)

STUART ROBERT
Born during 1785 in
Callander, Perthshire.
Emigrated from Scotland
to Canada during 1806. Fur
trader in Canada and Oregon.
Public official in Detroit,
Michigan, c1834. Father of
David, born in Brooklyn,
New York, during 1816.
Died in Chicago, Illinois,
in 1848.
(TSA)

STUART WILLIAM
Born in Scotland.
Hudson Bay Company employee
from 1691 to 1719. Died at
York Fort 25 October 1719.
(HBRS)

STUART WILLIAM
Born in Glasgow in 1800.
Died in Jamaica 6 May 1835.
Buried in the Scots Cemetery,
Kingston, Jamaica.
(MIBWI)

SUMMERS JACOB
Emigrated from Scotland to
Canada. Received a land
grant in Charlottenburg,
St Raphael, Quebec, on
24 November 1787.
(PAO)

SUTHERLAND ALEXANDER
Born c1770. Farmer.
Emigrated from Scotland,
with his wife and four
children, to Canada.
Settled at Scott's Hill,
Pictou, Nova Scotia, 1815.
(PANS/RG1)

SUTHERLAND ALEXANDER
Born c1775. Labourer.
Emigrated from Scotland,
with his wife and three
children, to Canada.
Settled at Lower Settle-
ment, Pictou, Nova Scotia,
in 1815.
(PANS/RG1)

SUTHERLAND ALEXANDER
Born c1793. Former soldier.
Emigrated from Scotland,
with his unmarried sister,
to Canada. Received a land
grant in Halifax, Nova Scotia,
in 1815.
(PANS/RG20)

SUTHERLAND ALEXANDER
Emigrated from Scotland
to Canada on the
Clifford 15 September 1816.
Received a land grant in
Drummond, Upper Canada,
on 9 December 1816.
(PAO)

SUTHERLAND ANGUS(?)
Born c1755. Farmer.
Emigrated from Scotland,
with his wife and two
children, to Canada.
Settled at Scott's Hill,
Pictou, Nova Scotia, 1815.
(PANS/RG1)

SUTHERLAND CHRISTY
Born c1779. Servant.
Emigrated from Scotland
to Canada. Settled in
Pictou Town, Nova Scotia,
during 1815.
(PANS/RG1)

SUTHERLAND DAVID
Emigrated from Scotland
to Canada on the George
Canning in June 1821.
Received a land grant in
Ramsay, Upper Canada, on
16 July 1821.
(PAO)

SUTHERLAND ELEANOR
Born c1794. Servant.
Emigrated from Scotland
to Canada. Received a land
grant in Pictou Town, Nova
Scotia, in 1815.
(PANS/RG1)

SUTHERLAND GEORGE
Emigrated from Scotland,
with his wife, three sons
and three daughters, to
Canada on the George
Canning in June 1821.
Received a land grant in
Ramsay, Upper Canada, on
16 July 1821.
(PAO)

SUTHERLAND JOHN
Born c1770. Labourer.
Emigrated from Scotland,
with his wife and four
children, to Canada.
Settled at Scott's Hill,
Pictou, Nova Scotia, 1815.
(PANS/RG1)

SUTHERLAND JOHN
Born c1793. Tailor.
Emigrated from Scotland,
with his wife, to Canada.
Settled in Pictou Town,
Nova Scotia, in 1815.
(PANS/RG1)

SUTHERLAND MARGARET
Born c1796. Servant.
Emigrated from Scotland
to Canada. Settled in
Pictou Town, Nova Scotia,
in 1815.
(PANS/RG1)

SUTHERLAND ROBERT
Born c1769. Labourer.
Emigrated from Scotland,
with his wife and six
children, to Canada.
Settled at Scott's Hill,
Pictou, Nova Scotia, 1815.
(PANS/RG1)

SUTHERLAND WILLIAM
Sutherlandshire. Educated
at King's College,
Aberdeen, - graduated M.A.
27 March 1800. Missionary
in North America.
(KCA)

SUTHERLAND WILLIAM
Born c1759. Labourer.
Emigrated from Scotland,
with his wife and three
children, to Canada.
Settled on West Branch,
East River, Pictou, Nova
Scotia, in 1815.
(PANS/RG1)

SUTHERLAND WILLIAM
Born c1795. Emigrated from
Scotland to Nova Scotia in
1815.
(PANS/RG20)

SWAN JAMES
Emigrated from Scotland,
with his wife, three sons
and a daughter, to Canada
on the Prompt. Received a
land grant in Dalhousie,
Upper Canada, on
27 November 1821.
(PAO)

SWAPE(?) WILLIAM
Emigrated from Scotland,
with his wife and son, to
Canada on the Commerce in
August 1820. Received a
land grant in Lanark,
Upper Canada, 5 September
1820.
(PAO)

SYM ROBERT
Emigrated from Scotland
to Canada on the Commerce
in June 1821. Received a
land grant in Sherbrook,
Upper Canada, 7 August 1821.
(PAO)

SYME SAMUEL
Old Kilpatrick, Dunbartonshire. Applied to settle
in Canada on 3 March 1815.
(SRO/RH9)

SYME WALTER
Emigrated from Scotland
to Canada. Received a
land grant in Sherbrook,
Upper Canada, on
10 August 1822.
(PAO)

TASKIE JAMES
Born in Scotland. Former
lieutenant in the 57th
Regiment. Military
settler. Received a land
grant in Drummond, Upper
Canada, 21 August 1817.
(PAO)

TATLOCK WILLIAM
Emigrated from Scotland
to Canada on the Prompt
in June 1820. Settled in
Upper Canada.
(PAO)

TAILOR ALEXANDER
Sailor. Died of fever on
the voyage from Scotland
to Darien on
28 October 1698.
(NLS)

TAYLOR EDWARD
Scottish indentured servant.
Land grant at Middleton,
Monmouth County, New Jersey,
13 January 1692.
(EJD/D)

TAYLOR JAMES
Fochabers, Morayshire.
Applied to settle in
Canada on 2 March 1815.
(SRO/RH9)

TAYLOR JOHN
Born in Scotland. Wife
three sons and three
daughters. Received a
land grant in Drummond,
Upper Canada, 3 March 1819.
(PAO)

TAYLOR JOHN
Emigrated from Scotland to
Canada on the Commerce in
August 1820. Received a
land grant in Lanark,
Upper Canada, 5 September
1820.
(PAO)

TAYLOR WILLIAM
Emigrated from Scotland to
Canada on the Earl of Buck-
ingham. Received a land
grant in Sherbrook, Upper
Canada, 1 August 1821.
(PAO)

TAIT JAMES
Emigrated from Scotland to
the eastern shore of
Virginia pre 1783.
(OD)

TAIT PATRICK
Indentured servant
imported from Scotland
to East New Jersey by
Lord Neil Campbell in
December 1685.
(EJD/A225)

TAWSE JOHN
Son of James Tawse, farmer
in Towie, Aberdeenshire.
Educated at Marischal
College, Aberdeen, from
1817 to 1821, graduated
M.A. Presbyterian minister
in Toronto, Canada.
(MCA)

TEGAN JOHN
Born in Scotland c1730.
Emigrated from Scotland
to America before 1756.
Farmer in Virginia.
(OD)

TELFAIR EDWARD
Born during 1735 in the
Stewartry of Kirkcudbright.
Educated at Kirkcudbright
Grammar School. Emigrated
from Scotland to America in
1758. Settled in Virginia,
North Carolina and Georgia.
Merchant and politician.
Father of Thomas. Died in
Savannah, Georgia, in 1807.
(TSA)

TELFER JAMES
Son of Robert Telfer, born
in Dumfries-shire in 1796.
Emigrated from Scotland to
Canada in 1821. Received a
land grant in Caverhill,
Queensbury, York County,
New Brunswick, in 1821.
(PANB)

TELFER JOHN
Son of Robert Telfer, born
in Dumfries-shire in 1799.
Emigrated from Scotland
to Canada in 1821.
Received a land grant in
Caverhill, Queensbury, York
County, New Brunswick, 1821.
(PANB)

TELFER PETER
Emigrated from Scotland
to Darien. Planter.Died
there 24 December 1698.
(NLS)

TELFER ROBERT
Born during 1771 in
Dumfries-shire. Carpenter
and farmer. Wife and two
sons. Emigrated from
Scotland to Canada in 1821.
Received a land grant in
Caverhill, Queensbury,
York County, New Brunswick,
in 1821.
(PANB)

TENLER DAVID
Royalist soldier captured
at Worcester. Transported
from Gravesend, Kent, to
Boston ,New England, on the
John and Sarah, master John
Greene, 13 May 1652.
(NER)

TENNANT EDWARD
Emigrated from Scotland,
with his wife, two sons
and two daughters, to
Canada on the David of
London in June 1821.
Received a land grant in
Dalhousie, Upper Canada,
on 9 September 1821.
(PAO)

TENNANT JAMES
Emigrated from Scotland
to Canada on the Brothers
on 13 August 1817.
Received a land grant in
Younge, Upper Canada, on
16 February 1818.
(PAO)

TENNANT WILLIAM
Emigrated from Scotland
to Canada on the Brothers
on 13 August 1817.
Received a land grant in
Younge, Upper Canada, on
16 February 1818.
(PAO)

TENTER WILLIAM
Emigrated from Scotland
to Darien. Died there on
11 December 1698.
(NLS)

THOM ADAM
Angus. Educated at King's
College, Aberdeen, graduated
M.A. in March 1823. LL.D.
Judge in Rupert's Land,
Canada.
(KCA)

THOM ALEXANDER
Born in Scotland. Staff
surgeon to the settlers.
Military settler. Received
land grants in Upper Canada
at - Bathurst in June 1816,
in Drummond 16 October 1816,
in Elmsley 30 June 1817, and
in Sherbrook 18 May 1819.
(PAO)

THOMAS JAMES
Born in Scotland c1730.
Emigrated from Scotland
to America. Farmer in
Virginia.
(OD)

THOMSON ALEXANDER
Indentured servant
imported from Scotland
to east New Jersey by
Lord Neil Campbell in
December 1685.
(EJD/A225)

THOMSON ALEXANDER
Son of James Thomson,
accountant in the Excise
Office. Savannah, Georgia,
married Mary Elisabeth
Spencer, daughter of
William Spencer, H.M.
Customs Collector of
Savannah, Georgia. Married
by Rev Samuel Frink,
minister of Christ Church,
Savannah, Georgia, on
24 November 1770.
(EMR)

THOMPSON ALEXANDER
Emigrated from Scotland,
with his wife, to Canada
on the Agincourt on
9 August 1817. Received
a land grant in Beckwith,
Upper Canada, 27 March 1818,
and in Drummond, Upper
Canada, 18 May 1820.
(PAO)

THOMSON ANDREW
Brother of David Thomson.
Emigrated from Dumfries-
shire(?), Scotland, to
Canada c1800.
(SO)

THOMSON of KINLOCH ANDREW
Son of Andrew Thomson of
Kinloch, Fife. Apprentice
to Robert Hill. Admitted
to the Society of Writers
to the Signet 2 June 1809.
Married Barbara Hunter on
20 February 1818. Died in
Saratoga, USA, August 1831.
(WS)

THOMSON ANDREW
Born in 1789, son of
John Thomson of Prior-
Letham, Fife.
Apprenticed to John
Russell. Admitted to the
Society of Writers to the
Signet on 23 June 1820.
Died in Florida on
14 July 1841.
(WS)

THOMSON A. G.
Emigrated from Scotland
to Canada in 1820.
(SRO/GD51.6.2122)

THOMSON ARCHIBALD
Brother of David Thomson.
Emigrated from Dumfries-
shire to Canada c1800.
(SO)

THOMPSON ARCHIBALD
Emigrated from Scotland,
with his wife and two sons,
to Canada on the Commerce
in June 1821. Received a
land grant in Dalhousie,
Upper Canada, 20 July 1821.
(PAO)

THOMPSON DAVID
Jedburgh, Roxburghshire.
Emigrated from Scotland
to America before 1749.
Merchant in Yorktown,
Virginia.
(OD)

THOMSON DAVID
Born in 1764. Stone-
mason. Emigrated from
Westerkirk, Dumfries-
shire, with his wife
Mary Glendinning and
four children, to Upper
Canada in 1795.
(SO)

THOMSON GEORGE
Aberdeen. Graduated
M.A. at the University
of Aberdeen in March
1822. Minister of the
Scots Church in MacNab,
Upper Canada.
(UKA)(MCA)

THOMPSON HENRY
Emigrated from Scotland,
with his wife, three sons
and three daughters, to
Canada on the Commerce in
June 1821. Received a land
grant in Sherbrook, Upper
Canada, on 1 August 1821.
(PAO)

THOMPSON JAMES
Born in Tain, Ross-shire,
in 1732. Sergeant in the
Fraser Highlanders. Fought
in Canada at Louisbourg in
1758 and at Quebec in 1759.
Settled in Quebec. Father
of James and John. Died in
1830.
(SNF)(SRO/GD45.422)

THOMPSON JAMES
Glasgow. Jailed at
Suffolk, Virginia, as
a suspected convict
servant 1 August 1771.
(Va. Gaz.)

THOMSON Rev JAMES
Born during 1779 in
Lockerbie, Dumfries-shire.
Ordained at Auchtergaven,
Perthshire, in 1806.
Emigrated from Scotland
to New Brunswick in 1816.
Minister at Newcastle and
Chatham on the Miramachi
River from 1817 to 1830.
Died 11 November 1830.
(HPC)

THOMPSON Mrs JAMES
A widow. Emigrated from
Scotland, with her son
and daughter, to Canada
on the Rothiemurcus
4 June 1818. Received a
land grant in Burgess,
Upper Canada, on
22 October 1818.
(PAO)

THOMPSON JAMES
Emigrated from Scotland,
with his wife, two sons
and a daughter, to
Canada on the Commerce
in August 1820. Received a
land grant in Lanark,
Upper Canada, on
5 September 1820.
(PAO)

THOMPSON JAMES
Emigrated from Scotland
to Canada on the David
in June 1821. Received
a land grant in Lanark,
Upper Canada, on
14 August 1821.
(PAO)

THOMSON JANET
Indentured servant
imported from Scotland
to East New Jersey by
Lord Neil Campbell in
December 1685.
(EJD/A225)

THOMSON JOHN
Son of John Thomson in
Aberdeen. Educated at
Marischal College,
Aberdeen, c1815. Settled
in the West Indies.
(MCA)

THOMPSON JOHN
Emigrated from Scotland
to Canada on the Success
on 8 September 1817.
Received land grants in
South Gower, Upper Canada,
on 13 October 1817, and
on 16 April 1818.
(PAO)

THOMSON JOHN
Emigrated from Scotland
to Canada on the Agincourt
on 12 August 1817. Received
a land grant in Upper
Canada on 9 February 1818.
(PAO)

THOMSON JOHN
Son of William Thomson
and Rachel Weir. Died
in Jamaica 29 July 1823.
(Lesmahowgow GS)

THOMSON MARGERY
Indentured servant
imported from Scotland
to East New Jersey by
Lord Neil Campbell in
December 1685.
(EJD/A225)

THOMPSON THOMAS
Emigrated from Scotland
to America before 1756.
Schoolmaster in Virginia.
(OD)

THOMPSON THOMAS
Emigrated from Scotland
to Canada on the
Anthea Morias 5 June 1817.
Received a land grant in
Burgess, Upper Canada, on
29 July 1818.
(PAO)

THOMSON WILLIAM
Indentured servant
imported from Scotland
to East New Jersey by
Lord Neil Campbell in
December 1685.
(EJD/A225)

THOMSON WILLIAM
Indentured servant
imported from Scotland
to East New Jersey by
Lord Neil Campbell in
December 1685.
(EJD/A225)

THOMSON WILLIAM
Born in Scotland in 1741.
Revolutionary soldier.
Married Sarah Patterson
in York County, Penn-
sylvania. Father of
Andrew, Mary, Nelly, John,
Margaret, Susanna, Jane,
William, Adam and Sarah.
Settled in Ohio in 1797.
Died during 1806. Buried
in Guernsey County, Ohio.
(ORIII)

THOMSON WILLIAM
Emigrated from Scotland
to Canada on the Agincourt
12 August 1817. Received
a land grant in Upper
Canada on 9 February 1818.
(PAO)

THOMPSON WILLIAM
Emigrated from Scotland
to Canada on the Success
on 8 September 1817.
Received land grants in
South Gower on 13 October
1817 and on 16 April 1818.
(PAO)

THOMPSON ....
Born c1761. Mason.
Emigrated from Scotland,
with his wife and four
children, to Canada.
Settled in Pictou Town,
Nova Scotia, 1815.
(PANS/RG1)

TOD JAMES
Born c1742 in Scotland(?)
Settled in Canada c1767.
Merchant in Quebec. Died
there on 16 October 1816.
(DCB)

TODD JAMES
Carpenter. Emigrated
from Scotland to Canada.
Received a land grant in
Smith, Newcastle, Upper
Canada, on 15 September
1818.
(PAO)

TODD JOHN
Emigrated from Scotland,
with his wife and seven
sons, to Canada on the
Prompt. Received a land
grant in Dalhousie,
Upper Canada, on
21 November 1821.
(PAO)

TOLMIE MURDOCH
Son of John Tolmie,
Dunvegan, Skye, Inver-
ness-shire. Settled in
Nova Scotia pre 1809.
(NRAS.2237)

TOLMIE NORMAN
Born in 1734, son of
William Mor Tolmie and
Katharine MacKenzie.
Master mariner. Settled
in New York. Married
Phoebe Comeris. Died
in 1787.
(MB)

TOMLINSON JONATHAN
Emigrated from Scotland,
with his wife, three sons
and four daughters, to
Canada on the Commerce
in June 1821. Received
a land grant in Ramsay,
Upper Canada, on
1 August 1821.
(PAO)

TOSH WILLIAM
Indentured servant
imported from Scotland
to East New Jersey by
Lord Neil Campbell in
December 1685.
(EJD/A225)

TOSHACH JOHN sr
Emigrated from Scotland,
with his wife, five sons
and four daughters, to
Canada on the Commerce.
Received a land grant in
Ramsay, Upper Canada, on
9 September 1821.
(PAO)

TOSHACH JOHN jr
Emigrated from Scotland
to Canada on the Commerce.
Received a land grant in
Ramsay, Upper Canada, on
9 September 1821.
(PAO)

TOSHACH WILLIAM
Emigrated from Scotland
to Canada on the Commerce.
Received a land grant in
Ramsay, Upper Canada, on
9 September 1821.
(PAO)

TOUGH ALASTAIR
Royalist soldier captured
at Worcester. Transported
from Gravesend, Kent, to
Boston, New England, on the
John and Sarah, master John
John Greene, 13 May 1652.
(NER)

TOWER ALEXANDER
Son of George Tower,
merchant in Aberdeen.
Educated at Marischal
College, Aberdeen, from
1815 to 1819 - graduated
M.A. Planter in Santa
Cruz.
(MCA)

TOWER JAMES
Son of John Tower in
Aberdeen. Educated at
Marischal College,
Aberdeen, c1774 to 1776.
Doctor in St Thomas,
West Indies.
(MCA)

TOWNSLEY JOHN
Born 12 September 1757 in
Scotland. Married Hester
Martin during 1784.
Father of James, Innes,
William, Alexander, John,
Thomas, Samuel and George.
Revolutionary soldier.
Died in Cedarville, Ohio,
on 27 December 1857.
Buried at Massie's Creek,
Ohio.
(ORIII)

TRAILL GEORGE
Born in 1746, second son
of Rev George Traill of
Hobbister, minister of
Dunnet, Caithness, and
Jean Murray. Emigrated
from Scotland to America.
Settled at St George,
Grenada. Died in 1774.
(GOT)

TRAILL JOHN
Born in 1694, son of
William Traill of
Westness, and Barbara
Balfour. Emigrated from
Scotland to America.
Merchant in Boston,
Massachusetts.
(GOT)

TRAILL ROBERT
Born 29 April 1744, son
of Rev George Traill of
Hobbister, D.D., and
Jean Murray. Emigrated
from Scotland to Phila-
delphia, Pennsylvania,
during 1763. Married
Elizabeth Grotz on
3 March 1774. Died in
Easton, Pennsylvania, on
31 July 1816.
(GOT)

TRAILL THOMAS
Born in 1749, son of Rev
George Traill of Hobbister,
D.D., minister of Dunnet,
Caithness, and Jean Murray.
Emigrated from Scotland to
St Vincent.
(GOT)

TRAN HUGH
Son of Arthur Tran. Merchant
in Glasgow, and from c1767
in St Kitts.
(SRA/B10.15.7141)

TROTTER Rev THOMAS
Born in Berwickshire 1782.
Educated at Edinburgh
University. Ordained in 1808
in Johnshaven, Kincardine.
Emigrated from Scotland to
Nova Scotia 1818. Minister
in Nova Scotia from 1818
to 1853. Died in 1855.
(HPC)

TROUP JOHN
Educated at Marischal
College, Aberdeen, -
graduated M.D. in 1770.
Doctor in Jamaica.
(MCA)

TULLIS JOHN
Emigrated from Scotland,
with his wife, five sons
and three daughters, to
Canada on the Commerce
in June 1821. Received
a land grant in
Dalhousie, Upper Canada,
on 20 July 1821.
(PAO)

TULLY JOHN
Emigrated from Scotland
to Canada. Received a
land grant in Monaghan,
Newcastle, Upper Canada,
18 February 1818.
(PAO)

TURNBULL CHARLES
Glasgow. Agent for
Buchanan, Murdoch and
Company in Virginia, 1747.
(SRA/B10.15.5943)

TURNBULL JOHN
Emigrated from Scotland,
with his wife and son, to
Canada on the Brock 1820.
Received a land grant in
Lanark, Upper Canada, on
21 October 1821.
(PAO)

TURNBULL THOMAS
Emigrated from Scotland
to Canada on the Earl of
Buckingham. Received a
land grant in Dalhousie,
Upper Canada, 3 September
1821.
(PAO)

TURNBULL WILLIAM
Born in Stirling 1751.
Emigrated from Scotland
to America in 1770.
Settled in Philadelphia,
Pennsylvania. Married (2)
Mary Nisbet. Father of
A. Nisbet Turnbull.
(BAF)

TURRIFF JOHN
Emigrated from Scotland,
with his wife and son, to
Canada on the Commerce
in June 1820. Received a
land grant in Lanark,
Upper Canada, on
3 September 1820.
(PAO)

TURRIFF WILLIAM
Emigrated from Scotland
to Canada on the Commerce
in June 1820. Received a
land grant in Lanark,
Upper Canada, on
3 September 1820.
(PAO)

TWADDLE ROBERT
Emigrated from Scotland
to Canada on the Earl of
Buckingham in June 1821.
Received a land grant in
Sherbrook, Upper Canada,
on 24 July 1821.
(PAO)

TWEEDIE JAMES
Born in Torthorwald,
Dumfries-shire, on
27 August 1797. Shoe-
maker. Married Margaret
Byars, 1799-1862. Father
of Thomas born on
13 September 1820.
Emigrated from Scotland,
with his wife and son,
to Canada during 1821.
Received a land grant in
Caverhill, Queensbury,
York County, New Brunswick,
in 1821. Died 14 March 1860.
Buried at Wicklow, New
Brunswick.
(PANB)

TYNETT WILLIAM
Indentured servant
imported from Scotland
to East New Jersey by
Charles Gordon during
October 1684. Headright
land grant in 1689.
Married Mary Stillwell.
(EJD/A255/B159)

UPTON THOMAS
Freeholder. Emigrated from
Scotland, with his family
and five indentured servants,
to Georgia, c1737.
(HGP)

URQUHART DONALD
Emigrated from Scotland,
with his wife, to Canada.
Born c1788. Labourer.
Settled at Harbourmouth,
Pictou, Nova Scotia, 1815.
(PANS/RG1)

URQUHART HUGH
Ross-shire. Graduated M.A.
at King's College, Aberdeen,
on 25 March 1814. Minister
of the Scots Church, Cornwall, Canada.
(UKA)

URQUHART ROBERT
Emigrated from Scotland,
with his wife, two sons
and a daughter, to Canada
on the Brock in 1820.
Received a land grant in
Lanark, Upper Canada, on
25 October 1821.
(PAO)

* USHER (see p. 312)

URQUHART Rev
Emigrated from Scotland
to Prince Edward Island
c1800. Minister there
from 1800 to 1802.
Minister in Miramachi, New
Brunswick, from 1802 to
1814. Died in 1814.
(HPC)

VEITCH JAMES
Born in 1628, third son of
Malcolm Veitch and Janet
Stewart. Emigrated from
Scotland to America in 1651.
Settled in Calvert County,
Maryland. Sheriff of
Putuxent St Maries and
Potomack from 1653 to 1657.
Married Mary Gakerlin 1657.
Father of four sons, including
Nathan, 1668-1705. Died
in 1685.
(BAF)

VEITCH JOHN
Son of Alexander Veitch in
Peebles. Emigrated from
Scotland to America in 1766.
Settled in Bladenburg,
Maryland.
(MHR.M1098)

VERNER HUGH
Born in Scotland(?)
Hudson Bay Company
employee from 1679
to c1694.
(HBRS)

WABER ROBERT
Indentured servant
imported from Scotland
to East New Jersey by
David Mudie November 1684.
(EJD/A196)

WADDELL ALEXANDER
Born in Scotland during
February 1732. Emigrated
from Scotland to America.
Married Eleanor Roush in
Virginia during 1770.
Father of William, James,
John, Alexander, Joseph,
Elizabeth, Ann, Miriam,
Jennie and Isabella.
Revolutionary soldier.
Died on 8 September 1834.
Buried at Waddell-Hulbert
Cemetery, Green, Ohio.
(ORIII)

WADDELL GEORGE
Emigrated from Scotland,
with his wife, two sons
and four daughters, to
Canada on the Brock 1820.
Received a land grant in
Lanark, Upper Canada, on
25 October 1821.
(PAO)

WALKER ALEXANDER
Son of John Walker and
Jane McKnight, born in
Wigtown. Emigrated from
Scotland, via Ireland, to
America c1726. Settled in
Chester County, Penn-
sylvania. Father of three
children.
(MCC)

WALKER ISABEL
Indentured servant
imported from Scotland
to East New Jersey by
Charles Gordon during
October 1684.
(EJD/A255)

WALKER JAMES
And his wife Isabel
Johnstone. Indentured
servants imported from
Scotland to East New
Jersey by Thomas Gordon
in October 1684. Sold to
Samuel Moore. Headright
land grant in 1689.
(EJD/A/B159)

WALKER JANET
Indentured servant
imported from Scotland
to East New Jersey by
Robert Fullerton during
October 1684.
(EJD/A)

WALKER JOHN
Born in Wigtown, son of
John Walker and Jane
McKnight. Married in
Wigtown on 1 January 1702
to Katharine Rutherford.
Emigrated from Scotland,
via Newry, Ireland, to
Maryland in May 1726.
Settled in Chester County,
Pennsylvania. Father of
Elizabeth, John, James,
Thomas, William, Jane,
Samuel, and Alexander.
Died in Pennsylvania 1734.
Buried in Nottingham.
(DAR/NC)

WALKER ROBERT
Kingston, Scotland.
Emigrated from Scotland
to Virginia before 1775.
Married Elizabeth Starke
c1745. Father of Robert,
Richard, David, Bolling,
Freeman, Starke, Louisa,
Martha, Mary and Clara.
(HBV)

WALKER WILLIAM
Emigrated from Scotland,
with two sons and a
daughter, to Canada on
the Commerce in June 1820.
Received a land grant in
Lanark, Upper Canada, on
5 September 1820.
(PAO)

WALLACE ANDREW
Emigrated from Scotland,
with his wife, five sons
and three daughters, to
Canada on the Prompt.
Received a land grant in
Dalhousie, Upper Canada,
on 21 November 1821.
(PAO)

WALLACE HUGH
Emigrated from Scotland,
with his wife and two
daughters, to Canada on
the David of London.
Received a land grant in
Lanark, Upper Canada, on
1 October 1821.
(PAO)

WALLACE HUGH
Emigrated from Scotland,
with his son, to Canada.
Received a land grant in
Dalhousie, Upper Canada,
on 24 August 1822.
(PAO)

WALLACE JOHN
Emigrated from Scotland
to America during 1771.
Miller in Nansedmond
County, Virginia.
(OD)

WALLACE MICHAEL
Emigrated from Scotland
to America in 1771.
Miller in Nansedmond
County, Virginia.
(OD)

WALLACE PETER
Emigrated from Scotland
to America after 1680.
Planter in Virginia.
(OD)

WALLACE WILLIAM
Born in Aberdeen in 1760.
Emigrated from Scotland
to America in 1788.
(HG)

WALLACE WILLIAM
Emigrated from Scotland
to Canada. Received a land
grant in Cavan, Newcastle,
Upper Canada, on 2 July
1818.
(PAO)

WALLACE WILLIAM
Emigrated from Scotland,
with his wife, two sons
and three daughters, to
Canada on the Earl of
Buckingham in June 1821.
Received a land grant in
Ramsay, Upper Canada, on
31 July 1821.
(PAO)

WARDLAW HARRY
Son of John Wardlaw and
Mary Gartshore. Writer
in Edinburgh c1742.
Jacobite in 1745.
Stationer in London c1755.
Settled in Jamaica.
(TWS)

WARDROP DANIEL
Born in Glasgow during
1765. Merchant. Emigrated
from Scotland to America.
Died in Virginia in 1791.
(SRA)

WARK ALEXANDER
Emigrated from Scotland,
with his wife, son and
two daughters, to Canada
on the Commerce. Received
a land grant in Lanark,
Upper Canada, on
22 August 1822.
(PAO)

WARNOCK JOHN
Emigrated from Scotland,
with his wife and son,
to Canada on the Commerce
in June 1821. Received a
land grant in Sherbrook,
Upper Canada, on 8 August
1821.
(PAO)

WARREN ....
A Scottish soldier.
Settled at Murray Bay or
Mount Murray, Quebec, after
the Siege of Quebec 1762.
(PRSC)

WATT JAMES
Emigrated from Scotland,
with his wife, to Canada
on the David of London
in June 1821. Received a
land grant in Lanark,
Upper Canada, 8 August 1821.
(PAO)

WATT JOHN
Emigrated from Scotland,
with his wife, to Canada
on the David of London in
June 1821. Received a land
grant in Lanark, Upper
Canada, 8 August 1821.
(PAO)

WATT WILLIAM
Born in 1745. Mason.
Brother of John Watt, 1738-
1782, mason in Symington,
Lanarkshire. Resident in
Tobago for 24 years. Died
in Brest 7 January 1795.
(Symington GS)

WATT WILLIAM
Born c1770, son of John
Watt, 1738-1782, mason in
Symington, Lanarkshire, and
Jean Fisher, 1745-1819.
Died in Tobago in 1793.
(Symington GS)

WATSON GEORGE
Emigrated from Scotland,
with his wife, two sons
and two daughters, to
Canada on the Earl of
Buckingham in June 1821.
Received a land grant in
Dalhousie, Upper Canada,
on 24 July 1821.
(PAO)

WATSON JAMES
Emigrated from Scotland,
with his wife, two sons
and two daughters, to
Canada on the Prompt in
June 1820. Received a land
grant in Dalhousie, Upper
Canada, 27 November 1821.
(PAO)

WATSON JOHN
Born in Scotland in 1685.
Emigrated from Scotland
to America c1715. Painter.
Settled Perth Amboy, New
Jersey. Died 22 August
1768. Buried at St Peter's
Church, Perth Amboy.
(Whitehead's 'Perth Amboy')

WATSON JOHN
Born in Scotland. Former
quartermaster in the
Glengarry Fencibles. Wife.
Military settler. Received
land grants in Upper Canada
at Beckwith 22 August 1816,
at Kitley 14 June 1817,
at Edwardsburgh 27 November
1818, and at Drummond on
9 July 1819.
(PAO)

WATSON JOHN
Emigrated from Scotland,
with his wife, three sons
and a daughter, to Canada
on the Earl of Buckingham
in June 1821. Received a
land grant in Ramsay,
Upper Canada, 25 July 1821.
(PAO)

WATSON JOHN
Emigrated from Scotland,
with his wife and four
daughters, to Canada on
the Earl of Buckingham in
June 1821. Received a land
grant in Dalhousie, Upper
Canada, 1 August 1821.
(PAO)

WATSON PETER
Emigrated from Leith, Mid-
lothian, to Staten Island,
New York, on the Exchange
Captain Peacock, during
December 1685. Indentured
servant. Settled at
Magnolia Farm, Freehold,
New Jersey. Married (1)?
(2)Agnes... Father of
Peter, William, Richard,
Gavin and David. Died 1729.
(MNJ)

WATSON THOMAS
Merchant in Arbroath, Angus.
Jacobite in 1745. Lieutenant
in Ogilvy's Forfarshire
Regiment. Possibly trans-
ported to the Plantations
in 1746.
(MR)

WEBSTER JAMES
Dundee, Angus. Merchant
in Richmond Vale, Cornwall,
Jamaica, c1780.
(TRA/TC/CC15.91)

WEBSTER JOHN
Indentured servant
imported from Scotland
to East New Jersey 1684.
(EJD/A)

WEBSTER PETER
Born in Scotland. Former
captain in the Royal
Artillery. Military
settler. Wife. Received
a land grant in Beckwith,
Upper Canada, 6 June 1817.
(PAO)

WEDDERBURN JOHN
Master of Blackness.
Jacobite. Captain of the
Glen Prosen Company in
Ogilvy's Forfarshire
Regiment, 1745. Escaped
from Scotland to America.
(MR)

WEEMS JAMES
Volunteer. Emigrated from
Scotland to Darien. Died
in Darien 9 November 1698.
(NLS)

WEIR JAMES
Born c1782. Farmer.
Barrachan, New Kilpatrick,
Stirlingshire. Emigrated
from Greenock, Renfrewshire,
to Canada on the Mary,
Captain Moore, in 1817.
(CO384.1)

WEIR JOHN
Graduated D.D. in Aberdeen
on 8 November 1794.
Surgeon in Jamaica.
(KCA)

WELCH MARGARET
Indentured servant
imported from Scotland
to East New Jersey by
James Johnston during
October 1685. Transferred
to Robert Turner in
Philadelphia, Pennsylvania,
on 10 March 1689.
(EJD/A226/B153)

WHARRIE HUGH
Son of Robert Wharrie of
Pathhead, 1748-1818,
surgeon, and Elizabeth
Smith, 1753-1825. Died
in Jamaica in 1809.
(Lesmahowgow GS)

WHITE ALEXANDER
PLanter. Emigrated from
Scotland to Darien. Died
in Darien 24 December 1698.
(NLS)

WHITE ALEXANDER
Born c1778, son of John
White, Bladnoch Bridge,
Wigton. Died in Mobile,
Alabama 2 March 1823.
(Wigtown GS)

WHITE ALEXANDER
Emigrated from Scotland,
with his wife, son and three
daughters, to Canada on
the George Canning in June
1821. Received a land grant
in Lanark, Upper Canada, on
16 July 1821.
(PAO)

WHITE DAVID
Planter. Emigrated from
Scotland to Darien. Died
in Darien 11 December 1698.
(NLS)

WHITE JAMES
Emigrated from Scotland,
with his wife, to Canada
on the Commerce. Received
a land grant in Dalhousie,
Upper Canada, 17 October 1821.
(PAO)

WHITE JOHN
Indentured servant
imported from Scotland
to East New Jersey by
Thomas Yallerton 1684.
(EJD/A)

WHITE JOHN
Leith, Midlothian.
Applied to settle in
Canada on 1 March 1815.
(SRO/RH9)

WHITE JOHN
Emigrated from Scotland
to Canada on the Commerce
in June 1820. Received a
land grant in Dalhousie,
Upper Canada, on
17 October 1821.
(PAO)

WHYTE WALTER
Emigrated from Glasgow
to Barbados in 1675.
(GR)

WHITE WILLIAM
Born in Scotland 1708.
Emigrated from Scotland
to America before 1750.
Planter in Virginia.
(OD)

WHITE WILLIAM
Emigrated from Scotland,
with his wife, to Canada
on the George Canning in
June 1821. Received a
land grant in Ramsay,
Upper Canada, on
16 July 1821.
(PAO)

WHITEBURN JOHN
Indentured servant
imported from Scotland
to East New Jersey by
John Campbell for Captain
Andrew Hamilton during
October 1684.
(EJD/A)

WHITFORD PASCO
Born in Scotland c1642.
Emigrated from Scotland,
with his wife Mary, to
America. Settled in East
Greenwich, Kingston and
Newport, Rhode Island.
Died in 1690.
(TV)

WHITEHEAD ALEXANDER
Educated in Glasgow c1798.
Emigrated from Scotland to
America. Doctor in Norfolk,
Virginia.
(SA)

WHITELAW THOMAS
Emigrated from Scotland,
with his two sons, to
Canada on the Brock in
1820. Received a land
grant in Lanark, Upper
Canada, 23 October 1821.
(PAO)

WHITTON ROBERT
Emigrated from Greenock,
Renfrewshire, to Canada,
on the David of London in
May 1821. Received a land
grant in Lanark, Upper
Canada, on 25 August 1821.
(PAO)

WILKIE ARCHIBALD
Emigrated from Scotland
to Canada. Received a
land grant in Ramsay,
Upper Canada, 4 April
1821.
(PAO)

WILKIE Rev DANIEL
Born in Tollcross 1777.
Educated at University of
Glasgow. Emigrated from
Scotland to Canada in 1803.
Settled in Quebec. Teacher
and editor of the 'Quebec
Star'. Died 10 May 1851.
Buried at Mount Herman
cemetery.
(SNF)(HPC)

WILKIE JAMES
Emigrated from Scotland,
with his wife, son and
daughter, to Canada on
the George Canning in
June 1821. Received a
land grant in Ramsay,
Upper Canada, on
18 July 1821.
(PAO)

WILKIE JOHN
Indentured servant
imported from Scotland
to East New Jersey by
Lord Neil Campbell in
December 1685.
(EJD/A225)

WILKIE JOHN
Emigrated from Scotland
to America before 1776.
Skipper based in
Gloucester County,
Virginia.
(OD)

WILLIAMS JAMES
Born in Kirkcudbright.
Married (1) ? (2)
Elizabeth Stewart in Prince
Edward Island. Agent for
Lord Selkirk. Emigrated
from Scotland to Canada
on the Oughton in 1803.
Possibly settled in
Louisiana during 1815.
(DCB)

WILLIAMS ROBERT
Son of Isabella Marshall
or Williams, Glasgow.
Emigrated from Scotland
to Jamaica c1819. Settled
on Sutton's Estate,
Clarendon parish, Jamaica.
Died in 1823.
(UNC/Williams pp)

WILLIAMSON CHARLES
Born in Edinburgh 1757.
Army officer. Emigrated
from Scotland to America
during 1790. Agent for
Pultenet estate, western
New York state, from 1790
to 1800. Died in New
Orleans, Louisiana, in
September 1808.
(TSA)

WILLOX ALEXANDER
Smith in Aberdeen.
Applied to settle in
Canada 4 March 1815.
(SRO/RH9)

WILLOCK FRANCIS
Born in Scotland. Former
soldier in the 103rd
Regiment. Military settler.
Received land grants in
Upper Canada at Oxford
on 31 July 1817, and in
Bathurst 4 November 1819.
(PAO)

WILLOCKS GEORGE
Aberdeen. Emigrated from
Scotland to America.
Settled in Perth-Amboy,
East New Jersey c1686.
Died c1728.
(EJD/B92)

WILLOX JAMES
M.D. Kemnay, Aberdeen-
shire. Land owner in
East New Jersey c1683.
(EJD/A)

WILSON EBENEZER
Emigrated from Scotland,
with his wife, two sons
and two daughters, to
Canada on the Earl of
Buckingham in June 1821.
Received a land grant in
Sherbrook, Upper Canada,
24 July 1821.
(PAO)

WILSON HUGH
Emigrated from Scotland,
with his wife, two sons
and two daughters, to
Canada on the David of
London. Received a land
grant in Lanark, Upper
Canada, 20 September 1821.
(PAO)

WILSON JACOB
Born in Scotland. Wife.
Military settler.
Received a land grant
in Bathurst, Upper Canada,
20 September 1816, and on
14 October 1816.
(PAO)

WILSON JAMES
Emigrated from Scotland
to Canada. Received a
land grant in Sherbrook,
Upper Canada, on
19 February 1821.
(PAO)

WILSON JAMES
Emigrated from Greenock,
Renfrewshire, to Canada,
on the David of London
in May 1821. Received a
land grant in Ramsay,
Upper Canada, on
10 September 1821.
(PAO)

WILSON JOHN
Royalist soldier captured
at Worcester. Transported
from Gravesend, Kent, to
Boston, New England, on the
John and Sarah, master John
Greene, 13 May 1652.
(NER)

WILSON JOHN
Paisley, Renfrewshire.
Applied to settle in
Canada on 2 March 1815.
(SRO/RH9)

WILSON JOHN
Emigrated from Scotland
to Canada on the David
of London. Received a
land grant in Ramsay,
Upper Canada, on
17 March 1822.
(PAO)

WILSON SAMUEL
Emigrated from Scotland
to Canada on the brig
Ann 1 September 1816.
Received land grants in
Upper Canada at Drummond
on 8 October 1816, and
at Bathurst 11 October
1816.
(PAO)

WILSON SAMUEL
Emigrated from Scotland,
with his wife and son,
to Canada on the Commerce
in June 1820. Received a
land grant in Lanark,
Upper Canada, on
8 September 1820.
(PAO)

WILSON WILLIAM
GLasgow. Applied to
settle in Canada on
26 February 1815.
(SRO/RH9)

WILSON WILLIAM
Born in Scotland. Former
soldier in the Canadian
Fencibles. Military
settler. Received a land
grant in Upper Canada,
on 30 September 1816.
(PAO)

WILSON WILLIAM
Emigrated from Scotland,
with his wife, son and
two daughters, to Canada
on the Earl of Buckingham
in June 1821. Received a
land grant in Ramsay,
Upper Canada, on
6 August 1821.
(PAO)

WILSON WILLIAM
Emigrated from Scotland,
with his wife, son and
two daughters, to Canada
on the Commerce. Received
a land grant in Lanark,
Upper Canada, on
11 October 1821.
(PAO)

WILSON WILLIAM R.
Born in Scotland in 1786.
Emigrated from Scotland
to America. School-teacher.
Died in New Jersey on
9 March 1856. Buried at
Tennant cemetery, Monmouth
County, New Jersey.
(Tennant GS)

WILSON WILLIAM
Emigrated from Scotland,
with his wife, two sons
and three daughters, to
Canada on the Earl of
Buckingham. Received
land grants in Ramsay,
Upper Canada, on
31 July 1821, and on
4 August 1822.
(PAO)

WODROW ALEXANDER
Fourth son of Robert
Wodrow, 1679-1734, and
Margaret Warner, died 1759.
Emigrated from Scotland to
America.
(HCA)

WODROW ANDREW
Eldest son of Robert
Wodrow, the Scottish church
historian. Emigrated from
Scotland to Virginia 1768.
Revolutionary cavalry
officer.
(TSA)

WOODROP WILLIAM
Glasgow. Merchant and
factor for James Ritchie
and Company at
Rappahannock, Virginia,
before 1776. Their
"attorney in fact" after
1783.
(SRA)

WOODS MICHAEL or ANDREW
Born in Scotland during
1684. Emigrated from
Scotland, via Ulster, to
America in 1724.
(BAF)

WRIGHT ARCHIBALD
Volunteer. Emigrated from
Scotland to Darien. Died
in Darien 6 November 1698.
(NLS)

WRIGHT GEORGE
Salton. Applied to settle
in Canada 27 February 1815.
(SRO/RH9)

WRIGHT JAMES McINTYRE
Shoemaker in Cupar, Fife(?)
Married Christian Walker in
Edinburgh. Emigrated from
Scotland to Canada in 1801.
Settled at English River,
Quebec, in 1802.
(CP)

WYLIE ALEXANDER
Emigrated from Scotland,
with his wife and daughter,
to Canada on the Commerce.
Received a land grant in
Lanark, Upper Canada, on
11 October 1821.
(PAO)

WYLLY ANTHONY
Inverness(?) Signed a
treaty with the Creek
Indians in Georgia on
11 August 1739.
(HGP)

WYLIE DAVID
Emigrated from Scotland,
with his wife and three
daughters, to Canada on
the Earl of Buckingham,
in June 1821. Received
a land grant in
Sherbrook, Upper Canada,
on 31 July 1821.
(PAO)

WYLIE J.
Ayr. Applied to settle in
Canada on 4 March 1815.
(SRO/RH9)

YALLERTON THOMAS
Emigrated from Scotland(?)
to East New Jersey in 1684.
(EJD/A)

YEAMAN GEORGE
Emigrated from Scotland
to Canada. Received a
land grant in Lanark,
Upper Canada, on
3 November 1821.
(PAO)

YEATES BENJAMIN
Born c1702. Berwick.
Indentured servant for
Virginia 9 April 1720.
(LGR)

YORBIS WILLIAM
Indentured servant
imported from Scotland
to East New Jersey 1684.
(EJD/A)

YORKLAND JACOB
Volunteer. Died of flux
on the voyage from
Scotland to Darien on
11 October 1698.
(NLS)

YORSTON JEANNIE
Edinburgh, married
George Thomson, merchant,
during December 1767.
(S.C. & Amer. Gen. Gaz.)

YOUNG ALEXANDER
Emigrated from Scotland,
with his wife, three sons
and three daughters, to
Canada on the Earl of
Buckingham in June 1821.
Received a land grant in
Sherbrook, Upper Canada,
on 31 July 1821.
(PAO)

YOUNG DAVID
Emigrated from Scotland,
with his wife, two sons
and two daughters, to
Canada on the David of
London in May 1821.
Received a land grant in
Lanark, Upper Canada, on
6 August 1821.
(PAO)

YOUNG EDWARD
Emigrated from Scotland
to Canada on the David of
London in June 1821.
Received a land grant in
Lanark, Upper Canada, on
10 September 1821.
(PAO)

YOUNG ISAAC
Emigrated from Scotland,
with his wife and seven
children, to Georgia
c1737.
(HGP)

YOUNG JAMES
Sailor. Died at Darien
on 27 November 1698.
(NLS)

YOUNG JAMES
Glasgow. Merchant in
Virginia c1745.
(SRA/portbooks)

YOUNG JAMES
Ayr. Applied to settle
in Canada on 4 March 1815.
(SRO/RH9)

YOUNG JAMES
Emigrated from Scotland,
with his wife, son and
seven daughters, to
Canada on the Commerce
in June 1821. Received a
land grant in Lanark,
Upper Canada, 26 July 1821.
(PAO)

YOUNG JOHN
Born during 1759 in Scot-
land(?) Settled in
Quebec c1783. Merchant
and public official. Died
in Quebec 14 September 1819.
(DCB)

YOUNG JOHN
Ayr. Applied to settle
in Canada on 4 March 1815.
(SRO/RH9)

YOUNG JOHN
Emigrated from Greenock,
Renfrewshire, with his wife,
to Canada on the David of
London in May 1821.
Received a land grant in
Ramsay, Upper Canada, on
17 August 1821.
(PAO)

YOUNG JOHN
Born in Ayr in 1811.
Emigrated from Scotland
to Canada during 1826.
Merchant and politician.
(BCB)

YOUNG ROBERT
Emigrated from Scotland
to Canada on the Commerce
in June 1821. Received a
land grant in Sherbrook,
Upper Canada, 1 August 1821.
(PAO)

YOUNG STEPHEN
Emigrated from Scotland
to Canada. Received a
land grant in Ramsay,
Upper Canada, on
11 October 1821.
(PAO)

YULE ALEXANDER
Emigrated from Scotland
to Canada on the George
Canning in June 1821.
Received a land grant in
Ramsay, Upper Canada, on
16 July 1821.
(PAO)

YULE JAMES sr
Emigrated from Scotland,
with his wife, two sons
and four daughters, to
Canada on the George
Canning in June 1821.
Received a land grant in
Ramsay, Upper Canada, on
16 July 1821.
(PAO)

YUILL JAMES jr
Emigrated from Greenock,
Renfrewshire, with his wife,
to Canada on the George
Canning in May 1821.
Received a land grant in
Ramsay, Upper Canada, on
16 July 1821.
(PAO)

YUILLE JOHN
Glasgow. Merchant in
Virginia c1745. Died in
Virginia.
(SRA/B10.15.5959)

YULE WILLIAM
Emigrated from Scotland,
with his wife, three sons
and a daughter, to Canada
on the Commerce in June
1820. Received a land grant
in Lanark, Upper Canada,
on 5 September 1820.
(PAO)

*
USHER GEORGE
Born 1777, fifth son of
James Usher of Toftfield,
and Margaret Grieve. Died
in Jamaica.
(U)

USHER THOMAS
Born 1774, fourth son of
James Usher of Toftfield,
and Margaret Grieve. Married
Eliza Stevenson. Merchant in
Cedar Valley, Jamaica.
(U)

CPSIA information can be obtained
at www.ICGtesting.com
Printed in the USA
FFOW04n1750080418
46201254-47478FF